COLLECTED PAPERS OF KENNETH J. ARROW

Volume 2 General Equilibrium

COLLECTED PAPERS OF KENNETH J. ARROW

General Equilibrium

The Belknap Press of Harvard University Press
Cambridge, Massachusetts 1983

Printed in the United States of America
10 9 8 7 6 5 4 3 2 1

This book is printed on acid-free paper,
and its binding materials have been chosen
for strength and durability.

Library of Congress Cataloging in Publication Data

Arrow, Kenneth Joseph, 1921–
Collected papers of Kenneth J. Arrow.

Includes bibliographical references and indexes.
Contents: v. 1. Social choice and justice—
v. 2. General equilibrium.
1. Welfare economics—Addresses, essays, lectures.
2. Social justice—Addresses, essays, lectures.
3. Distributive justice—Addresses, essays, lectures.
4. Equilibrium (Economics)—Addresses, essays, lectures.
I. Title.
HB846.A7725 1983 330.1 83-2688
ISBN 0-674-13760-4 (v. 1)
ISBN 0-674-13761-2 (v. 2)

Preface

The mutual connection, direct and indirect, of all parts of the economy is recognized in the classical economics of Adam Smith, Ricardo, and especially John Stuart Mill, though their analytic methods made the interrelations very simple indeed. A full explicit statement of general equilibrium was first achieved by Léon Walras, who stated clearly many of the leading problems, though with unsatisfactory resolutions: the existence of equilibrium, the efficiency of competitive equilibrium, its stability, its possible nonuniqueness, and the laws of its variation with respect to various parameters.

The subject, however, for all its intellectual grandeur, remained sterile. Little progress was made for many years, except for some insights of Pareto, who certainly clarified the relevant meaning of efficiency. The history is discussed more fully in Chapter 6; suffice it to say here that many of the basic issues were raised in the German literature of the 1930s and that the contributions of Abraham Wald and John von Neumann were basic to subsequent developments, to which Gerard Debreu, Leonid Hurwicz, and Lionel McKenzie were such major contributors.

The logic of general competitive equilibrium is closely related to that of economic planning. Leonid Hurwicz and I collaborated on a number of papers stimulated by this subject and leading to such questions as dynamic processes for achieving a maximum and the stability of competitive equilibrium. Our joint papers, together with other papers by each of us, have been collected in *Studies in Resource Allocation Processes* (1977), and have not been reprinted here. Chapter 12 here is a sample of work in this area.

The efficiency of competitive equilibrium holds under appropriate circumstances, but not under others, especially, as is well known, when there are externalities. In some papers, especially Chapter 7, I have sought to present the inefficiencies of the competitive system in a systematic form.

The papers that follow are among those I have published in technical journals, or as chapters in various types of collections, or as separate pamphlets. (Portions of books of which I was primary author are not included.) I am grateful to the publishers for permission to reproduce them here. The papers have been edited lightly, and a few have been supplied with headnotes to give the reader some insight into the circumstances that motivated the writing.

I would like to thank Mary Ellen Geer for her careful and thorough editing of this volume, Camille Smith for shepherding it through the publication process, and Michael Barclay and Robert Wood for preparing the index.

Contents

1 Alternative Proof of the Substitution Theorem for Leontief Models in the General Case *1*

2 An Extension of the Basic Theorems of Classical Welfare Economics *13*

3 The Role of Securities in the Optimal Allocation of Risk Bearing *46*

4 Existence of an Equilibrium for a Competitive Economy *58*

5 Import Substitution in Leontief Models *92*

6 Economic Equilibrium *107*

7 The Organization of Economic Activity: Issues Pertinent to the Choice of Market versus Nonmarket Allocation *133*

8 The Firm in General Equilibrium Theory *156*

9 General Economic Equilibrium: Purpose, Analytic Techniques, Collective Choice *199*

10 Cost-theoretical and Demand-theoretical Approaches to the Theory of Price Determination *227*

11 The Genesis of Dynamic Systems Governed by Metzler Matrices *245*

12 Quantity Adjustments in Resource Allocation: A Statistical Interpretation *265*

13 The Future and the Present in Economic Life *275*

14 Pareto Efficiency with Costly Transfers *290*

Index *303*

General Equilibrium

1 Alternative Proof of the Substitution Theorem for Leontief Models in the General Case

It is of some interest to state and prove, in a manner which does not involve the use of the calculus, the theorem concerning substitutability in Leontief models stated elsewhere by Samuelson (1951). The chief virtue of such restatement is not the generalization to nondifferentiable production functions but the greater clarity given to the importance of the special conditions of the problem. This approach has been developed by Koopmans (1951, chap. 8) for the case of three outputs; the present chapter seeks to generalize his results.

The Assumptions of the Samuelson-Leontief Model

Samuelson's assumptions will be restated here in the terminology of linear programming. We shall let $n + 1$ be the total number of commodities involved; the first n will be termed "products" and the $(n + 1)$th "labor."

ASSUMPTION 1. *There is a collection of basic activities, each represented by a vector with $n + 1$ components, such that every possible state of production is represented by a linear combination of a finite number of the basic activities with nonnegative coefficients.*[1] *The collection of basic activities from which such combinations are formed need not itself be finite.*

1. The restriction to linear combinations of a *finite* number of basic activities is unnecessary. The generalization of a set of nonnegative weights is a *measure* over the space of basic activities.

Reprinted from *Activity Analysis of Production and Allocation*, ed. T. C. Koopmans (New York: Wiley, 1951), pp. 155–164.

ASSUMPTION 2. *No basic activity has more than one output.*

ASSUMPTION 3. *In every basic activity labor is a nonzero input.*

ASSUMPTION 4. *There is a given supply of labor from outside the system, but none of any product.*

Assumption 1 is that of constant returns to scale; 2 states the absence of joint production in the basic activities; 3 states that labor appears solely as a primary input; and 4 states that no product is a primary input.

In the vector representation of activities, let the $(n + 1)$th component be labor. As usual, inputs will be represented by negative numbers, outputs by positive ones. By an activity of the ith industry we shall understand an activity in which no component other than the ith is positive. Clearly, any linear combination of the basic activities of the ith industry with nonnegative coefficients is itself an activity of the ith industry. Further, let y be any activity. Then, by Assumption 1,

$$y = \sum_k x_k b^k, \tag{1-1}$$

where $x_k \geqq 0$ and b^k is a vector representing a basic activity.[2] Number the activities b^k in such a way that those with $k = 1, \ldots, n_1$ are basic activities of the first industry, and, in general, those with $k = n_{i-1} + 1, \ldots, n_i$ are basic activities of the ith industry, where $n_0 = 0$. Then, from (1-1),

$$y = \sum_{i=1}^{n} \sum_{k=n_{i-1}+1}^{n_i} x_k b^k. \tag{1-2}$$

As noted,

$$\sum_{k=n_{i-1}+1}^{n_i} x_k b^k$$

(For the definition of a measure, see Saks, 1937, pp. 7–17.) If b stands for a variable basic activity and μ is a measure over the space of basic activities, then any state of production is of the form $\int b \, d\mu$. All subsequent results apply equally well to this more general case, with completely analogous proofs.

2. In this chapter all vectors are column vectors. For future reference, note that the prime symbol will not denote transposition but will serve to distinguish different column vectors.

is an activity of the ith industry. Hence, every activity is expressible as a sum of n activities, one from each industry.

Further, let a normalized activity be one in which the labor input is 1. From Assumption 1 it follows that every activity of the ith industry is the nonnegative multiple of a normalized activity of that industry, and conversely. Hence every activity is a linear combination of n normalized activities, one from each industry, with nonnegative coefficients. The amount of labor used in any activity is therefore the sum of these coefficients. If, finally, we choose the units of labor so that the total supply of labor available, as guaranteed by Assumption 4, is 1, we may say that any activity y is expressible in the form

$$y = \sum_{j=1}^{n} x_j a^j, \tag{1-3}$$

where

$$x_j \geqq 0, \qquad \sum_{j=1}^{n} x_j = 1 \tag{1-4}$$

and a^j is a normalized activity of the jth industry. As now defined, all vectors y, a^j have -1 as their $(n + 1)$th component; let us redefine them to have only their first n components.

Note that the set of all normalized activities of the jth industry is a convex set; call it S_j. From Assumption 2,

$$\text{if} \quad a \in S_j, \quad \text{then} \quad a_k \leqq 0 \quad \text{for all } k \neq j. \tag{1-5}$$

(Here the symbol ϵ means "belongs to"; a_k denotes the kth component of a.) Finally, it follows from Assumption 4 that

$$y \geqq 0. \tag{1-6}$$

(Following Koopmans [1951, chap. 3, sec. 2.5], we use this notation for partial ordering relations among vectors: $x \geqq y$ means $x_i \geqq y_i$, all i; $x \geq y$ means $x \geqq y$, $x \neq y$; $x > y$ means $x_i > y_i$, all i.)

The set S of feasible points in the product space is that satisfying (1-3), (1-4), and (1-6). The problem is to characterize the set of efficient points of S if the assumption contained in (1-5) is made.[3]

---

3. For the relevant definition of an efficient point see Koopmans (1951, chap. 3, sec. 5.2), considering labor as the only primary commodity.

The set of all points satisfying (1-3) and (1-4) will be referred to as the *convex hull of the union* of $S_1, \ldots, S_n$. S is then the intersection of the nonnegative orthant (of Euclidean n-space) with the convex hull of the union of $S_1, \ldots, S_n$.

The following notation and terminology will be used: A will denote a square matrix of order n, a_i^j will be the element in the ith row and jth column of A, and a^j will be the vector which is the jth column of A. A will be said to be *admissible* if $a^j \in S_j$ for every j. A *weight vector,* x, has the properties $x \geqq 0$, $\Sigma_{j=1}^n x_j = 1$. A pair (A,x) is said to be a *representation* if A is admissible, x is a weight vector, and $Ax \geqq 0$. A vector y for which there exists a representation (A,x) such that $y = Ax$ is termed *feasible;* this definition agrees with that given in the first sentence of the preceding paragraph.

In the light of (1-3)–(1-6), the economic significance of these definitions is obvious. In particular, the set of feasible points, or vectors, is precisely S; a representation is a mode of industrial organization which will achieve a given feasible point. Note that, in view of (1-5), $a_i^j \leqq 0$ for all $i \neq j$.

Two forms of Samuelson's theorem will be established, corresponding to Koopmans' "strong" and "weak" assumptions, respectively (1951, sec. 3.6). In the first case we assume that it is possible to produce a positive net output of all products; in the second we assume only that some net production is possible.

The Substitution Theorem under Strong Assumptions

THEOREM 1. *For each $j = 1, \ldots, n$, let S_j be a convex set in Euclidean n-space such that, if $a \in S_j$, then $a_i \leqq 0$ for $i \neq j$. Let S be the intersection of the convex hull of the union of $S_1, \ldots, S_n$ with the nonnegative orthant. If S is a compact set*[4] *with at least one positive element, then the set of efficient points of S is the intersection with the nonnegative orthant of an $(n-1)$-dimensional hyperplane the direction coefficients of whose outward normal are all positive.*

LEMMA 1. *If y' belongs to the compact set S, there is an efficient point y'' of S such that $y'' \geqq y'$.*[5]

Proof. Let U be the set of points y such that $y \in S$, $y \geqq y'$. U is a compact

4. That is, closed and bounded.

5. This lemma has been proved by von Neumann and Morgenstern (1947, p. 593) for the case where S has a finite number of elements.

set, so that the continuous function $\Sigma_{i=1}^n y_i$ attains a maximum in U, say at y''. Since $y'' \in U$, $y'' \geqq y'$. If y'' were not efficient, there would be a point $\bar{y}$ of S such that $\bar{y} \geq y''$; but then $\bar{y} \in U$, $\Sigma_{i=1}^n \bar{y}_i > \Sigma_{i=1}^n y_i''$, contrary to the construction of y''.

LEMMA 2. *If A is a (square) matrix such that $a_i^j \leqq 0$ for $i \neq j$, and x and y are vectors such that $Ax = y$, $x \geqq 0$, $y \geqq 0$, $y_i > 0$, then $x_i > 0$.*

Proof. By hypothesis, $a_i^j x_j \leqq 0$ for $i \neq j$, so that $\Sigma_{j \neq i} a_i^j x_j \leqq 0$. Hence $0 < y_i = a_i^i x_i + \Sigma_{j \neq i} a_i^j x_j \leqq a_i^i x_i$. Since $x_i \geqq 0$, we must have $x_i > 0$.

LEMMA 3. *Let A be a matrix such that $a_i^j \leqq 0$ for $i \neq j$ and for which there exists a vector x such that $Ax > 0$. Then (a) $Ax' \geqq 0$ implies $x' \geqq 0$; (b) $Ax' \geq 0$ implies $x' \geq 0$.*[6]

Proof. By Lemma 2, the hypothesis $Ax > 0$ implies $x > 0$. The ratios x_j'/x_j are therefore defined; let

$$m = \min_j (x_j'/x_j), \tag{1-7}$$

where j varies from 1 to n, and choose i so that

$$x_i'/x_i = m. \tag{1-8}$$

From (1-7) and the hypotheses,

$$a_i^j x_j' = a_i^j x_j (x_j'/x_j) \leqq a_i^j x_j m \qquad (j \neq i). \tag{1-9}$$

Suppose $Ax' \geqq 0$. Then, from (1-8) and (1-9),

$$0 \leqq \sum_{j=1}^n a_i^j x_j' \leqq a_i^i x_i m + \sum_{j \neq i} a_i^j x_j m = m \sum_{j=1}^n a_i^j x_j.$$

By hypothesis, $\Sigma_{j=1}^n a_i^j x_j > 0$, so that $m \geqq 0$. From (1-7), $x_j' \geqq 0$, since $x_j > 0$ for all j, establishing (a).

If $Ax' \geq 0$, then, clearly, $x' \geqq 0$ by (a), $x' \neq 0$, so that $x' \geq 0$.

LEMMA 4. *If A is a matrix such that $Ax \geqq 0$ only if $x \geqq 0$, then A is nonsingular.*

Proof. If x is such that $Ax = 0$, then $A(-x) = 0$. By hypothesis, $x \geqq 0$, $-x \geqq 0$, so that $x = 0$. Hence $Ax = 0$ implies $x = 0$, so that A must be nonsingular.

---

6. Recall that in this chapter the prime is not used as a transposition sign.

LEMMA 5. *If (A,x) is a representation of $y > 0$, let Q be the set of points $y' \geqq 0$ for which there exists a vector x' such that $Ax' = y'$, $\Sigma_{j=1}^{n} x'_j = 1$. Then every point of Q is feasible.*

Proof. By hypothesis,

(1-10) $\quad a_i^j \leqq 0 \quad \text{for} \quad i \neq j,$

(1-11) $\quad Ax = y > 0.$

From (1-10), (1-11), and Lemma 3, $Ax' \geq 0$ implies $x' \geq 0$. Since $\Sigma_{j=1}^{n} x'_j = 1$, x' is a weight vector. Therefore (A,x') is a representation, and y' is a feasible point.

LEMMA 6. *If Q is defined as in Lemma 5, there do not exist two points y', y'', in Q such that $y' \geq y''$.*

Proof. Suppose the contrary. Let $y' = Ax'$, $y'' = Ax''$, where

$$\text{(1-12)} \qquad \sum_{j=1}^{n} x'_j = 1 = \sum_{j=1}^{n} x''_j,$$

$A(x' - x'') \geq 0$. By the proof of Lemma 5, A satisfies the hypotheses of Lemma 3, so that $x' - x'' \geq 0$; but then, $\Sigma_{j=1}^{n}(x'_j - x''_j) > 0$, contrary to (1-12).

LEMMA 7. *If, for each $k = 1, \ldots, p$, $y^{(k)}$ has representation $(A^{(k)}, x^{(k)})$, and $t_k > 0$, and if $\Sigma_{k=1}^{p} t_k = 1$, then $y = \Sigma_{k=1}^{p} t_k y^{(k)}$ is feasible and has a representation (A,x), where $x = \Sigma_{k=1}^{p} t_k x^{(k)}$, and $a^j = (\Sigma_{k=1}^{p} t_k x_j^{(k)} a^{(k)j})/x_j$, for all j for which $x_j > 0$.*

Proof. Define x and a^j as in the hypothesis; for all j such that $x_j = 0$, choose a^j to be any element of S_j. Since the sets S_j are convex, it follows that $a^j \in S_j$ for each j, so that A is admissible. It is also easy to see that x is a weight vector, that $y = Ax$, and that $y \geq 0$, so that (A,x) is a representation of y.

LEMMA 8. *Let $y > 0$ be an efficient point with representation (A,x), and let T be defined in terms of y in the same way that Q is defined in Lemma 5. Then, (a) A is nonsingular; (b) every efficient point of S belongs to T.*

Proof. By the proof of Lemma 5, A satisfies the hypotheses of Lemma 3 and hence is nonsingular by Lemmas 3 and 4.

Let y' be any efficient point. Since there is a positive efficient point, we cannot have $y' = 0$. Since A is nonsingular, there is a vector x' such that

$Ax' = y' \geq 0$. By Lemma 3, $x' \geq 0$, and therefore $\Sigma_{j=1}^{n} x'_j > 0$. Let $t_0 = 1/\Sigma_{j=1}^{n} x'_j$. Then, $A(t_0 x') = t_0 y' \geq 0$, $\Sigma_{j=1}^{n} t_0 x'_j = 1$, so that

(1-13) $\quad t_0 y' \in T.$

By (1-13) and Lemma 5, $t_0 y'$ is feasible. If $t_0 > 1$, then $t_0 y' \geq y'$, which is impossible for an efficient point y'. Hence

(1-14) $\quad 0 < t_0 \leqq 1.$

The variable point $t t_0 y' + (1 - t)y > 0$ for $t = 0$. Hence we can choose t_1 so that

(1-15) $\quad t_1 < 0,$

(1-16) $\quad y'' = t_1 t_0 y' + (1 - t_1)y > 0.$

Let $x'' = t_1 t_0 x' + (1 - t_1)x$; then, by the definition of t_0 and the fact that x is a weight vector, $\Sigma_{j=1}^{n} x''_j = 1$; also, $y'' = Ax''$. From (1-16) and the definition of T, $y'' \in T$. By Lemma 5,

(1-17) $\quad y''$ is a feasible point.

Let $t_2 = (t_1 t_0)/(t_1 t_0 - 1)$, $t_3 = (1 - t_1)/(1 - t_1 t_0)$. From (1-14) and (1-15),

(1-18) $\quad 0 < t_2 < 1,$

(1-19) $\quad t_3 \geqq 1.$

From (1-16),

(1-20) $\quad t_3 y = t_2 y' + (1 - t_2)y''.$

From (1-18), (1-20), (1-17), and Lemma 7, $t_3 y$ is a feasible point. If $t_3 > 1$, then $t_3 y > y$, so that y would not be efficient, contrary to hypothesis. Hence, from (1-19), $t_3 = 1$, which implies that $t_0 = 1$. From (1-13), then, $y' \in T$.

Proof of Theorem 1. By hypothesis, there is at least one positive feasible point. By Lemma 1, there is an efficient point $y > 0$. Let T be defined as in Lemma 8. Then every efficient point of S belongs to T. Conversely, let y' be any point of T. If y' is not efficient, there is, by Lemma 1, an efficient point $y'' \geq y'$. Since y'' is efficient, it belongs to T by Lemma 8; but this contradicts Lemma 6. Hence y' is efficient, so that T is precisely the set of efficient points.

T is the intersection with the nonnegative orthant of the hyperplane defined parametrically by the equations $Ax' = y$, $\Sigma_{j=1}^{n} x'_j = 1$. By Lemma 8,

A is nonsingular, so that $x' = A^{-1}y$. Let A_j^i be the element in the jth row and ith column of A^{-1}, and A^i be the ith column. Then the equation of the hyperplane is

$$\sum_{i=1}^{n}\left(\sum_{j=1}^{n} A_j^i\right) y_i = 1.$$

Hence the numbers $\Sigma_{j=1}^{n} A_j^i$ are the direction numbers of the outward normal to T. For each i, AA^i is a vector all of whose components are zero except for the ith, which is 1. Therefore $AA^i \geq 0$; by Lemma 3, $A^i \geq 0$, so that $\Sigma_{j=1}^{n} A_j^i > 0$ for all i.

The Substitution Theorem under Weak Assumptions

A generalization of Theorem 1 in which it is assumed only that there is a feasible point $y \geq 0$ (instead of $y > 0$) will be developed in this section. Some new terminology and notation will be needed.

A representation (A,x) will be said to be *trivial* if there is a nonnull set of integers, I, such that $x_i > 0$ for some i in I, and $\Sigma_{j \epsilon I} a_i^j x_j = 0$ for all i in I. The mode of industrial organization displayed by a trivial representation has the property that there is a collection of industries in which there is some net input of labor and possibly of other commodities and such that the output of any one industry in the group is completely absorbed by the other industries in the group. This group, then, is only a drain on the net resources of the nation. The main result of this section is that any industry which can be used in any system of industrial organization not of the degenerate type just described can yield a positive net output; therefore Samuelson's theorem applies.

LEMMA 9. *Let A be a matrix such that $a_i^j \leqq 0$ when $i \neq j$; x and y vectors such that $x \geqq 0$, $y \geqq 0$, $y = Ax$; I a set of integers (between 1 and n); and i an element of I. Then, (a) $\Sigma_{j \epsilon I} a_i^j x_j \geqq y_i \geqq 0$; (b) if $\Sigma_{j \epsilon I} a_i^j x_j = 0$, then $y_i = 0$, and $a_i^j = 0$ for all $j \epsilon -I$ such that $x_j > 0$. (By $-I$ is meant the set of integers between 1 and n not in I.)*

Proof. From the hypothesis,

$$a_i^j x_j \leqq 0 \quad \text{for} \quad i \neq j, \tag{1-21}$$

so that

$$\sum_{j \epsilon -I} a_i^j x_j \leqq 0. \tag{1-22}$$

From (1-22) and the hypotheses,

$$0 \leqq y_i = \sum_{j\epsilon I} a_i^j x_j + \sum_{j\epsilon -I} a_i^j x_j \leqq \sum_{j\epsilon I} a_i^j x_j,$$

establishing (a). If $\Sigma_{j\epsilon I} a_i^j x_j = 0$, then clearly $y_i = 0$, and $\Sigma_{j\epsilon -I} a_i^j x_j = 0$, so that, from (1-21), $a_i^j x_j = 0$ for $j \epsilon -I$, from which (b) follows.

Lemma 9 is a generalization of Lemma 2.

LEMMA 10. *If $y \geq 0$ has a trivial representation (A,x), then y is not efficient.*

Proof. By hypothesis, there is a set of integers, I, such that

(1-23) $\quad x_i > 0 \quad$ for some $\quad i \epsilon I,$

(1-24) $\quad \sum_{j\epsilon I} a_i^j x_j = 0 \quad$ for all $\quad i \epsilon I.$

From (1-24) and Lemma 9b, $y_i = 0$ for all i in I; since $y_k > 0$ for some k, we must have k in $-I$. By Lemma 2, then, $x_k > 0$ for some k not in I. Together with (1-4), this shows that $0 < \Sigma_{j\epsilon I} x_j < 1$. Let $t = 1/(1 - \Sigma_{j\epsilon I} x_j)$, and define $x_j' = 0$ for $j \epsilon I$, $x_j' = t x_j$ for $j \epsilon -I$. Then

(1-25) $\quad t > 1,$

(1-26) $\quad x'$ is a weight vector.

Let $y' = Ax'$. For i in I, it follows from (1-24) and Lemma 9b that $a_i^j x_j = 0$ for j in $-I$. Hence

(1-27) $$y_i' = \sum_{j\epsilon I} a_i^j x_j' + \sum_{j\epsilon -I} a_i^j x_j' = 0 = t y_i,$$

for i in I. For $i \epsilon -I$, $a_i^j x_j \leqq 0$ for j in I. Therefore

$$0 \leqq y_i = \sum_{j\epsilon I} a_i^j x_j + \sum_{j\epsilon -I} a_i^j x_j \leqq \sum_{j\epsilon -I} a_i^j x_j,$$

so that

$$y_i' = \sum_{j\epsilon I} a_i^j x_j' + \sum_{j\epsilon -I} a_i^j x_j' = t \sum_{j\epsilon -I} a_i^j x_j \geqq t y_i,$$

for i in $-I$, or, with (1-27),

(1-28) $\quad y' \geqq t y.$

A is an admissible matrix by hypothesis; x' is a weight vector, by (1-26); and from (1-28), (1-25), and the hypothesis, $y' \geqq 0$, so that y' is a feasible point.

Furthermore, from (1-28), (1-25), and the hypothesis that $y \geq 0$, it follows that $y' \geq y$, so that y is not efficient.

The proof of Lemma 10 amounts to saying that the industrial organization represented by a trivial representation can always be improved by shutting down the group of industries which yields no net aggregate output and distributing the released labor to the other industries in proportion to the numbers already employed.

We shall also need the following generalization of Lemma 3:

LEMMA 11. *Let A be a matrix such that $a_i^j \leqq 0$ for $i \neq j$ and for which there exists a vector $x > 0$ such that (A,x) is a nontrivial representation. Then (a) $Ax' \geqq 0$ implies $x' \geqq 0$; and (b) $Ax' \geq 0$ implies $x' \geq 0$.*

Proof. Since $x > 0$, the ratios x_j'/x_j are defined. Let

$$m = \min_j (x_j'/x_j), \tag{1-29}$$

and let I be the set of integers such that $x_j'/x_j = m$; I is nonnull. From the hypothesis, $a_i^j x_j < 0$ for i in I, j in $-I$, if $a_i^j \neq 0$. We then have

$$x_j'/x_j = m \quad \text{for} \quad j \in I, \tag{1-30}$$

$$a_i^j x_j' = a_i^j x_j (x_j'/x_j) < m a_i^j x_j, \tag{1-31}$$

if i is in I, j in $-I$, and $a_i^j \neq 0$. Suppose that for all i in I, $\Sigma_{j \epsilon I} a_i^j x_j = 0$; since $x_j > 0$ for all j, it would follow that (A,x) is trivial, contrary to hypothesis. Hence, by Lemma 9a, there is some i in I such that

$$\sum_{j \epsilon I} a_i^j x_j > 0. \tag{1-32}$$

From (1-31),

$$\sum_{j \epsilon -I} a_i^j x_j' < m \sum_{j \epsilon -I} a_i^j x_j, \tag{1-33}$$

if $a_i^j \neq 0$ for some j in $-I$. Suppose $Ax' \geqq 0$. Then, using (1-30),

$$0 \leqq \sum_{j \epsilon I} a_i^j x_j' + \sum_{j \epsilon -I} a_i^j x_j' = m \sum_{j \epsilon I} a_i^j x_j + \sum_{j \epsilon -I} a_i^j x_j'. \tag{1-34}$$

If $a_i^j = 0$ for all j in $-I$, then, from (1-32) and (1-34), it follows that $m \geqq 0$. If $a_i^j \neq 0$ for some j in $-I$, then, from (1-33) and (1-34),

$$0 < m \sum_{j=1}^{n} a_i^j x_j.$$

Since $\Sigma_{j=1}^{n} a_i^j x_j \geqq 0$ by the hypothesis that (A,x) is a representation, we must have $m > 0$. Hence, in either case, it follows from (1-29) that $x' \geqq 0$. Part (b) follows from (a) as in Lemma 3.

An integer, i, between 1 and n will be said to denote a *useful industry* if there is some nontrivial representation (A,x) in which $x_i > 0$. Lemma 10 guarantees us that, in the search for efficient points, industries which are not useful can be regarded as nonexistent, so there is no loss of generality in assuming that all numbers denote useful industries.

It is possible that the set of feasible points is empty, in which case Samuelson's theorem naturally has no particular content. Hence we shall assume that there is at least one useful industry.

THEOREM 2. *For each $j = 1, \ldots, n$, let S_j be a convex set in Euclidean n-space such that if $a \in S_j$, then $a_i \leqq 0$ for $i \neq j$. Let S be the intersection of the nonnegative orthant with the convex hull of the union of $S_1, \ldots, S_n$. If S is a compact set, and if every number from 1 to n denotes a useful industry, then the set of efficient points of S is the intersection with the nonnegative orthant of a hyperplane the direction coefficients of whose outward normal are all positive.*

Proof. For each k, let $y^{(k)}$ be a feasible point with a nontrivial representation $(A^{(k)},x^{(k)})$ such that $x_k^{(k)} > 0$ for each k; the existence of these points follows from the hypothesis that every number from 1 to n denotes a useful industry. Let $y = (\Sigma_{k=1}^{n} y^{(k)})/n$; by Lemma 7, y is a feasible point with representation (A,x), where $x = (\Sigma_{k=1}^{n} x^{(k)})/n$, so that $x > 0$, and $a^j = (\Sigma_{k=1}^{n} x_j^{(k)} a^{(k)j})/nx_j$. Suppose (A,x) is trivial; then, for some set of integers I, $\Sigma_{j \in I} a_i^j x_j = 0$ for all i in I. From this, it follows that

$$\sum_{k=1}^{n} \left(\sum_{j \in I} a_i^{(k)j} x_j^{(k)} \right) = 0,$$

for all i in I. From Lemma 9a, then, $\Sigma_{j \in I} a_i^{(k)j} x_j^{(k)} = 0$ for each k and all i in I; in particular, the equation holds for any k in I. Since $x_k^{(k)} > 0$, and therefore $x_i^{(k)} > 0$ for at least one i in I, we would have $(A^{(k)}, x^{(k)})$, a trivial representation, contrary to hypothesis. Hence (A,x) is a nontrivial representation with $x > 0$. All the conditions of Lemma 11 are satisfied, so that, by Lemmas 11 and 4, A is nonsingular.

Let y' be any positive vector. Then there is a vector x' such that $Ax' = y' > 0$. By Lemma 11, $x' \geq 0$; let $t = 1/(\Sigma_{j=1}^{n} x_j') > 0$. Then tx' is a weight vector, and $ty' = A(tx')$ is a positive feasible point with representation

(A,tx'). All the hypotheses of Theorem 1 are then fulfilled, and the conclusion follows.

References

T. C. Koopmans, "Analysis of Production as an Efficient Combination of Activities." In *Activity Analysis of Production and Allocation,* ed. T. C. Koopmans. Cowles Commission Monograph no. 13. New York: Wiley, 1951, chap. 3, pp. 33–97.

T. C. Koopmans, "Alternative Proof of the Substitution Theorem for Leontief Models in the Case of Three Industries." In *Activity Analysis of Production and Allocation,* ed. T. C. Koopmans. Cowles Commission Monograph no. 13. New York: Wiley, 1951, chap. 8, pp. 147–154.

J. von Neumann and O. Morgenstern, *Theory of Games and Economic Behavior,* 2nd ed. Princeton: Princeton University Press, 1947.

S. Saks, *Theory of the Integral,* 2nd ed. Warsaw, Lwow, and New York: Stechert, 1937.

P. A. Samuelson, "Abstract of a Theorem concerning Substitutability in Open Leontief Models." In *Activity Analysis of Production and Allocation,* ed. T. C. Koopmans. Cowles Commission Monograph no. 13. New York: Wiley, 1951, chap. 7, pp. 142–146.

2 An Extension of the Basic Theorems of Classical Welfare Economics

This paper, like a number of others of mine, arose from putting together different ideas to which I had been exposed. My introduction to welfare economics (indeed, to economic theory in general) was a course in mathematical economics given by my master, Harold Hotelling, at Columbia University in the fall of 1941. In the course he presented the analysis of his presidential address to the Econometric Society (1938). I became acquainted also with the papers of Bergson and Lange, which were based, like those of Hotelling, on the first-order conditions of the calculus for interior maxima.

In the summer of 1948 I was brought by Meyer A. Girshick, the theoretical statistician who died at an early age, to the then-new Rand Corporation. Game theory was new at the time, and the halls rang with discussions and theorems by David Blackwell, Lloyd Shapley, Seymour Sherman, and many others. In particular, zero-sum game theory was being developed, and I learned, especially from Sherman, about the central role of convex sets and, in particular, of the separating-hyperplane theorem.

During the academic year 1948–49, at the University of Chicago,

Reprinted from *Proceedings of the Second Berkeley Symposium on Mathematical Statistics and Probability,* ed. J. Neyman (Berkeley: University of California Press, 1951), pp. 507–532.

I wish to thank Gerard Debreu, Cowles Commission for Research in Economics, for helpful comments.

I attended a debate on rent control in which Franco Modigliani was one of the participants. While I was listening, it occurred to me that if different kinds of housing are thought of as different commodities (as they should be in a rigorous analysis), then individuals are typically buying zero of most kinds. The usual proofs of the optimality of competition did not cover this case. A few weeks later Paul Samuelson gave a seminar, an exposition of the fundamental theorems of welfare economics. I was about to ask his opinion of my conundrum when I realized from his diagram that the separating-hyperplane theorem supplied the answer.

I did not have a chance to work out the details until the next academic year, at Stanford, when I was invited by Jerzy Neyman (in the belief that I was primarily a statistician) to participate in the second of the Berkeley Symposia on Mathematical Statistics and Probability. The writing process was educational; I understood for the first time the difference between the necessity and the sufficiency conditions and also found that there could be problems with corner equilibria—in effect seeing, though without full understanding, the possible discontinuity in the demand functions which later played a role in my joint paper with Gerard Debreu on existence of competitive equilibrium.

The presentation and circulation of my paper revealed two overlaps with the work of others. The first was with Debreu, who had come to the Cowles Commission in 1949 after I left. He was working on the same topic as I was, with essentially the same results. Second, at the symposium Albert Tucker presented his famous joint work with Harold Kuhn on nonlinear programming. The Kuhn-Tucker results are of course more general in many ways (and different, because they use differentiability), but not completely so; they assumed concavity of the objective function and the constraints, whereas Debreu and I assumed only quasi-concavity of the utility functions. This discrepancy bothered me; it was only in 1961 that Alain Enthoven and I showed that the Kuhn-Tucker theory could be extended, with some limitations, to quasi-concave functions.

The simultaneous work of Debreu, Kuhn and Tucker, and myself is a classic example of what Robert K. Merton calls a multiple discovery. Obviously, we all were stimulated by the emphasis on convex sets by John von Neumann and Oskar Morgenstern in their great book on game theory.

In regard to the distribution of a fixed stock of goods among a number of individuals, classical welfare economics asserts that a necessary and sufficient condition for the distribution to be optimal (in the sense that no other distribution will make everyone better off, according to his utility scale) is that the marginal rate of substitution between any two commodities be the same for every individual.[1] Similarly, a necessary and sufficient condition for optimal production from given resources (in the sense that no other organization of production will yield greater quantities of every commodity) is stated to be that the marginal rate of transformation for every pair of commodities be the same for all firms in the economy.[2]

Let it be assumed that for each consumer and each firm there is no divergence between social and private benefits or costs, that is, a given act of consumption or production yields neither satisfaction nor loss to any member of the society other than the consumer or producer in question. Then, it is usually argued, equality of the marginal rates of substitution between different commodities will be achieved if each consumer acts so as to maximize his utility subject to a budget restraint of a fixed money income and fixed prices, the same for all individuals. Similarly, equalization of the marginal rates of transformation will be accomplished if each firm maximizes profits, subject to technological restraints, where the prices paid and received for commodities are given to each firm and are the same for all. Possible wastage of resources by producing commodities which are left unsold is avoided by setting the prices so that the supply of commodities offered by producers acting under the impulse of profit maximization equals the demand for commodities by utility-maximizing consumers. So, perfect competition, combined with the equalization of supply and demand by suitable price adjustments, yields a social optimum.[3]

There is, however, one important point on which the proofs which have

1. By marginal rate of substitution between any commodity *A* and commodity *B* is meant the additional amount of commodity *A* needed to keep an individual as well off as he was before losing one unit of *B*, the amounts of all other commodities being held constant. If the preference scale for commodity bundles is expressed by means of a utility indicator, then the marginal rate of substitution between *A* and *B* equals the marginal utility of *A* divided by the marginal utility of *B*. See, for example, Hicks (1939, pp. 19–20).

2. The marginal rate of transformation between commodities *A* and *B* is the amount by which the output of *A* can be increased when the output of *B* is decreased by one unit, all other outputs remaining constant. In this definition, an input is regarded as a negative output. See Hicks (1939, pp. 79–81).

3. For a compact summary presentation of the proofs of the theorems sketched above, see O. Lange (1942) and the earlier literature referred to there, particularly the works of Pareto as well as Lerner and Hotelling.

been given of the above theorems are deficient. The choices made by an individual consumer and the range of possible social distributions of goods to consumers are restricted by the condition that negative consumption is meaningless. Social optimization or the utility maximization of the individual must therefore be carried out subject to the constraint that all quantities be nonnegative. Now all the proofs which have been offered, whether mathematical in form, such as Lange's, or graphical, such as Lerner's, implicitly amount to finding maxima or optima by the use of the calculus (Lerner, 1934, pp. 162–165). Since the problem is one of maximization under constraints, the method of Lagrange multipliers in its usual form is employed. Implicitly, then, it is assumed that the maxima are attained at points at which the inequality conditions that consumption of each commodity be nonnegative are ineffective; thus all maxima are interior maxima.

Let us illustrate by considering the distribution of fixed stocks of two commodities between two individuals. Let the preference system of individual i be represented by the utility indicator $U_i(x_1, x_2)$, where x_1 and x_2 are quantities of the two commodities, respectively. Let X_1 and X_2 be the total stocks of the two goods available for distribution. Then, if individual 1 receives quantities x_1 and x_2, individual 2 receives quantities $X_1 - x_1$ and $X_2 - x_2$ of the two goods, respectively. Then an optimal point can be defined by finding the distribution which will maximize the utility of individual 1 subject to the condition that the utility of individual 2 be held constant, that is, we maximize $U_1(x_1, x_2)$ subject to the condition that $U_2(X_1 - x_1, X_2 - x_2) = c$. The second relation implicitly defines x_2 as a function of x_1. Taking the total derivative with respect to x_1 and setting it equal to zero yields the relation

$$\frac{dx_2}{dx_1} = -\frac{\dfrac{\partial U_2}{\partial x_1}}{\dfrac{\partial U_2}{\partial x_2}},$$

the partial derivatives being evaluated at the point $(X_1 - x_1, X_2 - x_2)$. We can then differentiate $U_1(x_1, x_2)$ totally with respect to x_1, if we consider x_2 as a function of x_1. The total derivative is

$$\frac{\partial U_1}{\partial x_1} - \frac{\partial U_1}{\partial x_2}\frac{\dfrac{\partial U_2}{\partial x_1}}{\dfrac{\partial U_2}{\partial x_2}}.$$

If we ignore the additional conditions that $x_1 \geq 0$, $x_2 \geq 0$, $X_1 - x_1 \geq 0$, $X_2 - x_2 \geq 0$, a necessary condition for a maximum is that this total derivative be zero. It then easily follows that the marginal rate of substitution for the two commodities is the same for both individuals.

If we introduce the restraints on the ranges of x_1 and x_2, however, it can happen that the maximum value of U_1 as a function of x_1, where x_2 is considered not as an independent variable but as a function of x_1, is attained at one endpoint of the range, for example, when $x_1 = 0$. For such a maximum, all that is required is that the value of U_1 when $x_1 = 0$ is greater than that for slightly larger values of x_1, but not necessarily for values of x_1 slightly smaller than 0; indeed, U_1 is not even defined for such values. Then all we can assert is that the total derivative of U_1 with respect to x_1 at the optimal point is nonpositive; it may be negative. Then it would follow that the marginal rate of substitution between commodities 1 and 2 is less for individual 1 than for individual 2.[4]

It therefore follows that the condition of equality of marginal rates of substitution between a given pair of commodities for all individuals is not a necessary condition for an optimal distribution of goods in general. The classical theorem essentially considers only the case where the optimal distribution is an *interior* maximum, that is, every individual consumes some positive quantity of every good, so that the restraint on the ranges of the variables are ineffective. Now if commodities are defined sharply, so that, for example, different types of bread are distinguished as different commodities, it is empirically obvious that most individuals consume nothing of at least one commodity. Indeed, for any one individual, it is quite likely that the number of commodities on the market of which he consumes nothing exceed the number which he uses in some degree. Similarly, the optimal conditions for production, as usually expressed in terms of equality of marginal rates of substitution, are not necessarily valid if not every firm produces every product, yet it is even more apparent from casual observa-

4. The importance of such *corner* maxima has been stressed in the "linear programming" approach to production theory, developed by J. von Neumann (1945–46), T. C. Koopmans (1948, 1951), M. K. Wood (1949), and G. B. Dantzig (1949). As was pointed out by von Neumann and by the authors of several of the papers in Koopmans (1951), the corner maxima occurring in the formulation of linear programming are closely related to the optimal strategies of zero sum two-person games; see J. von Neumann and O. Morgenstern (1947, chap. 3). A generalization of linear programming closely related in spirit to the ideas of the present chapter is contained in a paper by H. W. Kuhn and A. W. Tucker (1951), which also relates corner maxima to the saddle points of a suitably chosen function.

tion that no firm engages in the production of more than a small fraction of the total number of commodities in existence.

On the face of it, then, the classical criteria for optimality in production and consumption have little relevance to the actual world. From the point of view of policy, the most important consequence of these criteria was the previously mentioned theorem that the use of the price system under a regime of perfect competition will lead to a socially optimal allocation of economic resources. The question is naturally raised of the continued validity of this theorem when the classical criteria are rejected.

It turns out that, broadly speaking, the optimal properties of the competitive price system remain even when social optima are achieved at corner maxima. In a sense, the role of prices in allocation is more fundamental than the equality of marginal rates of substitution or transformation, to which it is usually subordinated. From a mathematical point of view, the trick is the replacement of methods of differential calculus by the use of elementary theorems in the theory of convex bodies in the development of criteria for an optimum.[5]

These results have a bearing on one aspect of the recent controversy between Hicks and Kuznets over the concept of real national income. Kuznets (1948, pp. 3–4) argues essentially that if an individual does not consume anything of a certain commodity, his marginal valuation of the commodity is, in general, less than that of someone who consumes a positive quantity of that commodity. The redistributions which Hicks has made use of in his treatment of real national income are therefore imperfect. Hicks, in his reply, essentially accepts the point (1948, pp. 163–164). But if the argument of the present chapter is correct, it is the prices and not the marginal utilities which are in some sense primary. What Kuznets is getting at is the valid statement that the Hicks criterion may lead to the assertion that one situation is both better and worse than another (for example, Scitovsky, 1941–42; Samuelson, 1950, pp. 2–3). But this possibility has no special connection with the existence of corner maxima in individual utility maximization or social welfare optimization.

It develops as a by-product of the main investigation that the use of convex set methods also enables the criteria for optimality to cover the cases where there are goods which are unwanted or which are positive nuisances.

5. A sketch of the relevant parts of the theory of convex bodies is given in the last section of this chapter.

The assumption usually implicit in past studies has been that any individual would prefer to have more of any one commodity, holding all other commodity flows constant, to less. Providing we consider negative and zero as well as positive prices, the theorem on the optimality of the competitive price system is still valid for commodities such that additional quantities are useless or worse.

It should be noted, however, that there is an exceptional case in which an optimal distribution is not achievable through the use of prices. This case seems not to have been noted previously.

In the next section, the problem of optimal economic systems is posed formally, and certain assumptions about the functions entering therein are made. Some mathematical tools are presented in the third section. The necessary and sufficient conditions for the achievement of optimal situations are then developed in the fourth and fifth sections. The case where it can be assumed that unwanted goods are disposable without cost is discussed in the sixth section and related to linear programming in its present form. Diagrammatic representations of the conclusions are presented in the seventh section. An assessment of the economic meaning and probable validity of the assumptions made in the second section is presented in the eighth section. Finally, the relevant portions of the theory of convex sets are quickly sketched in the last section.

Formulation of the Problem of Optimal Distribution

We suppose that we have m individuals and n commodities in the society. By a *commodity bundle* will be meant a vector of n components expressing the quantity some individual will receive of each of the n commodities, the ith component designating the quantity of the ith commodity.

ASSUMPTION 1. *All quantities consumed must be nonnegative.*

The behavior and desires of each individual are assumed to be expressed by a system of rules specifying for each pair of commodity bundles either a preference for one over the other or indifference between them. This preference pattern is assumed to possess the usual properties of a (weak) complete ordering[6] and also suitable continuity properties. The pattern

6. That is, (1) for any two commodity bundles A and B, either A is preferred to B or B to A or the two are indifferent; (2) if A is preferred or indifferent to B and B is preferred or indifferent to C, then A is preferred or indifferent to C (transitivity).

therefore can be represented by a *utility indicator* $U(x)$ defined for all commodity bundles x in the nonnegative octant of Euclidean space and continuous in its domain of definition, with the property that bundle x is preferred to bundle y if and only if $U(x) > U(y)$; see, for example, Wold (1943).

By a *distribution* is meant an assignment of the n commodities among the m individuals. A distribution X is thus an array of mn numbers X_{ij}, designating the amount of commodity i to be given to individual j. For fixed j, the numbers $X_{1j}, \ldots, X_{nj}$ form the commodity bundle to be given to individual j; for a given X, this bundle will be designated by X_j. Implicit in the above notation for utility is the following important assumption:

ASSUMPTION 2. *The desirability of a distribution X to individual j is solely dictated by the desirability to him of the commodity bundle X_j.*

This is the assumption that individuals act selfishly. Hence, for any given distribution X, the desirabilities to individuals $1, \ldots, m$ are represented by the numbers $U_1(X_1), \ldots, U_m(X_m)$, respectively.

If x and y are commodity bundles and t a real number between 0 and 1, we shall understand by the notation $tx + (1 - t)y$ the commodity bundle whose ith component is $tx_i + (1 - t)y_i$. If x and y are indifferent in the judgment of an individual, then it is usually assumed in economic theory that the *convex combination* $tx + (1 - t)y$ is preferred to either x or y if t is different from 0 and 1.

ASSUMPTION 3. *For all j, if $U_j(x) = U_j(y)$, and $0 < t < 1$, then $U_j[tx + (1 - t)y] > U_j(x)$.*

Naturally, the possibilities for a social choice among alternative distributions are limited by the limitations on production. Such limitations can be phrased by saying that the social commodity bundle $\Sigma_{j=1}^{m} X_j$ must lie in a set T, where by the notation $\Sigma_{j=1}^{m} X_j$ is meant a bundle whose ith component is the sum of the ith components of the bundles $X_1, \ldots, X_m$. The set T will be known as the *transformation set*.

ASSUMPTION 4. *The transformation set T is nonnull, convex, and compact;*[7] *further, if x is a bundle in T, $x_i \geqq 0$ for every component of x.*

---

7. A set is said to be nonnull if it contains at least one element. It is said to be convex if for any two bundles x and y in the set and any t such that $0 \leq t \leq 1$, the bundle $tx + (1 - t)y$ also belongs to the set. Finally, a compact set is a bounded set such that no sequence of points in the set converges to a point outside the set.

DEFINITION. *A distribution X^* is said to be optimal in T if* (a) $\Sigma_{j=1}^{m} X_j^*$ *belongs to T; and* (b) *if there is no other distribution X such that* $\Sigma_{j=1}^{m} X_j$ *belongs to T and* $U_j(X_j) \geqq U_j(X_j^*)$ *for all j, with the strict inequality holding for at least one j.*

It is clear that for any distribution which is nonoptimal, there is another distribution in which everybody is at least as well off and at least one person better off. The optimal distribution of a fixed stock of goods is the special case where T consists of a single point.

Some Preliminary Lemmas

An elementary mathematical consequence of the assumptions and other statements from the elementary theory of convex sets will be presented here for later use.

LEMMA 1. *For given j and given number U, the set of vectors x for which* $U_j(x) \geqq U$ *is closed and convex; further, if x and y belong to the set and* $0 < t < 1$, *then* $U_j[tx + (1 - t)y] > U$.

Proof. Let x and y both belong to the indicated set. Without loss of generality, we may suppose

$$U \leqq U_j(x) \leqq U_j(y). \tag{2-1}$$

Define $f(t) = U_j[tx + (1 - t)y]$; this is a continuous function on the closed interval (0, 1) and so has a minimum there at some point t_0. Suppose $0 < t_0 < 1$; then we can obviously choose t_1, t_2 so that $0 < t_1 < t_0 < t_2 < 1$, $f(t_1) = f(t_2) \geqq f(t_0)$. But from the definition of $f(t)$ and Assumption 3, $f(t_0) > f(t_1)$ under these circumstances. Hence, it must be that $t_0 = 0$ or $t_0 = 1$; since $f(0) \geqq f(1)$ by (2-1), $f(t) > f(1) \geqq U$ for all t such that $0 < t < 1$, so that the set is convex.

That this set is closed follows immediately from the continuity of the function $U_j(x)$.

LEMMA 2. *Let A be any closed convex set and x^* a boundary point of A. Then there is a vector* $(p_1, \ldots, p_n)$, $p_i \neq 0$ *for some i, such that for all x in A,* $\Sigma_{i=1}^{n} p_i x_i \leqq \Sigma_{i=1}^{n} p_i x_i^*$.

LEMMA 3. *Let A and B be closed convex sets such that A has at least two points and no internal point of A is also a point of B. Then there is a vector* $p = (p_1, \ldots, p_n)$, *not all of whose components are zero, and a number c such that*

$$\sum_{i=1}^{n} p_i x_i \geqq c \quad \text{for all } x \text{ in } A,$$

$$\sum_{i=1}^{n} p_i x_i \leqq c \quad \text{for all } x \text{ in } B.$$

These lemmas and the definitions of internal and external points are discussed in the last section of this chapter.

The Case of a Single Individual

If $m = 1$, the distribution X reduces to a single vector or commodity bundle x. Then x^* is optimal in T if $U(x^*) \geqq U(x)$ for all x in T, that is, if x^* maximizes $U(x)$ for x in T. (Here, the subscript 1 on $U_1(x)$ has been omitted.) This case is of some interest because in certain respects the general case can be reduced to it.

THEOREM 1. *There is a unique optimal point x^* in any T.*

Proof. Since $U(x)$ is continuous and T is nonnull and compact, there is at least one maximum of $U(x)$ and therefore at least one optimal point. Suppose x^* and y^* are both optimal; then $U(x^*) \geqq U(y^*)$, $U(y^*) \geqq U(x^*)$, and therefore $U(x^*) = U(y^*)$. Let $z^* = \frac{1}{2}x^* + \frac{1}{2}y^*$. Since T is convex and x^* and y^* both belong to T, z^* belongs to T. By Assumption 3, $U(z^*) > U(x^*)$, contrary to the assumption that x^* and y^* are both optimal. Hence, the optimal point is unique.

DEFINITION. *The bundle x^* is said to be a point of bliss if $U(x^*) \geqq U(x)$ for all x.*

Clearly, if the point of bliss belongs to the transformation set T, it is optimal. Usually, an optimal point is not a point of bliss; that is, the optimal point for a given set of production restraints is not the best point the individual would wish for were he unrestrained.

LEMMA 4. *If x^* is optimal in T but not a point of bliss, then there is a vector p such that (a) $\Sigma_{i=1}^{n} p_i x_i \geqq \Sigma_{i=1}^{n} p_i x_i^*$ for all x such that $U(x) \geqq U(x^*)$; (b) $\Sigma_{i=1}^{n} p_i x_i \leqq \Sigma_{i=1}^{n} p_i x_i^*$ for all x in T; $p_i \neq 0$ for at least one i.*

Proof. Let V be the set of vectors x such that $U(x) \geqq U(x^*)$. From Theorem 1 and the definition of an optimal point, V and T have only the point x^* in common. Suppose x^* were an internal point of V. Then, by definition, in some linear subspace of the commodity n-space, x^* would be surrounded by a neighborhood of points all in V, and therefore there would exist two points x and y in V such that $x^* = tx + (1 - t)y$, where $0 < t < 1$. By Lemma 1, $U(x^*) > U(x^*)$, a contradiction. Therefore, x^* is an external point of V, and hence no internal point of V belongs to T. Since x^* is not a point of bliss, V contains at least one point besides x^*. By Lemma 1 and Assumption 4, V and T are closed convex sets. Lemma 4 then follows from Lemma 3, since x^* belongs to both V and T, so that $\Sigma_{i=1}^n p_i x_i^* = c$.

LEMMA 5. *For a given x^*, let p be such that $\Sigma_{i=1}^n p_i x_i \geqq \Sigma_{i=1}^n p_i x_i^*$ for all x for which $U(x) \geqq U(x^*)$ and such that $p_k x_k^* \neq 0$ for some k. Then x^* uniquely maximizes $U(x)$ subject to the condition that $\Sigma_{i=1}^n p_i x_i \leqq \Sigma_{i=1}^n p_i x_i^*$.*

Proof. Suppose the conclusion is false. Then, for some $x \neq x^*$,

$$\sum_{i=1}^{n} p_i x_i \leqq \sum_{i=1}^{n} p_i x_i^*, \tag{2-2}$$

$$U(x) \geqq U(x^*). \tag{2-3}$$

From the hypothesis, (2-3) implies that $\Sigma_{i=1}^n p_i x_i \geqq \Sigma_{i=1}^n p_i x_i^*$, so that, from (2-2), $\Sigma_{i=1}^n p_i x_i = \Sigma_{i=1}^n p_i x_i^*$. Let $y = \frac{1}{2}x + \frac{1}{2}x^*$. Then,

$$\sum_{i=1}^{n} p_i y_i = \sum_{i=1}^{n} p_i x_i^*. \tag{2-4}$$

By hypothesis, $x_k^* > 0$; therefore, $y_k > 0$. Define the vector z as follows: $z_i = y_i$ for $i \neq k$, $z_k = y_k + \epsilon$. For all ϵ sufficiently close to 0, $z_i \geqq 0$ for all i. From (2-3) and Lemma 1, $U(y) > U(x^*)$; therefore, for all ϵ sufficiently close to 0,

$$U(z) \geqq U(x^*). \tag{2-5}$$

By hypothesis, $p_k \neq 0$. Choose ϵ sufficiently close to 0 to satisfy (2-5) and of a sign opposite to p_k. Then, by (2-4),

$$\sum_{i=1}^{n} p_i z_i = \sum_{i=1}^{n} p_i y_i + \epsilon p_k < \sum_{i=1}^{n} p_i x_i^*. \tag{2-6}$$

But the existence of a vector z with properties (2-5) and (2-6) contradicts the hypotheses of the lemma.

DEFINITION. *The "price" vector p is said to equate supply and demand at x^* if (a) x^* uniquely maximizes $U(x)$ subject to the condition $\Sigma_{i=1}^n p_i x_i \leqq \Sigma_{i=1}^n p_i x_i^*$, (b) x^* maximizes $\Sigma_{i=1}^n p_i x_i$ subject to the condition that x belongs to T.*

If we interpret the vector p as a set of prices, one for each commodity, then clearly (a) states that x^* constitutes the quantities demanded of each commodity at the given price levels, provided sufficient income is supplied to purchase x^* but no more, under conditions of perfect competition, while (b) states that x^* will also be the quantities supplied under the assumption of profit maximization under competitive conditions. It is not implied that the price vector is unique, nor, of course, need there exist a price vector with the above properties for every x in T. Indeed, such price vectors will only exist for optimal points, as we shall see.

THEOREM 2. *If there is a vector p which equates supply and demand at x^*, then x^* is an optimal point.*

Proof. Suppose x^* is not optimal. Then for some y in T, $U(y) > U(x^*)$. Since x^* uniquely maximizes $U(x)$ subject to the conditions $\Sigma_{i=1}^{n} p_i x_i \leqq \Sigma_{i=1}^{n} p_i x_i^*$, it must be that $\Sigma_{i=1}^{n} p_i y_i > \Sigma_{i=1}^{n} p_i x_i^*$. But this contradicts the hypothesis that x^* maximizes the linear function $\Sigma_{i=1}^{n} p_i x_i$ for x in T.

Theorem 2 states that if a set of prices can be found which equate supply and demand, then the resulting situation is optimal. The triviality of the reasoning leading to this sufficient condition for optimality is in contrast with the more complicated proof leading to the converse theorem, which in fact is not valid in complete generality. The precise statement follows.

THEOREM 3. *For any optimal point x^*, there is a vector p with at least one nonzero component with the following properties:* (a) $\Sigma_{i=1}^{n} p_i x_i \geqq \Sigma_{i=1}^{n} p_i x_i^*$ *for all x such that $U(x) \geqq U(x^*)$;* (b) *there is a commodity bundle y^*, where $y_i^* \geqq x_i^*$ for all i, which maximizes the profit function $\Sigma_{i=1}^{n} p_i x_i$ subject to the condition that x be in T;* (c) *if x^* is not a point of bliss, then $y_i^* = x_i^*$ for all i in* (b); (d) *if either $p_k x_k^* \neq 0$ for some k or x^* is a point of bliss, then x^* uniquely maximizes $U(x)$ subject to the condition that $\Sigma_{i=1}^{n} p_i x_i \leqq \Sigma_{i=1}^{n} p_i x_i^*$.*

Proof. If x^* is not a point of bliss, then statements (a)–(c) are made in Lemma 4. Suppose x^* is a point of bliss which is optimal in T. Let τ be the least upper bound of values of t for which tx^* belongs to T. Since T is a closed set, τx^* belongs to T; also, clearly, $\tau \geqq 1$. Let $y^* = \tau x^*$. Since $x_i^* \geqq 0$ for each i, by Assumption 4, $y_i^* \geqq x_i^*$ for each i. For $t > \tau$, tx^* does not belong to T. Therefore every neighborhood of y^* contains points not in T, so that y^* is a boundary point of T. By Lemma 2, there is a price vector p

such that $\Sigma_{i=1}^{n} p_i x_i \leqq \Sigma_{i=1}^{n} p_i y_i^*$ for all x in T, establishing (b). Now suppose for some $x \neq x^*$, $U(x) \geqq U(x^*)$. Then if $y = \frac{1}{2}x + \frac{1}{2}x^*$, $U(y) > U(x^*)$ by Lemma 1, which contradicts the assumption that x^* is a point of bliss. Therefore, the set of points for which $U(x) \geqq U(x^*)$ contains just the point of bliss x^*, so that (a) is trivial. Part (c) is irrelevant if x^* is a point of bliss. Finally, the previous argument shows that $U(x^*) > U(x)$ for all $x \neq x^*$, so that (d) follows trivially in case x^* is a point of bliss.

If x^* is not a point of bliss, then (d) follows from (a) by Lemma 5.

Parts (a)–(c), particularly, characterize optimal points. For a point of bliss, it is possible to set prices so that at least as much will be produced, under the assumption of profit maximization, of each commodity as is used at the point of bliss. Then, if enough income is given the consumer so that he can purchase the quantities at the point of bliss evaluated at the prices just set, he will in fact purchase them. The more interesting case is that in which the point of bliss, if any, is not contained within the available production possibilities. Then prices can be set so that simultaneously the optimal point will maximize profits to producers and minimize the cost of achieving the associated (optimal) utility level to consumers. Apart from an exceptional case, that is, when the optimal bundle contains positive quantities only of those goods with zero price, it is also true that this minimum cost property is equivalent to the proposition that the individual maximizing his utility subject to the constraint that his expenditures at given prices not exceed a quantity sufficient to purchase the optimal bundle, will in fact choose that bundle.

Theorem 3 says, in effect, that an optimal point can be achieved by suitable choice of prices under a competitive system. By itself, this hardly distinguishes the price system from others. For example, obviously any point in T, and in particular the optimal point, can be achieved by rationing. Theorem 2 adds, however, the important quality that once a bundle has been chosen by means of the price system, we know that it is optimal, a quality not shared in as direct a way, at least, by direct controls. Of course, the validity of these theorems is dependent on the validity of Assumptions 1–4.

It is to be noted that no assumptions or conclusions as to the signs of the prices were made or drawn. At this stage, the presence of unwanted commodities in consumption or of goods whose production is made easier rather than harder by the employment of resources to produce other goods is not excluded.

The Case of Many Individuals

We will now return to the general case, where m, the number of individuals, may be more than 1.

DEFINITION. *For a given optimal distribution X^* and a given individual k, let T_k be the set of all vectors x for which there exists a distribution X such that* (a) $x = X_k$; (b) $U_j(X_j) \geqq U_j(X_j^*)$ *for all* $j \neq k$; (c) $\Sigma_{j=1}^{m} X_j$ *belongs to* T.

If we start from a given optimal distribution X^*, then T_k is the set of all possible bundles which individual k can secure for himself if he is given complete charge of the distribution of goods subject only to the conditions that the distribution be compatible with the production possibilities and at the same time not bring any other individual to a position in which the latter is worse off than he would be under the given optimal distribution. In order that X^* be in fact optimal, it is clear that individual k must find that the best vector x in T_k with respect to his utility function be X_k^*, for otherwise there would be another distribution compatible with the production possibilities in which no individual other than k is worse off than he would be at X^*, while individual k would have a way of being better off. For an optimal distribution, then, X_k^* must maximize $U_k(x)$ subject to the condition that x belongs to T_k; this must hold for each k. The set T_k then plays, in effect, the role of the production possibilities open to individual k, and the results of the previous one individual case can be used here. Incidentally, there is one difference between the sets T_k and the set T; the former, but not the latter, may (and usually will) include bundles with negative components. Their inclusion in T_k is in fact essential to the proof following. However, their exclusion from T was not in fact made use of in the proofs of the fourth section, so that the theorems there proved are still applicable where relevant.

LEMMA 6. *The sets T_k are nonnull, closed, and convex.*

Proof. By definition, the bundle X_k^* belongs to T_k, so that it is nonnull. Let x^n be a sequence of points in T_k which converge to a given point or bundle x. For each x^n, then, by definition of T_k, there is a distribution X^n such that

(2-7) $$\sum_{j=1}^{m} X_j^n \text{ belongs to } T,$$

(2-8) $$U_j(X_j^n) \geqq U_j(X_j^*) \quad \text{for all } j \neq k,$$

(2-9) $$x^n = X_k^n \quad \text{for each } n.$$

Since by Assumption 1, $X_{ij}^n \geqq 0$ for each n, i, and $j \neq k$, it follows that

(2-10) $$0 \leqq X_{ij}^n \leqq \sum_{j=1}^{m} X_{ij}^n - x_i^n \quad \text{for } j \neq k.$$

Since T is a bounded set by Assumption 4 and x_i^n a bounded sequence, it follows from (2-10) and (2-8) that the sequence X_{ij}^n is bounded for each fixed i and $j \neq k$. Then we can choose a subsequence of the integers, $n_1, \ldots, n_r, \ldots$, such that each of the sequences $X_{ij}^{n_r}$ converge; by (2-9), the sequences $X_{ik}^{n_r}$ also converge. Let $X_{ij} = \lim_{r\to\infty} X_{ij}^{n_r}$. From (2-9), it follows that, for each i,

(2-11) $$X_{ik} = x_i, \quad \text{or} \quad x = X_k.$$

From (2-8) and the continuity of $U_j(x)$,

(2-12) $$U_j(X_j) \geqq U_j(X_j^*) \quad \text{for all } j \neq k.$$

From (2-7), $\sum_{j=1}^{m} X_j^{n_r}$ belongs to T for each r. Since T is a closed set, it follows that in the limit,

(2-13) $$\sum_{j=1}^{m} X_j \text{ belongs to } T.$$

From (2-11)–(2-13), x belongs to T_k, so that T_k is closed.

Now let x and y be any two elements of T_k. Then, there exist distributions X and Y such that

(2-14) $$x = X_k, \qquad y = Y_k$$

(2-15) $$U_j(X_j) \geqq U_j(X_j^*), \qquad U_j(Y_j) \geqq U_j(X_j^*) \text{ for all } j \neq k,$$

(2-16) $$\sum_{j=1}^{m} X_j \text{ and } \sum_{j=1}^{m} Y_j \text{ both belong to } T.$$

Let $z = tx + (1-t)y$. Define the distribution Z so that $Z_j = tX_j + (1-t)Y_j$. Then by (2-14),

(2-17) $$z = Z_k.$$

Assume $0 \leqq t \leqq 1$. By Lemma 1, the set of all bundles for which $U_j(x) \geqq U_j(X_j^*)$ is convex. From (2-15),

(2-18) $$U_j(Z_j) \geqq U(X_j^*) \quad \text{for all } j \neq k.$$

Finally, since T is convex by Assumption 4, it follows from (2-16) that

(2-19) $$\sum_{j=1}^{m} Z_j \text{ belongs to } T.$$

From (2-17)–(2-19), z belongs to T_k, so that T_k is convex.

Lemma 6 formally establishes that T_k has all the relevant properties of T.

LEMMA 7. *If X^* is optimal in T, then X_j^* is optimal in T_j for each j.*

Proof. Suppose not. Then there is some individual k and some bundle x in T_k such that $U_k(x) > U_k(X_k^*)$, and hence a distribution X such that

(2-20) $$U_k(X_k) > U_k(X_k^*),$$

(2-21) $$U_j(X_j) \geqq U_j(X_j^*) \quad \text{for all } j \neq k,$$

(2-22) $$\sum_{j=1}^{m} X_j \text{ belongs to } T.$$

(2-20)–(2-22) contradict the statement that X^* is optimal in T.

Lemma 7 formally reduces the optimality problem for the society to that for single individuals. Without further argument, it could be deduced that there is a set of prices for each individual such that utility maximization under a budget constraint would lead him to choose the given optimal point (subject to the minor exception noted in Theorem 3d). However, a stronger statement can be made; the same set of prices will do for all individuals.

THEOREM 4. *If X^* is optimal in T, there is a vector p, for which $p_i \neq 0$ for some i, with the following properties:* (a) *for each j, $\Sigma_{i=1}^{n} p_i x_i \geqq \Sigma_{i=1}^{n} p_i X_{ij}^*$ for all x such that $U_j(x) \geqq U_j(X_j^*)$;* (b) *there is a vector y^* such that $\Sigma_{j=1}^{m} X_{ij}^* \leqq y_i^*$ for all commodities i and $\Sigma_{i=1}^{n} p_i x_i \leqq \Sigma_{i=1}^{n} p_i y_i^*$ for all x in T;* (c) *if, for some j, X_j^* is not a point of bliss, then $y^* = \Sigma_{j=1}^{m} X_j^*$ in* (b); (d) *for any individual j for whom either $p_k X_{kj}^* \neq 0$ for some k or X_j^* is a point of bliss, X_j^* uniquely maximizes $U_j(x)$ subject to the budget condition $\Sigma_{i=1}^{n} p_i x_i \leqq \Sigma_{i=1}^{n} p_i X_{ij}^*$.*

Proof. Let V_j be the set of all bundles x for which $U_j(x) \geqq U_j(X_j^*)$. We will consider two cases in proving the theorem.

Case 1. For some j, X_j^* is not a point of bliss. Let k be the value of j in question. By Lemma 7, X_k^* is optimal in T_k. By Lemma 4,

(2-23) $$\sum_{i=1}^{n} p_i x_i \leqq \sum_{i=1}^{n} p_i X_{ik}^* \quad \text{for all } x \text{ in } T_k,$$

(2-24) $$\sum_{i=1}^{n} p_i x_i \geqq \sum_{i=1}^{n} p_i X_{ik}^* \quad \text{for all } x \text{ in } V_k.$$

Choose an individual q distinct from k. Let x belong to V_q, which is nonnull since it contains X_q^*. Then $U_q(x) \geqq U_q(X_q^*)$. Define the distribution X as follows: $X_k = X_k^* + X_q^* - x$, $X_q = x$, $X_j = X_j^*$ for j distinct from both q and k. Then, it is easy to see that X_k belongs to T_k; by (2-23),

$$\sum_{i=1}^{n} p_i(X_{ik}^* + X_{iq}^* - x_i) \leqq \sum_{i=1}^{n} p_i X_{ik}^*,$$

or

$$\sum_{i=1}^{n} p_i x_i \geqq \sum_{i=1}^{n} p_i X_{iq}^*. \tag{2-25}$$

(2-25) holds for any x in V_q, where q is any individual distinct from k. From (2-24), then,

$$\sum_{i=1}^{n} p_i x_i \geqq \sum_{i=1}^{n} p_i X_{ij}^* \quad \text{for all } j \text{ and all } x \text{ in } V_j, \tag{2-26}$$

which is (a) in Theorem 4.

Now let x be any element of T. Define the distribution Y as follows: $Y_j = X_j^*$ for all $j \neq k$, $Y_k = x - \Sigma_{j \neq k} X_j^*$. Clearly Y_k belongs to T_k. By (2-23),

$$\sum_{i=1}^{n} p_i \left(x_i - \sum_{j \neq k} X_{ij}^* \right) \leqq \sum_{i=1}^{n} p_i(X_{ik}^*),$$

or

$$\sum_{i=1}^{n} p_i x_i \leqq \sum_{i=1}^{n} p_i \left(\sum_{j=1}^{n} X_{ij}^* \right) \quad \text{for all } x \text{ in } T, \tag{2-27}$$

which establishes (b) and (c). Finally, (d) follows from (a) by Lemma 5.

Case 2. X_j^* is a point of bliss for all j. Let τ be the least upper bound of the values of t such that $t(\Sigma_{j=1}^{m} X_j^*)$ belongs to T, $y^* = \tau(\Sigma_{j=1}^{m} X_j^*)$. Then $\tau \geqq 1$. As in Theorem 3, y^* is a boundary point of T, so that, by Lemma 2, we can choose p so that

$$\sum_{i=1}^{n} p_i x_i \leqq \sum_{i=1}^{n} p_i y_i^* \quad \text{for all } x \text{ in } T. \tag{2-28}$$

Clearly,

$$\sum_{j=1}^{m} X_{ij}^* \leqq y_i^* \quad \text{for all } i, \tag{2-29}$$

so that (b) is valid. As shown in the proof of Theorem 3, (a) and (d) are trivial in this case.

DEFINITION. *The vector p is said to equate supply and demand for the distribution X^* if* (a) *for each j, X_j^* uniquely maximizes $U_j(x)$ under the constraint $\Sigma_{i=1}^n p_i x_i \leqq \Sigma_{i=1}^n p_i X_{ij}^*$;* (b) *for all x in T, $\Sigma_{i=1}^n p_i x_i \leqq \Sigma_{i=1}^n p_i(\Sigma_{j=1}^m X_{ij}^*)$.*

THEOREM 5. *If there is a vector p which equates supply and demand for X^*, then X^* is optimal.*

Proof. Suppose not. Then there is a distribution X such that

(2-30) $U_k(X_k) > U_k(X_k^*)$ for some k,

(2-31) $U_j(X_j) \geqq U_j(X_j^*)$ for all $j \neq k$,

(2-32) $\sum_{j=1}^m X_j$ belongs to T.

From (2-30) and condition (a) of the preceding definition, it follows that

(2-33) $$\sum_{i=1}^n p_i X_{ik} > \sum_{i=1}^n p_i X_{ik}^*.$$

From (2-31) and condition (a), for $j \neq k$, either $\Sigma_{i=1}^n p_i X_{ij} > \Sigma_{i=1}^n p_i X_{ij}^*$, or $X_j = X_j^*$, so that

(2-34) $$\sum_{i=1}^n p_i X_{ij} \geqq \sum_{i=1}^n p_i X_{ij}^* \quad \text{for all } j \neq k.$$

From (2-33) and (2-34),

(2-35) $$\sum_{i=1}^n p_i \left(\sum_{j=1}^m X_{ij} \right) > \sum_{i=1}^n p_i \left(\sum_{j=1}^m X_{ij}^* \right).$$

But (2-32) and condition (b) imply that (2-35) is false. Hence, the theorem is true.

Theorems 4 and 5 together define the role of the price system in the same way as for a single individual in the fourth section. Disregarding the existence of points of bliss (for all too good empirical reasons) leaves only the case where $p_i X_{ij}^* = 0$ for all i for some individual j as an exceptional case of an optimal point unreachable by the price system. In this case, the optimal situation requires that individual j consume only free goods. The individuals for whom the conclusion of Theorem 4(d) is valid have the right to consume as much of the free goods as they wish in maximizing their utility under the budget constraint. Hence, it must be that at the bundles to which they are entitled under the optimal situation they are saturated with respect to the free goods; either an increase or a decrease in the quantity of any of the free goods, holding the quantities of other goods constant, would decrease satisfaction. The reason that the price system fails is that the prices of the goods consumed by individual j must be zero to permit other individuals to become saturated with those goods, but at the same time there is no restraint compelling individual j to stick to the quantity of free goods allotted to him under the optimal conditions, since, of course, he could, under the price system, consume as much of these as he pleases. Only by coincidence would he also be saturated with those free goods at a zero level of other goods.

The Case of Free Disposal

It is common in discussions of production to make implicitly or explicitly the following assumption.

ASSUMPTION 5. *If x belongs to T and y is a vector such that $0 \leqq y_i \leqq x_i$ for every commodity i, then y belongs to T.*

The argument generally runs that, if necessary, one could always produce y by producing x and then discarding the quantities $x_i - y_i$ of the commodities i. This amounts to assuming that there is a method of disposal of surplus products which is costless to producers. Under these conditions, it turns out that we can confine ourselves to nonnegative prices.

For the following lemma, let us define for a given integer $q \leqq n$, the *projection* of an n-vector x to be the q-vector whose components are $x_1, \ldots, x_q$. The projection of a set T will be the set of all points in q-dimensional space which are projections of points of the set T.

LEMMA 8. *Let x^* belong to the transformation set T, and suppose $x_i^* > 0$ for $i = 1, \ldots, q$, $x_i^* = 0$ for $i = q + 1, \ldots, n$. Let $x^{*\prime}$ and T' be the projections of x^* and T, respectively. Then, if $x^{*\prime}$ is a boundary point of T' in q-dimensional space and if Assumption 5 holds, there is a vector p such that x^* maximizes $\Sigma_{i=1}^{n} p_i x_i$ for x in T, and such that $p_i \geqq 0$ for all i, $p_i > 0$ for some i.*

Proof. Clearly, T' is closed, convex, and nonnull. By Lemma 2, there exists a vector $(p_1, \ldots, p_q)$ such that

$$(2\text{-}36) \qquad \sum_{i=1}^{q} p_i x_i \leqq \sum_{i=1}^{q} p_i x_i^* \quad \text{for all } x \text{ in } T', \qquad p_i \neq 0 \quad \text{for some } i,$$

since $x^{*\prime}$ is a boundary point of T'. For a given r such that $1 \leqq r \leqq q$, define the n-vector y in T so that $y_i = x_i^*$ for $i \neq r$, $y_r = 0$. By Assumption 5, y belongs to T. Let y' be the projection of y; by (2-36), it follows that $p_r x_r^* \geqq 0$. By construction $x_r^* > 0$, so that $p_r \geqq 0$. This holds for all r between 1 and q, inclusive. From (2-36), then, $p_i > 0$ for at least one value of i. Define $p_i = 0$ for $i = q + 1, \ldots, n$. If x belongs to T and x' is the projection of x, then $\Sigma_{i=1}^n p_i x_i = \Sigma_{i=1}^q p_i x_i'$. The lemma then follows from (2-36).

LEMMA 9. *Let X^* be an optimal distribution in which, for some individual k, X_k^* is not a point of bliss. If p satisfies the conclusions of Theorem 4 and if Assumption 5 holds, then $p_i > 0$ for at least one value of i.*

Proof. Suppose $p_i \leqq 0$ for all i. Then $\Sigma_{i=1}^n p_i X_{ij}^* \leqq 0$ for all j, and $\Sigma_{i=1}^n p_i(\Sigma_{j=1}^m X_{ij}^*) \leqq 0$. But by Assumption 5, the point $(0, \ldots, 0)$ belongs to T; since the point $\Sigma_{j=1}^m X_j^*$ maximizes $\Sigma_{i=1}^n p_i x_i$ for x in T, $\Sigma_{i=1}^n p_i(\Sigma_{j=1}^m X_{ij}^*) \geqq 0$, and therefore $\Sigma_{i=1}^n p_i(\Sigma_{j=1}^m X_{ij}^*) = 0$, so that for each j, $\Sigma_{i=1}^n p_i X_{ij}^* = 0$. Since p satisfies Theorem 4(a),

$$(2\text{-}37) \qquad \sum_{i=1}^{n} p_i x_i \geqq 0 \quad \text{for all } x \text{ in } V_k.$$

By hypothesis, there is a vector y for which

$$(2\text{-}38) \qquad U_k(y) > U_k(X_k^*).$$

Since $p_i \neq 0$ for some i, there is an r such that $p_r < 0$. Let z be any vector for which $z_r > 0$; let $w = ty + (1 - t)z$. For all $t < 1$, $w_r > 0$; but for t sufficiently close to 1, it follows by continuity from (2-38) that $U_k(w) \geqq U_k(X_k^*)$, so that $\Sigma_{i=1}^n p_i w_i \geqq 0$ by (2-37). But since $p_i \leqq 0$ for all i, $p_r < 0$, $\Sigma_{i=1}^n p_i w_i < 0$, a contradiction.

THEOREM 6. *If X^* is an optimal distribution and if Assumption 5 is valid, then there is a set of prices p satisfying the conclusions of Theorem 4 for which $p_i \geqq 0$ for all i, $p_i > 0$ for at least one i.*

Proof. First suppose that X_j^* is a point of bliss for all j. Let y^* be the point in T which enters into Theorem 4(b). By renumbering the commodities, it may be supposed that $y_i^* > 0$ for $i = 1, \ldots, q$, $y_i^* = 0$ for $i = q + 1, \ldots, n$. Let $y^{*\prime}$ and T' be the projections of y^* and T respectively. Suppose that for some $t > 1$, the point $ty^{*\prime}$ belongs to T'. Then there is a point z in T such that $z_i = ty_i^*$ for $i = 1, \ldots, q$, $z_i \geqq 0$ for $i = q + 1, \ldots, n$. By construction, the point ty^* has the same first q coordinates as z, while the last $n - q$ are zero, so that ty^* belongs to T by Assumption 5 contrary to the construction of y^*. Hence, for all $t > 1$, $ty^{*\prime}$ does not belong to T', and $y^{*\prime}$ is a boundary point of T'. Conclusion (b) of Theorem 4 then follows from Lemma 8. Conclusions (a) and (d) follow trivially in this case, as before.

Now suppose that for some j, X_j^* is not a point of bliss for individual j. By Lemma 9, there is a vector p' satisfying the conclusions of Theorem 4 with $p_i' > 0$ for at least one value of i. It will be shown that any negative price in this vector can be replaced by a zero price without changing the conclusions of this theorem. Suppose $p_r' < 0$. Define p so that $p_i = p_i'$ for $i \neq r$, $p_r = 0$; it will be shown that p has the same properties as p'. By Theorem 4(b) and (c),

$$\text{(2-39)} \qquad \sum_{i=1}^{n} p_i' x_i \leqq \sum_{i=1}^{n} p_i' \left(\sum_{j=1}^{m} X_{ij}^* \right) \quad \text{for all } x \text{ in } T.$$

In (2-39), first let x be such that $x_i = \Sigma_{j=1}^m X_{ij}^*$ for $i \neq r$, $x_r = 0$. By Assumption 5, x belongs to T. Then $p_r'(\Sigma_{j=1}^m X_{rj}^*) \geqq 0$; since $p_r' < 0$, $\Sigma_{j=1}^m X_{rj}^* = 0$, so that

$$\text{(2-40)} \qquad X_{rj}^* = 0 \quad \text{for all } j,$$

$$\text{(2-41)} \qquad \sum_{i=1}^{n} p_i' \left(\sum_{j=1}^{m} X_{ij}^* \right) = \sum_{i=1}^{n} p_i \left(\sum_{j=1}^{m} X_{ij}^* \right).$$

Now, for any x in T, define y so that $y_i = x_i$ for $i \neq r$, $y_r = 0$. By Assumption 5, y belongs to T; by (2-39),

$$\text{(2-42)} \qquad \sum_{i=1}^{n} p_i' y_i \leqq \sum_{i=1}^{n} p_i' \left(\sum_{j=1}^{m} X_{ij}^* \right).$$

But $\Sigma_{i=1}^n p_i' y_i = \Sigma_{i=1}^n p_i x_i$; from (2-41) and (2-42),

$$\text{(2-43)} \qquad \sum_{i=1}^{n} p_i x_i \leqq \sum_{i=1}^{n} p_i \left(\sum_{j=1}^{m} X_{ij}^* \right) \quad \text{for all } x \text{ in } T,$$

which is conclusion (c).

By Theorem 4(a)

$$\text{(2-44)} \qquad \sum_{i=1}^{n} p_i' x_i \geqq \sum_{i=1}^{n} p_i' X_{ij}^* \quad \text{for all } j \text{ and all } x \text{ in } V_j.$$

From (2-40),

$$\text{(2-45)} \qquad \sum_{i=1}^{n} p_i' X_{ij}^* = \sum_{i=1}^{n} p_i X_{ij}^*.$$

Since $x_r \geqq 0$ and $p_r' < p_r$, $\Sigma_{i=1}^n p_i x_i \geqq \Sigma_{i=1}^n p_i' x_i$. From (2-44) and (2-45), then, $\Sigma_{i=1}^n p_i x_i \geqq \Sigma_{i=1}^n p_i X_{ij}^*$ for all j and all x such that $U_j(x) \geqq U_j(X_j^*)$, which is conclusion (a). As in the proof of Theorem 4, part (d) follows from (a) by Lemma 5.

If the new vector p still has negative components, they may be removed by the above process. Since p' had at least one positive component, which is undisturbed by subsequent operations, each of the successive price vectors has at least one nonzero component.

DEFINITION. *A bundle x^* of goods in the transformation set T will be said to be efficient if for some set of utility functions $U_j(x)(j = 1, \ldots, m)$, there is a distribution X^* such that* (a) *X^* is optimal in T;* (b) *$\Sigma_{j=1}^m X_j^* = x^*$; and* (c) *for some j, X_j^* is not a point of bliss for individual j.*

This definition of efficient points is not precisely equivalent to that used in linear programming by T. C. Koopmans and others (Koopmans, 1948, 1951; Dantzig, 1949; Wood and Dantzig, 1949) but conveys the same general meaning. The efficient points of T are just those which could be used in some optimal distribution. Clause (c) is inserted to exclude trivialities. Without it, by suitable choice of the functions $U_j(x)$, every point of T would be efficient. Of course, when every individual is at his point of maximum absolute satisfaction, the concept of economic efficiency becomes meaningless.

THEOREM 7. *Under Assumption 5, the following are each a necessary and sufficient condition for x^* to be efficient:* (a) *$\Sigma_{i=1}^n p_i x_i \leqq \Sigma_{i=1}^n p_i x_i^*$ for all x in T and for some p for which $p_i \geqq 0$ for all i, $p_i > 0$ for some i;* (b) *there is no y in T for which $x_i^* < y_i$ for all i.*

Proof. First, it will be shown that (a) is a necessary and sufficient condition for x^* to be optimal. The necessity has already been shown in Theorem 6. For the sufficiency, let X^* be a distribution which gives x^*/m to each individual. For each individual j, let $U_j(x) = -\Sigma_{i=1}^n (x_i - x_i^*/m - p_i)^2$, defined only for those values of x for which $x_i \geq 0$ for all i. This utility function has an absolute maximum at the point $x^*/m + p$, and its indifference surfaces are concentric spheres about that point. From the geometric picture, or algebraically with the aid of Schwarz's inequality, it is easy to see that Assumption 3 is verified. By simple algebraic manipulation, it can be seen that x^*/m uniquely maximizes $U_j(x)$ subject to the condition $\Sigma_{i=1}^n p_i x_i \leqq \Sigma_{i=1}^n p_i(x_i^*/m)$. From the statement of condition (a), and Theorem 5, it follows that X^* is an optimal distribution for the given set of utility functions and therefore that x is an efficient point.

To show that (b) is also a necessary and sufficient condition for x^* to be an efficient point, it will be shown that (b) is equivalent to (a). If there were a y in T such that $y_i > x_i^*$ for all i, then, if $p_i \geqq 0$ for all i, $p_i > 0$ for some i, $\Sigma_{i=1}^n p_i x_i^* < \Sigma_{i=1}^n p_i y_i$, contrary to (a). Hence, (a) implies (b).

For the converse, renumber the commodities so that $x_i^* > 0$ for $i = 1, \ldots, q$, $x_i^* = 0$ for $i = q + 1, \ldots, n$.

Case 1. For some y in T, $x_i^* < y_i$ for $i = 1, \ldots, q$. Suppose that for each $i = q + 1, \ldots, n$, there is a vector $x^{(i)}$ in T such that $x_i^{(i)} > 0$. Let $z = \Sigma_{i=q+1}^n t_i x^{(i)} + t_0 y$, where $t_i \geqq 0$ $(i = 0, \ldots, n)$, $\Sigma_{i=0}^n t_i = 1$. Since T is convex, z belongs to T. For t_i sufficiently small $(i \neq 0)$, $x_i^* < z_i$ for all i, contrary to (b). Hence, for some r between $q + 1$ and n, $x_r = 0$ for all x in T. Let $p_r = 1$, $p_i = 0$ for $i \neq r$; then $\Sigma_{i=1}^n p_i x_i = 0$ for all x in T, and (a) holds trivially.

Case 2. There is no y in T such that $x_i^* < y_i$ for all $i \leqq q$. Let $x^{*\prime}$ and T' be the projections of x^* and T, respectively. Let z be a q-vector with $z_i = x_i^* + \epsilon$; then for all positive ϵ, z does not belong to T'. Hence, $x^{*\prime}$ is a boundary point of T', and (a) holds by Lemma 8.

Assumption 5 relates to free disposal on the part of the producers. It might instead be presupposed that it is the consumers who can dispose without cost of otherwise unwanted goods.

ASSUMPTION 6. *For each j, if $x_i \leqq y_i$ for all i, $U_j(x) \leqq U_j(y)$.*

For convenience, let $x \leq y$ mean that $x_i \leqq y_i$ for all i, $x_i < y_i$ for some i. Because of Assumption 3, it easily follows that increasing the stock of one commodity, holding all others fixed, actually increases the desirability of a bundle. Hence, Assumption 6 really implies insatiability of wants.

LEMMA 10. *If $x \leq y$, then under Assumption 6, $U_j(x) < U_j(y)$.*

Proof. By Assumption 6, $U_j(x) \leqq U_j(y)$. Suppose $U_j(x) = U_j(y)$. Let $z = \frac{1}{2}x + \frac{1}{2}y$; by Assumption 3, $U_j(z) > U_j(y)$, which is impossible since $z_i \leqq y_i$ for all i.

If Assumption 6 holds, we will understand in the definition of an efficient point that the utility functions referred to must satisfy that assumption.

THEOREM 8. *Under Assumption 6, a necessary and sufficient condition that* x^* *be an efficient point is that for some* p *such that* $p_i > 0$ *for all* i, $\sum_{i=1}^{n} p_i x_i \leqq \sum_{i=1}^{n} p_i x_i^*$ *for all* x *in* T.

Proof. Suppose x^* an efficient point. Then there is an optimal distribution X^* and a price vector p satisfying the conclusions of Theorem 4. By Lemma 10, X_j^* is not a point of bliss for any j. For any j,

(2-46) $$\sum_{i=1}^{n} p_i x_i \geqq \sum_{i=1}^{n} p_i X_{ij}^* \quad \text{for all } x \text{ in } V_j.$$

For any $r = 1, \ldots, n$, let $y_i = X_{ij}^*$ for $i \neq r$, $y_r > X_{rj}^*$. By Assumption 6, y belongs to V_j. By (2-46), $p_r(y_r - X_{rj}^*) \geqq 0$, so that $p_r \geqq 0$, or

(2-47) $$p_i \geqq 0 \quad \text{for all } i.$$

By Theorem 4, $p_s \neq 0$ for some s; by (2-47), $p_s > 0$. For any $r \neq s$, let $z_i = y_i$ for $i \neq s$, $z_s = y_s - \epsilon$. By Lemma 10, $U_j(y) > U_j(X_j^*)$; by continuity, $U_j(z) \geqq U_j(X_j^*)$ for ϵ sufficiently small but positive. By (2-46), $p_r(y_r - X_{rj}^*) \geqq p_s\epsilon > 0$, or $p_i > 0$ for all i. Since p also has properties (b) and (c) of Theorem 4, the conclusion follows from the assumption that x^* is an efficient point.

Conversely, for each individual j, let $U_j(x) = \sum_{i=1}^{n} a_i \log (x_i + 1/m)$, defined only for those values of x for which $x_i \geqq 0$ for all i. If we define $f(t)$ as in the proof of Lemma 1, it is easy to verify that $f''(t) < 0$ for all t if $a_i > 0$ for all i. Hence, the minimum attained by $f(t)$ over the closed interval (0, 1) must be attained at an endpoint; if $f(0) = f(1)$, then $f(t) > f(0)$ for $0 < t < 1$, so that Assumption 3 is fulfilled. Choose $a_i = p_i(x_i^* + 1)/\sum_{i=1}^{n} p_i x_i^*$. Since $U_j(x)$ increases with each variable x_i, its maximum under a budget constraint will occur on the boundary of the constraint. The maximum can therefore be obtained by using Lagrangian multipliers with the constraint $\sum_{i=1}^{n} p_i x_i = \sum_{i=1}^{n} p_i(x_i^*/m)$, and the maximum turns out to be attained uniquely at x^*/m.

THEOREM 9. *If Assumption 6 holds, then a necessary and sufficient condition that* X^* *be an optimal distribution is that there exists a set of prices* p, *with* $p_i > 0$ *for all* i, *such that* $\sum_{j=1}^{m} X_j^*$ *maximizes* $\sum_{i=1}^{n} p_i x_i$ *for* x *in* T *and such that* X_j^* *maximizes* $U_j(x)$ *for all* x *such that* $\sum_{i=1}^{n} p_i x_i \leqq \sum_{j=1}^{m} p_i X_{ij}^*$.

Proof. This theorem follows easily from Theorems 4, 5, and 8; since $p_i > 0$

for all i, the exceptional case in Theorem 4(d) does not arise unless $X_{ij}^* = 0$ for all i; but in that case the theorem is trivially valid.

This theorem is, of course, the classical theorem of the applicability of the price system under insatiable wants extended to include corner maxima.

In connection with free disposal, it may be remarked that the use of the price system to achieve a distribution where all individuals are at a point of bliss, as in Theorem 4(b), implied a mechanism of free disposal somewhere in the system, since producers' profit maximization will, in general, lead to an excessive supply.

Some Diagrammatic Representations

In the case of two individuals, two commodities, and a set T containing just one point, the various theorems can be best illustrated by a diagram

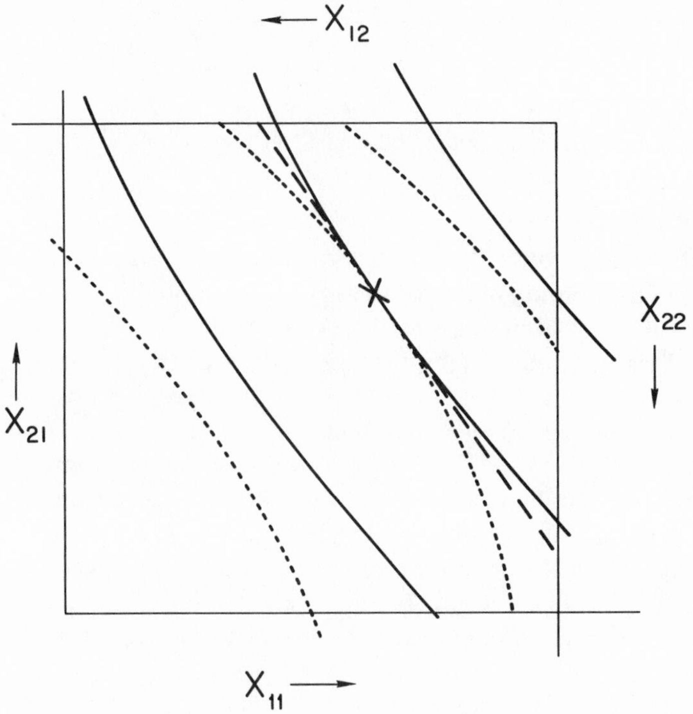

Figure 2.1 The standard case of an interior maximum, both individuals receiving positive quantities of each commodity

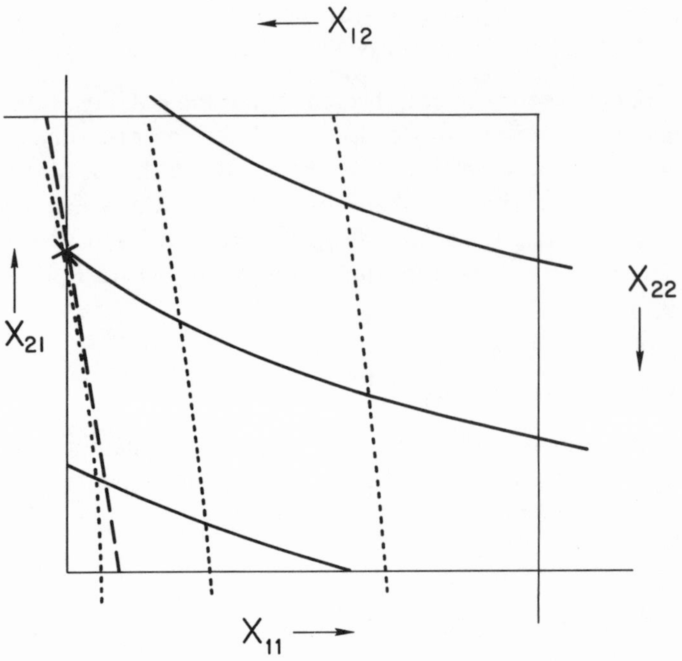

Figure 2.2 The case of corner maximum, individual 1 getting nothing of commodity 1

introduced by F. Y. Edgeworth (1932). When T contains just one point, the problem is that of distribution of a fixed stock of two commodities among the two individuals. A distribution X has four components, X_{11}, X_{12}, X_{21}, and X_{22}, where X_{ij} is the amount of the ith commodity given to individual j. In this case, the two sums $X_{11} + X_{12}$ and $X_{21} + X_{22}$ are given, so that a distribution can be represented by a point in a plane. In the following box diagrams, the variables X_{11}, X_{21}, X_{12}, and X_{22} are measured along the lower, left-hand, upper, and right-hand axes respectively, the last two being measured in the opposite direction to the usual manner. The solid indifference curves pertain to individual 1 and so are read with respect to the lower and left-hand axes, the dotted curves to individual 2 and the upper and right-hand axes. Sample optimal distributions are marked with crosses. Any point within the box is a distribution. Note that the indifference curves for either individual may go outside the axes relating to the other. Dashed straight lines denote the boundaries of budget restraints.

Figure 2.1 illustrates the standard case of an interior maximum, with both

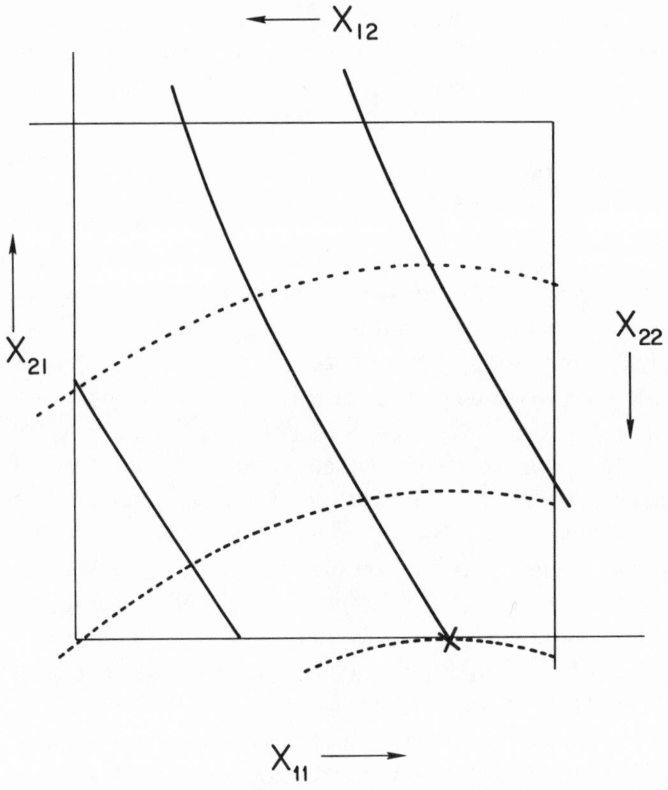

Figure 2.3 The exceptional case in which conclusion (d) of Theorem 4 does not hold

individuals receiving positive quantities of each commodity. By setting prices positive and proportional to the direction numbers of the normal to the line separating the indifference curves at their point of tangency, the indicated optimal distribution can be obtained by the workings of the price system.

In Figure 2.2 is shown the case of a corner maximum, with individual 1 getting nothing of commodity 1. The separating line is not tangent to the indifference curve of individual 1 through the optimal point; nevertheless, there is a price vector (indeed, unique up to a factor of proportionality) which will drive both individuals to the optimal point.

Figure 2.3 shows the exceptional case in which conclusion (d) of Theorem 4 does not hold, that is, the optimal point is not a point of utility maximization for both individuals for some pair of prices. Individual 2 will only choose the indicated point if $p_1 = 0$, but then individual 1 will seek a point further out on the X_{11}-axis than is consistent with the claims of individual 2.

Comments on the Assumptions

Assumptions 2–4 have played a vital role in the analysis. The most critical is probably Assumption 2, that the desirability of a distribution to any individual depends only on the commodity apportionment to him. If any component of X entered as a variable into the utility functions of more than one individual, the whole analysis would be vitiated as it stands. Conspicuous consumption of the type envisioned by Veblen is a case where there is a negative interrelation between the consumption of one individual and the welfare of another. The drive for income equality and similar concepts of social equity, to the extent that it is shared by individuals who stand to lose from a purely individualistic viewpoint, represents another case of this type.

The empirical importance of this phenomenon has been stressed by Veblen (1899) and more recently by J. S. Duesenberry (1949); references to other studies are to be found in a paper by H. Leibenstein (1950, especially pp. 184–186). Some of the formal implications for the problem of optimal allocation are discussed by Pigou, Meade, Reder (see the references in Leibenstein), Tintner (1946), and Duesenberry (1949, pp. 92–104). The general feeling is that in these cases, optimal allocation can be achieved by a price system, accompanied by a suitable system of taxes and bounties. However, the problem has only been discussed in simple cases; and no system has been shown to have, in the general case, the important property possessed by the price system and expressed in Theorem 5; not only can optimal distributions (usually) be achieved by the price system but any distribution so achieved is optimal.

I have argued elsewhere (Arrow, 1950, 1951) that if we seek distributions which are not merely optimal in the above sense but uniquely best in some social sense, then it must be assumed that the utility functions are interdependent, to the extent, at least, that each individual has standards of social equity. These imply that preferences as among distributions depend not only on the consumption of the individual but also among the distribution of welfare as related to the individual's social ideals.

The as yet unachieved hope of the type of analysis of which this chapter is a sample, the so-called "new welfare economics," is that the problems of social welfare can be divided into two parts: a preliminary social value judgment as to the distribution of welfare followed by a detailed division of commodities taking interpersonal comparisons made by the first step as given. It is in the second step that the present type of analysis may be useful. The preceding paragraphs suggest some of the difficulties.

Assumptions 3 and 4 are convexity assumptions in the field of consumption and production, respectively. Assumption 3 is invariably made in discussions of consumer's demand theory; it is a lineal descendant of the postulate of diminishing marginal utility, made when it was customary to regard utility as measurable. The justification for the assumption, however, is usually given little consideration. A common one, given for example by Hicks (1939, pp. 23–24) is that the demand function is known empirically to be single-valued and continuous and that for every commodity bundle there is a set of prices and an income level for which that bundle will be demanded. It may be doubted that this assumption is really empirically verifiable, and in any case, it is an assumption of a totally different logical order from that of utility maximization itself. The older discussions of diminishing marginal utility as arising from the satisfaction of more intense wants first make more sense, although they are bound up with the untenable notion of measurable utility. However, their fundamental point seems well taken. We must imagine that the individual has the choice of alternative uses of a given stock of goods to maximize his well-being. The preferences for alternative bundles rest then on the *best* use that can be made of each. This preliminary maximization, so to speak, gives rise to the convexity of the indifference curves.

This argument has been given a more definite form by T. C. Koopmans (verbal communication). Let x and y be two indifferent bundles. If it is supposed that the goods can be stored, even if only for a very short time, then a flow of goods at the rate $tx + (1 - t)y$ $(0 \leqq t \leqq 1)$ can be consumed at the rate of x for fraction of time t and at the rate of y for fraction of time $1 - t$. Since in each part the individual is as well off as he would be with consuming at the rate x (by the assumption that the two bundles are indifferent), the satisfaction from the flow $tx + (1 - t)y$ should be at least as great as that from x; and in general, if $0 < t < 1$, one would expect that there would be some rearrangement of the time order of consumption to yield still greater satisfaction.

Assumption 4 is usually derived from the two hypotheses of constant returns to scale (that is, for a given production process, multiplying all inputs in the same proportion will lead to a multiplication of outputs by the same proportion) and additivity of distinct production processes (that is, if process

1 yields a [vector] output x_1 and process 2 yields an output x_2, then both processes may be operated simultaneously to yield output $x_1 + x_2$). Convexity of the transformation set may, however, hold under more general hypotheses. For example, diminishing returns to scale will not violate the convexity assumption so long as the additivity postulate holds; even if the activities are rival (that is, if performance of both will yield less than the sum of the outputs of the two separately), the set T will be convex provided returns to scale diminish sufficiently rapidly. Similarly, increasing returns to scale may still not violate the convexity assumption if there is sufficient complementarity among activities.[8]

Convex Sets

To make the discussion self-contained, some definitions and the proofs of Lemmas 2 and 3 will be sketched here. For a more complete treatment see Bonnesen and Fenchel (1939, especially chapter 1).

DEFINITION. *The dimension of a convex set A is the dimension of that linear subspace of the original space containing A which has the smallest dimension.*

DEFINITION. *An external point of a convex set is a point which is a boundary point of the set in the space of smallest dimension containing the set.*

DEFINITION. *An internal point of a convex set is a point of the set which is not an external point.*

DEFINITION. *By the convex hull of a set S is meant the set of all points which belong to every convex set containing S.*

It is easy to see that the convex hull of S is itself a convex set; it is the same as the set of all convex combinations of a finite number of elements of S. Also, if a convex set A has at least two points, it possesses an internal point since its dimension is at least 1.

Proof of Lemma 3. For any r, define A_r as the (closed) set of all points of A whose distance from the nearest external point of A was at least $1/r$. Any given internal point of A has a distance greater than zero from every external point; hence A_r is nonnull for r sufficiently large. Let A'_r be the convex hull of

8. The general problem of rivalry and complementarity among activities has been discussed in an unpublished manuscript by my colleague, Stanley Reiter.

A; it too is nonnull for r sufficiently large. Clearly no external point belongs to A_r for any r. Since no external point is a convex combination of internal points, the closed set A'_r contains only internal points for every r, and therefore is disjoint from B for every r. Find the shortest line segment between a point of B and a point of A'_r, and construct a plane $\Sigma_{i=1}^n p_i^r x_i = c_r$ through the midpoint of the line segment and normal to it. Clearly, by proper choice of sign,

$$\sum_{i=1}^{n} p_i^r x_i > c_r \quad \text{for } x \text{ in } A'_r, \tag{2-48}$$

$$\sum_{i=1}^{n} p_i^r x_i < c_r \quad \text{for } x \text{ in } B, \tag{2-49}$$

since A'_r lies on one side of the plane and B on the other. Further, since for some i, $p_i^r \neq 0$, we can assume

$$\sum_{i=1}^{n} (p_i^r)^2 = 1. \tag{2-50}$$

From (2-50), the sequence of vectors $\{p^r\}$ is bounded; it can be inferred from (2-48) and (2-49) that the same is true of $\{c_r\}$. Hence, there is a subsequence of the integers r for which the two sequences converge, say to p and c, respectively. From (2-49),

$$\sum_{i=1}^{n} p_i x_i \leqq c \quad \text{for } x \text{ in } B. \tag{2-51}$$

Any given internal point of A belongs to A'_r for r sufficiently large, so that, from (2-48),

$$\sum_{i=1}^{n} p_i x_i \geqq c \quad \text{for all internal points of } A. \tag{2-52}$$

Since an external point of A is the limit of a sequence of internal points, (2-52) holds for all x in A. Finally, from (2-50), by taking limits $\Sigma_{i=1}^n p_i^2 = 1$, so that $p_i \neq 0$ for some i.

Proof of Lemma 2. If the dimension of A is less than n, then all the points of A lie in a hyperplane $\Sigma_{i=1}^n p_i x_i = c$. In particular, $\Sigma_{i=1}^n p_i x_i^* = c$, and the lemma is trivially true. If the dimension of A equals n, then A has at least two points. Let B be the set consisting of the point x^* alone. Then the conditions of Lemma 3 are satisfied. Since x^* belongs to both A and B, $c = \Sigma_{i=1}^n p_i x_i^*$, and Lemma 2 holds.

References

K. J. Arrow, "A difficulty in the concept of social welfare," *Jour. of Political Economy,* vol. 58 (1950), pp. 328–346.

K. J. Arrow, *Social Choice and Individual Values,* Cowles Commission Monograph 12, Wiley, New York, 1951.

K. J. Arrow and A. C. Enthoven, "Quasi-concave programming," *Econometrica,* vol. 29 (1961), pp. 779–800. Reprinted in K. J. Arrow and L. Hurwicz (eds.), *Studies in Resource Allocation Processes,* Cambridge University Press, Cambridge, 1977, pp. 112–133.

T. Bonnesen and W. Fenchel, *Theorie der Konvexen Körper,* Springer, Berlin, 1939; Chelsea, New York, 1948.

G. B. Dantzig, "Programming of interdependent activities: II. Mathematical model," *Econometrica,* vol. 17 (1949), pp. 200–211.

G. Debreu, "The coefficient of resource utilization," *Econometrica,* vol. 19 (1951), pp. 273–292.

J. S. Duesenberry, *Income, Saving, and the Theory of Consumer Behavior,* Harvard University Press, Cambridge, 1949.

F. Y. Edgeworth, *Mathematical Psychics,* reprint, London School of Economics, London, 1932.

J. R. Hicks, "The valuation of the social income—a comment on Professor Kuznets' reflections," *Economica,* new series, vol. 15 (1948), pp. 163–172.

J. R. Hicks, *Value and Capital,* Clarendon Press, Oxford, 1939.

T. C. Koopmans (ed.), *Activity Analysis of Production and Allocation,* Cowles Commission Monograph 13, Wiley, New York, 1951.

T. C. Koopmans, "Optimum utilization of the transportation system," abstract, *Econometrica,* vol. 16 (1948), pp. 66–68.

H. W. Kuhn and A. W. Tucker, "Nonlinear programming," in J. Neyman (ed.), *Second Berkeley Symposium on Mathematical Statistics and Probability,* University of California Press, Berkeley, 1951, pp. 481–492.

S. Kuznets, "On the valuation of social income—reflections on Professor Hicks' article, Part I," *Economica,* new series, vol. 15 (1948), pp. 1–16.

O. Lange, "The foundations of welfare economics," *Econometrica,* vol. 10 (1942), pp. 215–228.

H. Leibenstein, "Bandwagon, Snob, and Veblen effects in the theory of consumers' demand," *Quarterly Jour. of Economics,* vol. 64 (1950), pp. 183–207.

A. P. Lerner, "The concept of monopoly and the measurement of monopoly power," *Review of Economic Studies,* vol. 1, no. 3 (1934), pp. 157–175.

J. von Neumann, "Über ein ökonomisches Gleichungssystem und eine Verallgemeinerung des Brouwerschen Fixpunktsatzes," *Ergebnisse eines mathematischen Kolloquiums,* Heft 8 (1935–36), pp. 73–83, translated as, "A model of general economic equilibrium," *Review of Economic Studies,* vol. 13 (1945–46), pp. 1–9.

J. von Neumann and O. Morgenstern, *Theory of Games and Economic Behavior,* 2nd ed., Princeton University Press, Princeton, 1947.

P. A. Samuelson, "Evaluation of real national income," *Oxford Economic Papers,* new series, vol. 2 (1950), pp. 1–29.

T. Scitovsky, "A note on welfare propositions in economics," *Review of Economic Studies* (1941–42), pp. 77–88.

G. Tintner, "A note of welfare economics," *Econometrica,* vol. 14 (1946), pp. 69–78.

T. Veblen, *The Theory of the Leisure Class,* Macmillan, Chicago, 1899.

H. Wold, "A synthesis of pure demand analysis. Part II," *Skandinavisk Aktuarie-tidskrift,* vol. 26 (1943), pp. 220–263.

M. K. Wood and G. B. Dantzig, "Programming of interdependent activities: I. General discussion," *Econometrica,* vol. 17 (1949), pp. 193–199.

3 The Role of Securities in the Optimal Allocation of Risk Bearing

Ever since I encountered Hicks's *Value and Capital* while I was still a graduate student, I had the aim of completing and extending his vision of the economic system in its purest form. This was not because I believed that the economic world was perfectly competitive or that it was clearly self-equilibrating; after all, Chamberlin, Robinson, and Keynes were dominant intellectual influences, and I had the even more powerful influence of the facts of massive unemployment and large corporations. But the idea that the economic world was a *general* system, with all parts interdependent, seemed (and seems) to me to be an essential of good analysis. I regret what appears to be a revival of single-market thinking both among monetarists and among some of the younger empirical analysts. Then as now, the only game in town that offered a general system of economic interdependence was general competitive equilibrium, an idea to which the name of Léon Walras is imperishably linked. At least, such a system would provide a starting point for analysis of the market's imperfections.

One lacuna in the theory of general competitive equilibrium was certainly an incapacity to include uncertainty. There had been a

Reprinted from *Review of Economic Studies,* 31 (1963–64): 91–96. Appeared originally in French translation in *Économetrie,* Colloques Internationaux du Centre National de la Recherche Scientifique, 11 (1953): 41–47. The research was carried out under contract Nonr-225 (50) of the U.S. Office of Naval Research at Stanford University.

limited literature on demand for particular risky assets, but none that could successfully incorporate the individual markets into a general system. I was strongly interested in theoretical statistics, having studied with both Harold Hotelling and Abraham Wald. The latter especially was devoted to the study of foundations. A standard viewpoint in probability theory by then was to consider a random variable to be a function on some underlying space. A statistical decision in the broadest sense could be regarded as defining a random variable, which also depended on the parameters of the distribution, and thus the choice among statistical decision procedures was a choice among functions depending on both the underlying sample space and the unknown parameters. Wald's views were adapted and revised by L. J. Savage, who revived the Bayesian concept that the parameters were also random variables. Hence, a decision under uncertainty could be regarded as a function of states of nature.

In trying to incorporate uncertainty into general equilibrium theory, I was led by the Wald-Savage viewpoint to consider an elementary decision as one that took a unit value for one state of nature and zero elsewhere; thus all general decisions could be regarded as bundles of elementary decisions. When I was beginning to develop this idea, but before I had had a chance to elaborate on it, I was invited on a few months' notice to a conference on the foundations of risk bearing sponsored by the Centre National de la Recherche Scientifique in June 1952. Jacob Marschak had recommended my name to the organizers. It was indeed an eventful conference, with an all-star set of participants (Maurice Allais, Milton Friedman, Pierre Massé, Jacob Marschak, and Leonard Savage, among others) and much controversy about the validity of the expected-utility and subjective-probability axioms. I rather hastily wrote up my notes; they were translated into French by the Institut des Sciences Economiques Appliquées, with some help from me, and thus the article appeared in French.

Subsequently the *Review of Economic Studies* asked to publish the work in English; I supplied them with my original manuscript, which has therefore appeared as an English "translation" of the original. When the paper was later reprinted in my collection *Essays in the Theory of Risk-Bearing,* a note and postscript were added.

The theory of the optimal allocation of resources under conditions of certainty is well known. In this chapter, an extension of the theory to conditions of subjective uncertainty is considered.

Attention is confined to the case of a pure exchange economy; the introduction of production would not be difficult. We suppose I individuals, and S possible states of nature. In the sth state, amount x_{sc} of commodity $c(c = 1, \ldots, C)$ is produced. It is assumed that each individual acts on the basis of subjective probabilities as to the states of nature; let π_{is} be the subjective probability of state s according to individual i. Further, let x_{isc} be the amount of commodity claimed by individual i if state s occurs. These claims are, of course, limited by available resources, so that

$$\sum_{i=1}^{I} x_{isc} = x_{sc}, \tag{3-1}$$

assuming the absence of saturation of individuals' desires.

The problem of optimal allocation of risk bearing is that of choosing the magnitudes x_{isc}, subject to restraints (3-1), in such a way that no other choice will make every individual better off. In the next section it is briefly argued that, if there exist markets for claims on all commodities, the competitive system will lead to an optimal allocation under certain hypotheses.

However, in the real world the allocation of risk bearing is accomplished by claims payable in money, not in commodities. In the third section it is shown that the von Neumann-Morgenstern theorem enables us to conclude that, under certain hypotheses, the allocation of risk bearing by competitive securities markets is in fact optimal.

In the fourth section, it is shown that the hypotheses used in the two previous sections contain an important implication: that the competitive allocation of risk bearing is guaranteed to be viable only if the individuals have attitudes of risk aversion.[1]

Allocation of Risk Bearing by Commodity Claims

Let $V_i(x_{i11}, \ldots, x_{i1C}, x_{i21}, \ldots, x_{iSC})$ be the utility of individual i if he is assigned claims of amount x_{isc} for commodity c if state s occurs $(c = 1, \ldots, C; s = 1, \ldots, S)$. This is exactly analogous to the utility function in the case of certainty except that the number of variables has

1. Note added for this translation. Since the above was written I have come to the conclusion that this statement needs very severe qualification, as explained in note 3.

increased from C to SC. We may therefore achieve any optimal allocation of risk bearing by a competitive system. Let x^*_{isc} ($i = 1, \ldots, I$; $s = 1, \ldots, S$; $c = 1, \ldots, C$) be any optimal allocation; then there exist a set of money incomes y_i for individual i, and prices $\bar{p}_{sc}$ for a unit claim on commodity c if state s occurs, such that if each individual i chooses values of the variables x_{isc} ($s = 1, \ldots, S$; $c = 1, \ldots, C$) subject to the restraint

$$\sum_{s=1}^{S} \sum_{c=1}^{C} \bar{p}_{sc} x_{isc} = y_i, \tag{3-2}$$

taking prices as given, the chosen values of the x_{isc}'s will be the given optimal allocation x^*_{isc} ($i = 1, \ldots, I$; $s = 1, \ldots, S$; $c = 1, \ldots, C$).

The argument is a trivial reformulation of the usual one in welfare economics.[2] However, there is one important qualification; the validity of the theorem depends on the assumption (not always made explicitly) that the indifference surfaces are convex to the origin, or, to state the condition equivalently, that $V_i(x_{i11}, \ldots, x_{iSC})$ is a *quasi-concave* function of its arguments. [The function $f(x_1, \ldots, x_n)$ is said to be quasi-concave if for every pair of points $(x^1_1, \ldots, x^1_n)$ and $(x^2_1, \ldots, x^2_n)$ such that $f(x^1_1, \ldots, x^1_n) \geqq f(x^2_1, \ldots, x^2_n)$ and every real number α,

$$0 \leqq \alpha \leqq 1;$$

$$f(\alpha x^1_1 + (1-\alpha)x^2_1, \ldots, \alpha x^1_n + (1-\alpha)x^2_n) \geqq f(x^2_1, \ldots, x^2_n).$$

It is easy to see geometrically the equivalence between this definition and the convexity of the indifference surfaces.]

THEOREM 1. *If $V_i(x_{i11}, \ldots, x_{iSC})$ is quasi-concave for every i, then any optimal allocation of risk bearing can be realized by a system of perfectly competitive markets in claims on commodities.*

The meaning of the hypothesis of Theorem 1 will be explored in the fourth section.

Allocation of Risk Bearing by Securities

In the actual world, risk bearing is not allocated by the sale of claims against specific commodities. A simplified picture would rather be the following:

2. See, for a simple exposition, O. Lange, "The Foundation of Welfare Economics," *Econometrica,* 10 (1942):215–228, or P. A. Samuelson, *Foundations of Economic Analysis,* chap. 8.

securities are sold which are payable in money, the amount depending on the state s which has actually occurred (this concept is obvious for stocks; for bonds, we have only to recall the possibility of default if certain states s occur); when the state s occurs, the money transfers determined by the securities take place, and then the allocation of commodities takes place through the market in the ordinary way, without further risk bearing.

It is not difficult to show that any optimal allocation of risk bearing can be achieved by such a competitive system involving securities payable in money. For the given optimal allocation, x^*_{isc}, let the prices $\bar{p}_{sc}$ and the incomes y_i be determined as in the previous section. For simplicity, assume there are precisely S types of securities, where a unit security of the sth type is a claim paying one monetary unit if state s occurs and nothing otherwise. Any security whatever may be regarded as a bundle of the elementary types just described.

Let q_s be the price of the sth security and p_{sc} the price of commodity c if state s occurs. Choose them so that

(3-3) $$q_s p_{sc} = \bar{p}_{sc}.$$

An individual confronted with these prices has the same range of alternatives available as he did under the system described in the previous section, taking $q_s p_{sc}$ as equivalent to the price of a claim on commodity c in state s. He will plan to acquire the same claims, and therefore, on the market for securities of the sth type, individual i will purchase sufficient securities of type s to realize the desired purchase of commodities if state s occurs, that is, he will purchase

(3-4) $$y^*_{is} = \sum_{c=1}^{C} p_{sc} x^*_{isc}$$

units of the sth type of security. His purchase of securities of all types is restricted by the restraint

$$\sum_{s=1}^{S} q_s y_{is} = y_i;$$

the allocation y^*_{is} $(s = 1, \ldots, S)$ satisfies this restraint, as can be seen from (3-2), (3-3), and (3-4).

The total monetary stock available is $\Sigma_{i=1}^{I} y_i = y$. The net volume of claims payable when any state s occurs must therefore be precisely y or

(3-5) $$\sum_{i=1}^{I} y_{is} = y \qquad (s = 1, \ldots, S).$$

Substitute (3-4) into (3-5) and multiply both sides by q_s/y, then, from (3-3),

(3-6) $$q_s = \frac{\sum_{i=1}^{I} \sum_{c=1}^{C} \bar{p}_{sc} x^*_{isc}}{y} \qquad (s = 1, \ldots, S).$$

The prices p_{sc} are then determined from (3-3).

With the prices q_s and p_{sc} thus determined, and the incomes y_i, the competitive system, operating first on the securities markets and then on the separate commodity markets, will lead to the allocation x^*_{isc}. For, as we have already seen, individual i will demand y^*_{is} of security s. Suppose state s occurs. He then has income y^*_{is} to allocate among commodities with prices $\bar{p}_{sc}$. Let $U_i(x_{is1}, \ldots, x_{isC})$ be a utility function of individual i for commodities, then he chooses a bundle so as to maximize U_i subject to the restraint

(3-7) $$\sum_{c=1}^{C} p_{sc} x_{isc} = y^*_{is}.$$

Let x^+_{isc} $(c = 1, \ldots, C)$ be the chosen commodity amounts. Since by (3-4) the quantities x^*_{isc} satisfy (3-7), it follows from the definition of a maximum that

(3-8) $$U_i(x^+_{is1}, \ldots, x^+_{isC}) \geqq U_i(x^*_{is1}, \ldots, x^*_{isC}).$$

The quantities x^+_{isc} are defined for all s.

By the von Neumann–Morgenstern theorem, the function U_i may be chosen so that

(3-9) $$V_i(x_{i11}, \ldots, x_{iSC}) = \sum_{s=1}^{S} \pi_{is} U_i(x_{is1}, \ldots, x_{isC}).$$

Suppose that in (3-8), the strict inequality holds for at least one s for which $\pi_{is} > 0$. Then by (3-9),

(3-10) $$V_i(x^+_{i11}, \ldots, x^+_{iSC}) > V_i(x^*_{i11}, \ldots, x^*_{iSC}).$$

On the other hand, if we multiply in (3-7) by q_s and sum over s, it is seen that the bundle of claims $(x^+_{i11}, \ldots, x^+_{iSC})$ satisfies restraint (3-2). But by construction the bundle $(x^*_{i11}, \ldots, x^*_{iSC})$ maximizes V_i subject to (3-2); hence (3-10) is a contradiction, and the equality holds in (3-8) for all states with positive subjective probability. If the *strict* quasi-concavity of U_i is assumed, as usual, the equality implies that $x^+_{isc} = x^*_{isc}$ for all c and all i and s for which $\pi_{is} > 0$. If $\pi_{is} = 0$, then obviously $x^*_{isc} = 0$ $(c = 1, \ldots, C)$, which implies that $y^*_{is} = 0$ and therefore $x^+_{isc} = 0$ $(c = 1, \ldots, C)$. Hence, once the state s occurs, individual i will in fact purchase the bundle prescribed under the optimal allocation.

THEOREM 2. *If* $\Sigma_{s=1}^{S} \pi_{is} U_i(x_{is1}, \ldots, x_{isC})$ *is quasi-concave in all its variables, then any optimal allocation of risk bearing can be achieved by perfect competition on the securities and commodity markets, where securities are payable in money.*

Socially, the significance of the theorem is that it permits economizing on markets; only $S + C$ markets are needed to achieve the optimal allocation, instead of the SC markets implied in Theorem 1.

One might wonder if any loopholes have been left through arbitrage between securities and hold of money; in the allocation of securities, an individual has the option of holding cash instead and using the hoarding in the commodity allocation.

If we sum over s in (3-6) and use (3-2),

$$\text{(3-11)} \qquad \sum_{s=1}^{S} q_s = \frac{\sum_{i=1}^{I} \sum_{s=1}^{S} \sum_{c=1}^{C} \bar{p}_{sc} x^*_{isc}}{y} = \frac{\sum_{i=1}^{I} y_i}{y} = 1.$$

A monetary unit is equivalent to a bundle of S unit securities, one of each type; to avoid arbitrage, then, such a bundle should have a unit price. This is ensured by (3-11).

Risk Aversion and the Competitive Allocation of Risk Bearing

What is the economic significance of the hypothesis that the utility functions

$$V_i = \sum_{s=1}^{S} \pi_{is} U_i$$

be quasi-concave? The easiest case to consider is that in which

$$S = 2, \qquad \pi_{is} = \tfrac{1}{2} \qquad (s = 1,2).$$

THEOREM 3. *If* $\frac{1}{2}[f(x_1, \ldots, x_C) + f(x_{C+1}, \ldots, x_{2C})]$ *is quasi-concave in all its variables, then* $f(x_1, \ldots, x_C)$ *is a concave function.*

The expression $f(x_1, \ldots, x_C)$ will be said to be concave if for every pair of points $(x_1^1, \ldots, x_C^1)$ and $(x_1^2, \ldots, x_C^2)$,

$$f(\tfrac{1}{2}x_1^1 + \tfrac{1}{2}x_1^2, \ldots, \tfrac{1}{2}x_C^1 + \tfrac{1}{2}x_C^2) \\ \geqq \tfrac{1}{2}[f(x_1^1, \ldots, x_C^1) + \tfrac{1}{2}f(x_1^2, \ldots, x_C^2)].$$

It is well known that a concave function is always quasi-concave, but not conversely.

Proof. Suppose $f(x_1, \ldots, x_C)$ is not concave. Then for some pair of points, $(x_1^1, \ldots, x_C^1)$ and $(x_1^2, \ldots, x_C^2)$,

$$(3\text{-}12) \qquad f\left(\frac{x_1^1 + x_1^2}{2}, \ldots, \frac{x_C^1 + x_C^2}{2}\right) < \tfrac{1}{2}f(x_1^1, \ldots, x_C^1) + \tfrac{1}{2}f(x_1^2, \ldots, x_C^2).$$

Let

$$(3\text{-}13) \qquad g(x_1, \ldots, x_{2C}) = \tfrac{1}{2}[f(x_1, \ldots, x_C) + f(x_{C+1}, \ldots, x_{2C})].$$

Then obviously

$$g(x_1^1, \ldots, x_C^1, x_1^2, \ldots, x_C^2) = g(x_1^2, \ldots, x_C^2, x_1^1, \ldots, x_C^1).$$

By the hypothesis that g is quasi-concave, then

$$(3\text{-}14) \qquad g\left(\frac{x_1^1 + x_1^2}{2}, \ldots, \frac{x_C^1 + x_C^2}{2}, \frac{x_1^2 + x_1^1}{2}, \ldots, \frac{x_C^2 + x_C^1}{2}\right) \geqq g(x_1^1, \ldots, x_C^1, x_1^2, \ldots, x_C^2).$$

But from (3-13) and (3-12),

$$\begin{aligned} & g\left(\frac{x_1^1 + x_1^2}{2}, \ldots, \frac{x_C^1 + x_C^2}{2}, \frac{x_1^2 + x_1^1}{2}, \ldots, \frac{x_C^2 + x_C^1}{2}\right) \\ &= \tfrac{1}{2}\left[f\left(\frac{x_1^1 + x_1^2}{2}, \ldots, \frac{x_C^1 + x_C^2}{2}\right) + f\left(\frac{x_1^2 + x_1^1}{2}, \ldots, \frac{x_C^2 + x_C^1}{2}\right)\right] \\ &= f\left(\frac{x_1^1 + x_1^2}{2}, \ldots, \frac{x_C^1 + x_C^2}{2}\right) \\ &< \tfrac{1}{2}[f(x_1^1, \ldots, x_C^1) + f(x_1^2, \ldots, x_C^2)] \\ &= g(x_1^1, \ldots, x_C^1, x_1^2, \ldots, x_C^2), \end{aligned}$$

which contradicts (3-14). Hence, $f(x_1, \ldots, x_C)$ must be concave.

In terms of the allocation of risk bearing, Theorem 3 implies that if one wishes to ensure the viability of the competitive allocation for all possible assignments of probabilities π_{is}, it must be assumed that the individual utility functions U_i must be concave. This condition, in turn, is obviously equivalent to the assumption of risk aversion; for the condition

$$U_i\left(\frac{x_1^1 + x_1^2}{2}, \ldots, \frac{x_C^1 + x_C^2}{2}\right)$$
$$\geqq \tfrac{1}{2}[U_i(x_1^1, \ldots, x_C^1) + U_i(x_1^2, \ldots, x_C^2)]$$

means that an even gamble as between two bundles is never preferred to the arithmetic mean of those bundles.

The hypothesis of quasi-concavity of the utility function has here only been indicated as a sufficient, not a necessary condition for the viability of competitive allocation. However, without the assumption of quasi-concavity, some optimal allocations cannot be achieved by competitive means, and in general, there would be only very special cases in which any competitive equilibrium is achievable. Consider the following simple examples:

There are one commodity, two individuals, and two states. Both individuals have the same utility function.

(3-15) $\qquad U_i(x) = x^2 \qquad (i = 1,2);$

this function is monotonic and hence quasi-concave, but not concave, since it implies risk preference. Assume further that $\pi_{is} = \frac{1}{2}(i = 1,2; s = 1,2)$, then

(3-16) $\qquad V_i(x_{i11}, x_{i21}) = \frac{1}{2}(x_{i11}^2 + x_{i21}^2) \qquad (i = 1,2).$

Finally, suppose that

(3-17) $\qquad x_{11} = 1, \qquad x_{21} = 2.$

It is easy to see that for any fixed set of prices on claims under alternative states, each individual will buy all of one claim or all of the other. Hence any optimal allocation in which both individuals possess positive claims in both states is unachievable by competitive means. Such optimal allocations do exist; we have only to choose the variables $x_{is1}(i = 1,2; s = 1,2)$ so as to maximize V_1 subject to the restraints, implied by (3-17),

$$x_{111} + x_{211} = 1, \qquad x_{121} + x_{221} = 2,$$

and the restraint V_2 = constant. If, for example, we fix $V_2 = \frac{1}{2}$, we have the optimal allocation,

$$x_{111} = \frac{\sqrt{5} - 1}{\sqrt{5}}, \qquad x_{121} = \frac{2\sqrt{5} - 2}{\sqrt{5}},$$

$$x_{211} = \frac{1}{\sqrt{5}}, \qquad x_{222} = \frac{2}{\sqrt{5}}.$$

In fact, for the functions given by (3-16), a competitive equilibrium usually does not exist. Let $y_i (i = 1,2)$ be the incomes of the two individuals. Let p be the price of a unit claim for state 1, taking the unit claim in state 2 as numéraire. Then in a competitive market, individual i maximizes V_i subject to

$$px_{i11} + x_{i21} = y_i.$$

He will then choose $x_{i11} = y_i/p$, $x_{i21} = 0$ if $p < 1$ and choose $x_{i11} = 0$, $x_{i21} = y_i$ if $p > 1$. Hence, if $p \neq 1$, there will be zero demand, and hence disequilibrium, on one market. If $p = 1$, each individual will be indifferent between the bundles $(y_i,0)$ and $(0,y_i)$. Except in the special case where $y_1 = 1, y_2 = 2$ (or vice versa), there is again no possible way of achieving equilibrium.[3]

Appendix

The previous discussion has been confined to the case of pure consumption. It is possible to introduce production decisions in a framework of essentially the same character. If we assume that the production takes place under random conditions, for example, those induced by weather or by accident, we can, in linear programming terminology, represent each activity by a vector whose components are the outputs or inputs of all commodities for all possible states of nature. If, as before, we substitute commodity options for commodities, the vector describing any particular activity can be formally identified with the commodity vector. An interesting point to be made is that under these circumstances production decisions of a firm do not depend on the probability judgments or utilities of the owners of the firms. Let q_s be the price of a security which promises \$1.00 in state s and nothing otherwise. Let p_{sc} be the price of commodity c in state s. Then among all the possible values of the variables x_{sc} available to the firm under its conditions of production the firm chooses so as to maximize,

---

3. Though there is nothing wrong formally with the analysis of this last section, I now consider it misleading. If there are a large number of consumers, the income of each being relatively small, it has now been established by the important work of Farrell and Rothenberg that the quasi-concavity of the indifference curves is unnecessary to the existence of competitive equilibrium; see M. J. Farrell, "The Convexity Assumption in the Theory of Competitive Markets," *Journal of Political Economy,* 67 (1959):377–391, and J. Rothenberg, "Non-Convexity, Aggregation and Pareto Optimality," ibid., 68 (1960):435–468.

$$\sum_{s=1}^{S} q_s \sum_{c=1}^{C} p_{sc} x_{sc}.$$

The values q_s might be interpreted as the market evaluation of the probability of state s. Then the rule for the firm is to compute for each possible state of nature the profit to be obtained from any given production plan, and weight these various profits for any given plan by the market evaluations of probabilities of that state of nature. The owners of the firm, if their evaluations of probabilities differ from that of the market, will be led to engage in other operations on the security market, but their decisions as to production will not be affected by these judgments.

However, the definition of a commodity is seriously affected on the production side by the nature of the theory of uncertainty. For two units to be regarded as part of the same commodity, they must have the same role of production for any possible state of nature. Let us consider two identical machines with independent probabilities of breakdown. There are from this point of view four possible states of nature: one where both machines are in action, one where machine 1 is in action while machine 2 is out, one where machine 2 is in action and machine 1 is out, and one where both are out of action. Since the two machines are not substitutable for each other in every state of nature, they must be regarded as different commodities. The number of commodities thus becomes enormously greater than is ordinarily supposed, and indivisibility becomes a much more prevalent phenomenon. If there are a great many units of a commodity, even though each unit is indivisible, the indivisibilities may be regarded as so small compared to the total flow that they can be disregarded. This is not so if each machine, for example, has to be regarded as a separate commodity. Hence the usual theory of allocation which presupposes convexity of the production structure will become inapplicable, and the theorems of welfare economics and competitive allocation will become false. Consider, for example, the following situation, which is greatly simplified from a case studied by a Swedish engineer, Palm. Suppose we have two machines, each with a fifty-fifty chance of breakdown, and one man. To operate, a machine has to be in action and have a man assigned to it. If neither machine has broken down, then only one machine can be used. Hence it is clear that one machine will be in operation with probability $\frac{3}{4}$ and 0 machines will be in operation with probability $\frac{1}{4}$ so that the expected output is $\frac{3}{4}$ of the potential output of one machine. Now suppose there are four machines and two men and again assume that each machine will break down with probability $\frac{1}{2}$; then 0 machines will be in action with probability $\frac{1}{16}$, one machine with probability $\frac{1}{4}$, and two machines with probability $\frac{11}{16}$. The expected output will therefore be $\frac{13}{8}$ of the potential output of a single machine, which is more than twice as much. In other words, by doubling the number of men and doubling the number of machines we have more than doubled the expected output. An analysis shows that this increasing return arises out of the consideration of indivisibility just advanced. Such increasing returns are, of course, incompatible with the competitive allocation of risk bearing. Other difficulties arise with the competitive allocation of risk bearing in the case where some members of society have a preference for risk. Also the spread of information which may alter subjective probabilities creates some difficulties in the whole theory. These topics need more explanation than can be given to them here.

To conclude, we have seen that it is possible to set up formal mechanisms which under certain conditions will achieve an optimal allocation of risk by competitive methods. However, the empirical validity of the conditions for the optimal character of competitive allocation is considerably less likely to be fulfilled in the case of uncertainty than in the case of certainty and, furthermore, many of the economic institutions which would be needed to carry out the competitive allocation in the case of uncertainty are in fact lacking.

References

Savage, L. J. 1954. *The Foundations of Statistics.* New York: Wiley.
Wald, A. 1950. *Statistical Decision Functions.* New York: Wiley.

4 Existence of an Equilibrium for a Competitive Economy

In the process of seeking a deeper foundation for general equilibrium theory, one obvious problem was a proof of existence. I became aware of it as a graduate student; I do not recall just how or from what source. I did know that Abraham Wald, who had been brought by Hotelling to join him in teaching mathematical statistics at Columbia, had worked on this problem. I obtained the references to his papers from him, but he regarded further progress as difficult, and I was discouraged from further work. In any case, Wald's assumption that the Weak Axiom of Revealed Preference held for the market was very strong, and his methods did not offer any suggestions for weakening it.

The paper of John von Neumann on the existence of balanced growth equilibrium, translated into English, seemed to be relevant, but the model was far indeed from normal economic reasoning, for consumption was not determined by any optimization considerations. It was the paper of John F. Nash, Jr., showing the existence of equilibrium points to games by the use of Kakutani's fixed-point theorem (equivalent to von Neumann's), that suggested to several of us the corresponding analysis for the concept of general competitive equilibrium. Gerard Debreu, Lionel McKenzie, and I all followed up this lead independently, each in his own way. My original

This chapter was written with Gerard Debreu. Reprinted from *Econometrica,* 22 (1954): 265–290.

approach, for what it is worth, was to formulate competitive equilibrium as the equilibrium of a suitably chosen game. The players of this fictitious game were the consumers, a set of "anticonsumers" (one for each consumer), producers, and a price chooser. Each consumer chose a consumption vector, each anticonsumer a nonnegative number (interpretable as the marginal utility of income), each firm a production vector, and the price chooser a price vector on the unit simplex. The payoff to a consumer was the utility of his consumption vector plus the budgetary surplus (possibly negative, of course) multiplied by the anticonsumer's chosen number. The payoff to an anticonsumer was the negative of the payoff to the corresponding consumer. The payoff to the firm was profit and to the price chooser the value of excess demand at the chosen prices. This is a well-defined game. The existence of equilibrium does not follow mechanically from Nash's theorem, since some of the strategy domains are unbounded.

Debreu and I sent our manuscripts to each other and so discovered our common purpose. We also detected the same flaw in each other's work; we had ignored the possibility of discontinuity when prices vary in such a way that some consumers' incomes approach zero. We then collaborated, mostly by correspondence, until we had come to some resolution of this problem. In the main body of the work we followed more closely Debreu's more elegant formulation, based on the concept of generalized games, which eliminated the need for "anticonsumers." McKenzie's paper was published in the issue of *Econometrica* previous to the one in which our paper appeared.

Léon Walras (1900) first formulated the state of the economic system at any point of time as the solution of a system of simultaneous equations representing the demand for goods by consumers, the supply of goods by producers, and the equilibrium condition that supply equal demand on every market. It was assumed that each consumer acts so as to maximize his utility, each producer acts so as to maximize his profit, and perfect competition prevails, in the sense that each producer and consumer regards the prices paid and received as independent of his own choices. Walras did not, however, give any conclusive arguments to show that the equations, as given, have a solution.

The investigation of the existence of solutions is of interest both for descriptive and for normative economics. Descriptively, the view that the competitive model is a reasonably accurate description of reality, at least for certain purposes, presupposes that the equations describing the model are consistent with each other. Hence, one check on the empirical usefulness of the model is the prescription of the conditions under which the equations of competitive equilibrium have a solution.

Perhaps as important is the relation between the existence of solutions to a competitive equilibrium and the problems of normative or welfare economics. It is well known that, under suitable assumptions on the preferences of consumers and the production possibilities of producers, the allocation of resources in a competitive equilibrium is optimal in the sense of Pareto (no redistribution of goods or productive resources can improve the position of one individual without making at least one other individual worse off), and conversely every Pareto-optimal allocation of resources can be realized by a competitive equilibrium (see, for example, Arrow, 1951; Debreu, 1951; and the references given there). From the point of view of normative economics the problem of existence of an equilibrium for a competitive system is therefore also basic.

To study this question, it is first necessary to specify more carefully than is generally done the precise assumptions of a competitive economy. The main results of this chapter are two theorems stating very general conditions under which a competitive equilibrium will exist. Loosely speaking, the first theorem asserts that if every individual has initially some positive quantity of every commodity available for sale, then a competitive equilibrium will exist. The second theorem asserts the existence of competitive equilibrium if there are some types of labor with the following two properties: (1) each individual can supply some positive amount of at least one such type of labor; and (2) each such type of labor has a positive usefulness in the production of desired commodities. The conditions of the second theorem, particularly, may be expected to be satisfied in a wide variety of actual situations, though not, for example, if there is insufficient substitutability in the structure of production.

The assumptions made below are, in several respects, weaker and closer to economic reality than A. Wald's (1951). Unlike his models, ours presents an integrated system of production and consumption which takes account of the circular flow of income. The proof of existence is also simpler than his. Neither the uniqueness nor the stability of the competitive solution is investigated in this chapter. The latter study would require specification of the dynamics of a competitive market as well as the definition of equilibrium.

Mathematical techniques are set-theoretical. A central concept is that of an abstract economy, a generalization of the concept of a game.

The last section contains a detailed historical note.

1. Statement of the First Existence Theorem for a Competitive Equilibrium

1.0. In this section a model of a competitive economy will be described, and certain assumptions will be made concerning the production and consumption units in the economy. The notion of equilibrium for such an economy will be defined, and a theorem stated about the existence of this equilibrium.

1.1. We suppose there are a finite number of distinct commodities (including all kinds of services). Each commodity may be bought or sold for delivery at one of a finite number of distinct locations and one of a finite number of future time points. For the present purposes, the same commodity at two different locations or two different points of time will be regarded as two different commodities. Hence, there are altogether a finite number of commodities (when the concept is used in the extended sense of including spatial and temporal specifications). Let the number of commodities be l; the letter h, which runs from 1 to l, will designate different commodities.

1.2.0. The commodities, or at least some of them, are produced in *production units* (for example, firms). The number of production units will be assumed to be a finite number n; different production units will be designated by the letter j. Certain basic assumptions will be made about the technological nature of the production process; before stating them, a few elements of vector and set notation will be given.

1.2.1. $x \geqq y$ means $x_h \geqq y_h$ for each component h;

$x \geq y$ means $x \geqq y$ but not $x = y$;

$x > y$ means $x_h > y_h$ for each component h.

R^l is the Euclidean space of l dimensions, that is, the set of all vectors with l components.

0 is the vector all of whose components are 0.

$\{x| \ \}$, where the blank is filled in by some statement involving x, means the set of all x's for which that statement is true.

$\Omega = \{x|x \epsilon R^l, x \geqq 0\}$.

For any set of vectors A, let $-A = \{x|-x \epsilon A\}$.

For any sets of vectors A_ι $(\iota = 1, \ldots, \nu)$, let

$\Sigma_{\iota=1}^{\nu} A_\iota = \{x|x = \Sigma_{\iota=1}^{\nu} x_\iota$ for some $x_1, \ldots, x_\nu$, where $x_\iota \epsilon A_\iota\}$.

1.2.2. For each production unit j, there is a set Y_j of possible production plans. An element y_j of Y_j is a vector in R^l, the hth component of which, y_{hj}, designates the output of commodity h according to that plan. Inputs are treated as negative components. Let $Y = \Sigma_{j=1}^{n} Y_j$; then the elements of Y represent all possible input-output schedules for the production sector as a whole. The following assumptions about the sets Y_j will be made:

ASSUMPTION 1. (a) *Y_j is a closed convex subset of R^l containing 0 $(j = 1, \ldots, n)$.*
(b) *$Y \cap \Omega = 0$.*
(c) *$Y \cap (-Y) = 0$.*

Assumption 1(a) implies nonincreasing returns to scale, for if $y_j \in Y_j$ and $0 \leq \lambda \leq 1$, then $\lambda y_j = \lambda y_j + (1 - \lambda)0 \in Y_j$, since $0 \in Y_j$ and Y_j is convex. If we assumed in addition the additivity of production possibility vectors, Y_j would be a convex cone, that is, constant returns to scale would prevail. If, however, we assume that among the factors used by a firm are some which are not transferable in the market and so do not appear in the list of commodities, the production possibility vectors, if we consider only the components which correspond to marketable commodities, will not satisfy the additivity axiom.[1] The closure of Y_j merely says if vectors arbitrarily close to y_j are in Y_j, then so is y_j. Naturally, $0 \in Y_j$, since a production unit can always go out of existence. It is to be noted that the list of production units should include not only actually existing ones but those that might enter the market under suitable price conditions.

Assumption 1(b) says that one cannot have an aggregate production possibility vector with a positive component unless at least one component is negative. That is, it is impossible to have any output unless there is some input.

Assumption 1(c) asserts the impossibility of two production possibility vectors which exactly cancel each other, in the sense that the outputs of one are exactly the inputs of the other. The simplest justification for 1(c) is to note that some type of labor is necessary for any production activity, while labor cannot be produced by production-units. If $y \in Y$, and $y \neq 0$, then $y_h < 0$ for some h corresponding to a type of labor, so that $-y_h > 0$, (here, y_h

1. The existence of factors private to the firm is the standard justification in economic theory for diminishing returns to scale. See, for example, the discussion of "free rationed goods" by Hart (1940, pp. 4, 38); also, Hicks (1939, pp. 82–83); Samuelson (1947, p. 84).

is the *h*th component of the vector y). Since labor cannot be produced, $-y$ cannot belong to Y.[2]

Since commodities are differentiated according to time as well as physical characteristics, investment plans which involve future planned purchases and sales are included in the model of production used here.

1.2.3. The preceding assumptions have related to the *technological* aspects of production. Under the usual assumptions of perfect competition, the *economic* motivation for production is the maximization of profits taking prices as given. One property of the competitive equilibrium must certainly be

CONDITION 1. *y_j^* maximizes $p^* \cdot y_j$ over the set Y_j, for each j.*

Here, the asterisks denote equilibrium values, and p^* denotes the equilibrium price vector.[3] The above condition is the first of a series which, taken together, define the notion of *competitive equilibrium.*

1.3.0. Analogously to production, we assume the existence of a number of *consumption units,* typically families or individuals but including also institutional consumers. The number of consumption units is m; different consumption units will be designated by the letter i. For any consumption unit i, the vector in R^l representing its consumption will be designated by x_i. The *h*th component, x_{hi}, represents the quantity of the *h*th commodity consumed by the *i*th individual. For any commodity, other than a labor service supplied by the individual, the rate of consumption is necessarily nonnegative. For labor services, the amount supplied may be regarded as the negative of the rate of "consumption," so that $x_{hi} \leqq 0$ if h denotes a labor service. Let $\mathcal{L}$ denote the set of commodities which are labor services. For any $h \in \mathcal{L}$, we may suppose there is some upper limit to the amount supplied, that is, a lower limit to x_{hi}, since, for example, he cannot supply more than 24 hours of labor in a day.

ASSUMPTION 2. *The set of consumption vectors X_i available to individual i*

2. The assumptions about production used here are a generalization of the "linear programming" assumptions. The present set is closely related to that given by Koopmans (1951). In particular, 1(b) is Koopmans' "Impossibility of the Land of Cockaigne," 1(c) is "Irreversibility"; see Koopmans (1951, pp. 48–50).

3. For any two vectors u, v, the notation $u \cdot v$ denotes their inner product, that is, $\Sigma_h u_h v_h$. Since y_{hj} is positive for outputs, negative for inputs, $p^* \cdot y_j$ denotes the profit from the production plan y_j at prices p^*.

(=1, . . . , m) is a closed convex subset of R^l *which is bounded from below; that is, there is a vector* ξ_i *such that* $\xi_i \leqq x_i$ *for all* $x_i \in X_i$.

The set X_i includes all consumption vectors among which the individual could conceivably choose if there were no budgetary restraints. Impossible combinations of commodities, such as the supplying of several types of labor to a total amount of more than 24 hours a day or the consumption of a bundle of commodities insufficient to maintain life, are regarded as excluded from X_i.

1.3.1. As is standard in economic theory, the choice by the consumer from a given set of alternative consumption vectors is supposed to be made in accordance with a preference scale for which there is a utility indicator function $u_i(x_i)$ such that $u_i(x_i) \geqq u_i(x_i')$ if and only if x_i is preferred or indifferent to x_i' according to individual i.

ASSUMPTION 3. (a) *$u_i(x_i)$ is a continuous function on X_i.*
(b) *For any $x_i \in X_i$, there is an $x_i' \in X_i$ such that $u_i(x_i') > u_i(x_i)$.*
(c) *If $u_i(x_i) > u_i(x_i')$ and $0 < t < 1$, then $u_i[tx_i + (1 - t)x_i'] > u_i(x_i')$.*

Assumption 3(a) is, of course, a standard assumption in consumers' demand theory. It is usually regarded as a self-evident corollary of the assumption that choices are made in accordance with an ordering, but this is not accurate. Actually, for X_i a subset of a Euclidean space (as is ordinarily taken for granted), the existence of a continuous utility indicator is equivalent to the following assumption: for all x_i', the sets $\{x_i \mid x_i \in X_i$ and x_i' preferred or indifferent to $x_i\}$ and $\{x_i \mid x_i \in X_i$ and x_i preferred or indifferent to $x_i'\}$ are closed (in X_i); see Debreu (1954). The assumption amounts to a continuity assumption on the preference relation.

Assumption 3(b) assumes that there is no point of saturation, no consumption vector which the individual would prefer to all others. It should be noted that this assumption can be weakened to state merely that no consumption vector attainable with the present technological and resource limitations is a point of saturation. Formally, the revised assumption would read as follows:

ASSUMPTION 3′(b). *For any $x_i \in \hat{X}_i$, there is an $x_i' \in X_i$ such that $u_i(x_i') > u_i(x_i)$,*

where $\hat{X}_i$ has the meaning given it in section 3.3.0 below.

Assumption 3(c) corresponds to the usual assumption that the indifference surfaces are convex in the sense that the set $\{x_i \mid x_i \in X_i$ and $u_i(x_i) \geqq \alpha\}$ is a convex set for any fixed real number α.

The last statement, which asserts the *quasi-concavity* of the function $u_i(x_i)$, is indeed implied by Assumption 3(c) (but is obviously weaker). For suppose x^1 and x^2 are such that $u_i(x^n) \geqq \alpha$ ($n = 1,2$) and $0 < t < 1$. Let $x^3 = tx^1 + (1 - t)x^2$. Without loss of generality, we may suppose that $u_i(x^1) \geqq u_i(x^2)$. If the strict inequality holds, then $u_i(x^3) > u_i(x^2) \geqq \alpha$, by Assumption 3(c). Suppose now $u_i(x^1) = u_i(x^2)$, and suppose $u_i(x^3) < u_i(x^2)$. Then, from Assumption 3(a), we can find x^4, a strict convex combination of x^3 and x^1, such that $u_i(x^3) < u_i(x^4) < u_i(x^1) = u_i(x^2)$. The point x^3 can be expressed as a strict convex combination of x^4 and x^2; since $u_i(x^4) < u_i(x^2)$, it follows from Assumption 3(c) that $u_i(x^3) > u_i(x^4)$, which contradicts the inequality just stated. Hence, the supposition that $u_i(x^3) < u_i(x^2)$ is false, so that $u_i(x^3) \geqq u_i(x^2) \geqq \alpha$.

Actually, it is customary in consumers' demand theory to make a slightly stronger assumption than the quasi-concavity of $u_i(x_i)$, namely, that $u_i(x_i)$ is *strictly* quasi-concave, by which is meant that if $u_i(x_i) \geqq u_i(x_i')$ and $0 < t < 1$, then $u_i[tx_i + (1 - t)x_i'] > u_i(x_i')$. This is equivalent to saying that the indifference surfaces do not contain any line segments, which again is equivalent to the assumption that for all sets of prices and incomes, the demand functions, which give the coordinates of the consumption vector that maximizes utility for a given set of prices and income, are single-valued. Clearly, strict quasi-concavity is a *stronger* assumption than 3(c).[4]

1.3.2. We also assume that the ith consumption unit is endowed with a vector ζ_i of initial holdings of the different types of commodities available and a contractual claim to the share α_{ij} of the profit of the jth production unit for each j.

ASSUMPTION 4. (a) $\zeta_i \in R^l$; *for some* $x_i \in X_i$, $x_i < \zeta_i$.
(b) *For all* i, j, $\alpha_{ij} \geqq 0$; *for all* j, $\Sigma_{i=1}^m \alpha_{ij} = 1$.

The component ζ_{hi} denotes the amount of commodity h held initially by individual i. We may extend this to include all debts payable in terms of commodity h, debts owed to individual i being added to ζ_{hi} and debts owed by him being deducted. Thus, for $h \in \mathcal{L}$, ζ_{hi} would differ from zero only by the amount of debts payable in terms of that particular labor service. (It is not necessary that the debts cancel out for the economy as a whole; thus

4. The remarks in the text show that strict quasi-concavity implies Assumption 3(c), while 3(c) implies quasi-concavity. To show that strict quasi-concavity is actually a stronger assumption than 3(c), we need only exhibit a utility function satisfying 3(c) but not strictly quasi-concave. The function $u_i(x_i) = \Sigma_{h=1}^l x_{hi}$ has these properties.

debts to or from foreigners may be included, provided they are payable in some commodity.)

The second half of Assumption 4(a) asserts in effect that every individual could consume out of his initial stock in some feasible way and still have a positive amount of *each* commodity available for trading in the market.[5] This assumption is clearly unrealistic. However, the necessity of this assumption or some parallel one for the validity of the existence theorem points up an important principle; to have equilibrium, it is necessary that each individual possess some asset or be capable of supplying some labor service which commands a positive price at equilibrium. In Assumption 4(a), this is guaranteed by insisting that an individual be capable of supplying something of each commodity; at least one will be valuable (in the sense of having a price greater than zero) at equilibrium since there will be at least one positive price at equilibrium, as guaranteed by the assumptions about the nature of the price system made in 1.4 below. A much weaker assumption of the same type is made in Theorem 2.

1.3.3. The basic economic motivation in the choice of a consumption vector is that of maximizing utility among all consumption vectors which satisfy the budget restraint, that is, whose cost at market prices does not exceed the individual's income. His income, in turn, can be regarded as having three components: wages, receipts from sales of initially-held stocks of commodities and claims expressible in terms of them, and dividends from the profits of production units. This economic principle must certainly hold for equilibrium values of prices and of the profits of the production units.

CONDITION 2. *x_i^* maximizes $u_i(x_i)$ over the set $\{x_i | x_i \in X_i,\ p^* \cdot x_i \leqq p^* \cdot \zeta_i + \Sigma_{j=1}^{n} \alpha_{ij} p^* \cdot y_j^*\}$.*

This, like Condition 1 in section 1.2.3, is a condition of a competitive equilibrium. Because of the definition of labor services supplied as negative components of x_i, $p^* \cdot x_i$ represents the excess of expenditures on commodities over wage income. The term $p^* \cdot \zeta_i$ represents the receipts from the sale of initially-held commodities. The term $\Sigma_{j=1}^{n} \alpha_{ij} p^* \cdot y_j^*$ denotes the revenue of consumption unit i from dividends.

---

5. This assumption plays the same role as the one made by von Neumann in his study of a dynamic model of production (1945–46) that each commodity enters into every production process either as an input or as an output.

1.4.0. It remains to discuss the system of prices and the meaning of an equilibrium on any market.

CONDITION 3. $p^* \in P = \{p | p \in R^l, p \geqq 0, \Sigma_{h=1}^l p_h = 1\}$.

Condition 3 basically expresses the requirement that prices be nonnegative and not all zero. Without any loss of generality, we may normalize the vector p^* by requiring that the sum of its coordinates be 1, since all relations are homogeneous (of the first order) in p.

1.4.1. Conditions 1 and 2 are the conditions for the equilibrium of the production and consumption units, respectively, for given p^*. Hence, the supply and demand for all commodities is determined as a function of p (not necessarily single-valued) if we vary p and at the same time instruct each production and consumption unit to behave as if the announced value of p were the equilibrium value. The market for any commodity is usually considered to be in equilibrium when the supply for that commodity equals the demand; however, we have to consider the possibility that at a zero price, supply will exceed demand. This is the classical case of a free good.

Let

$$x = \sum_i x_i,\ y = \sum_j y_j,\ \zeta = \sum_i \zeta_i, \qquad z = x - y - \zeta.$$

The vector z has as its components the excess of demand over supply (including both produced and initially-available supply) for the various commodities.

CONDITION 4. $z^* \leqq 0,\ p^* \cdot z^* = 0$.

Condition 4 expresses the discussion of the preceding paragraph. We have broadly the dynamic picture of the classical "law of supply and demand"; see, for example, Samuelson (1947), p. 263. That is, the price of a commodity rises if demand exceeds supply, falls if supply exceeds demand. Equilibrium is therefore incompatible with excess demand on any market, since price would simply rise; hence the first part of Condition 4 for equilibrium is justified. An excess of supply over demand drives price down, but, in view of Condition 3, no price can be driven below zero. Hence, $z_h^* < 0$ for some commodity h is possible, but only if $p_h^* = 0$. Since $p_h^* \geqq 0$ for all h and $z_h^* \leqq 0$ for all h, $p^* \cdot z^* = \Sigma_h p_h^* z_h^*$ is a sum of nonpositive terms. This sum can be zero if and only if $p_h^* z_h^* = 0$ for all h, that is, either $z_h^* = 0$ or $z_h^* < 0$

and $p_h^* = 0$. Condition 4, therefore, sums up precisely the equilibrium conditions that are desired.[6]

1.4.2. In the preceding paragraph, it was implicitly assumed that for a commodity with a positive price the entire initial stock held by a consumption unit was available as a supply on the market along with amounts supplied by production and consumption units as a result of profit maximization and utility maximization respectively (in this context, consumption by a consumption unit out of its own stocks counts both as supply on the market and as demand to the same numerical amount).

This becomes evident on noting that each individual spends his entire *potential* income because of the absence of saturation (and since the model covers his entire economic life). More precisely, Assumption 3(b) shows that there exists an x_i' such that $u_i(x_i') > u_i(x_i^*)$, where x_i^* is the equilibrium value of x_i. Let t be an arbitrarily small positive number; by Assumption 3(c), $u_i[tx_i' + (1-t)x_i^*] > u_i(x_i^*)$. That is, in every neighborhood of x_i^*, there is a point of X_i preferred to x_i^*. From Condition 2,

$$p^* \cdot x_i^* \leqq p^* \cdot \zeta_i + \sum_j \alpha_{ij} p^* \cdot y_j^*.$$

Suppose the strict inequality held. Then we could choose a point of X_i for which the inequality still held and which was preferred to x_i^*, a contradiction of Condition 2.

$$p^* \cdot x_i^* = p^* \cdot \zeta_i + \sum_j \alpha_{ij} p^* \cdot y_j^*. \tag{4-1}$$

To achieve his equilibrium consumption plan, x_i^*, individual i must actually receive the total income given on the right-hand side. He cannot, therefore, withhold any initial holdings of commodity h from the market if $p_h^* > 0$.

DEFINITION 1. *A set of vectors* $(x_1^*, \ldots, x_m^*, y_1^*, \ldots, y_n^*, p^*)$ *is said to be a competitive equilibrium if it satisfies Conditions 1–4.*

THEOREM 1. *For any economic system satisfying Assumptions 1–4, there is a competitive equilibrium.*

6. The view that some commodities might be free goods because supply always exceeded demand goes back to the origins of marginal utility theory; see Menger (1950, pp. 98–100). The critical importance of rephrasing the equilibrium condition for prices in the form of Condition 4 for the problem of the existence of a solution to the Walrasian equilibrium equations was first perceived by Schlesinger (1933–34).

2. A Lemma on Abstract Economies

2.0. In this section the concept of an *abstract economy,* a generalization of that of a *game,* will be introduced, and a definition of equilibrium given. A lemma giving conditions for the existence of equilibrium of an abstract economy will be stated. The lemma is central in the proofs of the theorems stated in this chapter.

2.1. Let there be ν subsets of R^l, $\mathfrak{A}_\iota (\iota = 1, \ldots, \nu)$. Let $\mathfrak{A} = \mathfrak{A}_1 \times \mathfrak{A}_2 \times \ldots \times \mathfrak{A}_\nu$, that is, $\mathfrak{A}$ is the set of ordered ν-tuples $a = (a_1, \ldots, a_\nu)$, where $a_\iota \in \mathfrak{A}_\iota$ for $\iota = 1, \ldots, \nu$. For each ι, suppose there is a real function f_ι defined over $\mathfrak{A}$. Let $\overline{\mathfrak{A}}_\iota = \mathfrak{A}_1 \times \mathfrak{A}_2 \times \ldots \times \mathfrak{A}_{\iota-1} \times \mathfrak{A}_{\iota+1} \times \ldots \times \mathfrak{A}_\nu$, that is, the set of ordered $(\nu - 1)$-tuples $\overline{a}_\iota = (a_1, \ldots, a_{\iota-1}, a_{\iota+1}, \ldots, a_\nu)$, where $a_{\iota'} \in \mathfrak{A}_{\iota'}$ for each $\iota' \neq \iota$. Let $A_\iota(\overline{a}_\iota)$ be a function defining for each point $\overline{a}_\iota \in \overline{\mathfrak{A}}_\iota$ a subset of $\mathfrak{A}_\iota$. Then the sequence $[\mathfrak{A}_1, \ldots, \mathfrak{A}_\nu, f_1, \ldots, f_\nu, A_1(\overline{a}_1), \ldots, A_\nu(\overline{a}_\nu)]$ will be termed an *abstract economy.*

2.2. To motivate the preceding definition, consider first the special case where the functions $A_\iota(\overline{a}_\iota)$ are in fact constants, that is, $A_\iota(\overline{a}_\iota)$ is a fixed subset of $\mathfrak{A}_\iota$, independent of $\overline{a}_\iota$; for simplicity, suppose that $A_\iota(\overline{a}_\iota) = \mathfrak{A}_\iota$. Then the following interpretation may be given: there are ν individuals; the ιth can choose any element $a_\iota \in \mathfrak{A}_\iota$; after the choices are made, the ιth individual receives an amount $f_\iota(a)$, where $a = (a_1, \ldots, a_\nu)$. In this case, obviously, the abstract economy reduces to a game.

In a game, the payoff to each player depends on the strategies chosen by all, but the domain from which strategies are to be chosen is given to each player independently of the strategies chosen by other players. An abstract economy, then, may be characterized as a generalization of a game in which the choice of an action by one agent affects both the payoff and the domain of actions of other agents.

The need for this generalization in the development of an abstract model of the economic system arises from the special position of the consumer. His "actions" can be regarded as alternative consumption vectors; but these are restricted by the budget restraint that the cost of the goods chosen at current prices not exceed his income. But the prices and possibly some or all of the components of his income are determined by choices made by other agents. Hence, for a consumer, who is one agent in the economic system, the function $A_\iota(\overline{a}_\iota)$ must not be regarded as a constant.

2.3. Nash (1950) has formally introduced the notion of an *equilibrium point* for a game.[7] The definition can easily be extended to an abstract economy (see Debreu, 1952, p. 888).

DEFINITION 2. *a^* is an equilibrium point of $[\mathfrak{A}_1, \ldots, \mathfrak{A}_\nu, f_1, \ldots, f_\nu, A_1(\bar{a}_1), \ldots, A_\nu(\bar{a}_\nu)]$ if, for all $\iota = 1, \ldots, \nu$, $a_\iota^* \in A_\iota(\bar{a}_\iota^*)$ and $f_\iota(\bar{a}_\iota^*, a_\iota^*) = \max_{a_\iota \in A_\iota(\bar{a}_\iota^*)} f_\iota(\bar{a}_\iota^*, a_\iota)$.*

Thus an equilibrium point is characterized by the property that each individual is maximizing the payoff to him, given the actions of the other agents, over the set of actions permitted him in view of the other agents' actions.

2.4. We repeat here some definitions from Debreu (1952, pp. 888–889).

The *graph* of $A_\iota(\bar{a}_\iota)$ is the set $\{a | a_\iota \in A_\iota(\bar{a}_\iota)\}$. This clearly generalizes to the multivalued functions $A_\iota(\bar{a}_\iota)$ the ordinary definition of the graph of a function.

The function $A_\iota(\bar{a}_\iota)$ is said to be *continuous* at $\bar{a}_\iota^0$ if for every $a_\iota^0 \in A_\iota(\bar{a}_\iota^0)$ and every sequence $\{\bar{a}_\iota^n\}$ converging to $\bar{a}_\iota^0$, there is a sequence $\{a_\iota^n\}$ converging to a_ι^0 such that $a_\iota^n \in A_\iota(\bar{a}_\iota^n)$ for all n. Again, if $A_\iota(\bar{a}_\iota)$ were a single-valued function, this definition would coincide with the ordinary definition of continuity.

LEMMA. *If, for each ι, $\mathfrak{A}_\iota$ is compact and convex, $f_\iota(\bar{a}_\iota, a_\iota)$ is continuous on $\mathfrak{A}$ and quasi-concave[8] in a_ι for every $\bar{a}_\iota$, $A_\iota(\bar{a}_\iota)$ is a continuous function whose graph is a closed set, and, for every $\bar{a}_\iota$, the set $A_\iota(\bar{a}_\iota)$ is convex and nonempty, then the abstract economy $[\mathfrak{A}_1, \ldots, \mathfrak{A}_\nu, f_1, \ldots, f_\nu, A_1(\bar{a}_1), \ldots, A_\nu(\bar{a}_\nu)]$ has an equilibrium point.*

This lemma generalizes Nash's theorem on the existence of equilibrium points for games (1950). It is a special case of the theorem in Debreu (1952), when taken in conjunction with the remark on p. 889 therein.[9]

---

7. Actually, the concept had been formulated by Cournot (1897) in the special case of an oligopolistic economy; see pp. 80–81.

8. For the definition of a quasi-concave function, see section 1.3.1 above.

9. To see this, we need only remark that a compact convex set is necessarily a contractible polyhedron (the definition of a contractible polyhedron is given in Debreu (1952), pp. 887–888), that the compactness of the graph of $A_\iota(\bar{a}_\iota)$ follows from its closure, as assumed here, and the compactness and hence boundedness of $\mathfrak{A}$ which contains the graph of $A_\iota(\bar{a}_\iota)$, and that the set $\{a_\iota | a_\iota \in A_\iota(\bar{a}_\iota), f_\iota(\bar{a}_\iota, a_\iota) = \max_{a_\iota' \in A_\iota(\bar{a}_\iota)} f_\iota(\bar{a}_\iota, a_\iota')\}$ is, for any given $\bar{a}_\iota$, a convex and therefore contractible set when $f_\iota(\bar{a}_\iota, a_\iota)$ is quasi-concave in a_ι.

3. Proof of Theorem 1

3.1.0. We will here define an abstract economy whose equilibrium points will have all the properties of a competitive equilibrium. There will be $m + n + 1$ participants, the m consumption units, the n production units, and a fictitious participant who chooses prices, and who may be termed the *market participant.*

For any consumption unit i, let $\bar{x}_i$ denote a point in $X_1 \times \ldots \times X_{i-1} \times X_{i+1} \times \ldots \times X_m \times Y_1 \times \ldots \times Y_n \times P$, that is, $\bar{x}_i$ has as components $x_{i'}(i' \neq i)$, $y_j(j = 1, \ldots, n)$, p. Define

$$A_i(\bar{x}_i) = \left\{ x_i | x_i \in X_i, p \cdot x_i \leqq p \cdot \zeta_i + \max \left[0, \sum_{j=1}^{n} \alpha_{ij} p \cdot y_j \right] \right\}.$$

We will then study the abstract economy $E = [X_1, \ldots, X_m, Y_1, \ldots, Y_n, P, u_1(x_1), \ldots, u_m(x_m), p \cdot y_1, \ldots, p \cdot y_n, p \cdot z, A_1(\bar{x}_1), \ldots, A_m(\bar{x}_m)]$. That is, each of the first m participants, the consumption units, chooses a vector x_i from X_i, subject to the restriction that $x_i \in A_i(\bar{x}_i)$, and receives a payoff $u_i(x_i)$; the jth out of the next n participants, the production units, chooses a vector y_j from Y_j (unrestricted by the actions of other participants), and receives a payoff $p \cdot y_j$; and the last agent, the market participant, chooses p from P (again the choice is unaffected by the choices of other participants), and receives $p \cdot z$. Here, z is defined as in section 1.4.1 in terms of $x_i(i = 1, \ldots, m)$ and $y_j(j = 1, \ldots, n)$. The domains X_i, Y_j, P have been defined in sections 1.3.0, 1.2.2, 1.4.0, respectively.

3.1.1. Only two of the component elements of the abstract economy E call for special comment. One is the payoff function of the market participant. Note that z is determined by x_i and y_j. Suppose the market participant does not maximize instantaneously but, taking other participants' choices as given, adjusts his choice of prices so as to increase his payoff. For given z, $p \cdot z$ is a linear function of p; it can be increased by increasing p_h for those commodities for which $z_h > 0$, decreasing p_h if $z_h < 0$ (provided p_h is not already 0). But this is precisely the classical "law of supply and demand" (see section 1.4.1 above), and so the motivation of the market participant corresponds to one of the elements of a competitive equilibrium. This intuitive comment is not, however, the justification for this *particular* choice of a market payoff; that justification will be found in section 3.2.[10]

10. A concept similar to that of the present market payoff is found in Debreu (1951), sections 11, 12.

3.1.2. In the definition of $A_i(\bar{x}_i)$, the expression $\Sigma_{j=1}^{n}\alpha_{ij}p \cdot y_j$ is replaced by max $[0, \Sigma_{j=1}^{n}\alpha_{ij}p \cdot y_j]$. For arbitrary choices of p and y_j (within their respective domains, P and Y_j), it is possible that $\{x_i | x_i \in X_i, p \cdot x_i \leqq p \cdot \zeta_i + \Sigma_{j=1}^{n}\alpha_{ij}p \cdot y_j\}$ is empty. To avoid this difficulty, we make the replacement indicated. Since, for some $x_i' \in X_i$, $\zeta_i \geqq x_i'$ (by Assumption 4(a), section 1.3.2 above), $p \cdot \zeta_i \geqq p \cdot x_i'$, and

$$p \cdot \zeta_i + \max\left[0, \sum_{j=1}^{n} \alpha_{ij}p \cdot y_j\right] \geqq p \cdot \zeta_i \geqq p \cdot x_i',$$

so that $A_i(\bar{x}_i)$ is nonempty.

Of course, it is necessary to show that the substitution makes no difference *at equilibrium*. By definition of E-equilibrium (see section 2.3 above), y_i^* maximizes $p^* \cdot y_j$ subject to the condition that $y_j \in Y_j$ (here asterisks denote E-equilibrium values). By Assumption 1(a) (see section 1.2.2 above), $0 \in Y_j$; hence, in particular

(4-2) $$p^* \cdot y_j^* \geqq p^* \cdot 0 = 0.$$

By Assumption 4(b), $\Sigma_{j=1}^{n}\alpha_{ij}p^* \cdot y_j^* \geqq 0$, and max $[0, \Sigma_{j=1}^{n}\alpha_{ij}p^* \cdot y_j^*] = \Sigma_{j=1}^{n}\alpha_{ij}p^* \cdot y_j^*$. Therefore,

$$A_i(\bar{x}_i^*) = \left\{x_i | x_i \in X_i, p^* \cdot x_i \leqq p^* \cdot \zeta_i + \sum_{j=1}^{n} \alpha_{ij}p^* \cdot y_j^*\right\}.$$

From the definition of an equilibrium point for an abstract economy and the payoff for a consumption unit,

Condition 2 is satisfied at an equilibrium point of the abstract economy E.

3.2. Before establishing the existence of an equilibrium point for E, it will be shown that such an equilibrium point is also a competitive equilibrium in the sense of Definition 1. It has already been shown that Condition 2 is satisfied, while Conditions 1 and 3 follow immediately from the definition of an equilibrium point and the payoffs specified.

In section 1.4.2, it was shown that Eq. (4-1) followed from Condition 2, which we have already shown to hold here, and Assumptions 3(b) and 3(c). Sum over i, and recall that, from Assumption 4(b), $\Sigma_{i=1}^{m}\alpha_{ij} = 1$. Then, from the definition of z

(4-3) $$p^* \cdot z^* = 0.$$

Let δ^h be the vector in which every component is 0, except the hth, which is

1. Then $\delta^h \in P$ (see Condition 3). Hence, by definition of an equilibrium point,

$$0 = p^* \cdot z^* \geqq \delta^h \cdot z^* = z_h^*,$$

or

$$z^* \leqq 0. \tag{4-4}$$

Equations (4-3) and (4-4) together assert Condition 4. It has been shown that any equilibrium point of E satisfies Conditions 1–4 and hence is a competitive equilibrium. The converse is obviously also true.

3.3.0. Unfortunately, the Lemma stated in the previous section is not directly applicable to E, since the action spaces are not compact.

Let

$$\hat{X}_i = \{x_i | x_i \in X_i, \text{ there exist } x_{i'} \in X_{i'} \text{ for each } i' \neq i \text{ and } y_j \in Y_j \text{ for each } j \text{ such that } z \leqq 0\},$$

$$\hat{Y}_j = \{y_j | y_j \in Y_j, \text{ there exist } x_i \in X_i \text{ for each } i, y_{j'} \in Y_{j'} \text{ for each } j' \neq j \text{ such that } z \leqq 0\}.$$

$\hat{X}_i$ is the set of consumption vectors available to individual i if he had complete control of the economy but had to take account of resource limitations. $\hat{Y}_j$ has a similar interpretation. We wish to prove that these sets are all bounded. It is clear that an E equilibrium x_i^* must belong to $\hat{X}_i$ and that an E equilibrium y_j^* must belong to $\hat{Y}_j$.

3.3.1. Suppose $\hat{Y}_1$ is unbounded. Then there exist sequences y_j^k, x_i^k such that

$$\lim_{k \to \infty} |y_1^k| = \infty, \qquad \sum_{j=1}^{n} y_j^k \geqq \sum_{i=1}^{m} x_i^k - \zeta, \qquad y_j^k \in Y_j, \qquad x_i^k \in X_i. \tag{4-5}$$

Let

$$\xi = \sum_{i=1}^{m} \xi_i.$$

Then, from Assumption 2, $\Sigma_{i=1}^m x_i^k \geqq \xi$, so that

$$\sum_{j=1}^{n} y_j^k \geqq \xi - \zeta. \tag{4-6}$$

Let $\mu^k = \max_j |y_j^k|$; for k sufficiently large, $\mu^k \geqq 1$. From Assumption 1(a), $(1/\mu^k)y_j^k + (1 - 1/\mu^k)0 \in Y_j$. From (4-5) and (4-6),

(4-7) $\sum_{j=1}^{n} (y_j^k/\mu^k) \geqq (\xi - \zeta)/\mu^k; \qquad y_j^k/\mu^k \in Y_j$ for k sufficiently large;

$\lim_{k \to \infty} \mu^k = \infty; \qquad |y_j^k/\mu^k| \leqq 1.$

From the last statement, a subsequence $\{k_q\}$ can be chosen so that for every j

(4-8) $\lim_{q \to \infty} y_j^{k_q}/\mu^{k_q} = y_j^o.$

From (4-7), (4-8), and the closure of Y_j (see Assumption 1(a)),

(4-9) $\sum_{j=1}^{n} y_j^o \geqq 0$ and $y_j^o \in Y_j$.

From (4-9), $\Sigma_{j=1}^n y_j^o \in Y$. From Assumption 1(b), $\Sigma_{j=1}^n y_j^o = 0$, or, for any given j',

(4-10) $\sum_{j \neq j'} y_j^o = -y_{j'}^o.$

Since $0 \in Y_j$ for all j, both the left-hand side and $y_{j'}^o$ belong to Y. The right-hand side therefore belongs to both Y and $-Y$; by Assumption 1(c), $y_{j'}^o = 0$ for any j'. From (4-8), then, the equality $|y_j^{k_q}| = \mu^{k_q}$ can hold for at most finitely many q for fixed j. But this is a contradiction since, from the definition of μ^{k_q}, the equality must hold for at least one j for each q, and hence for infinitely many q for some j. It has therefore been shown that $\hat{Y}_1$ is bounded, and, by the same argument,

(4-11) $\hat{Y}_j$ is bounded for all j.

3.3.2. Let $x_i \in \hat{X}_i$. By definition,

(4-12) $\xi_i \leqq x_i \leqq \sum_{j=1}^{n} y_j - \sum_{i' \neq i} x_{i'} + \zeta, \qquad (x_{i'} \in X_{i'}, y_j \in Y_j)$

By definition again, it follows that $y_j \in \hat{Y}_j$ for all j; also $x_{i'} \geqq \xi_{i'}$.

$$\xi_i \leqq x_i \leqq \sum_{j=1}^{n} y_j - \sum_{i' \neq i} \xi_{i'} + \zeta, \qquad (y_j \in \hat{Y}_j).$$

From (4-11), the right-hand side is bounded.

(4-13) $\hat{X}_i$ is bounded for all i.

3.3.3. We can therefore choose a positive real number c so that the cube $C = \{x \mid |x_h| \leqq c \text{ for all } h\}$ contains in its *interior* all $\hat{X}_i$ and all $\hat{Y}_j$. Let $\tilde{X}_i = X_i \cap C$, $\tilde{Y}_j = Y_j \cap C$.

3.3.4. Now introduce a new abstract economy $\tilde{E}$, identical with E in section 3.1, except that X_i is replaced by $\tilde{X}_i$ and Y_j by $\tilde{Y}_j$ everywhere. Let $\tilde{A}_i(\bar{x}_i)$ be the resultant modification of $A_i(\bar{x}_i)$ (see 3.1.0). It will now be verified that all the conditions of the Lemma are satisfied for this new abstract economy.

From Assumptions 2 and 1(a), X_i and Y_j are closed convex sets; the set C is a compact convex set; therefore, $\tilde{X}_i$ and $\tilde{Y}_j$ are compact convex sets. P is obviously compact and convex.

For a consumption unit, the continuity and quasi-concavity of $u_i(x_i)$ are assured by Assumptions 3(a) and 3(c) (see the discussion in section 1.3.1). For a production unit or the market participant, the continuity is trivial, and the quasi-concavity holds for any linear function.

For a production unit or the market participant, Y_j or P is a constant and therefore trivially continuous; the closure of the graph is simply the closure of $\tilde{\mathfrak{A}} = \tilde{X}_1 \times \ldots \times \tilde{X}_m \times \tilde{Y}_1 \times \ldots \times \tilde{Y}_n \times P$. The sets Y_j, P are certainly convex and nonempty.

For a consumption unit, the set $\tilde{A}_i(\bar{x}_i)$ is defined by a linear inequality in x_i (section 3.1.0) and hence is certainly convex. For each i, let x_i' have the property $x_i' \leqq \zeta_i$, $x_i' \in X_i$ (see Assumption 4(a)); set $y_j' = 0$. Since $\Sigma_{i=1}^m x_i' - \Sigma_{j=1}^n y_j' - \zeta \leqq 0$, $x_i' \in \hat{X}_i$ for each i, by definition, and hence $x_i' \in C$. It was shown in section 3.1.2 that $x_i' \in A_i(\bar{x}_i)$ for all $\bar{x}_i$; since $\tilde{A}_i(\bar{x}_i) = [A_i(\bar{x}_i)] \cap C$, $\tilde{A}_i(\bar{x}_i)$ contains x_i' and therefore is nonnull.

Since the budget restraint is a weak inequality between two continuous functions of a, it is obvious that the graph of $\tilde{A}_i(\bar{x}_i)$ is closed.

3.3.5. It remains only to show that $\tilde{A}_i(\bar{x}_i)$ is continuous.

Remark. If $p \cdot \zeta_i > \min_{x_i \in \tilde{X}_i} p \cdot x_i$, then $\tilde{A}_i(\bar{x}_i)$ is continuous at the point $\bar{x}_i = (x_1, \ldots, x_{i-1}, x_{i+1}, \ldots, x_m, y_1, \ldots, y_n, p)$.

Proof. Let $r_i = p \cdot \zeta_i + \max\,[0, \Sigma_{j=1}^n \alpha_{ij} p \cdot y_j]$. When $\bar{x}_i^k$ converges to $\bar{x}_i$, $\lim_{k\to\infty} p^k = p$, $\lim_{k\to\infty} r_i^k = r_i$. Consider a point $x_i \in \tilde{A}_i(\bar{x}_i)$; then,

(4-14) $$x_i \in \tilde{X}_i, \qquad p \cdot x_i \leqq r_i.$$

(a) If $p \cdot x_i < r_i$, then $p^k \cdot x_i < r_i^k$ for all k sufficiently large, and $x_i \in \tilde{A}_i(\bar{x}_i^k)$. Then we need only choose $x_i^k = x_i$ for all k sufficiently large. (See the definition of continuity in section 2.4).

(b) If $p \cdot x_i = r_i$, choose x_i', by hypothesis, so that $x_i' \in \tilde{X}_i$, $p \cdot x_i' < p \cdot \zeta_i \leqq r_i$. For k sufficiently large, $p^k \cdot x_i' < r_i^k$. Define $x_i(\lambda) = \lambda x_i + (1-\lambda)x_i'$, and consider the set of values of λ for which $0 \leqq \lambda \leqq 1$, $x_i(\lambda) \in \tilde{A}_i(\bar{x}_i^k)$. Since $\tilde{X}_i$ is convex, $x_i(\lambda) \in \tilde{X}_i$. Then one must have

$$p^k \cdot [\lambda x_i + (1-\lambda)x_i'] \leqq r_i^k$$

or

$$\lambda \leqq (r_i^k - p^k \cdot x_i')/(p^k \cdot x_i - p^k \cdot x_i'),$$

if we note that the denominator is positive for k sufficiently large, since $p \cdot x_i = r_i > p \cdot x_i'$. The largest value of λ satisfying the above conditions is, then,

$$\lambda^k = \min [1,(r_i^k - p^k \cdot x_i')/(p^k \cdot x_i - p^k \cdot x_i')].$$

For k sufficiently large, $\lambda^k > 0$. Then $x_i(\lambda^k) \in \tilde{A}_i(\overline{x}_i^k)$ for all k sufficiently large. But also

$$\lim_{k\to\infty} r_i^k = r_i = \lim_{k\to\infty} p^k \cdot x_i, \quad \text{so that} \quad \lim_{k\to\infty} \lambda^k = 1,$$
$$\text{and} \quad \lim_{k\to\infty} x_i(\lambda^k) = x_i.$$

The continuity of $\tilde{A}_i(\overline{x}_i)$ is therefore established.

If Assumption 4(a) holds, then the condition of the Remark is trivially satisfied for any $p \in P$, and $y_j \in \tilde{Y}_j(j = 1, \ldots, n)$.

3.4.0. The existence of an equilibrium point $(x_1^*, \ldots, x_m^*, y_1^*, \ldots, y_n^*, p^*)$ for the abstract economy $\tilde{E}$ has, therefore, been demonstrated. It will now be shown that this point is also an equilibrium point for the abstract economy E described in section 3.1. The converse is obvious; therefore a competitive equilibrium is *equivalent* to an $\tilde{E}$ equilibrium. (See the end of section 3.2.)

3.4.1. From Assumption 1(a) and the definition of C (section 3.3.3) it follows that $0 \in \tilde{Y}_j$ for each j. So that, as in section 3.1.2,

$$\max\left[0, \sum_{j=1}^{n} \alpha_{ij} p^* \cdot y_j^*\right] = \sum_{j=1}^{n} \alpha_{ij} p^* \cdot y_j^*.$$

From the definition of $\tilde{A}_i(\overline{x}_i)$,

$$p^* \cdot x_i^* \leqq p^* \cdot \zeta_i + \sum_{j=1}^{n} \alpha_{ij} p^* \cdot y_j^*.$$

Sum over i; then $p^* \cdot x^* \leqq p^* \cdot \zeta + p^* \cdot y^*$, or $p^* \cdot z^* \leqq 0$. For fixed z^*, p^* maximizes $p \cdot z^*$ for $p \in P$; by an argument similar to that used in section 3.2, this implies that

$$\text{(4-14)} \qquad z^* \leqq 0.$$

From (4-14) and the definitions in section 3.3.0, $x_i^* \in \hat{X}_i$, $y_j^* \in \hat{Y}_j$ for all i and j, and, by section 3.3.3, x_i^* and y_j^* are *interior* points of C.

Suppose, for some $x_i' \in A_i(\bar{x}_i^*)$, $u_i(x_i') > u_i(x_i^*)$. By Assumption 3(c), $u_i[tx_i' + (1-t)x_i^*] > u_i(x_i^*)$ if $0 < t < 1$. But for t sufficiently small, $tx_i' + (1-t)x_i^*$ belongs to C. Since $tx_i' + (1-t)x_i^* \in A_i(\bar{x}_i^*)$, by the convexity of the latter set, $tx_i' + (1-t)x_i^* \in \tilde{A}_i(\bar{x}_i^*)$, for t small enough, which contradicts the definition of x_i^* as an equilibrium value for $\tilde{E}$.

(4-15) x_i^* maximizes $u_i(x_i)$ for $x_i \in A_i(\bar{x}_i^*)$.

Suppose, for some $y_j' \in Y_j$, $p^* \cdot y_j' > p^* \cdot y_j^*$. Then, $p^* \cdot [ty_j' + (1-t)y_j^*] > p^* \cdot y_j^*$ for $0 < t < 1$. As in the preceding paragraph, the convex combination belongs to $\tilde{Y}_j$ for t sufficiently small, a contradiction to the equilibrium character of y_j^* for $\tilde{E}$.

(4-16) y_j^* maximizes $p^* \cdot y_j$ for $y_j \in Y_j$.

That p^* maximizes $p \cdot z^*$ for $p \in P$ is directly implied by the definition of equilibrium point for $\tilde{E}$, since the domain of p is the same in both abstract economies.

It has been shown, therefore, that the point $(x_1^*, \ldots, x_m^*, y_1^*, \ldots, y_n^*, p^*)$ is also an equilibrium point for E; as shown in section 3.2, it is, therefore, a competitive equilibrium. Theorem 1 has thus been proved.

4. Statement of the Second Existence Theorem for a Competitive Equilibrium

4.0. As noted in section 1.3.2, Assumption 4(a), which states in effect that a consumption unit has initially a positive amount of every commodity available for trading, is clearly unrealistic, and a weakening is very desirable. Theorem 2 accomplishes this goal, though at the cost of making certain additional assumptions in different directions and complicating the proof. Assumptions 1–3 are retained. The remaining assumptions for Theorem 2 are given in the following paragraphs of this section.

4.1. Assumption 4(a) is replaced by the following:

ASSUMPTION 4′(a). *$\zeta_i \in R^l$; for some $x_i \in X_i$, $x_i \leqq \zeta_i$ and, for at least one $h \in \mathcal{P}$, $x_{hi} < \zeta_{hi}$.*

The set $\mathcal{P}$ is defined more closely in section 4.4 below; briefly, it consists of all types of labor that are always productive. Assumption 4′(a) is a weakening of 4(a); it is now only supposed that the individual is capable of supplying at least one type of productive labor. Assumptions 4′(a) and 4(b) together will be denoted by 4′.

4.2. Let $X = \Sigma_{i=1}^{m} X_i$.

ASSUMPTION 5. *There exist $x \in X$ and $y \in Y$ such that $x < y + \zeta$.*

Assumption 5 asserts that it is possible to arrange the economic system by choice of production and consumption vectors so that an excess supply of all commodities can be achieved.

4.3. As in section 3.2, δ^h will be the positive unit vector of the hth axis in R^l. For any $\lambda > 0$, $x_i + \lambda\delta^h$ represents an increase λ in the amount of the hth commodity over x_i, with all other commodities remaining unchanged in consumption.

DEFINITION 3. *Let $\mathcal{D}$ be the set of commodities such that if $i = 1, \ldots, m$, $x_i \in X_i$, $h \in \mathcal{D}$, then there exists $\lambda > 0$ such that $x_i + \lambda\delta^h \in X_i$ and*

$$u_i(x_i + \lambda\delta^h) > u_i(x_i).$$

$\mathcal{D}$ is the set of commodities which are always desired by every consumer.

ASSUMPTION 6. *The set $\mathcal{D}$ is not empty.*

Assumption 6 is a stronger form of 3(b) as given in section 1.3.1. In the same manner as noted there, Assumption 6 can be weakened to assert that the set $\mathcal{D}'$ of commodities desired for all consumption vectors compatible with existing resource and technological conditions is not empty. Formally we could introduce the following definition:

DEFINITION 4. *Let $\mathcal{D}'$ be the set of commodities such that if $i = 1, \ldots, m$, $x_i \in \hat{X}_i$, $h \in \mathcal{D}'$, then there exists $\lambda > 0$ such that $x_i + \lambda\delta^h \in X_i$ and*

$$u_i(x_i + \lambda\delta^h) > u_i(x_i).$$

Assumption 6 can then be replaced by:

ASSUMPTION 6′. *The set $\mathcal{D}'$ is not empty.*

DEFINITION 5. *Let $\mathcal{P}$ be the set of commodities such that if $y \in Y$, $h \in \mathcal{P}$, then* (a) *$y_h \leqq 0$ and* (b) *for some $y' \in Y$ and all $h' \neq h$, $y'_{h'} \geqq y_{h'}$, while for at least one $h'' \in \mathcal{D}$, $y'_{h''} > y_{h''}$.*

ASSUMPTION 7. *The set $\mathcal{P}$ is not empty.*

Assumption 7 plays a key role in the following proof. We interpret the set $\mathcal{P}$ as consisting of some types of labor. Part (a) simply asserts that no labor service, at least of those included in $\mathcal{P}$, can be produced by a production unit. Part (b) asserts that, if no restriction is imposed on the amount (consumed) of some one type of "productive" labor, then it is possible to increase the output of at least one "desired" commodity (a commodity in $\mathcal{D}$) without decreasing the output or increasing the input of any commodity other than the type of productive labor under consideration.

A case where Assumption 7 might not hold is an economic system with fixed technological coefficients where production requiring a given type of labor also requires, directly or indirectly, some complementary factors. It is easy to see intuitively in this case how an equilibrium may be impossible. Given the amount of complementary resources initially available,[11] there will be a maximum to the quantity of labor that can be employed in the sense that no further increase in the labor force will increase the output of any commodity. Now, as is well known, the supply of labor may vary either way as real wages vary (see Robbins, 1930) and broadly speaking is rather inelastic with respect to real wages. In particular, as real wages tend to zero, the supply will not necessarily become zero; on the contrary, as real incomes decrease, the necessity of satisfying more and more pressing needs may even work in the direction of increasing the willingness to work despite the increasingly less favorable terms offered. It is, therefore, quite possible that for any positive level of real wages, the supply of labor will exceed the maximum employable and hence *a fortiori* the demand by firms. Thus, there can be no equilibrium at positive levels of real wages. At zero real wages, on the contrary, demand will indeed be positive but of course supply of labor will be zero, so that again there will be no equilibrium. The critical point in the argument is the discontinuity of the supply curve for labor as real wages go to zero.

Assumption 7 rules out any situation of limitational factors in which the marginal productivity of all types of labor in terms of desired commodities is zero. In conjunction with Assumption 4′(a), on the one hand, and Assumption 6, on the other, it ensures that any individual possesses the ability to supply a commodity which has at least derived value.

11. These complementary resources may be land, raw materials critical in certain industrial processes, or initial capital equipment.

It may be remarked that Assumption 7 is satisfied if there is a productive process turning a form of labor into a desired commodity without the need of complementary commodities. Domestic service or other personal services may fall in this category.[12]

Let $\hat{Y} = \{y | y \in Y$, there exists $x_i \in X_i$ for all i such that $z \leqq 0\}$. It may be remarked that Assumption 7 can be effectively weakened (in the same way that 6 could be weakened to 6′) to

ASSUMPTION 7′. *The set $\mathcal{P}'$ is not empty,* where

DEFINITION 6. *Let $\mathcal{P}'$ be the set of commodities such that if $h \in \mathcal{P}'$ and*

(a) $y \in Y$, then $y_h \leqq 0$,

(b) $y \in \hat{Y}$, then for some $y' \in Y$ and all $h' \neq h$, $y'_{h'} \geqq y_{h'}$, while for at least one $h'' \in \mathcal{D}$, $y'_{h''} > y_{h''}$.

Note that Assumptions 3(b), 6, and 7 can *simultaneously* be weakened to 3′(b), 6′, and 7′.

THEOREM 2. *For an economic system satisfying Assumptions 1–3, 4′, and 5–7, there is a competitive equilibrium.*

5. Proof of Theorem 2

5.0. Let π be the number of elements of $\mathcal{P}$. For any ε, $0 < \varepsilon \leq \frac{1}{2\pi}$, define

$$P^{\varepsilon} = \{p | p \in P, p_h \geq \varepsilon \quad \text{for all } h \in \mathcal{P}\}.$$

From Assumption 4′(a), we can choose $x_i \in X_i$ so that $x_{hi} \leqq \zeta_{hi}$ for all h, $x_{h'i} < \zeta_{h'i}$ for some $h' \in \mathcal{P}$. For any $p \in P^{\varepsilon}$,

$$p \cdot (\zeta_i - x_i) = \sum_h p_h(\zeta_{hi} - x_{hi}) \geqq p_{h'}(\zeta_{h'i} - x_{h'i}) > 0$$

or

(4-17) $\qquad$ for some $x_i \in X_i$, $p \cdot x_i < p \cdot \zeta_i$.

5.1.0. The basic method of proof of Theorem 2 will be similar to that of Theorem 1. We seek to show that an equilibrium point for the abstract economy E, defined in section 3.1.0, exists. As already shown in 3.2, such an equilibrium point would define a competitive equilibrium. First, the econ-

---

12. The possibility of disequilibrium and therefore unemployment through failure of Assumption 7 to hold corresponds to so-called "structural unemployment."

omy E is replaced by the economy $E^{\varepsilon} = [X_1, \ldots, X_m, Y_1, \ldots, Y_n, P^{\varepsilon}, u_1(x_1), \ldots, u_m(x_m), p \cdot y_1, \ldots, p \cdot y_n, p \cdot z, A_1(\bar{x}_1), \ldots, A_m(\bar{x}_m)]$. Clearly, E^{ε} is the same as E, except that the price domain has been contracted to P^{ε}. The existence of an equilibrium point for E^{ε} for each ε will first be shown; then, it will be shown that for some ε, an equilibrium point of E^{ε} is also an equilibrium point of E.[13]

To show the existence of an equilibrium point for E^{ε}, the same technique will be used as in proving the existence of an equilibrium point for E in Theorem 1. The argument is that the equilibrium point, if it exists at all, must lie in a certain bounded domain. Hence, if we alter the abstract economy E^{ε} by intersecting the action domains with a suitably chosen hypercube, we will not disturb the equilibrium points, if any; but the Lemma of the second section will now be applicable, and the existence of an equilibrium point shown (see section 3.3 above).

5.1.1. This section will be purely heuristic, designed to motivate the choice of the hypercube mentioned in the previous paragraph. Suppose an equilibrium point $[x_1^*, \ldots, x_m^*, y_1^*, \ldots, y_n^*, p^*]$ exists for the abstract economy E^{ε}. Since $x_i^* \in A_i(\bar{x}_i^*)$ for all i, by definition (see section 3.1.0),

$$p^* \cdot x_i^* \leqq p^* \cdot \zeta_i + \sum_{j=1}^{n} \alpha_{ij} p^* \cdot y_j^*$$

(see also 3.1.2). If we sum over i and recall that $\Sigma_{i=1}^{m} \alpha_{ij} = 1$,

$$p^* \cdot \left(\sum_{i=1}^{m} x_i^* - \sum_{i=1}^{m} \zeta_i - \sum_{j=1}^{n} y_j^* \right) \leqq 0,$$

or $p^* \cdot z^* \leqq 0$.

Since p^* maximizes $p \cdot z^*$ for $p \in P^{\varepsilon}$, by definition of equilibrium, $p \cdot z^* \leqq 0$ for all $p \in P^{\varepsilon}$, or,

(4-18) $$p_{h'} z_{h'}^* \leqq \sum_{h \neq h'} p_h(\zeta_h - x_h^* + y_h^*), \quad \text{for any } h'.$$

Note that, since $y_h^* \leqq 0$ for $h \in \mathcal{P}$, by (a) of Definition 5

(4-19) $$x_h^* - y_h^* \geqq x_h^* \geqq \xi_h, \quad \text{for } h \in \mathcal{P},$$

13. The introduction of E^{ε} is made necessary by the following fact: Exp. (4-17) may not hold for all $p \in P$ and the condition of the Remark in section 3.3.5 may not be satisfied for all $p \in P$.

by Assumption 2. ζ and ξ are defined in sections 1.4.1 and 3.3.1, respectively.

For any given h', define p as follows: $p_h = \varepsilon$ for $h \in \mathcal{P}$ and $h \neq h'$; $p_h = 0$ for $h \notin \mathcal{P}$ and $h \neq h'$; $p_{h'} = 1 - \Sigma_{h \neq h'} p_h$. Then, if $h' \in \mathcal{P}$, $p_{h'} = 1 - (\pi - 1)\varepsilon$ (which is indeed $\geqq \varepsilon$ if $\varepsilon \leqq \frac{1}{2\pi}$); if $h' \notin \mathcal{P}$, $p_{h'} = 1 - \pi\varepsilon$. From (4-18) and (4-19),

$$\text{(4-20)} \qquad \text{if } h' \in \mathcal{P}, [1 - (\pi - 1)\varepsilon] z^*_{h'} \leqq \varepsilon \sum_{\substack{h \in \mathcal{P} \\ h \neq h'}} (\zeta_h - \xi_h),$$

$$\text{if } h' \notin \mathcal{P}, (1 - \pi\varepsilon) z^*_{h'} \leqq \varepsilon \sum_{h \in \mathcal{P}} (\zeta_h - \xi_h).$$

If $0 < \varepsilon \leq (\frac{1}{2\pi})$, then certainly $1 - \pi\varepsilon > 0$, $1 - (\pi - 1)\varepsilon > 0$, and necessarily

$$\varepsilon/[1 - (\pi - 1)\varepsilon] < \varepsilon/(1 - \pi\varepsilon).$$

Finally, for any h, $\zeta_h - \xi_h \geqq 0$ from Assumptions 4′(a) and 2. If we divide through the first inequality in (4-20) by $[1 - (\pi - 1)\varepsilon]$,

$$\text{(4-21)} \qquad z^*_{h'} \leqq \{\varepsilon/[1 - (\pi - 1)\varepsilon] \sum_{\substack{h \in \mathcal{P} \\ h \neq h'}} (\zeta_h - \xi_h)$$

$$\leqq [\varepsilon/(1 - \pi\varepsilon)] \sum_{h \in \mathcal{P}} (\zeta_h - \xi_h), \quad \text{for } h' \in \mathcal{P}.$$

The same inequality between the extreme items holds for $h' \notin \mathcal{P}$, as can be seen by dividing through in the second inequality in (4-20) by $(1 - \pi\varepsilon)$. But if $\varepsilon \leq (\frac{1}{2\pi})$, then we see in turn that $2\pi\varepsilon \leqq 1$, $\pi\varepsilon \leqq 1 - \pi\varepsilon$, and, by division by $\pi(1 - \pi\varepsilon)$, $\varepsilon/(1 - \pi\varepsilon) \leqq 1/\pi$. From (4-21),

$$z^*_{h'} \leqq (1/\pi) \sum_{h \in \mathcal{P}} (\zeta_h - \xi_h).$$

Let $\zeta'_h = \zeta_h + (1/\pi) \Sigma_{h \in \mathcal{P}} (\zeta_h - \xi_h)$, with ζ' being the vector whose components are $\zeta_1, \ldots, \zeta_l$; then

$$\text{(4-22)} \qquad x^* - y^* \leqq \zeta'.$$

The equilibrium point then will lie in a region defined by (4-22) and the conditions $x^*_i \in X_i$, $y^*_j \in Y_j$, $p^* \in P^\varepsilon$. These are exactly the same as the requirements for E in the proof of Theorem 1, except that ζ has been replaced by ζ', and P by P^ε.

5.2.0. The proof will now be resumed. Define

$$\hat{X}_i' = \{x_i | x_i \in X_i, \quad \text{and there exist } x_{i'} \in X_{i'} \text{ for all } i' \neq i,\ y_j \in Y_j \quad \text{for all } j \text{ such that } x - y \leqq \zeta'\},$$

$$\hat{Y}_j' = \{y_j | y_j \in Y_j, \quad \text{and there exist } x_i \in X_i \text{ for all } i,\ y_{j'} \in Y_{j'} \quad \text{for all } j' \neq j \text{ such that } x - y \leqq \zeta'\}.$$

These definitions are identical with those of $\hat{X}_i$, $\hat{Y}_j$ in section 3.3.0, except that ζ has been replaced by ζ'. The arguments of sections 3.3.0–3.3.3 may therefore be repeated exactly. We can choose a positive real number c' so that the cube

$$C' = \{x | |x_h| \leqq c' \quad \text{for all } h\}$$

contains in its *interior* all $\hat{X}_i'$ and all $\hat{Y}_j'$. Let $\tilde{X}_i' = X_i \cap C'$, $\tilde{Y}_j' = Y_j \cap C'$.

5.2.1. Let $\tilde{E}^\varepsilon$ be an abstract economy identical with E^ε in section 5.1.0, except that X_i is replaced by $\tilde{X}_i'$ and Y_j by $\tilde{Y}_j'$ everywhere. Let $\tilde{A}_i'(\bar{x}_i)$ be the resultant modification of $A_i(\bar{x}_i)$. It is easy to see that the argument of 3.3.4 remains completely applicable in showing that all the requirements of the Lemma are satisfied other than the continuity of $\tilde{A}_i'(\bar{x}_i)$. The last follows immediately from the Remark of section 3.3.5, and Exp. (4-17), since $x_i \in \hat{X}_i'$ and hence to $\tilde{X}_i'$. Hence, $\tilde{E}^\varepsilon$ has an equilibrium point $[x_1^*, \ldots, x_m^*, y_1^*, \ldots, y_n^*, p^*]$ for each ε, $0 < \varepsilon \leqq (\frac{1}{2\pi})$. We show now that an equilibrium point of $\tilde{E}^\varepsilon$ is an equilibrium point of E^ε (the converse is obvious).

5.2.2. Since $0 \in \tilde{Y}_j'$,

$$p^* \cdot y_j^* \geqq p^* \cdot 0 = 0, \tag{4-23}$$

so that $\sum_{j=1}^m \alpha_{ij} p^* \cdot y_j^* \geqq 0$, and, as in section 5.1.1, $p^* \cdot z^* \leqq 0$, from which it can be concluded that, as in Eq. (4-22), $x^* - y^* \leqq \zeta'$. From the definitions of $\hat{X}_i'$, $\hat{Y}_j'$ in section 5.2.0, $x_i^* \in \hat{X}_i'$, $y_j^* \in \hat{Y}_j'$ for all i and j; hence, as shown in that section,

(4-24) x_i^*, y_j^* are interior points of C'.

From the definition of an equilibrium point, x_i^* maximizes $u_i(x_i)$ for $x_i \in \tilde{A}_i'(\bar{x}_i^*)$. From (4-24), it follows exactly as in section 3.4.1 that

(4-25) x_i^* maximizes $u_i(x_i)$ for $x_i \in A_i(\bar{x}_i^*)$.

In the same way,

(4-26) y_j^* maximizes $p^* \cdot y_j$ for $y_j \in Y_j$.

From the definition of equilibrium for $\tilde{E}^\varepsilon$,

(4-27) p^* maximizes $p \cdot z^*$ for $p \in P^\varepsilon$.

5.3.0. Suppose that, for some ε, $0 < \varepsilon \leqq \frac{1}{2\pi}$,

(4-28) $p_h^* > \varepsilon$ for all $h \in \mathcal{P}$.

Let p be any element of P, $p' = tp + (1 - t)p^*$, where $0 < t \leqq 1$. Suppose $p \cdot z^* > p^* \cdot z^*$; then $p' \cdot z^* > p^* \cdot z^*$. But, from (4-28), $p' \in P^\varepsilon$ for t sufficiently small, which contradicts (4-27). Thus, if (4-28) holds for some ε, $p \cdot z^* \leqq p^* \cdot z^*$ for all $p \in P$, that is, p^* maximizes $p \cdot z^*$ for $p \in P$ (and not merely $p \in P^\varepsilon$). In conjunction with (4-25) and (4-26), this shows that the abstract economy E has an equilibrium point and therefore, as shown in section 3.2,

(4-29) If (4-28) holds, there is a competitive equilibrium.

5.3.1. It will therefore now be assumed that (4-28) does not hold for any $\varepsilon > 0$. Then, for each ε, $0 < \varepsilon \leqq \frac{1}{2\pi}$,

(4-30) $p_h^* = \varepsilon$ for at least one $h \in \mathcal{P}$.

For all ε, $p^* \in P$, $x_i^* \in C'$, $y_j^* \in C'$ (see [4-24]). P and C' are compact sets; a set of converging sequences can therefore be chosen so that

(4-31) $$\lim_{k \to \infty} \varepsilon_k = 0, \qquad (x_1^k, \ldots, x_m^k, y_1^k, \ldots, y_n^k, p^k)$$

is an equilibrium point for E^{ε_k}, $\lim_{k \to \infty} x_i^k = x_i^0$,

$$\lim_{k \to \infty} y_j^k = y_j^0, \qquad \lim_{k \to \infty} p^k = p^0.$$

Since the sets X_i, Y_j, P are closed, $x_i^0 \in X_i$, $y_j^0 \in Y_j$, $p^0 \in P$. From (4-30), there must be at least one $h \in \mathcal{P}$ for which $p_h^k = \varepsilon_k$ for infinitely many k, and hence by (4-31), $p_h^0 = 0$ for that h. For convenience, let $h = 1$.

(4-32) $p_1^0 = 0, \quad 1 \in \mathcal{P}$.

As shown in section 3.2, statement (4-25) of 5.2.2, which is Condition 2, implies Eq. (4-3) of 3.2, namely, $p^k \cdot z^k = 0$. Let k approach ∞; by (4-31),

(4-33) $p^0 \cdot z^0 = 0$.

For any fixed y_j, statement (4-26) tells us that $p^k \cdot y_j^k \geqq p^k \cdot y_j$. Let k approach ∞; then $p^0 \cdot y_j^0 \geqq p^0 \cdot y_j$.

(4-34) y_j^0 maximizes $p^0 \cdot y_j$ for $y_j \in Y_j$.

5.3.2. Choose any $x_i \in X_i$ such that $u_i(x_i) > u_i(x_i^0)$. For k sufficiently large, $u_i(x_i) > u_i(x_i^k)$, from (4-31) and the continuity of u_i. This is not compatible with the statement that $x_i \in A_i(\bar{x}_i^k)$, by (4-25), so that $p^k \cdot x_i > p^k \cdot x_i^k$. Let k approach ∞.

(4-35) If $x_i \in X_i$ and $u_i(x_i) > u_i(x_i^0)$, then $p^0 \cdot x_i \geqq p^0 \cdot x_i^0$.

5.3.3. This section is a digression which may be of some interest for general techniques in the theory of the consumer. It can easily be shown that from (4-35),

(4-36) x_i^0 minimizes $p^0 \cdot x_i$ on $\{x_i | \; x_i \in X_i, \quad u_i(x_i) \geqq u_i(x_i^0)\}$

and that p^0 maximizes $p \cdot z^0$ for $p \in P$. In conjunction with (4-34), it is then shown that all the conditions for a competitive equilibrium are satisfied, except that utility maximization by a consumption unit under a budget restraint has been replaced by minimization of cost for a given utility level (compare [4-36] with Condition 2). The duality between cost minimization and utility maximization is indeed valid almost everywhere, that is, in the interior of P, where all prices are positive, but not everywhere.

From the viewpoint of welfare economics, it is the principle that the consumption vector chosen should be the one which achieves the given utility at least cost which is primary, and the principle of maximizing utility at a given cost only relevant when the two give identical results.[14] For a descriptive theory of behavior under perfect competition, on the other hand, it is, of course, the concept of utility maximization which is primary. To the extent that the duality is valid, the principle of cost minimization leads to much simpler derivations, for example, of Slutzky's relations. Actually, minimization of cost for a given utility is essentially minimization of a linear function when the argument is limited to a convex set; mathematically, the problem is identical with that of maximizing profits subject to the transformation conditions, so that the theories of the consumer and the firm become

14. See Arrow (1951), lemma 4, p. 513; a brief discussion of the conditions for the duality to be valid is given in lemma 5, pp. 513–514. See also Debreu (1951); Friedman (1952).

identical.[15] However, the failure of the duality to hold in all cases shows that there are delicate questions for which the principle of utility maximization cannot be replaced by that of cost minimization.

5.3.4. From (4-32), $1 \in \mathcal{P}$. By (b) of Definition 5, there exists $y' \in Y$ such that

(4-37) $\quad y'_h \geqq y^0_h$ for all $h \neq 1$; $\quad y'_{h'} > y^0_{h'}$ for some $h' \in \mathfrak{D}$.

Here, $y^0 = \sum_{j=1}^n y_j^0$. From (4-34), $p^0 \cdot y'_j \leqq p^0 \cdot y^0_j$ for all j. Summing over j then gives

(4-38) $\quad p^0 \cdot y' \leqq p^0 \cdot y^0$.

With the aid of (4-37) and (4-32),

$$p^0 \cdot (y' - y^0) = \sum_h p^0_h(y'_h - y^0_h)$$
$$= \sum_{h \neq 1} p^0_h(y'_h - y^0_h) \geqq p^0_{h'}(y'_{h'} - y^0_{h'}).$$

Since $y'_{h'} - y^0_{h'} > 0$, (4-38) requires that $p^0_{h'} = 0$.

(4-39) $\quad p^0_{h'} = 0$ for at least one $h' \in \mathfrak{D}$.

Let $x_i \in X_i$, $x_i(t) = tx_i + (1 - t)x^0_i$, where $0 < t \leqq 1$. From Definition 3, there exists

(4-40) $\quad \lambda > 0, \quad u_i(x^0_i + \lambda\delta^{h'}) > u_i(x^0_i)$.

Since $x_i(t) + \lambda\delta^{h'}$ approaches $x^0_i + \lambda\delta^{h'}$ as t approaches 0, it follows from (4-40) that

(4-41) $\quad u_i[x_i(t) + \lambda\delta^{h'}] > u_i(x^0_i)$ for t sufficiently small.

From (4-41) and (4-35), $p^0 \cdot [x_i(t) + \lambda\delta^{h'}] \geqq p^0 \cdot x^0_i$. But, from (4-39),

$$p^0 \cdot (\lambda\delta^{h'}) = \lambda p^0_{h'} = 0.$$

Since $p^0 \cdot [x_i(t) + \lambda\delta^{h'}] = tp^0 \cdot x_i + (1 - t)p^0 \cdot x^0_i + p^0 \cdot (\lambda\delta^{h'})$, it follows easily that $p^0 \cdot x_i \geqq p^0 \cdot x^0_i$.

(4-42) $\quad x^0_i$ minimizes $p^0 \cdot x_i$ over X_i.

---

15. Knight (1944) and Friedman (1949, esp. pp. 469–474) have therefore gone so far as to argue that it is always better to draw up demand functions as of a given real income (that is, utility) instead of a given money income.

Let X be defined as in section 4.2. Since $p^0 \cdot x = \Sigma_{i=1}^m p^0 \cdot x_i$, it follows immediately from (4-42) that

(4-43) $\quad x^0$ minimizes $p^0 \cdot x$ over X.

5.3.5. In accordance with Assumption 5, choose $x \epsilon X$, $y \epsilon Y$ so that $x < y + \zeta$. Then, with the aid of (4-43), $p^0 \cdot (y + \zeta) > p^0 \cdot x \geqq p^0 \cdot x^0$, or

(4-44) $\quad p^0 \cdot y > p^0 \cdot (x^0 - \zeta)$.

From (4-33),

(4-45) $\quad p^0 \cdot (x^0 - y^0 - \zeta) = 0$.

This, combined with (4-44) gives

(4-46) $\quad p^0 \cdot y > p^0 \cdot y^0$.

But this implies that, for some j, $p^0 \cdot y_j > p^0 \cdot y_j^0$, while $y_j \epsilon Y_j$, a contradiction to (4-34). Thus, the assumption made at the beginning of section 5.3.1, that for every $\varepsilon > 0$, $p_h^* = \varepsilon$ for at least one $h \epsilon \mathcal{P}$, has led to a contradiction and must be false. Statement (4-28) must then be valid, and by statement (4-29), Theorem 2 has been proved.

5.3.6. The following theorem, slightly more general than Theorem 2, can easily be proved in a way practically identical to the above.

Assumption 4′(a) is replaced by

ASSUMPTION 4″(a). *$\zeta_i \epsilon R^l$; for some $x_i \epsilon X_i$, $x_i \leqq \zeta_i$ and, for at least one $h \epsilon \mathfrak{D} \cup \mathcal{P}$, $x_{hi} < \zeta_{hi}$.*

Assumptions 4″(a) and 4(b) together are denoted by 4″.

THEOREM 2′. *For an economic system satisfying Assumptions 1–3, 4″, 5, and 6 there is a competitive equilibrium.*

6. Historical Note

The earliest discussion of the existence of competitive equilibrium centered around the version presented by Cassel (1924). There are four basic principles of his system: (1) demand for each final good is a function of the prices of all final goods; (2) zero profits for all producers; (3) fixed technical coefficients relating use of primary resources to output of final commodities; and (4) equality of supply and demand on each market. Let x_i be the demand for final commodity i, p_i the price of final commodity i, a_{ij} the amount of primary resource j used in the production of one unit of commodity i,, q_j the price of resource j, and r_j the amount of resource j available initially. Then Cassel's system may be written

$$x_i = f_i(p_1, \ldots, p_m) \tag{4-47}$$

$$\sum_j a_{ij} q_j = p_i \quad \text{for all } i, \tag{4-48}$$

$$\sum_i a_{ij} x_i = r_j \quad \text{for all } j. \tag{4-49}$$

Neisser remarked that the Casselian system might have negative values of prices or quantities as solutions (1932, pp. 424–425). Negative quantities are clearly meaningless and, at least in the case of labor and capital, negative prices cannot be regarded as acceptable solutions since the supply at those prices will be zero. Neisser also observed that even some variability in the technical coefficients might not be sufficient to remove the inconsistency (pp. 448–453).

Stackelberg (1933) pointed out that if there were fewer commodities than resources, the equations (4-49) would constitute a set of linear equations with more equations than unknowns and therefore possess, in general, no solution. He correctly noted that the economic meaning of this inconsistency was that some of the equations in (4-49) would become inequalities, with the corresponding resources becoming free goods. He argued that this meant the loss of a certain number of equations and hence the indeterminacy of the rest of the system. For this reason, he held that the assumption of fixed coefficients could not be maintained and the possibility of substitution in production must be admitted. This reasoning is incorrect; the loss of the equations (4-49) which are replaced by inequalities is exactly balanced by the addition of an equal number of equations stating that the prices of the corresponding resources must be zero.

Indeed, this suggestion had already been made by Zeuthen (1933; see pp. 2–3, 6), though not in connection with the existence of solutions. He argued that the resources which appeared in the Casselian system were properly only the scarce resources; but it could not be regarded as known a priori which resources are free and which are not. Hence Eqs. (4-49) should be rewritten as inequalities,

$$\sum_i a_{ij} x_i \leqq r_j,$$

with the additional statement that if the strict inequality holds for any j, then the corresponding price $q_j = 0$.

Schlesinger (1933–34) took up Zeuthen's modification and suggested that it might resolve the difficulties found by Neisser and Stackelberg. It was in this form that the problem was investigated by Wald (1933–34, 1934–35) under various specialized assumptions. These studies are summarized and commented on in Wald (1951).

From a strictly mathematical point of view the first theorem proved by Wald (1951, pp. 372–373) neither contains nor is contained in our results. In the assumptions concerning the productive system, the present chapter is much more general since Wald assumes fixed proportions among the inputs and the single output of every process. On the demand side, he makes assumptions concerning the demand functions instead of deriving them, as we do, from a utility maximization assumption. It is on this point that no direct comparison is possible. The assumptions made by Wald are somewhat specialized (1951, p. 373, assumptions 4, 5, and 6). One of them, interestingly enough, is the same as Samuelson's postulate (1947, pp. 108–111), but applied to the collective demand functions rather than to individual ones. Wald gives a heuristic argument for this assumption which is based essentially on utility-maximization grounds. In the same model, he also assumes that the demand functions are independent of the distribution of income, depending solely on the total. In effect, then, he assumes a single consumption unit.

In his second theorem (1951, pp. 382–383), about the pure exchange case, Wald assumes utility maximization but postulates that the marginal utility of each commodity depends on that commodity alone and is a strictly decreasing nonnegative function of the amount of that commodity. The last clause implies both the convexity of the indifference map and nonsaturation with respect to every commodity. This theorem is a special case of our Theorem 2′, when $\mathcal{P}$ is the null set and $\mathfrak{D}$ contains all commodities (see section 5.3.6).

Wald gives an example, under the pure exchange case, where competitive equilibrium does not exist (1951, pp. 389–391). In this case, each individual has an initial stock of only one commodity, so that Theorem 1 is not applicable.

At the same time only one commodity is always desired by all, but two of the three consumers have a null initial stock of that commodity. Hence Theorem 2′ is not applicable.

It may be added that Wald has also investigated the uniqueness of the solutions; this has not been done here.

References

Arrow, K. J., "An Extension of the Basic Theorems of Classical Welfare Economics," in *Proceedings of the Second Berkeley Symposium on Mathematical Statistics and Probability,* J. Neyman (ed.), Berkeley and Los Angeles: University of California Press, 1951, pp. 507–532.

Cassel, G., *The Theory of Social Economy,* New York: Harcourt, Brace and Company, 1924.

Cournot, A. A., *Researches into the Mathematical Principles of the Theory of Wealth,* New York and London: Macmillan, 1897.

Debreu, G., "The Coefficient of Resource Utilization," *Econometrica,* vol. 19, July 1951, pp. 273–292.

Debreu, G., "A Social Equilibrium Existence Theorem," *Proceedings of the National Academy of Sciences,* vol. 38, no. 10, 1952, pp. 886–893.

Debreu, G., "Representation of a Preference Ordering by a Numerical Function," in *Decision Processes,* R. M. Thrall, C. H. Coombs, and R. L. Davis, eds., New York: Wiley, 1954.

Friedman, M., "The Marshallian Demand Curve," *Journal of Political Economy,* vol. 57 (1949), pp. 463–495.

Friedman, M., "The 'Welfare' Effects of an Income Tax and an Excise Tax," *Journal of Political Economy,* vol. 60, February 1952, pp. 25–33.

Hart, A. G., *Anticipations, Uncertainty, and Dynamic Planning,* Chicago: University of Chicago Press, 1940.

Hicks, J. R., *Value and Capital,* Oxford: The Clarendon Press, 1939.

Knight, F. H., "Realism and Relevance in the Theory of Demand," *Journal of Political Economy,* vol. 52 (1944), pp. 289–318.

Koopmans, T. C., "Analysis of Production as an Efficient Combination of Activities," in *Activity Analysis of Production and Allocation,* Cowles Commission Monograph no. 13, T. C. Koopmans, ed., New York: Wiley, 1951, chap. 3, pp. 33–97.

McKenzie, L., "On Equilibrium in Graham's Model of World Trade and Other Competitive Systems," *Econometrica,* vol. 22 (1954), pp. 147–161.

Menger, C., *Principles of Economics* (tr.), Glencoe, Illinois: The Free Press, 1950.

Nash, J. F., Jr., "Equilibrium Points in N-Person Games," *Proceedings of the National Academy of Sciences,* vol. 36 (1950), pp. 48–49.

Neisser, H., "Lohnhöhe und Beschäftigungsgrad im Marktgleichgewicht," *Weltwirtschaftliches Archiv,* vol. 36, 1932, pp. 415–455.

von Neumann, J., "Über ein ökonomisches Gleichungssystem und eine Verallgemeinerung des Brouwerschen Fixpunktsatzes," *Ergebnisse eines mathematischen Kolloquiums,* no. 8 (1937), pp. 73–83, translated as, "A Model of General Economic Equilibrium," *Review of Economic Studies,* vol. 13, no. 33, 1945–46, pp. 1–9.

Robbins, L., "On the Elasticity of Demand for Income in Terms of Effort," *Economica,* vol. 10 (1930), pp. 123–129.

Samuelson, P. A., *Foundations of Economic Analysis,* Cambridge, Massachusetts: Harvard University Press, 1947.

Schlesinger, K., "Über die Produktionsgleichungen der ökonomischen Wertlehre," *Ergebnisse eines mathematischen Kolloquiums,* no. 6 (1933–34), pp. 10–11.

Stackelberg, H., "Zwei Kritische Bemerkurgen zur Preistheorie Gustav Cassels," *Zeitschrift für Nationalökonomie,* vol. 4, 1933, pp. 456–472.

Wald, A., "Über die eindeutige positive Lösbarkeit der neuen Produktionsgleichungen," *Ergebnisse eines mathematischen Kolloquiums,* no. 6 (1933–34), pp. 12–20.

Wald, A., "Über die Produktionsgleichungen der ökonomischen Wertlehre," *Ergebnisse eines mathematischen Kolloquiums,* no. 7 (1934–35), pp. 1–6.

Wald, A., "Über einige Gleichungssysteme der mathematischen Ökonomie," *Zeitschrift für Nationalökonomie,* vol. 7 (1936), pp. 637–670, translated as "On Some Systems of Equations of Mathematical Economics," *Econometrica,* vol. 19, October 1951, pp. 368–403.

Walras, L., *Éléments d'économie politique pure,* 4th ed., Lausanne, Paris, 1900.

Zeuthen, F., "Das Prinzip der Knappheit, technische Kombination, and Ökonomische Qualität," *Zeitschrift für Nationalökonomie,* vol. 4, 1933, pp. 1–24.

5 Import Substitution in Leontief Models

In a typical Leontief model, there is a unique method of production for each product. Hence, if a given bill of final goods is specified, the output of each industry is uniquely determined, there being no possibilities of substitution. Chenery, in a contribution to a study of the industrial structure of the Italian economy (*Structure and Growth of the Italian Economy,* 1953, chap. 2, sec. E), has considered a model more general in that each commodity may be either produced domestically by a unique process or imported, which involves a drain on foreign exchange. Some, at least, of the domestic industries operate under capacity limitations. There are then alternative ways of producing a given bill of goods; choice among them is to be made on the basis of minimizing the cost of imports in foreign currency. One would expect that the choice of production and import program would depend on the relative prices of imports. The procedure actually used by Chenery is, however, independent of these prices. The purpose of this chapter is to demonstrate that his procedure is correct under a wide variety of circumstances, that is, that in spite of the presence of a substitution possibility, the optimal choice is independent of relative prices.

1. Basic Assumptions of the Model

I will briefly sketch the characteristics of the economy being analyzed. I will not argue its realism, though it is, I think, a rough approximation to the

Reprinted from *Econometrica,* 22 (1954):481–492.

condition of Italy and certain other European countries. The main purpose of this chapter, however, is the analytic contribution, which, it is hoped, may be capable of further extension.

The outstanding relevant features of the present model are the presence of unemployed labor and the imperfect competition on the market for exports due to import quotas in foreign countries. It is further assumed that the domestic production system can be described by a Leontief model, that is, that each commodity can be produced in just one way, the inputs being proportional to the scale of the output. It is assumed that foreign relative prices are not grossly out of line, in a sense to be made more exact below, with what domestic prices would be under competitive conditions. Finally, it is assumed that at least some industries have short-run capacity limitations. The aim of planning is to minimize the drain on foreign exchange. These assumptions will now be stated in a more precise way.

First of all, there are n commodities, each producible by a unique process which has only one output. Let a_{ij} be the amount of commodity i used in producing one unit of commodity j. As usual (see Leontief, 1951), we measure the quantities in dollars of some fixed base year. Since we are considering only commodities that are produced, so that labor and capital are excluded, the price of a unit produced must exceed the cost of the produced commodities used in production.

$$(5\text{-}1) \qquad a_{ij} \geqq 0, \qquad a_{ii} = 0, \qquad \sum_{i=1}^{n} a_{ij} < 1.$$

For analytic convenience, the assumption that exports cannot be expanded indefinitely at fixed prices will be stated in an extreme form. It will be assumed that exports can be sold at world prices freely up to a maximum beyond which none can be sold. This is an approximation to a declining demand curve, and, in view of widespread quantitative restrictions on imports, may have a certain degree of realism. Some such assumption is certainly widely made by planning authorities. The world prices in question are the prices in foreign markets less transport cost (in foreign currency). These prices will be referred to as "export prices." It will also be assumed that commodities can be imported in unlimited quantities at fixed prices, which are equal to foreign prices plus transport costs.[1]

1. I am indebted to a referee for *Econometrica* for stressing the distinction between export and import prices.

In symbols, let y_i^e be the export of the ith commodity, y_i^i the import of the ith commodity, η_i the maximum possible export of the ith commodity, π_i^e the export price, and π_i^i the import price of the ith commodity. Correspondingly, let y^e, y^i, η, π^e, and π^i be the vectors of exports, imports, maximum possible exports, export prices, and import prices, respectively.[2] From the discussions in the previous paragraph, it is assumed that[3]

$$y^e \leqq \eta. \tag{5-2}$$

From the definitions of import and export prices,

$$\pi^i \geqq \pi^e. \tag{5-3}$$

The net drain on foreign currency is given by

$$(\pi^i)' \, y^i - (\pi^e)' \, y^e. \tag{5-4}$$

Let ζ_i be the final demand (consumption plus investment) for the ith commodity, ζ the vector of final demands, x_i the domestic output of the ith commodity, and x the vector of domestic outputs. The demand by industry j for commodity i is then $a_{ij}x_j$, and the net domestic output of commodity i, which is total domestic output less derived demand by other industries, is $x_i - \Sigma_{j=1}^{n} a_{ij}x_j$. In vector notation, the vector of net domestic output is $(I - A)x$, where I is the identity matrix of order n and A is the matrix (a_{ij}). The net domestic output vector must be such that, together with imports, it suffices to take care of final demands and exports.

$$(I - A)x + y^i - y^e \geqq \zeta. \tag{5-5}$$

For each industry, let ξ_i be the total capacity. For an industry in which there are no capacity limitations, that is, where even in the short run output can be increased by a proportional increase in all inputs, ξ_i can be regarded as equal to infinity. Let ξ be the vector of capacities. Then,

$$0 \leqq x \leqq \xi. \tag{5-6}$$

Next, we will make a critically important assumption on import and export prices. It is assumed that, for each product, if the inputs (other than labor) are imported and the product then exported at the going import and

2. All vectors are considered to be column vectors unless a prime is attached to the symbol, in which case the transpose is taken.

3. By the notation below is meant, as usual, that $y_i^e \leqq \eta_i$ for all i; see Koopmans (1951, p. 45).

export prices, there will be a net gain in foreign exchange. To see why this assumption may be reasonable, consider the excess of the export price over the import cost of the produced inputs for the *j*th product. Then we can write it as

$$\pi_j^e - \sum_{i=1}^{n} a_{ij}\pi_i^i.$$

Let b_{ij} be the foreign input-output coefficient, that is, the amount of commodity i used in producing one unit of commodity j in the foreign world. Let π be the vector of prices in the foreign country. Then, purely as an identity,

$$\pi_j^e - \sum_{i=1}^{n} a_{ij}\pi_i^i = (\pi_j - \sum_{i=1}^{n} b_{ij}\pi_i) - (\pi_j - \pi_j^e) - \sum_{i=1}^{n} a_{ij}(\pi_i^i - \pi_i) + \sum_{i=1}^{n} (b_{ij} - a_{ij})\pi_i.$$

The "export surplus" obtainable by producing commodity j out of foreign components is thus expressed as the value added abroad less the transport cost of the final product less the transport cost of the inputs needed for the product plus a term which depends on the difference between the foreign and domestic technologies. Now, since labor certainly enters into the costs of production abroad and there are normally profit elements also, the first term, which is value added per unit output abroad, is certainly positive and usually fairly considerable. If we can assume that transport costs are relatively small, the second and third terms will be small; while if the technology abroad does not differ too greatly from that domestically, the fourth term will be small because the b_{ij}'s will be close to the a_{ij}'s. The negligibility of transport costs and the identity of foreign and domestic production structures are, of course, standard assumptions of foreign trade theory. If this is accepted, the second, third, and fourth terms will be small, while the first term, the value added, must be definitely positive. Hence we can assume that the export surplus must be positive.

$$\pi_j^e > \sum_{i=1}^{n} a_{ij}\pi_i^i. \tag{5-7}$$

Finally, we assume that the only factor of production other than the produced commodities is labor and that there is unemployment, so that labor is a free good from the national point of view. Under these conditions, any triplet of vectors x, y^e, y^i, is feasible if it satisfies (5-2), (5-5), and (5-6).

Among the feasible programs, the optimal one is that which minimizes the drain on foreign currency, given by (5-4).

THEOREM. *Under the above assumptions (5-1), (5-3), and (5-7) on the technology and the import and export prices, the optimal program has the following properties: (1) no commodity is both imported and exported; (2) there is no industry such that simultaneously the domestic industry has excess capacity and the exports are less than the maximum possible.*[4] *There is precisely one feasible program satisfying these conditions, so that the optimal program is independent of import and export prices so long as they satisfy (5-3) and (5-7).*

The theorem is demonstrated in the next section. To avoid misapprehension, it should be remarked that the theorem does not imply, even when applicable, that relative import and export prices are of no relevance for the planner. The theorem permits a considerable simplification of the planning process in that, within the limits of the theorem's validity, the minimum-cost import program for a *given* set of final demands can be determined in a fairly simple manner. But the cost itself depends on import and export prices, so that the choice among *alternative* bills of final demands will still depend on those prices.

2. Mathematical Analysis

The problem of minimizing the linear form $(\pi^i)' \, y^i - (\pi^e)' \, y^e$ subject to (5-2), (5-5), and (5-6) is of course a problem in linear programming. In the present case, some preliminary considerations lead to a relatively simple solution.

2.1. First of all, we can assume without loss that in an optimal program, there is no commodity which is both exported and imported. For suppose there were, and we reduced both exports and imports of that commodity slightly by the same amount. The upper bound (5-2) on exports would certainly be maintained. In the condition (5-5) that the given final demands be at least met, only the difference between exports and imports enters, so

---

4. Under certain unimportant circumstances, there may be other optimal programs equally as good (in terms of minimizing the adverse trade balance) as the one satisfying (1) and (2), but there is never any loss in restricting oneself to such programs. For the circumstances, see the next section.

(5-5) is still satisfied. In (5-6), the export and imports do not enter explicitly. Hence, the new program is still feasible. Further, from (5-3), which states that import prices are at least as high as export prices, adverse trade balance cannot be increased and will in fact be reduced if the import price is actually greater than the export price, as we would expect if transport costs are significant. Hence, we can assume without loss of generality that

(5-8) $\quad$ for any j, $\quad$ either $y_j^e = 0 \quad \text{or} \quad y_j^i = 0.$

In view of (5-8) we can simplify the formulation of the problem by introducing the vector

(5-9) $\quad y = \eta + y^i - y^e.$

The vector y may be interpreted as the excess of maximum possible exports over actual exports, imports being taken as negative exports. Given the vector y, we can easily find the vectors y^i and y^e from which it was derived; since $y - \eta = y^i - y^e$, where both latter vectors are nonnegative, then it follows from (5-8) that y^i can be obtained by replacing all negative components of $y - \eta$ by 0, while y^e can be obtained from $y - \eta$ by replacing all positive components by 0 and changing the sign of all negative components. If $y \geqq 0$, then each negative component of $y - \eta$ will be greater than or equal to the corresponding component of $-\eta$, so that $y^e \leqq \eta$, that is, (5-2) is satisfied. Conversely, if (5-2) is satisfied, it follows from (5-9) that $y \geqq 0$. Hence, (5-2) is equivalent to the condition that

(5-10) $\quad y \geqq 0.$

Condition (5-5) can be written,

(5-11) $\quad (I - A)x + y \geqq \zeta + \eta.$

A feasible program can then be characterized by a pair of vectors x, y, satisfying (5-6), (5-10), and (5-11). For each such program, the corresponding import and export vectors y^i and y^e can be derived, as noted above, and the loss of foreign exchange evaluated from (5-4).

2.2. We will make use of a fundamental property of Leontief matrices. If we consider a matrix A having the properties stated in (5-1), that is, a nonnegative matrix whose column sums are all less than one, then it is well known that the matrix $I - A$ is nonsingular and the elements of $(I - A)^{-1}$ are all nonnegative (see, for example, Solow, 1952, p. 37). Any principal minor $\bar{A}$ of A (formed by deleting rows and corresponding columns) also enjoys the properties (5-1), so that $(I - \bar{A})^{-1}$ is also defined and consists of nonnegative elements.

2.3. Suppose the vectors x, y constitute an optimal program, so that (5-6), (5-10), and (5-11) are satisfied. In particular, (5-11) may be satisfied with the inequality holding for at least one component, that is, production plus imports exceeds required final demand plus exports for at least one commodity. A new program will be constructed which will also be feasible, will be at least as good from the viewpoint of minimizing loss of foreign exchange, and will involve equality in all components of (5-11), that is, no excess production. Assume then that (5-11) holds with an inequality in at least one component.[5]

(5-12) $$(I - A)x + y \geq \zeta + \eta.$$

(5-12) can also be written,

(5-13) $$(I - A)x + y = \zeta + \eta + u, \quad \text{where } u \geq 0.$$

If a program is optimal, there cannot be another feasible program $\bar{x}$, $\bar{y}$ for which $y \geq \bar{y}$, for a decrease in one component of y implies either an increase in exports or a decrease in imports, either of which reduces the drain on foreign exchange. Let v be defined by letting $v_i = \min (y_i, u_i)$; subtract v from both sides of (5-13), so that

$$(I - A)x + (y - v) = \zeta + \eta + (u - v) \geqq \zeta + \eta,$$

since $u \geqq v$. As also $y - v \geq 0$, the program x, $y - v$ is feasible. If $v_i > 0$ for any component i, then $y - v \leq y$, which is impossible if, as assumed, the program x, y is optimal. Hence, $v = 0$; that is,

(5-14) $$\text{if} \quad y_i > 0, \qquad u_i = 0.$$

Partition the vectors x, y, and u so that all the positive components of y are in $y^{(2)}$ and the zero components in $y^{(1)}$. With the aid of (5-14), then,

(5-15) $$y^{(1)} = 0, \qquad y^{(2)} > 0, \qquad u^{(1)} \geq 0, \qquad u^{(2)} = 0.$$

Partition the matrix A correspondingly, both as to rows and as to columns. Then (5-13) can be written,

---

5. By the symbol $u \geq v$, where u and v are vectors, is meant $u_i \geq v_i$ for all i, $u_i > y_i$ for at least one i. Similarly, by $u > v$ is meant $u_i > v_i$ for all i. See Koopmans (1951), p. 45.

(5-16) $$(I - A_{11})x^{(1)} - A_{12}x^{(2)} = \zeta^{(1)} + \eta^{(1)} + u^{(1)},$$
$$-A_{21}x^{(1)} + (I - A_{22})x^{(2)} + y^{(2)} = \zeta^{(2)} + \eta^{(2)}.$$

Define vector functions $x(t)$, $y(t)$ of the real variable t over the interval from 0 to 1, as follows:

(5-17) $$x^{(1)}(t) = (I - A_{11})^{-1}[A_{12}x^{(2)} + \zeta^{(1)} + \eta^{(1)} + (1 - t)u^{(1)}],$$
$$x^{(2)}(t) \equiv x^{(2)},$$
$$y^{(1)}(t) \equiv 0,$$
$$y^{(2)}(t) = A_{21}x^{(1)}(t) - (I - A_{22})x^{(2)} + \zeta^{(2)} + \eta^{(2)}.$$

By solving for $x^{(1)}$ in the first equation of (5-16) and for $y^{(2)}$ in the second, it is easily verified that

(5-18) $$x(0) = x, \qquad y(0) = y.$$

The expression in brackets in the first equation of (5-17) is composed of nonnegative elements; since $(I - A_{11})^{-1}$ has only nonnegative elements, $x^{(1)}(t) \geqq 0$. Further, since $u^{(1)} \geq 0$, the expression in brackets is decreasing in at least one component as t increases; from the nonnegativity of $(I - A_{11})^{-1}$, each component of $x^{(1)}(t)$ must be nonincreasing as t increases. Since x, y was feasible, $x \leqq \xi$, by (5-6).

(5-19) $$0 \leqq x(t) \leqq \xi \quad \text{for} \quad 0 \leqq t \leqq 1.$$

If we multiply through the first equation in (5-17) by $I - A_{11}$ and perform some obvious transpositions, it is easily seen that

(5-20) $$(I - A)x(t) + y(t) = \zeta + \eta + (1 - t)u \geqq \zeta + \eta$$
$$(0 \leqq t \leqq 1).$$

The matrix A_{21} has only nonnegative components; since all components of $x^{(1)}(t)$ are nonincreasing, all components of $y^{(2)}(t)$ are also nonincreasing, by the last line of (5-17). From (5-17), (5-18), and (5-15), for t sufficiently small but positive, $y(t) \geqq 0$; in conjunction with (5-19) and (5-20), then, the program $x(t)$, $y(t)$ is feasible. If $y(t)$ had one component which is strictly decreasing in t, then $y \geq y(t)$, which is impossible since it was assumed that x, y is optimal. Hence each component of $y(t)$ is neither increasing nor decreasing, so that $y(1) = y \geqq 0$. If t is set equal to 1 in (5-20),

(5-21) $$(I - A)x(1) + y = \zeta + \eta.$$

With the aid of (5-19), it is clear that the program $x(1)$, y is feasible. Since the net drain on foreign exchange depends only on y, it appears that starting with an optimal program we can find another as good by imposing the restriction that equality hold in every component in (5-11). That is, in searching for an optimal program, we may replace (5-11) by the stronger conditions,

$$(5\text{-}22) \qquad (I - A)x + y = \zeta + \eta.$$

It may be interesting to inquire to what extent the condition (5-22) is actually essential for an optimum. That is, how can it happen that there is more than one optimal program, not all satisfying (5-22)? To answer this question, subtract (5-21) from (5-13). Then,

$$(I - A)[x - x(1)] = u.$$

Multiply both sides by $(I - A)^{-1}$. Since $(I - A)^{-1}$ has only nonnegative elements and $u \geq 0$ (that is, u has at least one positive element),

$$x - x(1) = (I - A)^{-1}u \geq 0,$$

so that $x(1) \leq x \leqq \xi$. One special case is that in which the strict inequality holds, that is, $x(1) < \xi$. It will appear in the next section that under these circumstances the program $x(1)$, y can be optimal only if $y = 0$. That is, if it is possible to satisfy all final demands and export the maximum possible of every commodity without any imports and without reaching capacity in any industry, then there exist alternative optimal programs with excess production in some industries. More complicated cases exist where there are optimal programs with excess production in which some industries operate at capacity and even with imports in some industries; a detailed analysis of these cases does not seem worthwhile.

2.4. As a result of the last section, the problem is reduced to selecting a pair of vectors x, y satisfying (5-6), (5-10), and (5-22) so as to minimize (5-4). We shall now make use of (5-7) to establish the basic property of an optimal program, property (2) in the statement of the Theorem.

Suppose some industry is not operating at full capacity and at the same time is exporting less than the maximum possible. Then by increasing the output of the industry slightly, exporting the increase, and importing all the inputs needed for the increase, there will be, according to (5-7), an improvement in the foreign exchange position. For the right-hand side gives the cost in foreign exchange of a unit increase in production, while the left-hand side gives the additional receipts of foreign exchange.

In an optimal program, for each commodity j,

$$\text{either} \quad x_j = \xi_j \quad \text{or} \quad y_j = 0. \tag{5-23}$$

Simple as this step is, it is the critical one. For it will be shown that there can be only one program satisfying (5-6), (5-10), (5-22), and (5-23) simultaneously.

2.5. Suppose there were two different programs which satisfied (5-6), (5-10), (5-22), and (5-23) simultaneously; denote them by x, y, and $\bar{x}$, $\bar{y}$, respectively. If $x = \bar{x}$, then $y = \bar{y}$, by (5-22); hence, we must have $x \neq \bar{x}$. Without loss of generality, we may suppose $x_i < \bar{x}_i$ for at least one i. Partition the vectors x, $\bar{x}$, y, $\bar{y}$, so that

$$x^{(1)} < \bar{x}^{(1)}, \qquad x^{(2)} \geqq \bar{x}^{(2)}. \tag{5-24}$$

Since $\bar{x}^{(1)} \leqq \xi^{(1)}$, $x^{(1)} < \xi^{(1)}$; by (5-23),

$$y^{(1)} = 0. \tag{5-25}$$

Partition the matrix A correspondingly. In (5-22), applied to the two programs in question, consider only those equations corresponding to elements of $y^{(1)}$.

$$(I - A_{11})x^{(1)} - A_{12}x^{(2)} + y^{(1)} = \zeta^{(1)} + \eta^{(1)},$$

$$(I - A_{11})\bar{x}^{(1)} - A_{12}\bar{x}^{(2)} + \bar{y}^{(1)} = \zeta^{(1)} + \eta^{(1)}.$$

Solve for $x^{(1)}$ in the first equation and for $\bar{x}^{(1)}$ in the second, and take account of (5-25).

$$x^{(1)} = (I - A_{11})^{-1}[A_{12}x^{(2)} + \zeta^{(1)} + \eta^{(1)}],$$

$$\bar{x}^{(1)} = (I - A_{11})^{-1}[A_{12}\bar{x}^{(2)} + \zeta^{(1)} + \eta^{(1)} - \bar{y}^{(1)}].$$

Since A_{12} contains only nonnegative elements, it follows from the second half of (5-24) that $A_{12}x^{(2)} \geqq A_{12}\bar{x}^{(2)}$; since also $\bar{y}^{(1)} \geqq 0$, by (5-10), the bracketed expression in the first equation is at least as large, in each component, as that in the second. Since $(I - A_{11})^{-1}$ has only nonnegative elements, it follows that $x^{(1)} \geqq \bar{x}^{(1)}$, which contradicts the first half of (5-24).

That is, it has been shown that there can be only one program which satisfies all the conditions (5-6), (5-10), (5-22), and (5-23). But on the one hand, under the present assumptions, any optimal program must satisfy these conditions, and on the other hand, the conditions do not involve the import and export prices, so long as they satisfy the conditions (5-3) and (5-7). Hence, the Theorem has been demonstrated.[6]

2.6. A simple diagram may illustrate the reasoning of the last section, in the special case of two commodities where export and import prices are equal, that is, $\pi^e = \pi^i$. The aim of minimizing the drain on foreign exchange, as given by (5-4), is then simplified to that of minimizing $\pi'(y^e - y^i)$, where π stands for the common value of export and import price vectors. If, as before, we let y represent the extent to which exports fall short of the maximum possible, where imports are counted as negative exports, then $y - \eta$ represents net imports, or $y^e - y^i$. The net drain on foreign exchange is thus given by

$$\pi_1(y_1 - \eta_1) + \pi_2(y_2 - \eta_2). \tag{5-26}$$

The restriction (5-7) on prices can be written

$$\pi_1 - a_{21}\pi_2 > 0, \qquad \pi_2 - a_{12}\pi_1 > 0. \tag{5-27}$$

These conditions say that if labor costs are disregarded, each commodity can be produced at a profit in terms of foreign prices. The condition (5-22), that net domestic output plus net imports equals given final demands, can be written

$$x_1 - a_{12}x_2 + y_1 - \eta_1 = \zeta_1, \qquad x_2 - a_{21}x_1 + y_2 - \eta_2 = \zeta_2,$$

which can be solved for y_1 and y_2,

$$\begin{aligned} -y_1 &= x_1 - a_{12}x_2 - (\zeta_1 + \eta_1), \\ -y_2 &= x_2 - a_{21}x_1 - (\zeta_2 + \eta_2). \end{aligned} \tag{5-28}$$

From (5-28) and (5-26), the optimal program can be characterized as maximizing

$$\pi_1(x_1 - a_{12}x_2 - \zeta_1) + \pi_2(x_2 - a_{21}x_1 - \zeta_2) = (\pi_1 - a_{21}\pi_2)x_1 + (\pi_2 - a_{12}\pi_1)x_2 - (\pi_1\zeta_1 + \pi_2\zeta_2).$$

Since the last term is a constant uninfluenced by the choice of program, the optimal program is that feasible program which maximizes

6. This proof, which is considerably simplified from my original argument, is due to John Fei.

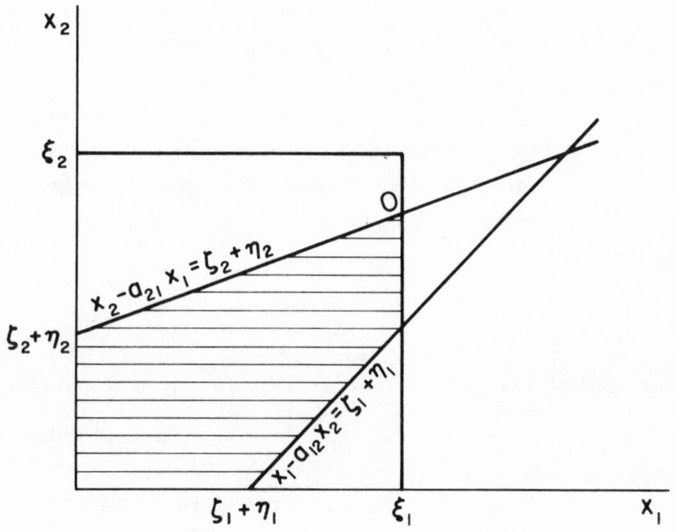

Figure 5.1

(5-29) $$(\pi_1 - a_{21}\pi_2)x_1 + (\pi_2 - a_{12}\pi_1)x_2.$$

A basic restriction on the choice of a program is that exports shall not exceed a certain quota η, which is expressed by the conditions $y_1 \geqq 0$, $y_2 \geqq 0$. In view of (5-28), these may be expressed as the following restrictions on x_1 and x_2:

(5-30) $$x_1 - a_{12}x_2 \leqq \zeta_1 + \eta_1, \qquad x_2 - a_{21}x_1 \leqq \zeta_2 + \eta_2.$$

The choice of x_1 and x_2 is further restricted by the capacity restrictions (5-6),

(5-31) $$0 \leqq x_1 \leqq \xi_1, \qquad 0 \leqq x_2 \leqq \xi_2.$$

The problem is to choose x_1 and x_2 satisfying (5-30) and (5-31) so as to maximize (5-29). The solutions of the equations

$$x_1 - a_{12}x_2 = \zeta_1 + \eta_1, \qquad x_2 - a_{21}x_1 = \zeta_2 + \eta_2$$

must lie in the positive quadrant since $0 < a_{12}, a_{21} < 1$. Hence, the feasible set is the horizontally shaded area in Figure 5.1. It is immediately apparent that the point O dominates any other feasible point, in the sense that each coordinate of O is at least as large as any other feasible point and at least one coordinate is actually larger. On the other hand, if (5-27) and (5-29) are compared, the objective is that of maximizing a positively-weighted sum of

x_1 and x_2 among all feasible points. Hence, point O must be better than any other feasible point for any set of prices, so long as they satisfy (5-27), which is the main content of the theorem. It is further to be noted that point O uses the full capacity of industry 1 but is below capacity in industry 2. It is on the line $x_2 - a_{21}x_1 = \zeta_2 + \eta_2$, which, from (5-28), implies that $y_2 = 0$, that is, that exports are at the maximum possible. That is, the commodity which is being produced domestically below capacity is being exported to the maximum possible extent.

3. Computational Methods

This section will justify the computational methods used by Chenery. Mathematically, they can be described as follows.

For two vectors u and v, let min (u,v) be the vector whose ith component is min (u_i,v_i). Define sequences w^n, x^n, y^n by the following recursive formulas:

(5-32) $$w^0 = x^0 = \min(\xi,\zeta + \eta), \qquad y^0 = \zeta + \eta - x^0,$$

(5-33) $$w^{n+1} = \min(Aw^n,\xi - x^n),$$

(5-34) $$x^{n+1} = x^n + w^{n+1},$$

(5-35) $$y^{n+1} = y^n + Aw^n - w^{n+1}.$$

In words, at the initial stage, we set the output of each industry equal to its capacity or the final demand for its product, including maximum possible exports, whichever is smaller. At each subsequent stage, the output of each industry is expanded to meet the derived demand of the previous round until capacity limits are reached; any remaining derived demand is met from imports. It will be shown that the sequences x^n, y^n converge to the optimal program.

From (5-33), $w^{n+1} \leqq Aw^n$; hence, from (5-35), $y^{n+1} \geqq y^n$. From (5-32), $y^0 \geqq 0$. Therefore,

(5-36) y^n is monotone increasing, $y^n \geqq 0$ for all n.

From (5-33), $w^{n+1} \leqq \xi - x^n$; then, $x^{n+1} = x^n + w^{n+1} \leqq x^n + \xi - x^n = \xi$. Hence,

(5-37) $x^n \leqq \xi$ for all n.

Also, $w^0 \geqq 0$. Suppose $w^n \geqq 0$; then $Aw^n \geqq 0$. With the aid of (5-37) and (5-33), $w^{n+1} \geqq 0$. Therefore, $w^n \geqq 0$ for all n; from (5-34), x^n is a monotone increasing sequence. But (5-37) implies that x^n is bounded. Hence,

(5-38) $\lim_{n\to\infty} x^n = x^*$ exists; $0 \leqq x^* \leqq \xi$; x^n is monotone increasing.

$$\begin{aligned} y^n &= \sum_{i=0}^{n-1} (y^{i+1} - y^i) + y^0 = y^0 + A \sum_{i=0}^{n-1} w^i - \sum_{i=1}^{n} w^i \\ &= y^0 + A \sum_{i=1}^{n-1} (x^i - x^{i-1}) + Aw^0 - \sum_{i=1}^{n} (x^i - x^{i-1}) \\ &= y^0 + Ax^{n-1} - Ax^0 + Aw^0 - x^n + x^0. \end{aligned}$$

Let n approach infinity. Let $y^* = \lim_{n\to\infty} y^n$.

$$\begin{aligned} y^* &= y^0 + Ax^* - Ax^0 + Aw^0 - x^* + x^0 \\ &= y^0 - (I - A)x^* + x^0. \end{aligned}$$

With the aid of (5-32),

(5-39) $(I - A)x^* + y^* = \zeta + \eta.$

From (5-36),

(5-40) $y^* \geqq 0.$

From (5-38)–(5-40), the program to which the sequences x^n, y^n converge satisfies (5-6), (5-10), and (5-22). We seek to show that this program is optimal. It suffices to show that it satisfies (5-23).

Suppose for some j that $x_j^* < \xi_j$. From (5-38), $x_j^n < \xi_j$ for all n. If n is replaced by $n + 1$, it follows from (5-34) that $w_j^{n+1} < \xi_j - x_j^n$, and therefore, from (5-33), that $w_j^{n+1} = \Sigma_i a_{ji} w_i^n$, for all n. From (5-35), then, $y_j^{n+1} = y_j^n$ for all n, or $y_j^n = y_j^0$ for all n, and therefore $y_j^* = y_j^0$. But since $x_j^0 < \xi_j$, $x_j^0 = \zeta_j + \eta_j$, and $y_j^0 = 0$. It has been shown that for all industries j for which $x_j^* < \xi_j$, $y_j^* = 0$, which is precisely (5-23). The limiting program x^*, y^* obtained from the iterative procedure (5-32)–(5-35) is then the optimal program so long as import prices satisfy condition (5-7).

References

Leontief, W. W. 1951. *The Structure of the American Economy* (2nd ed.). New York: Oxford University Press.

Koopmans, T. C. 1951. "Analysis of Production as an Efficient Combination of Activities," in T. C. Koopmans (ed.), *Activity Analysis of Production and*

Allocation. Cowles Commission Monograph no. 13. New York: Wiley. Pp. 33–97.
Solow, R. (1952). "On the Structure of Linear Models." *Econometrica,* 20:29–46.
The Structure and Growth of the Italian Economy. 1953. Prepared by the Program Division, Special Mission to Italy for Economic Cooperation, Mutual Security Agency, United States Government (mimeographed).

6 Economic Equilibrium

There are perhaps two basic, though incompletely separable, aspects of the notion of general equilibrium as it has been used in economics: (1) the simple notion of determinateness—that is, the relations that describe the economic system must form a system sufficiently complete to determine the values of its variables—and (2) the more specific notion that each relation represents a balance of forces. The last usually, though not always, is taken to mean that a violation of any one relation sets in motion forces tending to restore the balance (as will be seen below, this is not the same as the stability of the entire system). In a sense, therefore, almost any attempt to give a theory of the whole economic system implies the acceptance of the first part of the equilibrium notion, and Adam Smith's "invisible hand" is a poetic expression of the most fundamental of economic balance relations, the equalization of rates of return, as enforced by the tendency of factors to move from low to high returns.

The notion of equilibrium ("equal weight," referring to the condition for balancing a lever pivoted at its center) and with it the notion that the effects of a force may annihilate the force (for example, water finding its own level) had been familiar in mechanics long before the appearance of Smith's *Wealth of Nations* in 1776, but there is no obvious evidence that Smith drew his ideas from any analogy with mechanics. Whatever the source of the concept, the notion that through the workings of an entire system effects may be very different from, and even opposed to, intentions is surely the

Reprinted by permission of the publisher from *International Encyclopedia of the Social Sciences,* ed. David L. Sills (New York: Crowell Collier and Macmillan, 1968), vol. 4, pp. 376–386.

most important intellectual contribution that economic thought has made to the general understanding of social processes.

History of the Concept

It can be maintained that Smith was a creator of general equilibrium theory, although the coherence and consistency of his work can be questioned. A fortiori, later systematic expositors of the classical system, such as Ricardo, J. S. Mill, and Marx, in whose work some of Smith's logical gaps were filled, can all be regarded as early expositors of general equilibrium theory. Marx, in his scheme of simple reproduction, read in combination with his development of relative price theory in volumes 1 and 3 of *Das Kapital,* has indeed come in some ways closer in form to modern theory than any other classical economist, though of course everything is confused by his attempt to maintain simultaneously a pure labor theory of value and an equalization of rates of return on capital. The view that the classical economists had a form of the general equilibrium principle is further bolstered by modern reconstructions (see, for example, Samuelson, 1957, 1959).

There is, however, a very important sense in which none of the classical economists had a true general equilibrium theory: none had an explicit role for demand conditions. No doubt the more systematic thinkers, most particularly Mill and Cournot, gave verbal homage to the role of demand and the influence of prices on it, but there was no genuine integration of demand with the essentially supply-oriented nature of classical theory. The neglect of demand was facilitated by the special simplifying assumptions made about supply. A general equilibrium theory, from the modern point of view, is a theory about both the quantities and the prices of all economic goods and services. However, the classical authors found that prices appeared to be determined by a system of relations not involving quantities, derived from the zero-profit condition. This is clear enough with fixed production coefficients and a single primary factor, labor, as in Smith's famous exchange of deer and beaver, and it was the great accomplishment of Malthus and Ricardo to show that land could be brought into the system. If, finally, Malthusian assumptions about population implied that the supply price of labor was fixed in terms of goods, then even the price of capital could be determined (although the presence of capital as a productive factor and recipient of rewards was clearly an embarrassment to the classical authors, as it remains to some extent today).

Thus, in a certain definite sense the classicists had no true theory of resource allocation, since the influence of prices on quantities was not studied and the reciprocal influence was denied. But the classical theory could solve neither the logical problem of explaining relative wages of heterogeneous types of labor nor the empirical problem of accounting for wages that were rising steadily above the subsistence level. It is in this context that the neoclassical theories emerged, with all primary resources having the role that land alone had before.

(In all fairness to the classical writers, it should be remarked that the theory of foreign trade, especially in the form that Mill gave it, was a genuine general equilibrium theory. But, of course, the assumptions that were made, particularly factor immobility, were very restrictive.)

Cournot (1838), and after him Jenkin (1870) and the neoclassical economists, employed extensively the partial equilibrium analysis of a single market. In such an analysis, the demand and supply of a single commodity are conceived of as functions of the price of that commodity alone; the equilibrium price is that for which demand and supply are equal. This form of analysis must be viewed either as a pedagogical device that takes advantage of the ease of graphical representation of one-variable relations or as a first approximation to general equilibrium analysis in which repercussions through other markets are neglected.

The Contributions of Walras

The full recognition of the general equilibrium concept can unmistakably be attributed to Walras (1874–1877), although many of the elements of the neoclassical system were worked out independently by W. Stanley Jevons and by Carl Menger. In Walras' analysis, the economic system is made up of households and firms. Each household owns a set of resources, commodities useful in production or consumption, including different kinds of labor. For any given set of prices a household has an income from the sale of its resources, and with this income it can choose among all alternative bundles of consumers' goods whose cost, at the given prices, does not exceed its income. Thus, Walras saw the demand by households for any consumers' good as a function of the prices of both consumers' goods and resources. The firms were—at least in the earlier versions—assumed to be operating under fixed coefficients. Then the demand for consumers' goods determined the demand for resources; and the combined assumptions of fixed coefficients and zero profits for a competitive system implied relations between the prices of consumers' goods and of resources. An *equilibrium* set of prices, then, was a set such that supply and demand were equated on each market; under the assumption of fixed coefficients of production, or more generally of constant returns to scale, this amounted to equating supply and demand on the resource markets, with prices constrained to satisfy the zero-profit conditions for firms. Subsequent work of Walras, J. B. Clark, Wicksteed, and others generalized the assumptions about production to include alternative methods of production, as expressed in a production function. In this context, the prices of resources were determined by marginal productivity considerations.

That there existed an equilibrium set of prices was argued from the equality of the number of prices to be determined with the number of equations expressing the equality of supply and demand on various markets. Both are equal to the number of commodities, say n. In this counting, Walras recognized that there were two offsetting complications: (1) Only relative prices affected the behavior of households and firms, hence the system of equations had only $n - 1$ variables, a point which Walras expressed by selecting one commodity to serve as numéraire, with the prices of all commodities being measured relative to it. (2) The budgetary balance of each household between income and the value of consumption and the zero-profit condition for firms together imply what has come to be known as Walras' law, that the market value of supply equals that of demand for any set of prices, not merely the equilibrium set; hence, the supply-demand relations are not independent. If supply equals demand on $n - 1$ markets, then the equality must hold on the nth.

Walras wished to go further and discussed the stability of equilibrium essentially for the first time (that is, apart from some brief discussions by Mill in the context of foreign trade) in his famous but rather clumsy theory of *tâtonnements* (literally, "gropings" or "tentative proceedings"). He starts by supposing a set of prices fixed arbitrarily; then supply may exceed demand on some markets and fall below on others (unless the initial set is in fact the equilibrium set, there must, by Walras' law, be at least one case of each). Suppose the markets are considered in some definite order. On the first market, adjust the price so that supply and demand are equal, given all other prices; this will normally require raising the price if demand initially exceeded supply, decreasing it in the opposite case. The change in the first price will, of course, change supply and demand on all other markets. Repeat the process with the second and subsequent markets. At the end of one round, the last market will be in equilibrium, but none of the others need be, since the adjustments on subsequent markets will destroy the equilibrium achieved on any one. However, Walras argues, the supply and demand functions for any given commodity will be affected more by the changes in its own price than by the changes in other prices; hence, after one round the markets should be more nearly in equilibrium than they were to begin with, and with successive rounds the supplies and demands on all markets will tend to equality.

It seems clear that Walras did not literally suppose that the markets came into equilibrium in some definite order. Rather, the story was a convenient way of showing how the market system could in fact solve the system of equilibrium relations. The dynamic system, more properly expressed, asserted that the price on any market rose when demand exceeded supply and fell in the opposite case; the price changes on the different markets were to be thought of as occurring simultaneously.

Finally, Walras had a still higher aim for general equilibrium analysis: to study what is now called *comparative statics,* that is, the laws by which the equilibrium prices and quantities vary with the underlying data (resources, production conditions, or utility functions). But little was actually done in this direction.

Important contributions were made by Walras' contemporaries, Edgeworth, Pareto, and Irving Fisher. One contribution perhaps calls for special mention, since it has again become the subject of significant research, the *contract curve* (Edgeworth, 1881), known in modern terminology as the *core* (see the third section below and Debreu and Scarf, 1963).

Developments during and after the 1930s

The next truly major advances did not come until the 1930s. There were two distinct streams of thought, one beginning in German-language literature and dealing primarily with the existence and uniqueness of equilibrium, the other primarily in English and dealing with stability and comparative statics. The former started with a thorough examination of Cassel's simplification (1918) of Walras' system, an interesting case of work which had no significance in itself and yet whose study turned out to be extraordinarily fruitful. Cassel assumed two kinds of goods: commodities which entered into the demand functions of consumers, and factors which were used to produce commodities (intermediate goods were not considered). Each commodity was produced from factors with constant input–output coefficients. Factor supplies were supposed totally inelastic. Let a_{ij} be the amount of factor i used in the production of one unit of commodity j; x_j the total output of commodity j; v_i the total initial supply of factor i; p_j the price of commodity j; and r_i the price of factor i. Then the condition that demand equal supply for all factors reads

$$\text{(6-1)} \qquad \sum_j a_{ij} x_j = v_i, \quad \text{for all } i,$$

while the condition that each commodity be produced with zero profits reads

$$\text{(6-2)} \qquad \sum_i a_{ij} r_i = p_j, \quad \text{for all } j.$$

The system is completed by the equations relating the demand for commodities to their prices and to total income from the sale of factors. In total, there are as many equations as unknowns. But three virtually simultaneous papers by Zeuthen (1932), Neisser (1932), and von Stackelberg (1933) showed in different ways that the problem of existence of meaningful equilibrium was deeper than equality of equations and unknowns. Neisser noted that even with perfectly plausible values of the input–output coefficients, a_{ij}, the prices or quantities which satisfied (6-1) and (6-2) might well be negative. Von Stackelberg noted that (6-1) constituted a complete system of equations in the outputs, x_j, since the factor supplies, v_i, were data; but nothing had been assumed about the numbers of distinct factors or distinct commodities. If, in particular, the number of commodities were less than that of factors, equations (6-1) would in general have no solutions.

Zeuthen reconsidered the meaning of equations (6-1). He noted that economists, at least since Carl Menger, had recognized that some factors (for example, air) were so abundant that there would be no price charged for them. These would not enter into the list of factors in Cassel's system. But, Zeuthen argued, the division of factors into free and scarce should not be taken as given a priori. Hence, all that can be said is that the use of a factor should not exceed its supply; but if it falls short, then the factor is free. In symbols, (6-1) is replaced by

$$\text{(6-1')} \qquad \sum_j a_{ij} x_j \leqq v_i;$$

if the strict inequality holds, then $r_i = 0$. To a later generation of economists, to whom linear programming and its generalizations are familiar, the crucial significance of this step will need no elaboration; equalities are replaced by inequalities, and the vital notion of the complementary slackness of quantities and prices is introduced.

Independently of Zeuthen, the Viennese banker and amateur economist K. Schlesinger came to the same conclusion. But he went much further and intuitively grasped the essential point that replacement of equalities by inequalities also resolved the problems raised by Neisser and von Stackelberg. Schlesinger realized the mathematical complexity of a rigorous treatment, and, at his request, Oskar Morgenstern put him in touch with a young mathematician, Abraham Wald. The result was the first rigorous analysis of general competitive equilibrium. In a series of papers (see Wald, 1936 for a summary), Wald demonstrated the existence of competitive equilibrium in a series of alternative models, including the Cassel model and a model of pure exchange. Competitive equilibrium was defined in the Zeuthen sense, and the essential role of that definition in the justification of existence is made clear in the mathematics. Wald also initiated the study of uniqueness. Indeed, both of his alternative sufficient conditions for the uniqueness of competitive equilibrium have since become major themes of the literature: (1) that the weak axiom of revealed preference hold for the market demand functions (the sums of the demand functions of all individuals), or (2) that all commodities be gross substitutes (see definitions below).

Wald's papers were of forbidding mathematical depth, not only in the use of sophisticated tools but also in the complexity of the argument. As they gradually came to be known among mathematical economists, they probably served as much to inhibit further research by their difficulty as to stimulate it. Help finally came from the development of a related line of research, John von Neumann's theory of games (first basic paper published in 1928; see von Neumann and Morgenstern, 1944). The historical relation between game theory and economic equilibrium theory is paradoxical. In principle, game theory is a very general notion of equilibrium which should either replace the principle of competitive equilibrium or include it as a special case. In fact, while game theory has turned out to be extraordinarily stimulating to equilibrium theory, it has been through the use of mathematical tools developed in the former and used in the latter with entirely different interpretations. It was von Neumann himself who made the first such application in his celebrated paper on balanced economic growth (1937). In this model, there were no demand functions, only production. The markets had to be in equilibrium in the Zeuthen sense. But beyond this, there was equilibrium in a second sense, which may be termed *stationary equilibrium* (see the section on equilibrium over time). To prove the existence of equilibrium, von Neumann demonstrated that a certain ratio of bilinear forms has a saddle point, a generalization of the theorem which shows the existence of equilibrium in two-person zero-sum games. But in game theory the variables of the problem are probabilities (of choosing alternative strategies), while in the application to equilibrium theory one set of variables is prices and the other is the levels at which productive activities are carried on.

Von Neumann deduced his saddle-point theorem from a generalization of Brouwer's fixed-point theorem, a famous proposition in the branch of mathematics known as topology. A simplified version of von Neumann's theorem was presented a few years later by the mathematician Shizuo Kakutani, and Kakutani's theorem has been the basic tool in virtually all subsequent work. With this foundation, and the influence of the rapid development of linear programming on both the mathematical—again closely related to saddle-point theorems—and economic sides (the work of George B. Dantzig, Albert W. Tucker, Harold W. Kuhn, Tjalling C. Koopmans, and others, collected for the most part in an influential volume, Cowles Commission for Research in Economics, 1951; and the work of John F. Nash, Jr., 1950), it was perceived independently by a number of scholars that existence theorems of greater simplicity and generality than Wald's were possible. The first papers were those of McKenzie (1954) and Arrow and Debreu (1954). Subsequent developments were due to Hukukane Nikaidô, Hirofumi Uzawa, Debreu, and McKenzie. (The most complete systematic account of the existence conditions is in Debreu, 1959; the most general version of the existence theorem is in Debreu, 1962.)

Independently of this development of the existence conditions for equilibrium, the Anglo-American literature contained an intensive study of the comparative statics and stability of general competitive equilibrium. Historically, it was closely related to analyses of the second-order conditions for maximization of profits by firms and of utility by consumers; the most important contributors were John R. Hicks, Harold Hotelling, Paul Samuelson, and R. G. D. Allen. In particular, Hicks (1939) introduced the argument that the stability of equilibrium carried with it some implications for the shapes of the supply and demand functions in the neighborhood of equilibrium; hence, the effects of small shifts in any one behavior relation may be predicted, at least as to sign. Hicks's definition of stability has been replaced in subsequent work by Samuelson's (1941–1942); however, Hicks showed that (locally) stability in his sense was equivalent to a condition which has played a considerable role in subsequent research. Let X_i be the excess demand (demand less supply) for the ith commodity; it is in general a function of $p_1, \ldots, p_n$, the prices of all n commodities. Then Hicks's definition of stability was equivalent to the condition that the principal minors of the matrix whose elements were $\partial X_i/\partial p_j$ had determinants which were positive or negative according as the number of rows or columns included was even or odd. Such matrices will be referred to as *Hicksian.* Hicks also sought to derive comparative-statics conclusions about the response of prices to changes in demand functions. Presently accepted theorems derive the same conclusions but from somewhat different premises (see the section on comparative statics).

Samuelson formulated the presently accepted definition of stability. It must be based, he argued, on an explicit dynamic model concerning the behavior of prices when the system is out of equilibrium. He formalized the implicit assumption of Walras and most of his successors: the price of each commodity increases at a rate proportional to excess demand for that commodity. This assumption defined a system of differential equations; if every path satisfying the system and starting sufficiently close to equilibrium converged to it, then the system was stable. Samuelson was able to demonstrate that Hicks's definition was neither necessary nor sufficient for his and that the economic system was stable if the income effects on consumption were sufficiently small. He enunciated a general *correspondence principle:* that all meaningful theorems in comparative statics were derived either from the second-order conditions on maximization of profits by firms or of utility by consumers or from the assumption that the observed equilibrium was stable.

The current period of work in comparative statics and stability dates from the work of Mosak (1944) and Metzler (1945). The emphasis has tended to be a little different from Samuelson's correspondence principle; rather, the tendency has been to formulate hypotheses about the excess demand functions which imply both stability and certain results in comparative statics.

The Existence of Competitive Equilibrium

Consider a system with n commodities, with prices $p_1, \ldots, p_n$, respectively. Let us first suppose that at each set of prices, each economic agent (firm or household) has a single chosen demand or supply. If supplies are treated as negative demands, then for each commodity the net total excess demand (excess of demand over supply) by all economic agents is obtained by summing the excess demands for the individual agents, and this is a function of all prices; let $X_i(p_1, \ldots, p_n)$ be the excess demand function for the ith commodity. At an equilibrium, excess demand cannot be positive since there is no way of meeting it. Further, if the excess demand is negative (that is, there is an excess of supply over demand), the good is free and should have a zero price. Formally, a set of nonnegative prices $\bar{p}_1, \ldots, \bar{p}_n$ constitutes an *equilibrium* if

(6-3) $$X_i(\bar{p}_1, \ldots, \bar{p}_n) \leqq 0 \quad \text{for all } i,$$

(6-4) $$\bar{p}_i = 0 \quad \text{for all } i \text{ such that } X_i(\bar{p}_1, \ldots, \bar{p}_n) < 0.$$

With this definition, the following assumptions are sufficient for the existence of equilibrium:

(H) The functions $X_i(p_1, \ldots, p_n)$ are (positively) homogeneous of degree zero, that is, $X_i(\lambda p_1, \ldots, \lambda p_n) = X_i(p_1, \ldots, p_n)$ for all $\lambda > 0$ and all $p_1, \ldots, p_n$.
(W) $\Sigma_i p_i X_i(p_1, \ldots, p_n) = 0$ for all sets of prices.
(C) The functions $X_i(p_1, \ldots, p_n)$ are continuous.
(B) The functions $X_i(p_1, \ldots, p_n)$ are bounded from below (that is, supply is always limited).

Assumption (H) is standard in consumers' demand theory; (W) is Walras' law referred to above. Assumption (C) is the type usually made in any applied work, although, as will be seen later, it is closely related to assumptions of convexity of preferences and production. Assumption (B) is trivially valid in a pure exchange economy, since each individual has a finite stock of goods to trade. In an economy where production takes place, the matter is less clear. At an arbitrarily given set of prices, a producer may find it profitable to offer an infinite supply; the realization of his plans will, of course, require him to demand at the same time an infinite amount of some factor of production. Such situations are of course incompatible with equilibrium, but since the existence of equilibrium is itself in question here, the analysis is necessarily delicate.

The current proofs that the assumptions listed above imply the existence of competitive equilibrium require the use of Brouwer's fixed-point theorem, a mathematical theorem which asserts that a continuous transformation of a triangle or similar figure in higher-dimensional spaces into itself must leave at least one point unaltered. The argument may be sketched as follows: From (H), an equilibrium is unaltered if all prices are multiplied by the same positive constant; hence, without loss of generality we can assume that the sum of the prices is one. The set of all price vectors with nonnegative components summing to one is clearly a generalized triangle (technically called a *simplex*). For each set of prices, compute the excess demands (positive or negative) and then form a new price vector in which those components with positive excess demands are increased and the others decreased (but not below zero). These new prices are then adjusted so that the sum is again one. This process defines a continuous transformation of the simplex into itself and thus has a fixed point, a price vector which remains unaltered under the adjustment process. It is easy to see that this price vector must be an equilibrium.

The point of view just sketched is not sufficiently general for most purposes. We have already seen that the boundedness assumption appears artificial in the case where production is possible. Closely related to this is a second issue; the assumption that supplies and demands are single-valued appears unduly restrictive. Consider the simplest case of production: one input and one output which is proportional to the input. The behavior of the profit-maximizing entrepreneur depends on the ratio of the input price to the output price. If the price ratio is greater than the output–input ratio, then the firm will lose money if it engages in any production; hence, the profit-maximizing point is zero output and zero input, which is indeed single-valued. If the two ratios are equal, however, all output levels make zero profit; hence, the profit-maximizing entrepreneur is indifferent among them, and the supply function of the output and the demand function for the input must be taken to be multivalued. If the price ratio is less than the output–input ratio, then the entrepreneur will make increasing profits as he increases the scale of activity. There is *no* finite level which could be described as profit-maximizing.

To state a general definition of competitive equilibrium more precisely, the following model can be formulated: there are presumed to exist a set of households and a set of firms; all production is carried on in the latter. Each household has a collection of initial assets (here assumed to include the ability to supply different kinds of labor) and also a claim to a given portion (possibly zero, of course) of the profits of each firm; it is assumed that for each firm there are claims for exactly the entire profits (these claims are interpretable as equities or partnership shares). For given prices and given production decisions of the firms, the profits of the firms and the value of each individual's initial assets are determined and, hence, so is the individual's total income. The commodity bundles available are those whose value, at the given prices, does not exceed income and whose individual components are nonnegative (or satisfy some still stronger condition independent of prices). It is further assumed that the household can express preferences among commodity bundles and that these preferences have suitable continuity properties. The aim of the household is taken to be selection of the most preferred bundle among those available.

The behavior of the firms is more simply described. Each firm has available to it a set of possible production bundles; conventionally, the components are taken to be positive for outputs and negative for inputs. For a fixed set of prices, the profits for each possible production bundle are determined; then the firm chooses the (or a) bundle which maximizes profits. Notice that the profit-maximizing bundle need not be unique. Indeed, under constant returns to scale, it is never unique unless the firm's best policy is to shut down completely. (Under constant returns, if any bundle is possible, the bundle obtained by doubling all components, inputs and outputs alike, is also possible. Then if any bundle makes positive profits, doubling the bundle will double the profits; hence, there can be no profit-maximizing bundle. The existence of a profit-maximizing bundle thus entails that maximum profits be nonpositive. Since zero profits are always possible by zero activity level, we must have zero profits at the maximum. Either profits are negative for all nonzero bundles, in which case shutting down is the unique optimal policy, or profits are zero for some nonzero bundle, in which case any nonnegative multiple also achieves zero and therefore maximum profits.)

In this terminology, a "firm" may actually be producing zero output and therefore may not be statistically observable; the firm is potentially capable of producing outputs and would find it profitable to do so at different sets of prices than those prevailing.

A *competitive equilibrium,* then, is a designation of nonnegative prices for all commodities, of a bundle for consumption for each household, and of a production bundle for each firm satisfying the following conditions:

(a) for each household, the designated bundle maximizes utility among all available bundles;

(b) for each firm, the designated bundle maximizes profit among all technically possible bundles;

(c) for each commodity, the total consumed by all households does not exceed the total initially available plus the net total produced by all firms ("net" here means that input uses by some firms are subtracted from outputs of others);

(d) for those commodities for which total consumed is strictly less than total initially available plus total produced, the price is zero.

The adjective "competitive" refers to the assumption that each household or firm takes prices as given and independent of its decision.

The following assumptions are sufficient to ensure the existence of competitive equilibrium:

(1) The preference ordering of each household is continuous (a strict preference between two bundles continues to hold if either is slightly altered), admits of no saturation (for each bundle, there is another preferred to it), and is convex (if a bundle is varied along a line segment in the commodity space, one of the end points is least preferred).

(2) The set of possible production bundles for each firm is convex (any weighted combination of two possible production bundles is possible) and closed (any bundle that can be approximated by possible bundles is itself possible); further, it is always possible to produce no outputs and use no inputs.

(3) No production bundle possible to society as a whole (a bundle is possible for society as a whole if it is the algebraic sum of production bundles, one chosen among those possible for each firm) can contain outputs but not inputs; there is at least one bundle possible for society that contains a positive net output of all commodities not possessed initially by any household.

(4) The economy is irreducible—a concept developed by Gale (1960) and McKenzie (1959)—in the sense that no matter how the households are divided into two groups, an increase in the initial assets held by the members of one group can be used to make feasible an allocation which will make no one worse off and at least one individual in the second group better off.

It is perhaps interesting to observe that "atomistic" assumptions concerning individual households and firms are not sufficient to establish the existence of equilibrium; "global" assumptions (3) and (4) are also needed (though they are surely unexceptionable). Thus, a limit is set to the tendency implicit in price theory, particularly in its mathematical versions, to deduce all properties of aggregate behavior from assumptions about individual economic agents.

The hypotheses of convexity in household preferences and in production are the empirically most vulnerable parts of the above assumptions. In production, convexity excludes indivisibilities or increasing returns to scale. In consumption, convexity excludes cases in which mixed bundles are inferior to extremes; for example, in the very short run, a mixture of whiskey and gin is regarded by many as inferior to either alone, or living part time in each of two distant cities may be inferior to living in either one alone. It is of interest to know how far these assumptions may be relaxed.

Convexity does play an essential role in the proof. This may be illustrated by considering the simplest case—one input and one output proportional to it. As noted earlier, there will be one ratio of output to input prices at which the entrepreneur will be indifferent among all levels of output. If the supply of the input is given, then the equilibrium levels of input and output, as well as price, are determined. Now suppose that production is possible only at integer-valued levels of input, so that the production possibility set is not convex. If the supply of the input is not an integer, there is no way of equating demand and supply for it. It should be noted, though, that the input (and output) level can be so chosen that the difference between supply and demand does not exceed one-half. In effect, convexity ensures that supply and demand are, in a suitable sense, continuous and thus can be adjusted to varying levels of initial assets.

The assumption of convexity cannot be dispensed with in general theorems concerning the existence of equilibrium strictly defined. However, a line of thought begun by Farrell (1959) and developed by Rothenberg (1960) and Aumann (1966) suggests that the gap between supply and demand does not tend to increase with the size of the economy. More explicitly, if each agent (household or firm) is small compared with the total economy, then by suitable choice of prices and of consumption and production bundles, the discrepancy between supply and demand can be made small relative to the economy. Each household is certainly small relative to the economy, so that nonconvexities in individual preferences have no significant effect on the existence of equilibrium. However, increasing returns to scale over a sufficiently wide range may mean that a competitive profit-maximizing firm will be large at a given set of prices if it produces at all; hence, there is a real possibility that equilibrium may not exist.

Optimality and the Core

Although the view that competitive equilibria have some special optimality properties is at least as old as Adam Smith's invisible hand, a clarification of the relation is fairly recent. Since the subject belongs to the field of welfare economics, only a brief statement is given here. An allocation (designation of bundles for all households and all firms) is *feasible* if each bundle is possible for the corresponding agent and if, in the aggregate, the net output of each commodity (including quantities initially available) is at least as great as the demand by consumers. Each allocation, then, determines the utility level of the consumption of each household. One allocation is *dominated* by a second if the latter is feasible and if each individual has a higher utility under the second than under the first (more frequently, in the literature, the condition is put in the more complicated form of having each individual at least as well off and one individual better off, but the difference is trifling). Then an allocation is said to be optimal if it is feasible but not dominated by any other (a definition due to Pareto).

There are two theorems relating competitive equilibrium and optimal allocations, one concerning sufficiency and the other concerning necessity; the two have not always been distinguished in the literature. They are stated here without some minor qualifications.

Sufficiency. Any competitive equilibrium is necessarily optimal.

Necessity. Given any optimal allocation, there is some assignment of society's initial assets among individuals such that the optimal allocation is a competitive equilibrium corresponding to that distribution, provided that the assumptions of the previous section which ensure the existence of equilibrium hold.

It is useful to note that the sufficiency theorem is valid even if the assumptions of the previous section do not hold.

The concept of optimality is defined without regard to a price system or any prescribed set of markets. The optimality theorems assert that even though prices do not enter into the definition of optimality, there happens to be an identity between optima and competitive equilibria (under suitable conditions). This relation has been brought into still sharper relief with the modern theory of the core (Debreu and Scarf, 1963), which also, however, serves to emphasize the special role of large numbers of economic agents in the theory of perfect competition.

We start with essentially the same model of the production and consumption structure as in the previous section, deleting, of course, all references to prices and to income. However, the analyses of the core have so far made one significant restriction on the relation between producers and consumers. It is assumed that any coalition of households has access to the same set of possible production vectors, which is further assumed to display constant returns to scale. Consider now any feasible allocation. It is said to be *blocked* by a coalition S (a set of households) if there is another allocation among the members of S feasible for them (using only the assets they collectively started with) which makes each of them better off. Notice that the coalition might consist of all households in the society; for that coalition, blocking reduces to domination in the sense used earlier. A coalition might also consist of one individual; then he can block an allocation if, with only his own resources and the universally accessible technological knowledge, he can produce a bundle whose utility is higher than that of the bundle allocated to him.

The *core,* then, consists of all allocations that are not blocked by any coalition. The first theorem concerning the core generalizes the sufficiency theorem for optimality: *Any competitive equilibrium belongs to the core.* More interesting is a sort of converse proposition, which may be loosely stated as follows: *If the hypotheses of the previous section which ensure the existence of equilibrium hold, and if each individual is small compared with the economy, then the allocations in the core are all approximately competitive equilibria.* (The words "small" and "approximately" are rigorously interpreted as referring to suitably chosen limiting processes.)

Some interpretive remarks are in order here. First, the natural interpretation of the core is that if any sort of bargains are permitted by the rules of the economic game, the allocation finally arrived at should be in the core, since otherwise some coalition would have both the power and the desire to prevent it. Hence, it would follow, very strikingly, that for large numbers of participants the outcome would be the competitive equilibrium, provided the assumptions of the previous section were satisfied. Even under nonconvexity some scattered results of L. S. Shapley and M. Shubik (unpublished) suggest that the same holds approximately (that is, there may be no core in the precise definition, but there is a set of allocations that can be blocked but only with very small preference on the part of the blocking coalition). Hence, the existence of monopoly must depend on one of the three factors: (1) specialized abilities that are scarce relative to the economy; (2) increasing returns on a scale comparable to that of the economy; or (3) costs of coalition formation that are relatively low among producers of the same good and high for coalitions involving consumers and producers.

Second, the assumption that the production possibilities are the same for all coalitions is one that has been used by McKenzie and, with suitable interpretation, is not as drastic as it seems. We can assume that some or all productive processes require as inputs "entrepreneurial skills" or special talents of some kind. The commodity space is enlarged to include these skills, which may be distributed very unequally in the population. It can then be argued that diminishing returns to scale in the observable variables really results from a combination of constant returns in all variables, including entrepreneurial skills and a fixed supply of the latter. Further, different coalitions will really have very different access to production possibilities because of their very different endowments of skills.

Uniqueness of Competitive Equilibrium

Results concerning the uniqueness and stability of competitive equilibrium have been stated only for the case where the excess demand functions are single-valued, as at the beginning of the second section. It will then be assumed that assumptions (*H*), (*W*), and (*B*) hold; in fact, (*C*) will be strengthened to require differentiability of the excess demand functions.

Without further assumptions, there is no need that equilibrium be unique, and examples of nonuniqueness have been known since Marshall. The mathematical basis for a fairly general uniqueness theorem has only recently been worked out by Gale and Nikaidô (1965), and the most appropriate economic theorem has not been fully explored. However, one theorem along these lines can be stated. Suppose there is one commodity for which the excess demand is positive whenever its price is zero, regardless of the prices of all other commodities. Such a commodity is an eminent candidate for Walras' role of numéraire, and we may choose its price to be 1, since it cannot be zero (and therefore will be positive) in any equilibrium, and, from the homogeneity of excess demand functions, multiplying any equilibrium set of prices by a positive number leads to a new equilibrium (uniqueness of price equilibrium is, of course, defined only up to positive multiples). Call this the *n*th commodity, and consider the excess demands for commodities $1, \ldots, n-1$ as functions of $p_1, \ldots, p_{n-1}$, with p_n held constant at 1. The Jacobian of this set of functions is defined in mathematics as the matrix with components $(\partial X_i/\partial p_j)$, where i and j range from 1 to $n-1$. As noted in the first section, a matrix is termed *Hicksian* if the determinant of a principal minor is positive when it has an even number of rows and negative otherwise.

UNIQUENESS THEOREM 1. *If the Jacobian of the excess demand functions, omitting a numéraire and holding its price constant, is Hicksian for all sets of prices, then the equilibrium is unique.*

A special case of this theorem originated in effect with Wald (1936). Commodity i will be said to be a *gross substitute* for commodity j if an increase in p_j, holding all other prices constant, increases X_i. It follows from (*H*) that if all commodities are gross substitutes, the Jacobian of the excess demand functions, omitting a numéraire, is Hicksian. Then a consequence of uniqueness theorem 1 is: *If all commodities are gross substitutes, then equilibrium is unique.*

Finally, an entirely different sufficient condition was also stated by Wald:

UNIQUENESS THEOREM 2. *If the weak axiom of revealed preference holds for consumers as a whole, then equilibrium is unique.*

What is now termed the weak axiom of revealed preference—developed independently by Samuelson (1938)—states that if the commodity bundle chosen at prices prevailing in situation 1 are no more expensive at the prices prevailing in situation 0 than the bundle chosen in situation 0, then the latter bundle must be more expensive than the former at the prices in situation 1. For an individual, this axiom is a simple consequence of rational behavior; both bundles were available to him in situation 0, and the bundle he chose in that situation must therefore have been preferred. If both bundles had also been available in situation 1, then the less preferred bundle could never have been chosen; hence, the bundle chosen in situation 0 must have been unavailable because of cost in situation 1. However, the statement that the axiom holds for the demand functions of the market as a whole is not a consequence of rational behavior but is an additional assumption that is valid, in effect, when income effects are not too large in the aggregate.

Stability

The stability problem, as formalized by Samuelson, can be stated as follows: Suppose that an arbitrary (in general, nonequilibrium) set of prices is given so that there are nonzero excess demands, some of which are positive. It is assumed that prices adjust under the influence of the excess demands, specifically rising when excess demand is positive and falling in the opposite case. This suggests the following dynamic system:

$$dp_i/dt = k_i X_i(p_1, \ldots, p_n), \qquad i = 1, \ldots, n, \tag{6-5}$$

that is, the changes in prices (t denoting time) are proportional to the excess demands. Notice that allowing for "speeds of adjustment," k_i, that are different from 1 and from each other is not merely due to a desire for generality but is virtually a logical necessity, for a careful dimensional analysis shows that k_i will change with changes in the units of measurement of commodity i. More general (nonlinear) adjustment models have been studied, for example, a model in which dp_i/dt has merely the same sign as X_i.

A variation of this system, which has often been studied, distinguishes one commodity as numéraire and assumes that its price is held fixed, say at 1:

$$dp_i/dt = k_i X_i(p_1, \ldots, p_n), \qquad i = 1, \ldots, n-1, \qquad p_n = 1. \tag{6-6}$$

One difficulty arises in either system when the rules call for a price to become negative, which can happen if, for some i, $X_i(p_1, \ldots, p_n) < 0$ with $p_i = 0$. Since the excess demand functions are not even defined for negative prices, the rules must be altered. It has become customary to modify (6-5) and (6-6) by requiring that a price remain at zero under these conditions; but whether the rules remain consistent is a difficult mathematical question, which has been studied only by Uzawa (1958) and Morishima (1960a), and then only for very special cases.

The systems (6-5) or (6-6) are systems of differential equations; their solutions are time paths of prices, which are determined by the specification of initial conditions as well as by the system. The stability question is whether or not the resulting time path converges to an equilibrium. Global stability means that convergence occurs for any initial conditions; local stability that the path converges for initial conditions sufficiently close to an equilibrium. However, at the present time the most interesting results are sufficient for global as well as local stability, so we need not distinguish the two.

It should first be noted that neither of the systems is necessarily stable even if all the hypotheses which ensure the existence of equilibrium are satisfied; examples have been supplied by Scarf (1960) and Gale (1963). Gale's example is particularly simple: Suppose there are two individuals and three commodities, and there is no production. Individual 1 starts with a supply of good 1 and individual 2 with supplies of goods 2 and 3. Individual 1 has a utility function involving only goods 2 and 3, while individual 2 wishes only good 1. It is easy to see that there is a unique equilibrium. Now suppose that Giffen's paradox holds with regard to good 2 for individual 1 (that is, a rise in the price of good 2, holding other prices constant, raises individual 1's demand). Then it is possible to show that, for suitably chosen adjustment speeds, the solution of system (6-5) or (6-6) remains away from the equilibrium.

There are three different conditions, due to Arrow, Block, and Hurwicz (1959), any one of which is sufficient for the stability of the system.

STABILITY THEOREM 1. *If all commodities are gross substitutes, then systems (6-5) and (6-6) are both stable.*

STABILITY THEOREM 2. *If the market satisfies the weak axiom of revealed preference, then systems (6-5) and (6-6) are both stable.*

To state the third theorem we have to introduce the mathematical concept of a matrix with dominant diagonal. A matrix (a_{ij}) is said to have a dominant diagonal if $|a_{ii}| > \Sigma_{j \neq i} |a_{ij}|$ for all i. (The diagonal element is more important than all others in the same row.)

STABILITY THEOREM 3. *If the Jacobian of the excess demand functions (excluding a numéraire) has a dominant diagonal, all elements of which are negative, then system (6-6) is stable.*

Whether the Jacobian has a dominant diagonal may depend on the units in which the commodities are measured; stability theorem 3 asserts stability if there is *any* way of choosing the units so as to achieve diagonal dominance.

Stability theorem 2 can be interpreted as meaning that the transfers of income which take place during the course of the time path produce broadly offsetting results on demand; income effects are not too asymmetrical. Stability theorem 3 is perhaps closest to Walras' initial concepts; stability holds when the excess demand for a commodity is much more affected by a change in its own price than by any other price change (holding the price of a numéraire constant).

In all discussion of stability so far it has been implicitly assumed that no transactions take place at nonequilibrium prices, for if they did the excess demand functions would shift. (An alternative interpretation is that all commodities are completely perishable and that utilities and production are independent as between time periods. Then any transactions occurring in one period will have no effect on transactions occurring in the next period.) This assumption is the classical one of "recontracting," in Edgeworth's terminology, and was made by him and by Walras. The problem raised by transactions at nonequilibrium prices was immediately recognized, but little analysis took place. Several recent writers, particularly Negishi (1961), Hahn and Negishi (1962), and Uzawa (1962), have considered this problem under the rather awkward title of "non-*tâtonnement* stability." The system, to be complete, has to specify the nature of the transactions; since the system is not at equilibrium there will have to be rationing of sellers or of buyers. If it is simply assumed that any transactions that do take place cannot change the value of any individual's holdings, then gross substitutability is again a sufficient condition for stability. Under more specific assumptions about transactions, stability can be shown in much wider classes of cases.

Comparative Statics

The question raised in comparative statics is, What can be said of the effect of a shift in the excess demand functions on the price system? As might be supposed from the nature of the question, answers can only be given in a limited range of cases. Suppose that a *binary* shift has occurred—that is, the excess demand for one commodity, say 1, has decreased at every set of prices; the excess demand for another commodity, say 2, has increased correspondingly (the money value of the increased demand for 2 exactly equals the decrease in money value of demand for 1 at any given set of prices); and the excess demand functions for all other commodities have remained unchanged. Then the only general result in the literature is the following (Morishima, 1960b): If all commodities are gross substitutes and there has occurred a binary shift in demand from commodity 1 to commodity 2, then all prices of commodities other than 1 rise relative to the price of 1 or do not fall, and no relative price rise is greater than that of commodity 2.

Partial Equilibrium

A great deal of economic analysis has been concerned with equilibrium of a single market. Demand and supply for a commodity are regarded as functions of a single price, and equilibrium is interpreted as equality of supply and demand or as an excess of supply over demand at zero price.

Partial equilibrium analysis is to be regarded as a special case of general equilibrium analysis. The existence of one market presupposes that there must be at least one commodity beyond that traded on that market, for a price must be stated as the rate at which an individual gives up something else for the commodity in question. If there were really only one commodity in the world, there would be no exchange and no market.

Suppose for the moment that there are only two commodities, say 1 and 2. Because of homogeneity, demand and supply (which may, as before, be multivalued) are determined by the ratio of the price of commodity 1 to that of commodity 2, that is, the price of commodity 1 with commodity 2 as numéraire. From Walras' law, equilibrium on market 1 ensures equilibrium on market 2. Partial equilibrium analysis of market 1 is, in the case of two commodities, fully equivalent to general equilibrium analysis. All the previous theorems hold, and one more theorem on stability may be stated (Arrow and Hurwicz, 1958): For two commodities, equilibrium is always globally stable in the sense that for any initial set of prices, systems (6-5) and (6-6) of the fifth section always converge to some set of equilibrium prices (if the equilibrium price set is not unique up to positive multiples, the prices to which the system converges will depend on the starting point). This theorem has not always been recognized in discussions of stability of equilibrium in foreign trade, where the analysis has frequently been confined to two commodities.

Analysis of a two-commodity world may have considerable didactic usefulness as a way of studying general equilibrium through a special case admitting of simple diagrammatic representation, but it may be asked if partial equilibrium analysis has any empirical interest for a world of many commodities. An answer is provided by the following theorem, due independently to Hicks (1939) and Leontief (1936): If the relative prices of some set of commodities remain constant, then for all analytical purposes the set can be regarded as a single composite commodity, the price of which can be regarded as proportional to the price of any member of the set and the quantity of which is then defined so that expenditure (price times quantity) on the composite commodity is equal to the sum of the expenditures on the individual commodities in the set. In symbols, if the prices $p_1, \ldots, p_m$ of a set of commodities $1, \ldots, m$ satisfy the conditions $p_i = \rho\bar{p}_i$ ($\bar{p}_i$ a constant for each i while ρ may vary), then we can take ρ to be the price of the composite commodity and $\Sigma_{i=1}^{m}\bar{p}_i q_i$ to be the quantity, where q_i is the quantity of the ith good.

The Hicks-Leontief aggregation theorem can be used to justify partial equilibrium analysis. Suppose that a change in the price of commodity 1 leaves the relative prices of all others unchanged. Then insofar as we are considering only disturbances to equilibrium from causes peculiar to the market for commodity 1, the remaining commodities can be regarded as a single composite commodity, and partial equilibrium analysis is valid.

The assumption of strict constancy of relative prices of the other commodities will not usually be valid, of course, but it may hold approximately in many cases of practical interest. It is sufficient for the purpose that the changes in the relative prices of other commodities induced by a change in the price of the commodity being studied do not in turn induce a significant shift in supply or demand conditions on the market for that commodity.

Equilibrium over Time

While the above summarizes the central part of the literature on general economic equilibrium, there is a related conceptual question that deserves brief mention. Consider an economy extending over time, with dated inputs and outputs and household plans that run into the future. What can be said about the equilibrium of such an economy and, indeed, what is meant by the term?

One straightforward answer is that originally due to Hicks. We may simply date all commodity transactions and regard the same physically defined commodity at two different times as being two different commodities. Then the formal model of the second section remains, with reinterpretation, and we can still argue that there is an equilibrium over time. Planned supplies and demands are equated in the usual way.

This is a legitimate and indeed important interpretation. Problems of optimality, the core, uniqueness, and comparative statics (perhaps to be renamed "comparative dynamics") are restatable with no difficulty. Stability theory faces a more serious challenge, since time now enters in two different ways—in the underlying model and in the adjustment process. If all markets are taken to be futures markets, so that all adjustments take place simultaneously, there is no difficulty, but otherwise there is a new range of problems which have been approached only in the most fragmentary way.

However, the simple redating has the important implication of perfect foresight (possibly achieved through having all future economic transactions determined in currently existing futures markets). This seems empirically most unsatisfactory and involves significant logical problems of knowledge (Morgenstern, 1935). An alternative is to assume that each individual has expectations about the future that are continuous functions of present observed variables. Then in each period there will be an equilibrium, although each individual's plans for the future generally will not in fact be carried out.

From either point of view, considerable interest has attached to another meaning of equilibrium, which we may term *stationary equilibrium.* The equilibrium over time in the case of perfect foresight defines a set of prices and quantities for each period. The same is true of the succession of short-run equilibria defined by individuals acting under expectations. The question is, does this time sequence have a stationary or equilibrium value? Is there a set of prices and quantities such that, if they governed in the initial period, they would remain equilibrium values for all subsequent periods? Or, in a growing economy, would at least the relative prices and quantities remain constant if the appropriate values held in the initial period? This might be called the question of existence of stationary equilibrium, frequently termed the *balanced growth path.* The distinction between equilibrium in general and the stationary state, implicit in classical economics, was first clarified by Frisch (1935–1936).

The stability of stationary equilibrium is a different problem from that of stability in the sense used earlier, in the fifth section. Suppose we have an arbitrary initial quantity configuration. The question then arises, will the equilibrium values of the successive periods tend to converge to the stationary equilibrium? The study of this problem has been a major preoccupation of modern growth and capital theory, and it will not be enlarged on here.

References

Arrow, Kenneth J.; Block, Henry D.; and Hurwicz, Leonid. 1959. On the Stability of the Competitive Equilibrium, pt. 2. *Econometrica* 27:82–109.

Arrow, Kenneth J.; and Debreu, Gerard. 1954. Existence of an Equilibrium for a Competitive Economy. *Econometrica* 22:265–290.

Arrow, Kenneth J.; and Hurwicz, Leonid. 1958. On the Stability of the Competitive Equilibrium, pt. 1. *Econometrica* 26:522–552.

Aumann, Robert J. 1966. Existence of Competitive Equilibria in Markets With a Continuum of Traders. *Econometrica* 34:1–17.

Cassel, Gustav. (1918) 1932. *The Theory of Social Economy,* new rev. ed. New York: Harcourt. Translated from the fifth edition of *Theoretische Sozialökonomie.*

Cournot, Antoine Augustin. (1838) 1960. *Researches into the Mathematical Principles of the Theory of Wealth.* New York: Kelley. First published in French.

Cowles Commission for Research in Economics. 1951. *Activity Analysis of Production and Allocation: Proceedings of a Conference,* ed. Tjalling C. Koopmans. New York: Wiley.

Debreu, Gerard. 1959. *Theory of Value: An Axiomatic Analysis of Economic Equilibrium.* New York: Wiley.

Debreu, Gerard. 1962. New Concepts and Techniques for Equilibrium Analysis. *International Economic Review* 3:257–273.

Debreu, Gerard; and Scarf, Herbert. 1963. A Limit Theorem on the Core of an Economy. *International Economic Review* 4:235–246.

Edgeworth, Francis Y. (1881) 1953. *Mathematical Psychics: An Essay on the Application of Mathematics to the Moral Sciences.* New York: Kelley.

Farrell, M. J. 1959. The Convexity Assumption in the Theory of Competitive Markets. *Journal of Political Economy* 67:377–391.

Frisch, Ragnar. 1935–1936. On the Notion of Equilibrium and Disequilibrium. *Review of Economic Studies* 3:100–105.

Gale, David. 1960. *The Theory of Linear Economic Models.* New York: McGraw-Hill.

Gale, David. 1963. A Note on Global Instability of Competitive Equilibrium. *Naval Research Logistics Quarterly* 10:81–87.

Gale, David; and Nikaidô, Hukukane. 1965. The Jacobian Matrix and Global Univalence of Mappings. *Mathematische Annalen* 159:81–93.

Hahn, Frank H.; and Negishi, Takashi. 1962. A Theorem on Non-*tâtonnement* Stability. *Econometrica* 30:463–469.

Hicks, John R. (1939) 1946. *Value and Capital: An Inquiry into Some Fundamental Principles of Economic Theory,* 2d ed. Oxford: Clarendon.

Jenkin, Fleeming. (1870) 1931. The Graphic Representation of the Laws of Supply and Demand, and Their Application to Labour. Vol. 2, pp. 76–106 in Fleeming Jenkin, *Papers: Literary, Scientific, etc.* London School of Economics and Political Science.

Kuenne, Robert E. 1963. *The Theory of General Economic Equilibrium.* Princeton, N.J.: Princeton University Press.

Leontief, Wassily W. 1936. Composite Commodities and the Problem of Index Numbers. *Econometrica* 4:39–59.

McKenzie, Lionel W. 1954. On Equilibrium in Graham's Model of World Trade and Other Competitive Systems. *Econometrica* 22:147–161.

McKenzie, Lionel W. 1959. On the Existence of General Equilibrium for a Competitive Market. *Econometrica* 27:54–71.

Metzler, Lloyd A. 1945. The Stability of Multiple Markets: The Hicks Conditions. *Econometrica* 13:277–292.

Morgenstern, Oskar. 1935. Vollkommene Voraussicht und wirtschaftliches Gleichgewicht. *Zeitschrift für Nationalökonomie* 6:337–357.

Morishima, Michio. 1960a. A Reconsideration of the Walras-Cassel-Leontief Model of General Equilibrium. Pages 63–76 in Stanford Symposium on Mathematical Methods in the Social Sciences, Stanford University, 1959, *Mathematical Methods in the Social Sciences,* ed. Kenneth J. Arrow, Samuel Karlin, and Patrick Suppes. Stanford: Stanford University Press.

Morishima, Michio. 1960b. On the Three Hicksian Laws of Comparative Statics. *Review of Economic Studies* 27:195–201.

Mosak, Jacob L. 1944. *General Equilibrium Theory in International Trade.* Bloomington, Ind.: Principia.

Nash, John F., Jr. 1950. Equilibrium in *n*-Person Games. National Academy of Sciences, *Proceedings* 36:48–49.

Negishi, Takashi. 1961. On the Formation of Prices. *International Economic Review* 2:122–126.

Negishi, Takashi. 1962. The Stability of a Competitive Economy: A Survey Article. *Econometrica* 30:635–669.

Neisser, Hans. 1932. Lohnhöhe und Beschäftigungsgrad im Marktgleichgewicht. *Weltwirtschaftliches Archiv* 36:415–455.

Rothenberg, Jerome. 1960. Non-convexity, Aggregation, and Pareto Optimality. *Journal of Political Economy* 68:435–468.

Samuelson, Paul A. 1938. A Note on the Pure Theory of Consumer's Behavior. *Economica,* new series, 5:61–71.

Samuelson, Paul A. 1941–1942. The Stability of Equilibrium. *Econometrica* 9:97–120; 10:1–25.

Samuelson, Paul A. 1957. Wages and Interest: A Modern Dissection of Marxian Economic Models. *American Economic Review* 47:884–912.

Samuelson, Paul A. 1959. A Modern Treatment of the Ricardian Economy. *Quarterly Journal of Economics* 73:1–35, 217–231.

Scarf, Herbert. 1960. Some Examples of Global Instability of the Competitive Equilibrium. *International Economic Review* 1:157–172.

Stackelberg, Heinrich von. 1933. Zwei kritische Bemerkungen zur Preistheorie Gustav Cassels. *Zeitschrift für Nationalökonomie* 4:456–472.

Uzawa, Hirofumi. 1958. Gradient Method for Concave Programming. Pages 117–126 in Kenneth J. Arrow, Leonid Hurwicz, and Hirofumi Uzawa, *Studies in Linear and Non-linear Programming.* Stanford: Stanford University Press.

Uzawa, Hirofumi. 1962. On the Stability of Edgeworth's Barter Process. *International Economic Review* 3:218–232.

von Neumann, John. (1937) 1945. A Model of General Economic Equilibrium. *Review of Economic Studies* 13:1–9. First published in German in vol. 8 of *Ergebnisse eines mathematischen Kolloquiums.*

von Neumann, John; and Morgenstern, Oskar. (1944) 1964. *Theory of Games and Economic Behavior,* 3d ed. New York: Wiley.

Wald, Abraham. (1936) 1951. On Some Systems of Equations of Mathematical Economics. *Econometrica* 19:368–403. First pubiished in German in vol. 7 of *Zeitschrift für Nationalökonomie.*

Walras, Léon. (1874–1877) 1954. *Elements of Pure Economics: Or, the Theory of Social Wealth,* trans. William Jaffé. Homewood, Ill.: Irwin; London: Allen & Unwin. First published in French as *Éléments d'économie politique pure.*

Zeuthen, F. 1932. Das Prinzip der Knappheit, technische Kombination und ökonomische Qualität. *Zeitschrift für Nationalökonomie* 4:1–24.

7 The Organization of Economic Activity: Issues Pertinent to the Choice of Market versus Nonmarket Allocation

The concept of public goods has been developed through successive refinement over a long period of time. Yet, surprisingly enough, nowhere in the literature does there appear to be a clear general definition of this concept or the more general one of "externality." The accounts given are usually either very general and discursive, difficult to interpret in specific contexts, or else they are rigorous accounts of very special situations. What exactly is the relation between externalities and such concepts as "appropriability" or "exclusion"?

Also, there is considerable ambiguity in the purpose of the analysis of externalities. The best-developed part of the theory relates to only a single problem: the statement of a set of conditions, as weak as possible, which ensure that a competitive equilibrium exists and is Pareto-efficient. Then the denial of any of these hypotheses is presumably a sufficient condition for considering resort to nonmarket channels of resource allocation—usually thought of as government expenditures, taxes, and subsidies.

At a second level the analysis of externalities should lead to criteria for nonmarket allocation. It is tempting to set forth these criteria in terms analogous to the profit-and-loss statements of private business; in this form, we are led to benefit-cost analysis. There are, moreover, two possible aims for benefit-cost analysis. One, more ambitious but theoretically simpler, is

Reprinted from Joint Economic Committee, United States Congress, *The Analysis and Evaluation of Public Expenditures: The PPB System,* vol. 1 (Washington, D.C.: Government Printing Office, 1969), pp. 47–64.

specification of the nonmarket actions which will restore Pareto efficiency. The second involves the recognition that the instruments available to the government or other nonmarket forces are scarce resources for one reason or another, so that all that can be achieved is a "second best."

Other concepts that seem to cluster closely to the concept of public goods are those of "increasing returns" and "market failure." These are related to Pareto inefficiency on the one hand and to the existence and optimality of competitive equilibrium on the other; sometimes the discussions in the literature do not adequately distinguish these two aspects. I contend that market failure is a more general category than externality; and both differ from increasing returns in a basic sense, since market failures in general and externalities in particular are relative to the mode of economic organization, while increasing returns are essentially a technological phenomenon.

Current writing has helped bring out the point that market failure is not absolute; it is better to consider a broader category, that of transaction costs, which in general impede and in particular cases completely block the formation of markets. It is usually though not always emphasized that transaction costs are costs of running the economic system. An incentive for vertical integration is the replacement of the costs of buying and selling on the market by the costs of intrafirm transfers; the existence of vertical integration may suggest that the costs of operating competitive markets are not zero, as is usually assumed in our theoretical analysis.

Monetary theory, unlike value theory, is heavily dependent on the assumption of positive transaction costs. The recurrent complaint about the difficulty of integrating these two branches of theory is certainly governed by the contradictory assumptions made about transaction costs. The creation of money is in many respects an example of a public good.

The identification of transaction costs in different contexts and under different systems of resource allocation should be a major item on the research agenda of the theory of public goods and indeed of the theory of resource allocation in general. Only the most rudimentary suggestions are made here. The "exclusion principle" is a limiting case of one kind of transaction cost, but the costliness of the information needed to enter and participate in any market, another type of cost, has received little attention. Information is closely related on the one hand to communication and on the other to uncertainty.

Given the existence of Pareto inefficiency in a free market equilibrium, there will be pressure in the system to overcome it by some sort of departure from the free market, that is, some form of collective action. This need not be undertaken by the government. I suggest that in fact there is a wide variety of social institutions—in particular, generally accepted social norms of behavior—which serve in some means as compensation for failure or limitation of the market, though each in turn involves transaction costs of its own. The question also arises of how the behavior of individual economic agents in a social institution (especially in voting) is related to their behavior on the market. A good deal of the theoretical literature of recent years seeks to describe political behavior as analogous to economic, and we may hope for a general theory of socioeconomic equilibrium. But it must always be kept in mind that the contexts of choice are radically different, particularly when the hypotheses of perfectly costless action and information are relaxed. It is not accidental that economic analysis has been successful only in certain limited areas.

Competitive Equilibrium and Pareto Efficiency

A quick review of the familiar theorems on the role of perfectly competitive equilibrium in the efficient allocation of resources will be useful at this point. Perfectly competitive equilibrium has its usual meaning: households, possessed of initial resources, including possibly claims to the profits of firms, choose consumption bundles to maximize utility at a given set of prices; firms choose production bundles so as to maximize profits at the same set of prices; the chosen production and consumption bundles must be consistent with each other in the sense that aggregate production plus initial resources must equal aggregate consumption.[1] The key points in the definition are the parametric role of the prices for each individual and the identity of prices for all individuals. Implicit are the assumptions that all prices can be known by all individuals and that the act of charging prices does not itself consume resources.

A number of additional assumptions are made at different points in the theory of equilibrium, but most clearly are factually valid in the usual contexts and need not be mentioned. The two hypotheses frequently not valid are *C*, the convexity of household indifference maps and firm production possibility sets, and *M*, the universality of markets. While the exact

1. Sometimes this is stated to permit an excess of supply over demand, with a zero price for such free goods; but this can be included in the above formulation by postulating the existence of production processes (disposal processes) which have such surpluses as inputs and no outputs.

meaning of the last assumption will be explored later at some length, for the present purposes we mean that the consumption bundle which determines the utility of an individual is the same as that which he purchases at given prices subject to his budget constraint, and that the set of production bundles among which a firm chooses is a given range independent of decisions made by other agents in the economy.

The relations between Pareto efficiency and competitive equilibrium are set forth in the following two theorems.

PROPOSITION 1. *If M holds, a competitive equilibrium is Pareto-efficient.*

This theorem is true even if *C* does not hold.

PROPOSITION 2. *If C and M hold, then any Pareto-efficient allocation can be achieved as a competitive equilibrium by a suitable reallocation of initial resources.*

When the assumptions of Proposition 2 are valid, then the case for the competitive price system is strongest. Any complaints about its operation can be reduced to complaints about the distribution of income, which should then be rectified by lump-sum transfers. Of course, as Pareto already emphasized, the proposition provides no basis for accepting the results of the market in the absence of accepted levels of income equality.

The central role of competitive equilibrium both as a normative guide and as at least partially descriptive of the real world raises an analytically difficult question: does a competitive equilibrium necessarily exist?

PROPOSITION 3. *If C holds, then there exists a competitive equilibrium.*

This theorem is true even if *M* does not hold.

If both *C* and *M* hold, we have a fairly complete and simple picture of the achievement of desirable goals, subject always to the major qualification of the achievement of a desirable income distribution. The price system itself determines the income distribution only in the sense of preserving the status quo. Even if costless lump-sum transfers are possible, there is needed a collective mechanism reallocating income if the status quo is not regarded as satisfactory.

Of course *C* is not a necessary condition for the existence of a competitive equilibrium, only a sufficient one. From Proposition 1, it is possible to have an equilibrium and therefore efficient allocation without convexity (when *M* holds). However, in view of the central role of *C* in these theorems, the implications of relaxing this hypothesis have been examined intensively in recent years by Farrell (1959), Rothenberg (1960), Aumann (1966), and Starr (1969). Their conclusions may be summarized as follows: Let C' be the weakened convexity assumption that there are no indivisibilities large relative to the economy.

PROPOSITION 4. *Propositions 2 and 3 remain approximately true if C is replaced by C'.*

Thus, the only nonconvexities that are important for the present purposes are increasing returns over a range large relative to the economy. In those circumstances, a competitive equilibrium cannot exist.

The price system, for all its virtues, is only one conceivable form of arranging trade, even in a system of private property. Bargaining can assume extremely general forms. Under the assumptions C' and M, we are assured that not everyone can be made better off by a bargain not derived from the price system; but the question arises whether some members of the economy will not find it in their interest and within their power to depart from the perfectly competitive price system. For example, both Knight (1921, pp. 190–194) and Samuelson (1967, p. 120) have noted that it would pay all the firms in a given industry to form a monopoly. But in fact it can be argued that unrestricted bargaining can only settle down to a resource allocation which could also be achieved as a perfectly competitive equilibrium, at least if the bargaining itself is costless and each agent is small compared to the entire economy. This line of argument originated with Edgeworth (1881, pp. 20–43) and has been developed recently by Shubik (1959), Debreu and Scarf (1963), and Aumann (1964).

More precisely, it is easy to show:

PROPOSITION 5. *If M holds and a competitive equilibrium prevails, then no set of economic agents will find any resource allocation which they can accomplish by themselves (without trade with the other agents) which they will all prefer to that prevailing under the equilibrium.*

Proposition 5 holds for any number of agents. A deeper proposition is the following converse:

PROPOSITION 6. *If C' and M hold, and if the resources of any economic agent are small compared with the total of the economy, then, given any allocation not approximately achievable as a competitive equilibrium, there will be some set of agents and some resource allocation they can achieve without any trade with others which each one will prefer to the given allocation.*

These two propositions, taken together, strongly suggest that when all the relevant hypotheses hold, (1) a competitive equilibrium, if achieved, will not be upset by bargaining even if permitted, and (2) for any bargain not achievable by a competitive equilibrium there is a set of agents who would benefit by change to another bargain which they have the full power to enforce.

The argument that a set of firms can form a monopoly overlooks the possibility that the consumers can also form a coalition, threaten not to buy, and seek mutually advantageous deals with a subset of the firms; such deals are possible since the monopoly allocation violates some marginal equivalences.

In real life, monopolizing cartels are possible for a reason not so far introduced into the analysis: bargaining costs between producers and consumers are high, those among producers low—a point made most emphatically by Adam Smith (1937, p. 128): "People of the same trade seldom meet together, even for merriment or diversion, but the conversation ends in a conspiracy against the public, or in some contrivance to raise prices." *It is not the presence of bargaining costs per se but their bias that is relevant.* If all bargaining costs are high, but competitive pricing and the markets are cheap, then we expect the perfectly competitive equilibrium to obtain, yielding an allocation identical with that under costless bargaining. But if bargaining costs are biased, then some bargains other than the competitive equilibrium can be arrived at which will not be upset by still other bargains if the latter but not the former are costly.

Finally, in this review of the elements of competitive equilibrium theory, let me repeat the obvious and well-known fact that in a world where time is relevant, the commodities which enter into the equilibrium system include those with future dates. In fact, the bulk of meaningful future transactions cannot be carried out on any existing present market, so that assumption *M*, the universality of markets, is not valid.

Imperfectly Competitive Equilibrium

There is no accepted and well-worked-out theory corresponding to the title of this section. From the previous section it is clear that such a theory is needed perforce in the presence of increasing returns on a scale large relative to the economy (hereafter, the phrase "increasing returns" will always be understood to include the prepositional phrase just employed), and is superfluous in its absence.

There are two approaches to a theory of general equilibrium in an imperfectly competitive environment; most writers who touch on public policy questions implicitly accept one or the other of these prototheories without always recognizing that they have made such a choice. One assumes that all transactions are made according to the price system, that is, the same price is charged for all units of the same commodity; this is the *monopolistic competition* approach. The alternative approach assumes unrestricted bargaining; this is the *game theory* approach. The first might be deemed appropriate if the costs of bargaining were high relative to the costs of ordinary pricing, while the second assumes costless bargaining.[2]

It cannot be too strongly emphasized that neither approach is, at the present stage, a fully developed theory, and it is misleading to state any implications about the working of these systems. Chamberlin's purpose (1933) was certainly the incorporation of monopoly into a general equilibrium system, together with a view that the commodity space should be considered infinite-dimensional, with the possibility of arbitrarily close substitutes in consumption; Triffin (1941) emphasized this aspect, but the only completely worked out model of general monopolistic equilibrium is that of Negishi (1960–61), who made the problem manageable by regarding the demand functions facing the monopolists as those perceived by them, with only loose relations to reality. Such a theory would have little in the way of deducible implications (unless there were a supplementary psychological theory to explain the perceptions of demand functions) and certainly no clear welfare implications.

Of course, whatever a monopolistic competitive equilibrium means, it must imply inefficiency in the Pareto sense if there are substantial increasing returns. For a firm can always make zero profits by not existing; hence, if it operates, price must at least equal average cost, which is greater than marginal cost. Kaldor (1935) and Demsetz (1964), however, have argued that in the "large numbers" case, the welfare loss may be supposed very small. I would conjecture that this conclusion is true, but it is not rigorously

2. Within the framework of each prototheory, attempts have been made to modify it in the direction of the other. Thus, price discrimination is a modification of the price system in the pure theory of monopoly, though I am aware of no attempt to study price discrimination in a competitive or otherwise general equilibrium context. Some game theorists (Luce, 1954, 1955a, 1955b; Aumann and Maschler, 1964) have attempted to introduce bargaining costs in some way by simply limiting the range of possible coalitions capable of making bargains.

established, and indeed the model has never been formulated in adequate detail to discuss it properly.[3]

With unrestricted bargaining it is usual to conclude that the equilibrium, whatever it may be, must be Pareto-efficient, for, by definition, it is in the interest of all economic agents to switch from a Pareto-inefficient allocation to a suitably chosen Pareto-efficient one. This argument seems plausible, but it is not easy to evaluate in the absence of a generally accepted concept of solution for game theory. Edgeworth (1881) held the outcome of bargaining to be indeterminate within limits, and von Neumann and Morgenstern (1944) have generalized this conclusion. But when there is indeterminacy, there is no natural or compelling point on the Pareto frontier at which to arrive. It is certainly a matter of common observation, perhaps most especially in the field of international relations, that mutually advantageous agreements are not arrived at because each party is seeking to engross as much as possible of the common gain for itself. In economic affairs a frequently cited illustration is the assembly of land parcels for large industrial or residential enterprises whose value (net of complementary costs) exceeds the total value of the land in its present uses. Then the owner of each small parcel whose acquisition is essential to the execution of the enterprise can demand the entire net benefit. An agreement may never be reached or may be long delayed; at positive discount rates even the latter outcome is not Pareto-efficient. It is to avoid such losses that the coercive powers of the state are invoked by condemnation proceedings.

There is, however, another tradition within game theory which argues for the determinacy of the outcome of bargaining. Zeuthen (1930, chap. 4) had early propounded one such solution. After von Neumann and Morgenstern, Nash (1950, 1953) offered a solution, which Harsanyi (1956) later showed to be identical with that of Zeuthen. Nash's analysis of bargaining has been extended by Harsanyi (1959, 1963, 1966); variant but related approaches have been studied by Shapley (1953) and Selten (1964). The analysis has proceeded at a very general level, and its specific application to resource allocation has yet to be spelled out. In the simplest situation, bargaining between two individuals who can cooperate but cannot injure each other except by withholding cooperation, and who can freely transfer benefits

3. Suppose that the degree of increasing returns is sufficient to prevent there being more than one producer of a given commodity narrowly defined, but not to prevent production of a close substitute. Is this degree of returns sufficiently substantial to upset the achievement of an approximately perfect competitive equilibrium, as discussed in the last section?

between them, the conclusion of the theories is the achievement of a joint optimum followed by equal splitting of the benefits of cooperation net of the amounts each bargainer could obtain without cooperation. Thus, in a land assembly, if the participation of all parcels is essential, each owner receives the value of his parcel in its present (or best alternative) use plus an equal share of the net benefits of the project. Without further analytic and empirical work it is not easy to judge the acceptability of this conclusion.

An elementary example may bring out the ambiguities of allocation with unrestricted bargaining. Since the perfectly competitive equilibrium theory is satisfactory (in the absence of marketing failures and costs) when increasing returns on a substantial scale are absent, the problem of imperfectly competitive equilibrium arises only when substantial increasing returns are present. In effect, then, there are small numbers of effective participants. Suppose there are only three agents. Production is assumed to take place in coalitions; the output of each coalition depends only on the number of members in it. If the average output of the members of a coalition does not increase with the number of members, then the equilibrium outcome is the perfectly competitive one, where each agent produces by himself and consumes his own product. If the average output of a coalition increases with the number of members, then clearly production will take place in the three-member coalition; but the allocation is not determined by the threats of individuals to leave the coalition and go on their own, nor by threats of pairs to form coalitions (for any one member can claim more than one-third of the total output and still leave the other two more than they could produce without him). But perhaps the most interesting case is that where the average output is higher for two individuals than for either one or three, that is, increasing returns followed by diminishing returns. For definiteness, suppose that one agent can produce one unit, two agents can produce four units, and all three agents together can produce five units. Clearly, Pareto efficiency requires the joint productive activity of all three. Since each pair can receive four units by leaving the third agent out, it would appear that each pair must receive at least four units. But this implies that the total allocated to keep the three-man coalition together must be at least six, more than is available for distribution.[4]

(Theories of the Nash-Harsanyi type arrive at solutions in cases like this

---

4. The general principle illustrated by this example has been briefly alluded to by Shapley and Shubik (1967, p. 98, n. 5).

by assuming that the economic agents foresee these possible instabilities and recognize that any attempt by any pair to break away from the total coalition can itself be overturned. If each is rational and assumes the others are equally rational, then they recognize, in the completely symmetric situation of the example, that only a symmetric allocation is possible.)

The point of this discussion of possible game theory concepts of equilibrium is to suggest caution in accepting the proposition that bargaining costs alone prevent the achievement of Pareto efficiency in the presence of increasing returns, as Buchanan and Tullock (1962, p. 88) and Demsetz (1968, p. 61) assert.

Risk and Information

The possible types of equilibria discussed in the previous two sections are not, in principle, altered in nature by the presence of risk. If an economic agent is uncertain as to which of several different states of the world will obtain, he can make contracts contingent on the occurrence of possible states. The real-world counterparts of these theoretical contingent contracts include insurance policies and common stocks. With these markets for contingent contracts, a competitive equilibrium will arise under the same general hypotheses as in the absence of uncertainty. It is not even necessary that the economic agents agree on the probability distribution for the unknown state of the world; each may have his own subjective probabilities. Further, the resulting allocation is Pareto-efficient if the utility of each individual is identified as his expected utility according to his own subjective probability distribution.

But, as Radner (1968) has pointed out, there is more to the story. Whenever we have uncertainty we have the possibility of information and, of course, also the possibility of its absence. No contingent contract can be made if, at the time of execution, either of the contracting parties does not know whether the specified contingency has occurred or not. This principle eliminates a much larger number of opportunities for mutually favorable exchanges than might perhaps be supposed at first glance. A simple case is that known in insurance literature as "adverse selection." Suppose, for example, there are two types of individuals, *A* and *B*, with different life expectancies, but the insurance company has no way to distinguish the two; it cannot in fact identify the present state of the world in all its relevant aspects. The optimal allocation of resources under uncertainty would require separate insurance policies for the two types, but these are clearly impossible. Suppose further that each individual knows which type he belongs to. The company might charge a rate based on the probability of death in the two types together, but the insurance buyers in the two types will respond differently; those in the type with the more favorable experience, say *A*, will buy less insurance than those in type *B*, other things (income and risk aversion) being equal. The insurance company's experience will be less favorable than it intended, and it will have to raise its rates. An equilibrium rate will be reached which is, in general, between those corresponding to types *A* and *B* separately but closer to the latter. Such an insurance arrangement is, of course, not Pareto-efficient. It is not a priori obvious in general that this free market arrangement is superior to compulsory insurance, even though the latter is also not Pareto-efficient, because it typically disregards individual differences in risk aversion.

As the above example shows, the critical impact of information on the optimal allocation of risk bearing is not merely its presence or absence but its inequality among economic agents. If neither side knew which type the insured belonged to, then the final allocation would be Pareto-efficient if it were considered that the two types were indistinguishable; but in the above example the market allocation is Pareto-efficient neither with the types regarded as indistinguishable nor as distinguishable.

There is one particular case of the effect of differential information on the workings of the market economy (or indeed any complex economy) which is so important as to deserve special comment: one agent can observe the joint effects of the unknown state of the world and of decisions by another economic agent, but not the state or the decision separately. This case is known in the insurance literature as "moral hazard," but because the insurance examples are only a small fraction of all the illustrations of this case and because, as Pauly (1968) has argued, the adjective "moral" is not always appropriate, the case will be referred to here as the "confounding of risks and decisions." An insurance company may easily observe that a fire has occurred but cannot, without special investigation, know whether the fire was due to causes exogenous to the insured or to decisions of his (arson, or at least carelessness). In general, any system which, in effect, insures against adverse final outcomes automatically reduces the incentives to good decision making.

In these circumstances there are two extreme possibilities (with all intermediate possibilities being present): full protection against uncertainty of final outcome (for example, cost-plus contracts for production or research) or absence of protection against uncertainty of final outcome (the one-person firm; the admiral who is shot for cowardice *pour encourager les autres*). Both policies produce inefficiency, though for different reasons. In the first, the incentive to good decision making is dulled for obvious reasons; in the second, the functions of control and risk bearing must be united, whereas specialization in these functions may be more efficient for the workings of the system.

The relations between principals and agents (for example, patients and physicians, owners and managers) further illustrate the confounding of risks and decisions. In the professions in particular they also illustrate the point to be emphasized later: that ethical standards may to a certain extent overcome the possible Pareto inefficiencies.

So far we have taken the information structure as given. But the fact that particular information structures give rise to Pareto inefficiency means that there is an economic value in transmitting information from one agent to another, as well as in the creation of new information. J. Marschak (1968), Hirshleifer (unpublished), and others have begun the study of the economics of information, but the whole subject is in its infancy. Only a few remarks relevant to the present purpose will be made here.

(1) As both communications engineering and psychology suggest, the transmission of information is not costless. Any professor who has tried to transmit some will be painfully aware of the resources he has expended and, perhaps more poignantly, of the difficulties students have in understanding. The physical costs of transmission may be low, though probably not negligible, as any book buyer knows; but the "coding" of the information for transmission and the limited channel capacity of the recipients are major costs.

(2) The costs of transmitting information vary with both the type of information transmitted and the recipient and sender. The first point implies a preference for inexpensive information, a point stressed in oligopolistic contexts by Kaysen (1949, pp. 294–295) and in other bargaining contexts by Schelling (1957). The second point is relevant to the value of education and to difficulties of transmission across cultural boundaries (so that production functions can differ so much across countries).

(3) Because the costs of transmission are nonnegligible, even situations which are basically certain become uncertain for the individual; the typical economic agent simply cannot acquire in a meaningful sense the knowledge of all possible prices, even where they are each somewhere available. Markets are thus costly to use, and therefore the multiplication of markets, as for contingent claims as suggested above, becomes inhibited.

Externalities Illustrated

After this long excursus into the present state of the theory of equilibrium and optimality, it is time to discuss some of the standard concepts of externality, market failure, and public goods generally. The clarification of these concepts is a long historical process, not yet concluded, in which the classic contributions of Knight (1924), Young (1913, pp. 676–684), and Robertson (1924) have in more recent times been enriched by those of Meade (1952), Scitovsky (1954), Coase (1960), Buchanan and Stubblebine (1962), and Demsetz (1966). The concept of externality and the extent to which it causes nonoptimal market behavior will be discussed here in terms of a simple model.

Consider a pure exchange economy. Let x_{ik} be the amount of the kth commodity consumed by the ith individual ($i = 1, \ldots, n$; $k = 1, \ldots, m$) and $\bar{x}_k$ be the amount of the kth commodity available. Suppose in general that the utility of the ith individual is a function of the consumption of all individuals (not all types of consumption for all individuals need actually enter into any given individual's utility function); the utility of the ith individual is $U_i(x_{11}, \ldots, x_{mn})$. We have the obvious constraints:

(7-1) $$\sum_i x_{ik} \leqq \bar{x}_k.$$

Introduce the following definitions:

(7-2) $$x_{jik} = x_{ik}.$$

With this notation a Pareto-efficient allocation is a vector maximum of the utility functions $U_j(x_{j11}, \ldots, x_{jmn})$, subject to the constraints (7-1) and (7-2). Because of the notation used, the variables appearing in the utility function relating to the jth individual are proper to him alone and appear in no one else's utility function. If we understand now that there are n^2m commodities, indexed by the triple subscript jik, then the Pareto efficiency problem has a thoroughly classical form. There are n^2m prices, p_{jik}, attached to the constraints (7-2), plus m prices, q_k, corresponding to constraints (7-1). Following the maximization procedure formally, we see, much as in Samuelson (1954), that Pareto efficiency is characterized by the conditions

(7-3) $$\lambda_j(\partial U_j/\partial x_{ik}) = p_{jik},$$

and

(7-4) $$\sum_j p_{jik} = q_k,$$

where λ_j is the reciprocal of the marginal utility of income for individual j. (These statements ignore corner conditions, which can easily be supplied.)

Condition (7-4) can be given the following economic interpretation: Imagine each individual i to be a producer with m production processes, indexed by the pair (i, k). Process (i, k) has one input, namely, commodity k, and n outputs, indexed by the triple (j, i, k). In other words, what we ordinarily call individual i's consumption is regarded as the production of joint outputs, one for each individual whose utility is affected by individual i's consumption.

The point of this exercise is to show that by suitable and indeed not unnatural reinterpretation of the commodity space, externalities can be regarded as ordinary commodities, and all the formal theory of competitive equilibrium is valid, including its optimality.

It is not the mere fact that one man's consumption enters into another man's utility that causes the failure of the market to achieve efficiency. There are two relevant factors which cannot be discovered by inspection of the utility structures of the individual. One, much explored in the literature, is the appropriability of the commodities which represent the external repercussions; the other, less stressed, is the fact that markets for externalities usually involve small numbers of buyers and sellers.

The first point, Musgrave's "exclusion principle" (1959, p. 86), is so well known as to need little elaboration. Pricing demands the possibility of excluding nonbuyers from the use of the product, and this exclusion may be technically impossible or may require the use of considerable resources. Pollution is the key example; the supply of clean air or water to each individual would have to be treated as a separate commodity, and it would have to be possible in principle to supply it to some and not to others (though the final equilibrium would involve equal supply to all). But this is technically impossible.

The second point comes out clearly in our case. Each commodity (j, i, k) has precisely one buyer and one seller. Even if a competitive equilibrium could be defined, there would be no force driving the system to it; we are in the realm of imperfectly competitive equilibrium.

In my view, the standard lighthouse example is best analyzed as a problem of small numbers rather than of the difficulty of exclusion, though both elements are present. To simplify matters, I will abstract from uncertainty so that the lighthouse keeper knows exactly when each ship will need its services, and also abstract from indivisibility (since the light is either on or off). Assume further that only one ship will be within range of the lighthouse at any moment. Then exclusion is perfectly possible; the keeper need only shut off the light when a nonpaying ship is coming into range. But there would be only one buyer and one seller and no competitive forces to drive the two into a competitive equilibrium. If in addition the costs of bargaining are high, then it may be most efficient to offer the service free.

If, as is typical, markets for the externalities do not exist, then the allocation from the point of view of the "buyer" is determined by a rationing process. We can determine a shadow price for the buyer; this will differ from the price, zero, received by the seller. Hence, formally, the failure of markets for externalities to exist can also be described as a difference of prices between buyer and seller.

In the example analyzed, the externalities related to particular named individuals; individual *i*'s utility function depended on what a particular individual, *j*, possessed. The case where it is only the total amount of some commodity (for example, handsome houses) in other people's hands that matters is a special case, which yields rather simpler results. In this case, $\partial U_j/\partial x_{ik}$ is independent of i for $i \neq j$, and hence, by condition (7-3), p_{jik} is independent of i for $i \neq j$. Let

$$p_{iik} = p_{ik}, \qquad p_{jik} = \overline{p}_{jk} \quad \text{for } i \neq j.$$

Then condition (7-4) becomes

$$p_{ik} + \sum_{j \neq i} \overline{p}_{jk} = q_k$$

or

$$(p_{ik} - \overline{p}_{ik}) + \sum_{j} \overline{p}_{jk} = q_k,$$

from which it follows that the difference, $p_{ik} - \overline{p}_{ik}$, is independent of i. There are two kinds of shadow prices, a price $\overline{p}_{ik}$, the price that individual i is willing to pay for an increase in the stock of commodity k in any other individual's hands, and the premium, $p_{ik} - \overline{p}_{ik}$, he is willing to pay to have the commodity in his possession rather than someone else's. At the optimum, this premium for private possession must be the same for all individuals.

Other types of externalities are associated with several commodities simultaneously and do not involve named individuals, as in the case of neighborhood effects, where an individual's utility depends both on others' behavior (for example, aesthetic, criminal) and on their location.

There is one deep problem in the interpretation of externalities which can only be signaled here. What aspects of others' behavior do we consider as affecting a utility function? If we take a hard-boiled revealed preference attitude, then if an individual expends resources in supporting legislation regulating another's behavior, it must be assumed that that behavior affects his utility. Yet in the cases that students of criminal law call "crimes without victims," such as homosexuality or drug taking, there is no direct relation between the parties. Do we have to extend the concept of externality to all matters that an individual cares about? Or, in the spirit of John Stuart Mill, is there a second-order value judgment which excludes some of these preferences from the formation of social policy as being illegitimate infringements of individual freedom?

Market Failure

The problem of externalities is thus a special case of a more general phenomenon, the failure of markets to exist. Not all examples of market failure can fruitfully be described as externalities. Two very important examples have already been alluded to; markets for many forms of risk bearing and for most future transactions do not exist, and their absence is surely suggestive of inefficiency.

Previous discussion has suggested two possible causes for market failure: (1) inability to exclude; (2) lack of the necessary information to permit market transactions to be concluded.

The failure of futures markets cannot be directly explained in these terms. Exclusion is no more a problem in the future than in the present. Any contract to be executed in the future is necessarily contingent on some events (for example, that the two agents are still both in business), but there must be many cases where no informational difficulty is presented. The absence of futures markets may be ascribed to a third possibility: (3) supply and demand are equated at zero; the highest price at which anyone would buy is below the lowest price at which anyone would sell.

This third case of market failure, unlike the first two, is by itself in no way presumptive of inefficiency. However, it may usually be assumed that its occurrence is the result of failures of the first two types on complementary markets. Specifically, the demand for future steel may be low because of uncertainties of all types: sales and technological uncertainty for the buyer's firm, prices and existence of competing goods, and the quality specification of the steel. If, however, adequate markets for risk bearing existed, the uncertainties could be removed, and the demand for future steel would rise.

Transaction Costs

Market failure has been presented as absolute, but in fact the situation is more complex than this. A more general formulation is that of transaction costs, which are attached to any market and indeed to any mode of resource allocation. Market failure is the particular case where transaction costs are so high that the existence of the market is no longer worthwhile. The distinction between transaction costs and production costs is that the former can be varied by a change in the mode of resource allocation, while the latter depend only on the technology and tastes, and would be the same in all economic systems.

The discussions in the preceding sections suggest two sources of transaction costs: (1) exclusion costs and (2) costs of communication and information, including both the supplying and the learning of the terms on which transactions can be carried out. An additional source is (3) the costs of disequilibrium; in any complex system, the market or authoritative allocation, even under perfect information, it takes time to compute the optimal allocation, and either transactions take place which are inconsistent with the final equilibrium or they are delayed until the computations are completed (see T. Marschak, 1959).

These costs vary from system to system; thus, one of the advantages of a price system over either bargaining or some form of authoritative allocation is usually stated to be the economy in costs of information and communication. But the costs of transmitting and especially of receiving a large number of price signals may be high; thus, there is a tendency not to differentiate prices as much as would be desirable from the efficiency viewpoint. For example, the same price is charged for peak and off-peak usage of transportation or electricity.

In a price system, transaction costs drive a wedge between buyers' and sellers' prices and thereby give rise to welfare losses as in the usual analysis. Removal of these welfare losses by changing to another system (for example, governmental allocation on benefit-cost criteria) must be weighed against any possible increase in transaction costs (for example, the need for elaborate and perhaps impossible studies to determine demand functions without the benefit of observing a market).

The welfare implications of transaction costs would exist even if they were proportional to the size of the transaction, but in fact they typically exhibit increasing returns. The cost of acquiring a piece of information, for example, a price, is independent of the scale of use to which it will be put.

Collective Action: The Political Process

The state may frequently have a special role to play in resource allocation because, by its nature, it has a monopoly of coercive power, and coercive power can be used to economize on transaction costs. The most important use of coercion in the economic context is the collection of taxes; others are regulatory legislation and eminent domain proceedings.

The state is not an entity but rather a system of individual agents, a widely extensive system in the case of democracy. It is appealing and fruitful to analyze its behavior in resource allocation in a manner analogous to that of the price system. Since the same agents appear in the two systems, it becomes equally natural to assume that they have the same motives. Hotelling (1929, pp. 54–55) and Schumpeter (1942, chap. 22) had sketched such politicoeconomic models, and von Neumann and Morgenstern's monumental work is certainly based on the idea that all social phenomena are governed by essentially the same motives as economics. The elaboration of more or less complete models of the political process along the lines of economic theory is more recent, the most prominent contributors being Black (1958), Downs (1957), Buchanan and Tullock (1962), and Rothenberg (1965).

I confine myself here to a few critical remarks on the possibilities of such theories. These are not intended to be negative but to suggest problems that have to be faced and are raised by some points in the preceding discussion.

1. If we take the allocative process to be governed by majority voting, then, as we well know, there are considerable possibilities of paradox. The possible intransitivity of majority voting was already pointed out by Condorcet (1785). If, instead of assuming that each individual votes according to his preferences, it is assumed that all bargain freely before voting (vote-selling), the paradox appears in another form, a variant of the bargaining problems already noted in the section on imperfectly competitive equilibrium. If a majority could do what it wanted, then it would be optimal to win with a bare majority and take everything; but any such bargain can always be broken up by another proposed majority.

Tullock (1967, chap. 3) has recently argued convincingly that if the distribution of opinions on social issues is fairly uniform and if the dimensionality of the space of social issues is much less than the number of individuals, then majority voting on a sincere basis will be transitive. The argument is not, however, applicable to income distribution, for such a policy has as many dimensions as there are individuals, so that the dimensionality of the issue space is equal to the number of individuals.

This last observation raises an interesting question. Why, in fact, in democratic systems has there been so little demand for income redistribution? The current discussion of a negative income tax is the first serious attempt at a purely redistributive policy. Hagström (1938) presented a mathematical model predicting on the basis of a self-interest model for voters that democracy would inevitably lead to radical egalitarianism.

2. Political policy is not made by voters, not even in the sense that they choose the vector of political actions which best suits them. It is in fact made by representatives in one form or another. Political representation is an outstanding example of the principal-agent relation. This means that the link between individual utility functions and social action is tenuous, though by no means completely absent. Representatives are no more a random sample of their constituents than physicians are of their patients.

Indeed, the question can be raised: to what extent is the voter, when acting in that capacity, a principal or an agent? To some extent, certainly, the voter is cast in a role in which he feels some obligation to consider the social good, not just his own. It is in fact somewhat hard to explain otherwise why an individual votes at all in a large election, since the probability that his vote will be decisive is so negligible.

Collective Action: Social Norms

It is a mistake to limit collective action to state action; many other departures from the anonymous atomism of the price system are observed regularly. Indeed, firms of any complexity are illustrations of collective action, the internal allocation of their resources being directed by authoritative and hierarchical controls.

I want, however, to conclude by calling attention to a less visible form of social action: norms of social behavior, including ethical and moral codes. I suggest as one possible interpretation that they are reactions of society to compensate for market failures. It is useful for individuals to have some trust in each other's word. In the absence of trust, it would become very costly to arrange for alternative sanctions and guarantees, and many opportunities for mutually beneficial cooperation would have to be forgone. Banfield (1958) has argued that lack of trust is indeed one of the causes of economic underdevelopment.

It is difficult to conceive of buying trust in any direct way (though it can happen indirectly, for example, a trusted employee will be paid more as being more valuable); indeed, there seems to be some inconsistency in the very concept. Nonmarket action might take the form of a mutual agreement. But the arrangement of these agreements and especially their continued extension to new individuals entering the social fabric can be costly. As an alternative, society may proceed by internalization of these norms to the achievement of the desired agreement on an unconscious level.

There is a whole set of customs and norms which might be similarly interpreted as agreements to improve the efficiency of the economic system (in the broad sense of satisfaction of individual values) by providing commodities to which the price system is inapplicable.

These social conventions may be adaptive in their origins, but they can become retrogressive. An agreement is costly to reach and therefore costly to modify; and the costs of modification may be especially large for unconscious agreements. Thus, codes of professional ethics, which arise out of the principal-agent relation and afford protection to the principals, can serve also as a cloak for monopoly by the agents.

References

Aumann, R. J., 1964. "Markets with a Continuum of Traders," *Econometrica,* vol. 32, pp. 39–50.

Aumann, R. J., 1966. "The Existence of Competitive Equilibria in Markets with a Continuum of Traders," *Econometrica,* vol. 34, pp. 1–17.

Aumann, R. J., and Maschler, M., 1964. "The Bargaining Set for Cooperative Games," in Dresher, M., Shapley, L. S., and Tucker, A. W. (eds.), *Advances in Game Theory. Annals of Mathematics Study,* Princeton, vol. 52, pp. 443–476.

Banfield, E. C., 1958. *The Moral Basis of a Backward Society,* Glencoe, Ill.

Black, D., 1958. *The Theory of Committees and Elections,* Cambridge, U.K.

Buchanan, J., and Stubblebine, W. C., 1962. "Externality," *Economica,* vol. 29, pp. 371–384.

Buchanan, J., and Tullock, G., 1962. *The Calculus of Consent,* Ann Arbor, Michigan.

Chamberlin, E. H., 1933. *The Theory of Monopolistic Competition,* 8th ed., Cambridge, Mass.

Coase, R. H., 1960. "The Problem of Social Cost," *Journal of Law and Economics,* vol. 3, pp. 1–44.

Condorcet, Marquis de, 1785. *Essai sur l'application de l'analyse à la probabilité des décisions rendues à la pluralité des voix,* Paris.

Debreu, G., and Scarf, H., 1963. "A Limit Theorem on the Core of an Economy," *International Economic Review,* vol. 4, pp. 236–246.

Demsetz, H., 1964. "The Welfare and Empirical Implications of Monopolistic Competition," *Economic Journal,* vol. 74, pp. 623–691.

Demsetz, H., 1966. "Some Aspects of Property Rights," *Journal of Law and Economics,* vol. 9, pp. 61–70.

Demsetz, H., 1968. "Why Regulate Utilities," *Journal of Law and Economics,* vol. 11, pp. 55–66.

Downs, A., 1957. *An Economic Theory of Democracy,* New York.

Edgeworth, F. Y., 1881. *Mathematical Psychics: An Essay on the Application of Mathematics to the Moral Sciences,* London.

Farrell, M. J., 1959. "The Convexity Assumption in the Theory of Competitive Markets," *Journal of Political Economy,* vol. 67, pp. 377–391.

Hagström, K. G., 1938. "A Mathematical Note on Democracy," *Econometrica,* vol. 6, pp. 381–383.

Harsanyi, J. C., 1956. "Approaches to the Bargaining Problem before and after the Theory of Games: A Critical Discussion of Zeuthen's, Hicks', and Nash's Theories," *Econometrica,* vol. 24, pp. 144–157.

Harsanyi, J. C., 1959. "A Bargaining Model for the Cooperative N-Person Game," in Tucker, A. W., and Luce, R. D. (eds.), *Contributions to the Theory of Games IV. Annals of Mathematics Study,* Princeton, pp. 325–355.

Harsanyi, J. C., 1963. "A Simplified Bargaining Model for the N-Person Cooperative Game," *International Economic Review,* vol. 4, pp. 194–220.

Harsanyi, J. C., 1966. "A General Theory of Rational Behavior in Game Situations," *Econometrica,* vol. 34, pp. 613–634.

Hotelling, H., 1929. "Stability in Competition," *Economic Journal,* vol. 39, pp. 41–57.

Kaldor, N., 1935. "Market Imperfection and Excess Capacity," *Economica,* vol. 2, pp. 33–50.

Kaysen, Carl, 1949. "Basing Point Pricing and Public Policy," *Quarterly Journal of Economics,* vol. 63, pp. 289–314.

Knight, F. H., 1921. *Risk, Uncertainty, and Profit,* Boston and New York.

Knight, F. H., 1924. "Some Fallacies in the Interpretation of Social Cost," *Quarterly Journal of Economics,* vol. 38, pp. 582–606.

Luce, R. D., 1954. "A Definition of Stability for N-Person Games," *Annals of Mathematics,* vol. 59, pp. 357–366.

Luce, R. D., 1955a. "Ψ-Stability: A New Equilibrium Concept for N-Person Game Theory," in *Mathematical Models of Human Behavior,* Stamford, Conn., pp. 32–44.

Luce, R. D., 1955b. "K-Stability of Symmetric and Quota Games," *Annals of Mathematics,* vol. 62, pp. 517–555.

Marschak, J., 1968. "Economics of Inquiring, Communicating, Deciding," *American Economic Review Papers and Proceedings,* vol. 58, pp. 1–18.

Marschak, T., 1959. "Centralization and Decentralization in Economic Organizations," *Econometrica,* vol. 27, pp. 399–430.

Meade, J. E., 1952. "External Economies and Diseconomies in a Competitive Situation," *Economic Journal,* vol. 62, pp. 59–67.

Musgrave, R. A., 1959. *The Theory of Public Finance: A Study in Public Economy,* New York.

Nash, J. F., Jr., 1950. "The Bargaining Problem," *Econometrica,* vol. 18, pp. 155–162.

Nash, J. F., Jr., 1953. "Two Person Cooperative Games," *Econometrica,* vol. 21, pp. 128–140.

Negishi, T., 1960–61. "Monopolistic Competition and General Equilibrium," *Review of Economic Studies,* vol. 28, pp. 196–201.

von Neumann, J., and Morgenstern, O., 1944. *Theory of Games and Economic Behavior,* Princeton, 2nd ed.

Pauly, M. V., 1968. "The Economics of Moral Hazard: Comment," *American Economic Review,* vol. 58, pp. 531–537.

Radner, R., 1968. "Competitive Equilibrium under Uncertainty," *Econometrica,* vol. 36, pp. 31–58.

Robertson, D. H., 1924. "Those Empty Boxes," *Economic Journal,* vol. 34, pp. 16–30.

Rothenberg, J., 1960. "Non-Convexity, Aggregation, and Pareto Optimality," *Journal of Political Economy,* vol. 68, pp. 435–468.

Rothenberg, J., 1965. "A Model of Economic and Political Decision-Making," in Margolis, J. (ed)., *The Public Economy of Urban Communities,* Washington, D. C.

Samuelson, P. A., 1954. "The Pure Theory of Public Expenditures," *Review of Economic Statistics,* vol. 36, pp. 387–389.

Samuelson, P. A., 1967. "The Monopolistic Competition Revolution," in Kuenne, R. E. (ed.), *Monopolistic Competition Theory: Studies in Impact,* New York, London, and Sydney, pp. 105–138.

Schelling, T., 1957. "Bargaining, Communication, and Limited War," *Journal of Conflict Resolution,* vol. 1, pp. 19–36.

Schumpeter, J., 1942. *Capitalism, Socialism, and Democracy,* 3rd ed., New York.

Scitovsky, T., 1954. "Two Concepts of External Economies," *Journal of Political Economy,* vol. 62, pp. 143–151.

Selten, R., 1964. "Valuation of N-Person Games," in Dresher, M., Shapley, L. S., and Tucker, A. W. (eds.), *Advances in Game Theory. Annals of Mathematics Study,* Princeton, vol. 52, pp. 577–626.

Shapley, L. S., 1953. "A Value for N-Person Games," in Kuhn, H. W., and Tucker, A. W. (eds.), *Contributions to the Theory of Games II. Annals of Mathematics Study,* Princeton, vol. 28, pp. 307–317.

Shapley, L. S., and Shubik, M., 1967. "Ownership and the Production Function," *Quarterly Journal of Economics,* vol. 81, pp. 88–111.

Shubik, M., 1959. "Edgeworth Market Games," in Tucker, A. W., and Luce, R. D. (eds.), *Contributions to the Theory of Games IV. Annals of Mathematics Study,* Princeton, vol. 40, pp. 267–278.

Smith, A., 1937. *An Enquiry Concerning the Causes of the Wealth of Nations,* New York.

Starr, R., 1969. "Quasi-Equilibria in Markets with Nonconvex Preferences," *Econometrica,* vol. 37, pp. 25–38.

Triffin, R., 1941. *Monopolistic Competition and General Equilibrium Theory,* Cambridge, Mass.

Tullock, G., 1967. *Toward a Mathematics of Politics,* Ann Arbor, Mich.

Young, A. A., 1913. "Pigou's Wealth and Welfare," *Quarterly Journal of Economics,* vol. 27, pp. 672–686.

Zeuthen, F., 1930. *Problems of Monopoly and Economic Warfare,* London.

8 The Firm in General Equilibrium Theory

In classical theory, from Smith to Mill, fixed coefficients in production are assumed. In such a context, the individual firm plays little role in the general equilibrium of the economy. The scale of any one firm is indeterminate, but the demand conditions determine the scale of the industry and the demand by the industry for inputs. The firm's role is purely passive, and no meaningful boundaries between firms are established. No doubt the firm or the entrepreneur was much discussed and indeed given a central role in the informal parts of the discussion; the role was that of overcoming disequilibria. When profit rates were unequal, profit-hungry entrepreneurs moved quickly, with the end result of eliminating their functions.

When Walras first gave explicit formulation to the grand vision of general equilibrium, he took over intact the fixed-coefficient assumptions and therewith the passive nature of the firm. In the last quarter of the nineteenth century, J. B. Clark, Wicksteed, Barone, and Walras himself recognized the possibility of alternative production activities in the form of the production function. However, so long as constant returns to scale were assumed, the size of the firm remained indeterminate. The firm did have now, even in equilibrium, a somewhat more active role than in earlier theory; it at least had the responsibility of minimizing costs at given output levels.

There were other economists, however, who were interested in the theory of the firm as such, the earliest being Cournot (1838). Anyone with an

Reprinted from *The Corporate Economy: Growth, Competition, and Innovative Potential,* ed. R. Marris and A. Wood (Cambridge, Mass.: Harvard University Press; London: Macmillan, 1971), pp. 68–110.

elementary knowledge of calculus and a theory that firms are maximizing profits under competitive conditions is led without thinking to the hypothesis of increasing marginal costs or diminishing returns to scale. As Cournot also knew, firms may be monopolists as well as competitors; and in those circumstances, profit maximization is compatible with increasing returns to scale.

As in other aspects of economics, both of these somewhat contradictory tendencies appear in Marshall's welter of imprecise insights. It would be tedious to follow the subsequent discussions of laws of return and their relation to competitive or other equilibrium, carried on intermittently by such authors as Wicksell, Pareto, Robertson, Sraffa, Shove, and Viner (with the famous assistance of Y. K. Wong). Among the literary economists in the Anglo-American tradition, a kind of orthodoxy has emerged, in the U-shaped cost curve for the firm plus free entry. In more modern language, the production possibility set of the typical firm displays an initial tendency toward increasing returns followed at higher scales by decreasing returns. The first phase is explained by indivisibilities, the second by the decreasing ability of the entrepreneur to control the firm. As one may put it, entrepreneurship should also be regarded as an input to the firm; then, after the initial phase at least, the firm would have constant returns to all inputs (including entrepreneurship), but, since by definition the firm has only one entrepreneur, there are diminishing returns to all other factors. (The indivisibility of the entrepreneur is sometimes invoked to explain the initial phase also, though of course there are typically also indivisibilities of a more definitely technological variety.) The assumption of free entry implies that the supply of entrepreneurship in the economy is infinite, or, more precisely, that it is sufficiently large that its demand price will fall to zero at a point at which supply still exceeds demand.

The exact relation of this model of the firm to a full general equilibrium model has never been explored; in particular, the notion of an infinite supply of entrepreneurship is no more reasonable than that of an infinite supply of anything else.

The first mathematical model of general equilibrium was the work of Wald, summarized in Wald (1936), though some of the basic considerations in the model were suggested to him by K. Schlesinger (1933–34). In Wald's work, to the extent that production was involved at all, fixed coefficients were assumed. After the mathematical tools available had been greatly improved by von Neumann and others as part of the development of game theory, more general models were developed by McKenzie (1954) and

Arrow and Debreu (1954). The best systematic account is that of Debreu (1959); detailed improvements are found in Debreu (1962) and a somewhat different viewpoint in McKenzie (1959).

The treatment of the firm in Arrow–Debreu is unchanged in Debreu's later work. The set of firms is regarded as fixed. It should be noted, though, that a firm might find it most profitable to produce nothing; hence, what is ordinarily called entry here appears as a change from zero to positive output levels. The production possibility sets of the firms are assumed to be convex. This assumption excludes the possibility of an initial phase of increasing returns; it is compatible with either constant or diminishing returns to scale. The treatment of entrepreneurship in the model can then be interpreted in several ways. The most natural is to assume that entrepreneurship per se is not included in the list of commodities. Then where there are constant returns, entrepreneurship is not a factor of production, or, alternatively, it is not scarce. However, diminishing returns plus a finite fixed set of (potential) firms imply scarcity of entrepreneurship and positive pure profits. In this interpretation, too, we are not constrained to identify entrepreneurship as being supplied by any particular set of individuals; the diminishing returns can be inherent in the operating properties of the organization.

Alternatively, we can assume that entrepreneurial resources are included among the list of commodities and are supplied by specific individuals. This is McKenzie's assumption (1959); he completes it naturally by assuming constant returns to scale in all commodities. Then firms are distinguished by their needs for specific entrepreneurial resources (it is not assumed that entrepreneurship for one firm is necessarily the same as for another) and are limited in scale by the limitations on these resources.

The two models differ in their implications for income distribution. The Arrow–Debreu model creates a category of pure profits which are distributed to the owners of the firm; it is not assumed that the owners are necessarily the entrepreneurs or managers. Since profit maximization is assumed, conflict of interest between the organization or its management, on the one hand, and the owners, on the other, is assumed always to be resolved in favor of the owners. The model is sufficiently flexible, however, to permit the managers to be included among the owners.

In the McKenzie model, on the other hand, the firm makes no pure profits (since it operates at constant returns); the equivalent of profits appears in the form of payments for the use of entrepreneurial resources, but there is no residual category of owners who receive profits without rendering either capital or entrepreneurial services.

Several writers, especially Farrell (1959) and Rothenberg (1960), have argued that "small" nonconvexities, such as a limited initial phase of increasing returns, are compatible with an "approximate" equilibrium, that is, one in which discrepancies between supply and demand are small relative to the size of the market. Hence, the U-shaped cost curve is not basically incompatible with competitive general equilibrium theory, though so far there has been no rigorous development of the relations.

Substantial increasing returns to the firm, on the other hand, are obviously incompatible with the existence of a perfectly competitive equilibrium. It is of course in situations like this that monopolies arise. The theory of the profit-maximizing monopoly in a single market was developed in its essentials by Cournot and has been developed further only on secondary points, the most important of which has been the possibility of price discrimination. But, apart from some remarks in Pareto, the first serious discussions of monopoly in a general equilibrium context are those of J. Robinson (1933) and Chamberlin (1956; originally published in 1933). The formulation of an explicit model of general equilibrium with monopolistic elements will be discussed in the third section of this chapter.

In static theories of general equilibrium and in the absence of monopoly, then, the individual firm has been characterized by diminishing returns, a phenomenon associated with the vague concept of entrepreneurship. Kalecki (1939, chap. 4) suggested long ago that the reasons for limitation on the size of the firm might be found in dynamic rather than static considerations. Recent years have seen the beginning of dynamic analysis of the firm (especially Penrose, 1959, and Marris, 1964). From the point of view of realism and of interpretation of observations, these are a major advance. But on the production side they still retain the basic structure of the static model, restated in dynamic terms. Specifically, while returns to scale are constant in the long run, there are diminishing returns to the rate of growth, which plays the same role as scale does in a static model. (This view of attaching costs to rates of change has also been urged by some of those close to operations research; see, *inter alios,* Hoffman and Jacobs, 1954; Holt et al., 1960, pp. 52–53; Arrow, Karlin, and Scarf, 1958, p. 22.) Hence, the analysis of stationary states of the dynamic system has strong formal resemblance to purely static analysis; or, to put the matter the other way, static analysis remains useful provided it is interpreted parabolically rather than literally.

However, dynamic analysis may have deeper implications if we depart from the analysis of stationary states. The firm must now serve some additional roles. In the absence of futures markets, the firm must serve as a forecaster and as a bearer of uncertainty. Further, from a general equilibrium point of view, the forecasts of others become relevant to the evaluation of the firm's shares and therefore possibly of the firm's behavior. The general equilibrium to be analyzed is, in the first instance, the equilibrium of a moment, *temporary equilibrium* in the terminology of Hicks.

Some of these topics will be discussed below; for others, only open questions can be mentioned. The analysis will always concern itself with the existence of equilibrium under each of varying sets of assumptions. Existence of equilibrium is of interest in itself; certainly a minimal property that a model purporting to describe an economic system ought to have is consistency. In practice, the development of conditions needed to ensure the existence of equilibrium turns out in many cases to be very revealing; until one has to construct an existence proof, the relevance of many of these conditions is not obvious.

The proofs will not be presented in detail, but their general outlines will be indicated. In the next section, a sketch will first be given of a proof of existence of competitive equilibrium under standard assumptions. In the third section, a model of monopolistic competitive equilibrium will be presented and analyzed for existence; this will display the role of the firm as price-maker. In the fourth section, the existence of temporary equilibrium and its preconditions are discussed. More detailed proofs of the results of these sections will be found in Arrow and Hahn (1971, chap. 6, secs. 4 and 3 respectively).

The Existence of General Competitive Equilibrium

Since proofs of existence of equilibrium in more extended contexts start from the methods used in the perfectly competitive case, it is indispensable to indicate the main lines of the proof in that case. Although it would doubtless be possible to use the proofs of Debreu or McKenzie (cited above) as starting points, I have in fact used a new form of the proof which will appear in Arrow and Hahn (1971, chaps. 3–4).

First, the assumptions made are listed. Production is assumed to be organized in firms; let Y_f be the production possibility set for firm f with typical element $\mathbf{y}_f$.

ASSUMPTION 1. *Y_f is a closed convex set, and $\mathbf{0}$ belongs to Y_f.*

The last clause means that a firm can go out of existence.

ASSUMPTION 2. *If $\Sigma_f \mathbf{y}_f \geqq \mathbf{0}$ and $\mathbf{y}_f$ belongs to Y_f, all f, then $\mathbf{y}_f = \mathbf{0}$, all f.*

To assert that a vector is nonnegative means that each element is nonnegative.

To see the meaning of Assumption 2, note first that if $\Sigma_f \mathbf{y}_f \geqq \mathbf{0}$ but not $\Sigma_f \mathbf{y}_f = \mathbf{0}$ then the productive sector as a whole is supplying positive amounts of some goods with no inputs, a physical impossibility. If $\Sigma_f \mathbf{y}_f = \mathbf{0}$ but not all **y**'s are **0**, then some firms are in effect undoing the productive activity of others. If we assume that there are some inputs such as labor that are not produced by any firm, then such cancellation is impossible.

In view of Assumption 2, production is possible only if the economy has some initial supply of nonproduced commodities; let $\bar{\mathbf{x}}$ be this vector of initial endowments. We now assume that with the initial endowment it is possible to have a positive net output of all commodities, that is, we can use part but less than all of each initially available commodity to produce something of each produced commodity after netting out interindustry flows.

ASSUMPTION 3. *It is possible to choose $\bar{\mathbf{y}}_f$ from Y_f for each f so that the net output vector, $\Sigma_f \bar{\mathbf{y}}_f + \bar{\mathbf{x}}$, has positive components for all commodities.*

Among the three production assumptions, really only the convexity assumed in Assumption 1 can be regarded as dubious.

By a *production allocation* will be meant a specification of $\mathbf{y}_f \in Y_f$ for each f. By a *feasible production allocation* will be meant a production allocation which does not require more net inputs than are available from the initial endowment:

$$\sum_f \mathbf{y}_f + \bar{\mathbf{x}} \geqq \mathbf{0}.$$

Then it is possible to demonstrate from Assumptions 1 and 2 that

> the set of feasible production allocations is convex, closed, and bounded.

To discuss the assumptions about consumers, let X_h be the set of consumption vectors possible to household h. For present purposes, it can simply be regarded as the set of all nonnegative vectors where leisure is taken as one good. (A somewhat more complicated description is required to take care of the possibility that an individual may be capable of offering more than one kind of labor.)

ASSUMPTION 4. *X_h is closed and convex and contains only nonnegative vectors.*

Each household is assumed to possess some part of society's initial endowment, say $\bar{\mathbf{x}}_h$.

A somewhat technical assumption is needed to ensure that in a certain sense households can make choices without any trade and even without using all of whatever initial endowment they possess.

ASSUMPTION 5. *For each h, there exists* $\bar{\bar{\mathbf{x}}}_h \in X_h$, *such that* $\mathbf{0} \leqq \bar{\bar{\mathbf{x}}}_h \leqq \bar{\mathbf{x}}_h$; *further, any positive component of* $\bar{\mathbf{x}}_h$ *is also a positive component of* $\bar{\mathbf{x}}_h - \bar{\bar{\mathbf{x}}}_h$.

If we take X_h to be the set of nonnegative vectors, then $\bar{\bar{\mathbf{x}}}_h$ can be taken equal to $\mathbf{0}$.

The final assumption about the consumer is the usual one about the continuity and convexity of consumer preferences.

ASSUMPTION 6. *The preferences of household h can be represented by a continuous utility function,* $U_h(\mathbf{x}_h)$, *with the following convexity property (referred to as semistrict quasi-concavity): if* $\mathbf{x}_h^1$ *and* $\mathbf{x}_h^2$ *are consumption vectors such that* $U_h(\mathbf{x}_h^1) > U_h(\mathbf{x}_h^2)$ *and if* α *is a scalar,* $0 < \alpha \leqq 1$, *then* $U_h[\alpha \mathbf{x}_h^1 + (1-\alpha)\mathbf{x}_h^2] > U_h(\mathbf{x}_h^2)$. *Further, assume that there is no satiation in all commodities simultaneously, that is, for every* $\mathbf{x}_h^1 \in X_h$, *there exists* $\mathbf{x}_h^2 \in X_h$ *for which* $U_h(\mathbf{x}_h^2) > U_h(\mathbf{x}_h^1)$.

The convexity condition implies that indifference surfaces are convex but not necessarily strictly so (thus, they may possess flat segments); however, there are no "thick" bands in which all sufficiently close vectors are indifferent. Permitting flat segments on the indifference surfaces is necessary if one is to avoid assuming that all commodities enter directly into each household's utility function. The nonsatiation condition is consistent with satiation in any specific commodity or group of commodities.

Assumption 6 is restrictive, but the consequences of dropping it do not appear to be severe. If it is assumed that the endowment of no household is large relative to total endowment, then the discontinuities of individual household demand functions relative to the economy as a whole are small, and so the Farrell–Rothenberg argument shows that equilibrium is approximately attained; a fully rigorous version for the case of a pure exchange economy is to be found in Starr (1969).

Finally, we need an assumption about the relation between the initial endowment held by a household and the possibility of its improving someone's welfare. A given household, h', holds some commodities initially in positive amount and others in zero amount. Call that set of commodities the *h′-assets.* Now consider any allocation of resources to firms and households which is feasible for the given endowment vector. Such an allocation defines a *utility allocation,* a specification of the utility level of each household. Now suppose that some increase in society's endowment of h'-assets, all other components of the initial endowment remaining constant, permits a new resource allocation in which every household is at least as well off and household h'' better off. If this improvement is possible starting from any feasible allocation, then household h' is said to be *resource-related* to household h''.

A weaker relation between two households is the following: household h' is said to be *indirectly resource-related* to household h'' if there exists some chain of households, beginning with h' and ending with h'', such that each household in the chain is resource-related to its successor. We now assume:

ASSUMPTION 7. *Every household is indirectly resource-related to every other.*

(This definition is related to, but not identical with, that of irreducibility of the economy in McKenzie, 1959 and 1961, and it generalizes assumptions introduced by Arrow and Debreu, 1954, pp. 279–281, assumptions VI and VII.)

This assumption is very weak; each household is assumed to have something to offer the market which is valuable to someone, who in turn is similarly linked to someone else, and so forth till everyone is reached. Certainly in an advanced economy, it can easily be accepted.

The income of the household, available for its consumption, derives in general from two sources: the sale of its endowment and its share of the profits of firms. Since we are assuming convexity but not necessarily constant returns to scale, it is possible for firms to have positive profits even at equilibrium. It is therefore assumed that each household h has the right to a share, d_{hf}, in the profits of firm f. Necessarily,

$$(8\text{-}1) \qquad d_{hf} \geqq 0, \qquad \sum_h d_{hf} = 1 \quad \text{for all } f.$$

Then the income of the household is defined by

$$(8\text{-}2) \qquad M_h = \mathbf{p}\,\bar{\mathbf{x}}_h + \sum_f d_{hf}(\mathbf{p}\,\mathbf{y}_f),$$

since the profits of firm f are defined by $\mathbf{p}\,\mathbf{y}_f$.

We now state formally the usual definition of competitive equilibrium:

DEFINITION 1. *A price vector* $\mathbf{p}^*$ *and an allocation* $(\mathbf{x}_h^*, \mathbf{y}_f^*)$ *constitute a competitive equilibrium if the following conditions are satisfied:*

(a) $\mathbf{p}^* \geqq \mathbf{0}$ but $\mathbf{p}^* \neq \mathbf{0}$;

(b) $\sum_h \mathbf{x}_h^* \leqq \sum_h \bar{\mathbf{x}}_h + \sum_f \mathbf{y}_f^*$;

(c) $\mathbf{y}_f^*$ maximizes $\mathbf{p}^*\mathbf{y}_f$ subject to $\mathbf{y}_f \in Y_f$;

(d) $\mathbf{x}_h^*$ maximizes $U_h(\mathbf{x}_h)$ subject to $\mathbf{x}_h \in X_h$, $\mathbf{p}^* \mathbf{x}_h \leqq \mathbf{p}^*\bar{\mathbf{x}}_h + \sum_f d_{hf}(\mathbf{p}^*\mathbf{y}_f^*) = M_h^*$.

It turns out that the demand functions of the consumer defined implicitly by (d) can be discontinuous if prices approach a limit at which $M_h^* = 0$. It is convenient first to introduce a slightly different and weaker definition of competitive equilibrium, prove its existence, and then show that under the assumptions made, particularly Assumption 7, it also satisfies the conditions of Definition 1 (D.1). The new definition amounts to replacing the uncompensated demand functions of D.1 by compensated demand functions, that is, the consumer's choice is that of minimizing the cost of achieving a given utility level. The relation between the two is the following: a demand vector which maximizes utility under a given budget constraint certainly minimizes the cost of achieving the resulting utility; but a demand vector which minimizes the cost of achieving some stated utility also maximizes utility without spending more if the amount spent is positive (but not in general if $M_h = 0$).

DEFINITION 2. *The price vector,* $\mathbf{p}^*$*, utility allocation* (u_h^*) *and allocation* $(\mathbf{x}_h^*, \mathbf{y}_f^*)$ *is a compensated equilibrium if:*

(a) $\mathbf{p}^* \geqq \mathbf{0}$ but $\mathbf{p}^* \neq \mathbf{0}$;

(b) $\sum_h \mathbf{x}_h^* \leqq \sum_h \bar{\mathbf{x}}_h + \sum_f \mathbf{y}_f^*$;

(c) $\mathbf{y}_f^*$ maximizes $\mathbf{p}^* \mathbf{y}_f$ subject to $\mathbf{y}_f \in Y_f$;

(d) $\mathbf{x}_h^*$ minimizes $\mathbf{p}^* \mathbf{x}_h$ subject to $U_h(\mathbf{x}_h) \geqq u_h^*$;

(e) $\mathbf{p}^* \mathbf{x}_h^* = M_h^*$.

From the previous remarks, we note:

LEMMA 1. *If* $(\mathbf{p}^*, \mathbf{x}_h^*, \mathbf{y}_f^*)$ *constitute a competitive equilibrium and* $u_h^* = U_h(\mathbf{x}_h^*)$*, all h, then* $(\mathbf{p}^*, u_h^*, \mathbf{x}_h^*, \mathbf{y}_f^*)$ *constitute a compensated equilibrium. If*

$(\mathbf{p}^*, u_h^*, \mathbf{x}_h^*, \mathbf{y}_f^*)$ constitute a compensated equilibrium and if $M_h^* > 0$, all h, then $(\mathbf{p}^*, u_h^*, \mathbf{x}_h^*, \mathbf{y}_f^*)$ constitute a competitive equilibrium.

Hence, to establish the existence of a competitive equilibrium, it suffices to establish the existence of a compensated equilibrium such that $M_h^* > 0$, all h. Two of the conditions stated above together are sufficient to ensure this.

LEMMA 2. *If Assumptions 3 and 7 hold, then $M_h^* > 0$, all h, at a compensated equilibrium, so that it is also a competitive equilibrium.*

The argument runs roughly as follows: At a compensated equilibrium, firms are maximizing profits, by D.2(c). Since the firm can always shut down, by Assumption 1, equilibrium profits must be nonnegative, so that, from (8-2),

(8-3) $$M_h^* \geqq 0, \quad \text{all } h.$$

Also, from profit maximization,

$$\mathbf{p}^* \mathbf{y}_f^* \geqq \mathbf{p}^* \bar{\mathbf{y}}_f,$$

where $\bar{\mathbf{y}}_f$ is the output-input vector for firm f referred to in Assumption 3. Sum over firms f and add $\mathbf{p}^* \bar{\mathbf{x}}$; from (8-2),

$$\sum_h M_h^* = \sum_h (\mathbf{p}^* \bar{\mathbf{x}}_h) + \sum_f \sum_h d_{hf}(\mathbf{p}^* \mathbf{y}_f^*)$$

$$= \mathbf{p}^* \bar{\mathbf{x}} + \sum_f (\mathbf{p}^* \mathbf{y}_f^*) \geqq \mathbf{p}^* \left(\bar{\mathbf{x}} + \sum_f \bar{\mathbf{y}}_f\right),$$

since $\Sigma_h d_{hf} = 1$, by (8-1). But from Assumption 3, all the components of $\bar{\mathbf{x}} + \Sigma_f \bar{\mathbf{y}}_f$ are positive, while from D.2(a), all components of $\mathbf{p}^*$ are nonnegative and at least one positive. Hence,

$$\sum_h M_h^* > 0,$$

which implies

(8-4) $$M_h^* > 0 \quad \text{for some } h = h'', \quad \text{say.}$$

Suppose household h' is resource-related to household h''. Then the assets held by h' are valuable to h'', in the sense that its utility could be made to increase if the h'-assets increased; also h'' has an effective demand, since it has a positive income. It is then reasonable to assert and can be proved rigorously that at least one of the h'-assets must command a positive price. But this means, from (8-2), that $M_h^* > 0$ for $h = h'$. In turn that implies that $M_h^* > 0$ for any h resource-related to h'. Continuing in this way leads to the conclusion that $M_h^* > 0$ for any h indirectly resource-related to h''; but by Assumption 7, that includes every household, so that Lemma 2 holds.

We can therefore confine attention to the existence of a compensated equilibrium. One possible way of proceeding is to make use of the familiar relations between the competitive price system and Pareto efficiency. To simplify the discussion, some notation will be used: an allocation $(\mathbf{x}_h, \mathbf{y}_f)$ will be abbreviated to $\boldsymbol{w}$. The set of all possible allocations will be denoted by $\boldsymbol{W}$; the set of *feasible allocations,* to be denoted by $\hat{\boldsymbol{W}}$, are those for which

$$\sum_h \mathbf{x}_h \leqq \bar{\mathbf{x}} + \sum_f \mathbf{y}_f.$$

Clearly, if $\boldsymbol{w} = (\mathbf{x}_h, \mathbf{y}_f)$ is a feasible allocation, then $(\mathbf{y}_f)$ is a feasible production allocation, since $\mathbf{x}_h \geq \mathbf{0}$, all h. As noted earlier, the set of feasible production allocations is closed, bounded, and convex; from this, it is immediate that

(8-5) $\hat{\boldsymbol{W}}$, the set of feasible allocations, is closed, bounded and convex.

Any feasible allocation $\boldsymbol{w} = (\mathbf{x}_h, \mathbf{y}_f)$ determines a utility level, $u_h = U_h(\mathbf{x}_h)$ for each household. The numbers (u_h) taken as a vector will be termed a *utility allocation,* denoted by $\mathbf{u}$. We define a *Pareto-efficient utility allocation* in a slight variation of the usual manner:

DEFINITION 3. *The utility allocation* $\mathbf{u}$ *is Pareto-efficient if there is no other (feasible) utility allocation,* $\mathbf{u}'$, *such that* $u'_h > u_h$ *for all* h.

By the basic theorem of welfare economics, there is associated with each Pareto-efficient utility allocation, $\mathbf{u}^0$, a price vector, $\mathbf{p}^0$, and a feasible allocation, $\boldsymbol{w}^0 = (\mathbf{x}_h^0, \mathbf{y}_f^0)$, such that:

(a) $\mathbf{p}^0 \geqq \mathbf{0}$, $\mathbf{p}^0 \neq \mathbf{0}$;

(b) $\mathbf{x}_h^0$ minimizes the cost, $\mathbf{p}^0\, \mathbf{x}_h$, of achieving a utility level, $U_h(\mathbf{x}_h)$, at least equal to u_h^0;

(c) $\mathbf{y}_f^0$ maximizes profits, $\mathbf{p}^0\, \mathbf{y}_f$, among production vectors in Y_f;

(d) aggregate expenditure equals aggregate income, that is,

$$\sum_h \mathbf{p}^0\, \mathbf{x}_h^0 = \sum_h \mathbf{p}^0\, \bar{\mathbf{x}}_h + \sum_f \mathbf{p}^0\, \mathbf{y}_f^0.$$

Actually, when there are constant returns to scale and/or production possibility sets formed from finitely many basic activities (the linear programming model), it is not difficult to see that the price vectors and allocations realizing an efficient utility allocation may not be unique. Thus we can state in formal language:

LEMMA 3. *For every Pareto-efficient utility allocation,* $\mathbf{u}^0$, *there is a set of prices,* $P(\mathbf{u}^0)$, *and a set of feasible allocations,* $\hat{W}(\mathbf{u}^0)$, *such that (a)–(d) above hold for every* $\mathbf{p}^0$ *in* $P(\mathbf{u}^0)$ *and* $\mathbf{w}$ *in* $\hat{W}(\mathbf{u}^0)$.

Notice that every price vector in $P(\mathbf{u}^0)$ supports every allocation in $\hat{W}(\mathbf{u}^0)$. It is not hard to observe from this that the sets $P(\mathbf{u}^0)$ and $\hat{W}(\mathbf{u}^0)$ are convex sets.

The lemma associates with each utility vector a set of prices (and similarly a set of allocations). This relation generalizes the usual concept of a function, which associates a number or vector with each vector. A relation which associates a set to each vector is sometimes termed a *set-valued function,* sometimes a *correspondence;* we follow Debreu (1959, sections 1.3, 1.8) in using the latter term here. The concept of continuity is important in dealing with ordinary functions; we will need a generalization of it here.

DEFINITION 4. *A correspondence, which associates the set* $\Phi(\mathbf{x})$ *to the vector* $\mathbf{x}$, *is said to be upper semi-continuous (u.s.c.) if, given a sequence* $\{\mathbf{x}^\nu\}$ *ap-*

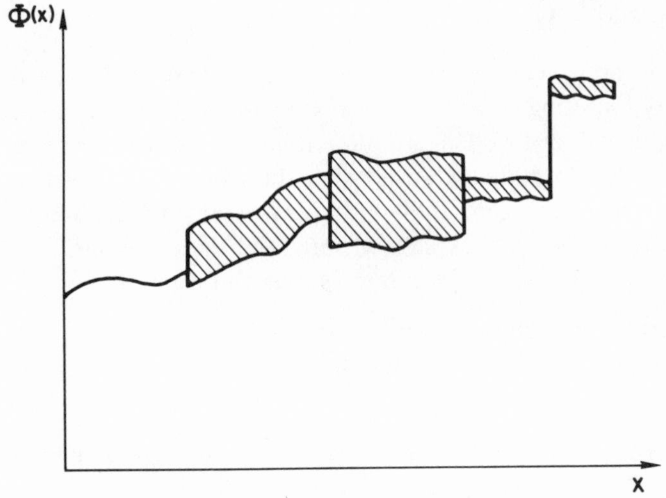

Figure 8.1

proaching $\mathbf{x}^0$ *and a sequence* $\{\mathbf{y}^\nu\}$ *approaching* $\mathbf{y}^0$, *where for each* ν, $\mathbf{y}^\nu$ *is an element of the set* $\Phi(\mathbf{x}^\nu)$ *associated with* $\mathbf{x}^\nu$, *then* $\mathbf{y}^0$ *belongs to* $\Phi(\mathbf{x}^0)$.

Figure 8.1 shows the graph of an upper semicontinuous correspondence where, in addition, $\Phi(\mathbf{x})$ is a convex set (possibly consisting of a single point) for each $\mathbf{x}$.

By straightforward if slightly tedious arguments, it can be shown that:

LEMMA 4. *The correspondences* $P(\mathbf{u})$ *and* $\hat{W}(\mathbf{u})$, *defined in Lemma 3, are u.s.c. and convex for each* $\mathbf{u}$.

Let us go back for a minute to Assumption 5; this guarantees the existence of a minimal consumption vector, $\bar{\bar{\mathbf{x}}}_h$, available to household h at any set of prices whatever. In discussing competitive equilibrium, then, we can confine ourselves to consumption vectors which yield at least as much utility as $\bar{\bar{\mathbf{x}}}_h$. We can assume, with no loss of generality, that

(8-6) $$U_h(\bar{\bar{\mathbf{x}}}_h) = 0,$$

and confine our attention to utility allocations which yield each household utility at least equal to 0. Let, therefore,

(8-7) U be the set of nonnegative Pareto-efficient utility allocations.

For any feasible allocation, $\mathbf{w}$ in $\hat{W}$, and any price vector $\mathbf{p}$, the expenditures of each household, $\mathbf{p}\ \mathbf{x}_h$, and its income, M_h, as given by (8-2), are defined, and hence so is its *budget surplus,*

(8-8) $$s_h(\mathbf{p},\mathbf{w}) = \mathbf{p}\ \mathbf{x}_h - M_h.$$

If we start with an arbitrary price vector and feasible allocation, we will "correct" them by imposing a penalty for violating the budget constraint, that is, for a negative value of s_h. This is done as follows: to each given price vector, $\mathbf{p}$, and feasible allocation, $\mathbf{w}$, we associate the set of all nonnegative utility allocations which yield zero utility for those households with budget deficits. (The correspondence thus defined might be said to punish the improvident while being neutral with regard to others.) Formally, define,

(8-9) $U(\mathbf{p},\mathbf{w})$ is the set of all nonnegative Pareto-efficient utility allocations, $\mathbf{u}$, such that $u_h = 0$ for all households, h, for which $s_h(\mathbf{p},\mathbf{w}) < 0$.

To show the existence of a compensated equilibrium, we use the method of fixed points. That is, we start with a set of values for interesting economic magnitudes (in the present application, prices, utilities, and allocations). To each vector in the set we associate a vector in the set, or more generally, a set of vectors which is a subset of the original set. In the terminology we have introduced, we have a correspondence which maps the elements of some set into subsets of that set. Then under certain continuity hypotheses we find that there is at least one point of the set which belongs to the subset into which it is mapped by the correspondence. If the correspondence has been suitably constructed, then it can be shown that its fixed point is in fact the desired compensated equilibrium. The fixed-point theorem used here is that due to the mathematician Kakutani (1941). Kakutani's theorem is in turn derived from the fixed-point theorem of Brouwer. An excellent reasonably elementary exposition of the proof of Brouwer's theorem is to be found in Tompkins (1964); simple self-contained proofs of both theorems are given in Burger (1963, appendix).

LEMMA 5. *(Kakutani's Fixed-Point Theorem.) Let S be a closed, bounded, and convex set and* $\Phi(\mathbf{x})$ *a correspondence defined for* $\mathbf{x}$ *in S and u.s.c. such that, for each* $\mathbf{x}$, $\Phi(\mathbf{x})$ *is nonnull, contained in S, and convex. Then there is some* $\mathbf{x}^0$ such that $\mathbf{x}^0$ *belongs to* $\Phi(\mathbf{x}^0)$.

In our application, the elements of S will be triples $(\mathbf{p}, \mathbf{u}, \boldsymbol{w})$ consisting of price vectors, $\mathbf{p}$, nonnegative Pareto-efficient utility allocations, $\mathbf{u}$ in U (see Assumption 7), and feasible allocations, $\boldsymbol{w}$ in $\hat{\boldsymbol{W}}$. The price vectors are assumed to be nonnegative and to have at least one positive component. Since multiplication of all prices by a positive constant has no economic significance, we can normalize the prices in some convenient way; we choose to make the sum of all prices equal to one. Then define the range of prices to be the set satisfying the conditions:

(8-10) $\quad P$ is the set of price vectors $\mathbf{p}$, with $\mathbf{p} \geqq 0$, and $\sum_i p_i = 1$.

The domain S is then the set of all triples $(\mathbf{p}, \mathbf{u}, \boldsymbol{w})$ with $\mathbf{p}$ in P, $\mathbf{u}$ in U, and $\boldsymbol{w}$ in $\hat{\boldsymbol{W}}$; each of the three components varies independently over its range. The set of all such triples is most conveniently denoted by $P \times U \times \boldsymbol{W}$, and is referred to as the *Cartesian product* of the three sets. More generally, given m sets, $X_1, \ldots, X_m$, their Cartesian product, $X_1 \times X_2 \times \ldots \times X_m$, is the set of all m-tuples of vectors, $(\mathbf{x}_1, \ldots, \mathbf{x}_m)$, such that $\mathbf{x}_1$ belongs to X_1, $\mathbf{x}_2$ to $X_2, \ldots, \mathbf{x}_m$ to X_m.

To each point $(\mathbf{p},\mathbf{u},\boldsymbol{w})$ in $P \times U \times \hat{\boldsymbol{W}}$, we associate a set which is the Cartesian product:

(8-11) $\quad P(\mathbf{u}) \times U(\mathbf{p},\boldsymbol{w}) \times \hat{\boldsymbol{W}}(\mathbf{u})$.

It is easy to see that P is a closed bounded set; since feasible allocations are bounded, by (8-5), it also follows that U is closed and bounded. Hence, the domain $P \times U \times \hat{W}$ is closed and bounded. The set P is convex, and the same is true of $\hat{W}$ by (8-5). It is not necessarily true that U is convex, however; it is after all simply the utility-possibility surface, and its shape is indeed dependent on the choice of the utility indicator for each household, a choice which depends on an arbitrary monotone transformation. For the moment, however, pretend that U is convex.

As asserted in Lemma 4, $P(\mathbf{u})$ and $\hat{W}(\mathbf{u})$ are u.s.c. and convex for each $\mathbf{u}$; they are nonnull by Lemma 3. It is easy to verify that $U(\mathbf{p}, w)$ is nonnull for each $\mathbf{p}$, w, and that it is a u.s.c. correspondence. Pretend again that it is also convex. Then the Cartesian product, (8-11), can easily be verified to be u.s.c. in the variables, $\mathbf{p}$, $\mathbf{u}$, w, and to be nonnull and convex for each set of values of the variables. Then Kakutani's theorem, Lemma 5, assures that there is a fixed point, that is, a triple, $(\mathbf{p}^*, \mathbf{u}^*, w^*)$ such that

$$(\mathbf{p}^*,\mathbf{u}^*,w^*) \quad \text{belongs to} \quad P(\mathbf{u}^*) \times U(\mathbf{p}^*,w^*) \times \hat{W}(\mathbf{u}^*).$$

By definition of a Cartesian product, this is equivalent to the three statements:

(8-12) $\mathbf{p}^*$ belongs to $P(\mathbf{u}^*)$,

(8-13) $\mathbf{u}^*$ belongs to $U(\mathbf{p}^*,w^*)$,

(8-14) w^* belongs to $\hat{W}(\mathbf{u}^*)$.

From (8-12) and (8-14), we can apply Lemma 3. Statements (a)–(c) of Lemma 3 together with the definition of $\hat{W}(\mathbf{u}^*)$ as containing only feasible allocations yield immediately statements (a)–(d) of D.2. It remains only to verify D.2(e). In view of (8-8), this is equivalent to showing that

(8-15) $s_h(\mathbf{p}^*,w^*) = 0$, all h.

On the other hand, statement (d) of Lemma 3 is equivalent to

$$\sum_h s_h(\mathbf{p}^*,w^*) = 0;$$

hence, to prove (8-15) it suffices to show that

(8-16) $s_h(\mathbf{p}^*,w^*) \geqq 0$, all h,

for, if a sum of nonnegative quantities is zero, each must be zero. Suppose then that (8-16) is false:

$$s_h(\mathbf{p}^*,w^*) < 0, \text{ some } h.$$

Then (8-13) and (8-9) together imply that $u_h^* = 0$ for any such h. But D.2(d) has already been demonstrated, that is, at a compensated equilibrium each household is attaining its utility at minimum cost. By our convention (8-6), $u_h^* = 0$ can always be attained by choosing the consumption vector $\bar{\bar{\mathbf{x}}}_h$, and this vector, by Assumption 5, can always be obtained without a budget deficit, so that (8-16) holds and therefore (8-15); condition (e) of D.2 is now verified and the demonstration of the existence of compensated equilibrium completed. From Lemma 2, then, the existence of a competitive equilibrium is now demonstrated.

One loose end remains: the application of Kakutani's theorem seems to require the convexity of U, the set of nonnegative Pareto-efficient allocations, and of $U(\mathbf{p},\mathbf{w})$, as defined in (8-9). We can relate U and $U(\mathbf{p},\mathbf{w})$, however, to convex sets in a straightforward way; the process is illustrated in Figure 8.2. Let V be the set of vectors $\mathbf{v}$, with as many components as households, such that

(8-17) V is the set of vectors $\mathbf{v}$ for which $\mathbf{v} \geqq \mathbf{0}$, $\sum_h v_h = 1$.

It is obvious that $\mathbf{0}$ is not a Pareto-efficient utility allocation. Hence, a line

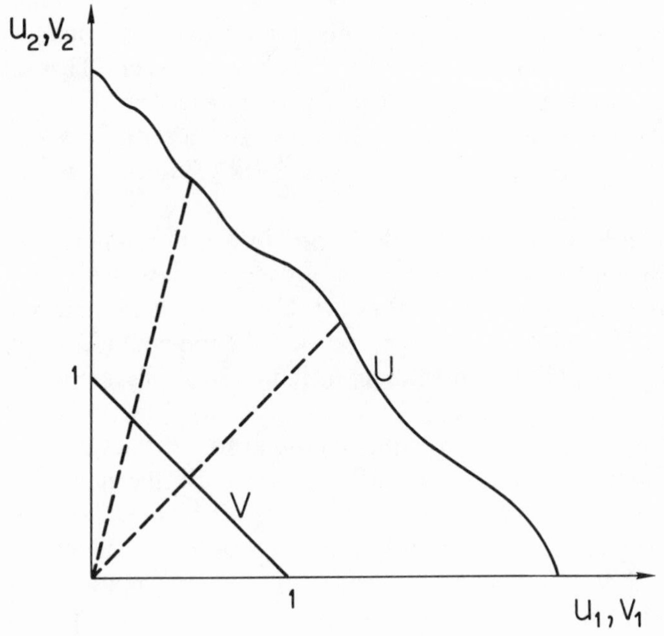

Figure 8.2

drawn from the origin to an element of U intersects V once and only once and can be used to associate a point of V to it. Therefore, selecting an element of U is equivalent to selecting an element of the convex set, V. Further, a member of U for which $u_h = 0$ is associated in this way with a point for which $v_h = 0$. By (8-9), $U(\mathbf{p},\mathbf{w})$ consists precisely of points of U for which $u_h = 0$ for certain h; it is therefore associated with a set, $V(\mathbf{p},\mathbf{w})$, which consists of those points of V for which $v_h = 0$ for the same h. (In Figure 8.2, if $U(\mathbf{p},\mathbf{w})$ is defined by the condition $u_1 = 0$, then it consists of the one point of U on the u_2-axis and is associated with the unique point of V for which $v_1 = 0$.) Then $V(\mathbf{p},\mathbf{w})$ is a convex set.

If then we replace U and $U(\mathbf{p},\mathbf{w})$ by V and $V(\mathbf{p},\mathbf{w})$ in the above mapping, all the conditions of Kakutani's theorem are strictly fulfilled.

The Firm as Price-Maker: Equilibrium under Monopolistic Competition

We now assume that there are some firms in the economy which are capable of exercising monopolistic or monopsonistic power over certain markets. We assume, however, the absence of interaction among the monopolistic firms. Each firm takes the current prices of products not under its control as given and perceives a demand (or supply) function, which may or may not be correct. The perception is made on the basis of observed prices and allocation. It is assumed that, at least at equilibrium, the demand functions are correct at the observed point, though not necessarily elsewhere. That is, for the quantities actually produced, the firm correctly perceives the prices which will clear the markets. However, it is not necessarily assumed that the monopolistic firms correctly perceive the elasticities of demand at the equilibrium point.

A model with these properties was developed in a brilliant paper by Negishi (1960–61) and an existence theorem proved for it, the only previous work of this type known to me. The assumptions made here are much weaker than those of Negishi; comparisons between the present model and earlier models of monopolistic competition, including Negishi's, are made at the end of this section.

The production possibility sets for monopolistic firms need not be convex; indeed, it is presumably the nonconvexity (in particular, the increasing returns to scale) which is the reason for the existence of monopoly. However, it is assumed that the prices charged by monopolistic firms are continuous functions of other prices and other production and consumption decisions. If we assume in the usual way that monopolists are maximizing profits according to their perceived demand curves, then this assumption amounts to saying that the perceived marginal revenue curves fall more sharply than marginal cost curves.

Though we weaken the convexity assumptions on the production possibility sets of the monopolists, we will still need to make some hypotheses which will ensure that the set of feasible production allocations satisfies some reasonable conditions, specifically that it is bounded if resources are bounded and that it is a set which does not break up into several parts or have holes in its middle. The second provision will be expressed more precisely by requiring that the set of those production possibility vectors for the monopolistic sector which are compatible with feasibility for the entire production sector can be expressed as the image of a closed bounded convex set under a continuous mapping.

The assumptions on the competitive sector will remain those made before.

There are then two kinds of firms, competitive and monopolistic. A subscript C will indicate a vector of *all* commodities which is possible for a competitive firm or for the competitive sector as a whole. Similarly, a subscript M will indicate a commodity vector for a monopolistic firm or for all monopolistic firms. Thus Y_{C_f} is the production possibility set for competitive firm f, Y_{M_g} for monopolistic firm g. The production possibility set for the competitive sector as a whole is $Y_C = \Sigma_f Y_{C_f}$, and similarly, $Y_M = \Sigma_g Y_{M_g}$. The elements of these sets are represented by lowercase boldface $\mathbf{y}$ with the appropriate subscripts. A monopolized commodity will of course not be the output of any vector in Y_C, but it may be an input. Also, the term "monopolized" is used to include "monopsonized."

ASSUMPTION 8. *Assumption 1 holds for the sets* Y_{C_f}.

ASSUMPTION 9. $\mathbf{0}$ *belongs to* Y_{M_g} *and* Y_{M_g} *is closed, for each* g.

It is possible to make assumptions parallel to Assumption 2 (impossibility of getting something for nothing) to include the monopolistic firms. To avoid complications, we will simply assume the implication we there drew from this assumption. By a *production allocation* $(\mathbf{y}_{C_f}, \mathbf{y}_{M_g})$ we mean a specification of the production vector for each firm, competitive or monopolistic. A production allocation is *feasible* if

$$\sum_f \mathbf{y}_{C_f} + \sum_g \mathbf{y}_{M_g} + \bar{\mathbf{x}} \geqq \mathbf{0}. \tag{8-18}$$

Then we assume:

ASSUMPTION 10. *The set of feasible production allocations is closed and bounded.*

An *allocation* is, as before, a consumption allocation and a production allocation, that is, a complete specification $(\mathbf{x}_h, \mathbf{y}_{C_f}, \mathbf{y}_{M_g})$.

(8-19) $\hat{W}$ is the set of feasible allocations, that is, those for which

$$\sum_h \mathbf{x}_h \leqq \bar{\mathbf{x}} + \sum_f \mathbf{y}_{C_f} + \sum_g \mathbf{y}_{M_g}.$$

If we continue to assume, as we will, that consumption vectors, $\mathbf{x}_h$, are always nonnegative, then from the definition (8-19) and Assumption 10, it follows immediately that

(8-20) $\hat{W}$ is a closed bounded set.

The concept of feasibility is introduced separately for the competitive sector (including households) and the monopolistic sector. An allocation in the competitive sector, $w_C = (\mathbf{x}_h, \mathbf{y}_{C_f})$ is *feasible* if there exists a monopolistic production allocation (not excluding $\mathbf{0}$) such that the entire allocation $(\mathbf{x}_h, \mathbf{y}_{C_f}, \mathbf{y}_{M_g})$ is feasible. Similarly, a *monopolistic production allocation,* $\mathbf{y}_M = (\mathbf{y}_{M_g})$, is feasible if there exists an allocation in the competitive sector, w_C, such that the entire allocation $(w_C, \mathbf{y}_M)$ is feasible. Let

(8-21) $\hat{W}_C$ be the set of feasible allocations in the competitive sector,

(8-22) $\hat{Y}_M$ be the set of feasible monopolistic production allocations.

Then (8-20) immediately implies:

(8-23) $\hat{W}_C$ is closed and bounded.

(8-24) $\hat{Y}_M$ is closed and bounded.

We now make a basic assumption on the structure of the monopolistic production possibility sets which amounts to saying that the extent of increasing returns there is not too great relative to the resources that the competitive sector would be capable of supplying. Let

$$\mathbf{z}_C = \sum_h \mathbf{x}_h - \bar{\mathbf{x}} - \sum_f \mathbf{y}_{C_f}$$

be any possible excess demand vector of the competitive sector, and Z_C be the set of such $\mathbf{z}_C$. In effect, $-\mathbf{z}_C$ is the vector of amounts made available to the monopolistic sector by the competitive sector. In general, $\mathbf{z}_C$ may have some positive components which denote net demands by the competitive sector. In particular, those positive components which represent monopolized goods measure demands by the competitive sector on the monopolistic sector. (If there are positive components of $\mathbf{z}_C$ which do not represent monopolized goods then the demands denoted cannot be met at all, and $\mathbf{z}_C$ certainly corresponds to an infeasible allocation.) For simplicity, suppose there is only one monopolistic firm and let Y_M be its production possibility set. Then from the definition of feasibility (8-19), $\mathbf{y}_M$ is feasible if and only if

(8-25) $\quad \mathbf{y}_M$ belongs to Y_M, $\quad \mathbf{y}_M \geqq \mathbf{z}_C$ for some $\mathbf{z}_C$ in Z_C.

For only one monopolistic firm, a monopolistic production allocation is simply the production vector for that firm, so that (8-25) characterizes the set of feasible monopolistic production allocations, $\hat{Y}_M$.

For simplicity, assume that there is free disposal in both the monopolistic and the competitive sectors. Then (8-25) states that $\hat{Y}_M$ is simply the intersection of the two sets, Y_M, the monopolist's production possibility set, and Z_C, the feasible excess demand vectors of the competitive sector. The set Z_C is convex by the assumptions made, but Y_M is not in general. The relation among these sets is illustrated in Figure 8.3. If the competitive sector is large relative to the monopolistic, then the set Z_C will tend to be shifted to the left. The intersection, $\hat{Y}_M$, will be "fat." It will then follow that if we inscribe a bounded closed convex set A, for example a sphere, as illustrated, every point of $\hat{Y}_M$ can be projected into some element of the sphere (including its interior) in a continuous way, and conversely every point in $\hat{Y}_M$ is the projection of some point in the sphere. We will make this an assumption, although it can be derived from more primitive assumptions.

ASSUMPTION 11. *There exists a continuous function, say* $\mathbf{y}_M(\mathbf{a})$, *which maps a closed bounded convex set, A, into all points of* $\hat{Y}_M$.

It is worth illustrating that if Z_C is not large relative to Y_M, then Assumption 11 need not hold: see Figure 8.4, which is the same as Figure 8.3 except for the location of the boundary of Z_C. Now $\hat{Y}_M$ breaks up into two parts, and certainly cannot be the continuous image of any one convex set. It is now certainly conceivable that no equilibrium will exist (though no example has been constructed); from an initial allocation corresponding to one area, the monopolist might always be motivated to choose a price which moves demand into the other area. At the very least, the weak assumptions we will

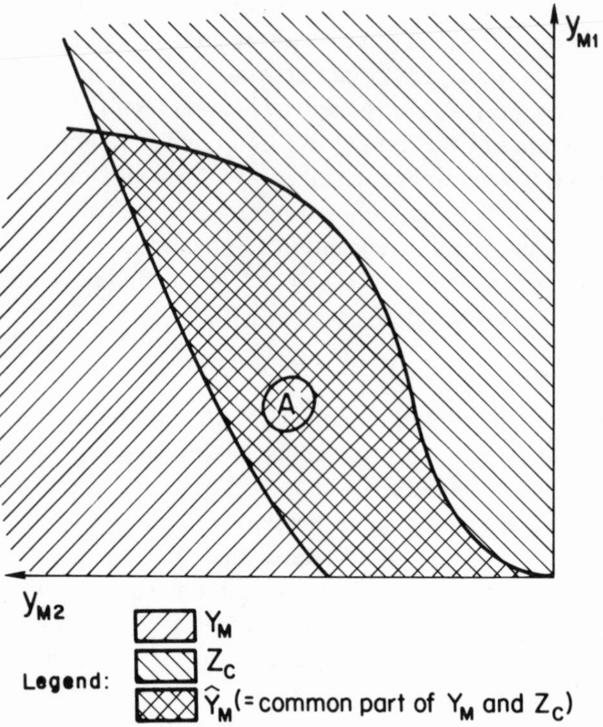

Figure 8.3

make on the monopolist's behavior will not suffice to exclude this possibility.

We now turn to the behavior of the monopolist. As a matter of notation, a superscript M will be used to denote those commodities which are monopolized or monopsonized, the superscript C for the remaining commodities. Thus, $\mathbf{p}^M$ is the vector of prices for the monopolized commodities alone; similarly, if P is a set of prices, P^C is the set of prices for competitive goods which is obtained by deleting from each $\mathbf{p} \in P$ the components corresponding to monopolized goods.

At any given moment, the monopolists observe current prices and the current allocation and (individually) decide on their prices. We do not here make any hypothesis of profit—or utility—maximization, but take their behavior for granted. The only conditions we impose are those indicated at the beginning of this section: monopolists' behavior is a continuous func-

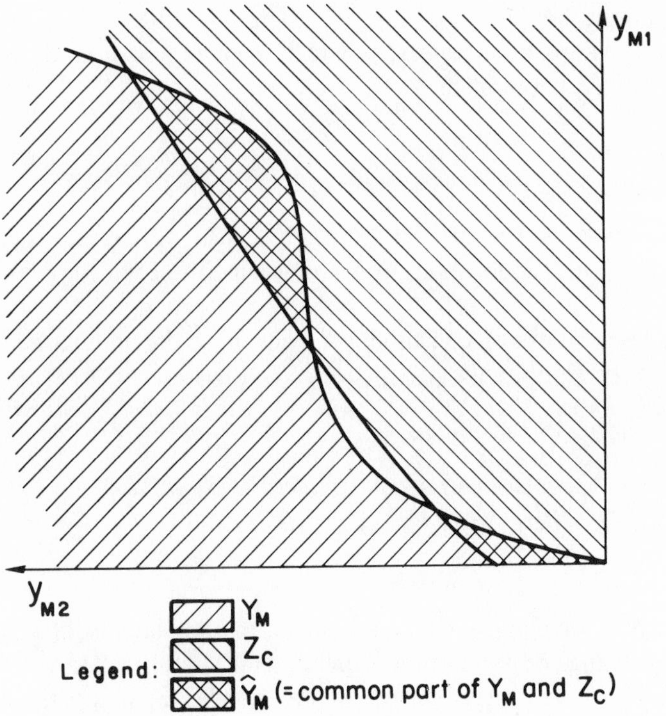

Figure 8.4

tion of their observations, and the monopolist will change prices if his markets are not clearing. The second provision is somewhat complicated to state precisely in a general equilibrium context. We take the following interpretation: suppose that the existing allocation is Pareto-efficient within the competitive sector (that is, taking the supplies and demands of monopolists as given) and that the relative prices of competitive goods correspond to a set of all prices which would sustain this allocation. Then if the entire set of prices (for monopolistic as well as competitive goods) will not sustain this allocation, the monopolistic prices (or at least one of them) will change. (A price vector is said to *sustain* a given allocation in the competitive sector if the production vector of each firm in the allocation is profit-maximizing at the given set of prices and the consumption vector of each household is utility-maximizing under the appropriate budget constraint at the given set of prices.)

Before stating the assumption, we need some further notation. For any fixed monopolistic production allocation, y_M, there is a range of feasible allocations for the competitive sectors, provided $\mathbf{y}_M \in Y_M$, namely those allocations, $w_C = (\mathbf{x}_h, \mathbf{y}_C)$, for which

$$\sum_h \mathbf{x}_h \leqq \sum_f \mathbf{y}_{C_f} + \bar{\mathbf{x}} + \sum_g \mathbf{y}_{M_g};$$

the productive activity of the monopolistic sector can be treated as a modification of the initial endowment from the viewpoint of the competitive sector.

We repeat the assumptions on consumer behavior in the previous section and add one mild condition:

ASSUMPTION 12. *Assumptions 4–6 hold.*

ASSUMPTION 13. *No household is satiated in competitive goods alone, that is, for every* $\mathbf{x}_h = (\mathbf{x}_h^C, \mathbf{x}_h^M)$, *there exists* $\mathbf{x}_h^{C\prime}$, *such that*

$$U_h(\mathbf{x}_h^{C\prime}, \mathbf{x}_h^M) > U_h(\mathbf{x}_h) = U_h(\mathbf{x}_h^C, \mathbf{x}_h^M).$$

For fixed $\mathbf{y}_M$, then, we can use the arguments of the previous section to note that there is a range of nonnegative Pareto-efficient utility allocations $U(\mathbf{y}_M)$, and, for each $\mathbf{u}$ in $U(\mathbf{y}_M)$, a set of Pareto-efficient competitive allocations, to be denoted by $\hat{W}_C(\mathbf{u}, \mathbf{y}_M)$, and a set of price vectors which sustain these allocations, $P_C(\mathbf{u}, \mathbf{y}_M)$. The "Pareto efficiency" in question has to do only with allocation within the competitive sector for any given production behavior on the part of the monopolistic sector, and in no way implies the obviously false proposition that the allocation as a whole is Pareto-efficient. Similarly, the price vectors in $P_C(\mathbf{u}, \mathbf{y}_M)$ only sustain the given allocation as far as the behavior of the competitive sector is concerned.

In accordance with our conventions about superscripts, the set $P_C^C(\mathbf{u}, \mathbf{y}_M)$ is obtained by considering only those components of the price vectors in $P_C(\mathbf{u}, \mathbf{y}_M)$ which represent prices of competitive commodities. Then our assumption about the pricing behavior of the monopolistic sector reads:

ASSUMPTION 14. *The prices charged by the monopolistic sector form a continuous function,* $\mathbf{p}^M(\mathbf{p}, w)$, *of prices and allocation. If* $\mathbf{p} = (\mathbf{p}^C, \mathbf{p}^M)$ *and* $w = (\mathbf{x}_h, \mathbf{y}_{C_f}, \mathbf{y}_{M_g})$ *have the properties that, for some* $\mathbf{u}$ *in* $U(\mathbf{y}_M)$,

$$\mathbf{p}^C = \lambda \mathbf{p}^{C\prime} \text{ for some } \lambda \geqq 0 \text{ and some } \mathbf{p}^{C\prime} \text{ in } P_C^C(\mathbf{u}, \mathbf{y}_M),$$

$$w_C = (\mathbf{x}_h, \mathbf{y}_{C_f}) \textit{ belongs to } \hat{W}_C(\mathbf{u}, y_M),$$

but

$$\mathbf{p} \textit{ does not belong to } P_C(\mathbf{u}, y_M),$$

then

$$\mathbf{p}^M(\mathbf{p}, w) \neq \mathbf{p}^M.$$

It is further assumed that, if $\mathbf{p}^M(\mathbf{p}, w) = \mathbf{p}^M$, *then* $\mathbf{p}\ \mathbf{y}_{M_g} \geqq 0$, *all g, and that the sum of prices charged by monopolists does not exceed 1.*

The next-to-last clause means that if monopolists are satisfied with their existing prices, they are not operating at a loss; the last clause means that monopolists, even though they make their decisions independently, will not, in total, demand more than is compatible with the normalization of prices.

Note that, from Assumption 13, the prices of competitive commodities cannot all be zero if they sustain efficient allocation within the competitive sector.

(8-26) For any y_M and any $\mathbf{u}$ in $U(y_M)$, $\mathbf{p}^C \neq \mathbf{0}$ for any $\mathbf{p}$ in $P_C(\mathbf{u}, y_M)$.

Finally, we make an assumption corresponding to Assumption 3, the ability of the economy to produce a positive amount of every good. We apply it, however, to the behavior of the competitive sector under the assumption that the monopolistic sector is not operating.

ASSUMPTION 15. *It is possible to choose* $\bar{\mathbf{y}}_{C_f}$ *from* Y_{C_f} *for each f so that* $\Sigma_f \bar{\mathbf{y}}_{C_f} + \bar{\mathbf{x}}$ *is strictly positive in every component representing a competitive commodity and zero in every component representing a monopolized commodity.*

In defining equilibrium for monopolistic competition, we must provide for the distribution of monopolistic profits to households. Hence, the income of the household is now given by

(8-27) $$M_h = \mathbf{p}\ \bar{\mathbf{x}}_h + \sum_f d^C_{hf}(\mathbf{p}\ \mathbf{y}_{C_f}) + \sum_g d^M_{hg}(\mathbf{p}\ \mathbf{y}_{M_g}),$$

where d^C_{hf} is the share of household h in the profits of competitive firm f and d^M_{hg} is the share of household h in the profits of monopolistic firm g, so that

$$d^C_{hf} \geq 0, \qquad d^M_{hg} \geq 0, \qquad \sum_h d^C_{hf} = 1, \qquad \sum_h d^M_{hg} = 1,$$

and therefore

$$\text{(8-28)} \qquad \sum_h M_h = \mathbf{p}\,\bar{\mathbf{x}} + \mathbf{p}\left(\sum_g \mathbf{y}_{C_f}\right) + \mathbf{p}\left(\sum_g \mathbf{y}_{M_g}\right).$$

DEFINITION 5. *A price vector, $\mathbf{p}^*$, and an allocation, $\boldsymbol{w}^* = (\mathbf{x}^*_h, \mathbf{y}^*_{C_f}, \mathbf{y}^*_{M_g})$, constitute a monopolistic competitive equilibrium if:*

(a) $\mathbf{p}^* \geqq 0$ and $\mathbf{p}^* \neq 0$;
(b) $\Sigma_h \mathbf{x}^*_h \leqq \Sigma_h \bar{\mathbf{x}}_h + \Sigma_f \mathbf{y}^*_{C_f} + \Sigma_g \mathbf{y}^*_{M_g}$;
(c) $\mathbf{y}^*_{C_f}$ maximizes $\mathbf{p}^* \mathbf{y}_{C_f}$ subject to $\mathbf{y}_{C_f}$ in Y_{C_f};
(d) $\mathbf{x}^*_h$ maximizes $U_h(\mathbf{x}_h)$ subject to $\mathbf{p}^* \mathbf{x}_h \leqq M^*_h$
$= \mathbf{p}^* \bar{\mathbf{x}}_h + \Sigma_f d^C_{hf}(\mathbf{p}^* \mathbf{y}^*_{C_f}) + \Sigma_g d^M_{hg}(\mathbf{p}^* \mathbf{y}^*_{M_g})$;
(e) $\mathbf{p}^{M*} = \mathbf{p}^M(\mathbf{p}^*, \boldsymbol{w}^*)$.

As in the previous section, it is convenient to demonstrate first the existence of a closely related type of equilibrium.

DEFINITION 6. *A price vector, $\mathbf{p}^*$, utility allocation, $\mathbf{u}^*$, and an allocation $\boldsymbol{w}^* = (\mathbf{x}^*_h, \mathbf{y}^*_{C_f}, \mathbf{y}^*_{M_g})$ constitute a compensated monopolistic equilibrium if (a), (b), (c), and (e) of D.5 hold, and, in addition,*

(d′) $\mathbf{x}^*_h$ minimizes $\mathbf{p}^* \mathbf{x}_h$ subject to $U_h(\mathbf{x}_h) \geqq u^*_h$;
(f) $\mathbf{p}^* \mathbf{x}^*_h = M^*_h$.

We now construct the mapping used to prove the existence of compensated monopolistic equilibrium.

An allocation, $\boldsymbol{w}$, specifies in particular a monopolistic production allocation, $\boldsymbol{y}_M$. Start, then, with an allocation, $\boldsymbol{w}$, a utility allocation $\mathbf{u}$ which is Pareto-efficient in the competitive sector for the given $\boldsymbol{y}_M$, that is, an element of $U(\boldsymbol{y}_M)$, and a price vector, $\mathbf{p}$. We form a set of price vectors associated with this triple as follows. The monopolistic components are assumed given by $\mathbf{p}^M(\mathbf{p}, \boldsymbol{w})$. For the given $\mathbf{u}$ and $\boldsymbol{y}_M$, the set $P_C(\mathbf{u}, \boldsymbol{y}_M)$ contains all vectors which would sustain that utility allocation in the competitive sector. For each $\mathbf{p}$ in $P_C(\mathbf{u}, \boldsymbol{y}_M)$, consider the corresponding vector, $\mathbf{p}^C$, containing just those components which represent competitive goods. By (8-26), $\mathbf{p}^C \neq \mathbf{0}$. Hence, each such vector can be rescaled so that, with the given monopolistic components, the final price vector satisfies the normalization condition that the sum of all prices (monopolistic and competitive) equals one (the last clause of Assumption 14 is also needed here). Formally,

(8-29) $\tilde{P}(\mathbf{u},\mathbf{p},\boldsymbol{w})$ is the set of all vectors $\mathbf{p}$ such that $\mathbf{p}^M = \mathbf{p}^M(\mathbf{p},\boldsymbol{w})$, $\mathbf{p}^C = \lambda \mathbf{p}^{C\prime}$ for some $\lambda \geqq 0$ and some $\mathbf{p}^{C\prime}$ in $P^C_{\mathcal{E}}(\mathbf{u},\boldsymbol{y}_M)$, and $\sum_i p_i = 1$.

Here, $\boldsymbol{y}_M$ are the monopolistic production components of $\boldsymbol{w}$, and $\mathbf{u}$ belongs to $U(\boldsymbol{y}_M)$. Now define

(8-30) $s_h(\mathbf{p},\boldsymbol{w}) = \mathbf{p}\ \mathbf{x}_h - M_h(\mathbf{p},\boldsymbol{w})$,

where M_h is defined by (8-27), and, as in the previous section, let

(8-31) $U(\mathbf{p},\boldsymbol{w})$ be the set of utility allocations in $U(\boldsymbol{y}_M)$ such that $u_h = 0$ if $s_h(\mathbf{p},\boldsymbol{w}) < 0$.

Define P as before (see (8-10)). We start now with the quadruples $(\mathbf{p},\mathbf{u},\boldsymbol{w}_C,\mathbf{a})$, where $\mathbf{p}$ belongs to P, $\mathbf{u}$ to $U(\boldsymbol{y}_M)$, $\boldsymbol{w}_C$ to $\hat{\boldsymbol{W}}_C$, and $\mathbf{a}$ to A. The set A has been introduced in Assumption 11. It will be recalled that $\boldsymbol{w}_C$ is an allocation in the competitive sector. From Assumption 11, $\mathbf{a}$ defines a monopolistic production allocation, $\boldsymbol{y}_M(\mathbf{a})$ in $\hat{\boldsymbol{Y}}_M$, so that $\boldsymbol{w}_C$ and $\mathbf{a}$, together, define an allocation, $\boldsymbol{w}$. Then the quadruple $(\mathbf{p},\mathbf{u},\boldsymbol{w}_C,\mathbf{a})$ is mapped into the Cartesian product

$$\tilde{P}(\mathbf{u},\mathbf{p},\boldsymbol{w}) \times U(\mathbf{p},\boldsymbol{w}) \times \hat{\boldsymbol{W}}_C(\mathbf{u},\boldsymbol{y}_M) \times \{\mathbf{a}\},$$

where $\{\mathbf{a}\}$ consists of the single point, $\mathbf{a}$. Kakutani's theorem can then be applied to show the existence of a fixed point $(\mathbf{p}^*, \mathbf{u}^*, \boldsymbol{w}^*_C, \mathbf{a}^*)$. Some difficult points in the proof are noted below. Let

(8-32) $\boldsymbol{y}^*_M = \boldsymbol{y}_M(\mathbf{a}^*), \qquad \boldsymbol{w}^* = (\boldsymbol{w}^*_C, \boldsymbol{y}^*_M)$.

By construction, $\mathbf{u}^*$ is Pareto-efficient in the competitive sector for the given $\boldsymbol{y}^*_M$. By definition of a fixed point,

(8-33) $\mathbf{p}^*$ belongs to $\tilde{P}(\mathbf{u}^*,\mathbf{p}^*,\boldsymbol{w}^*)$,

(8-34) $\mathbf{u}^*$ belongs to $U(\mathbf{p}^*,\boldsymbol{w}^*)$,

(8-35) $\boldsymbol{w}^*_C$ belongs to $\hat{\boldsymbol{W}}_C(\mathbf{u}^*,\boldsymbol{y}^*_M)$.

From the definition of $\tilde{P}(\mathbf{u},\mathbf{p},\boldsymbol{w})$ in (8-29), (8-33) states that

$$\mathbf{p}^{C*} = \lambda \mathbf{p}^{C\prime} \text{ for some } \lambda \geqq 0 \text{ and some } \mathbf{p}^{C\prime} \text{ in } P^C_{\mathcal{E}}(\mathbf{u}^*, \boldsymbol{y}^*_M),$$

and

(8-36) $\mathbf{p}^{M*} = \mathbf{p}^M(\mathbf{p}^*,\boldsymbol{w}^*)$.

From Assumption 14, (8-35) and (8-36) could not both hold if $\mathbf{p}^*$ did not belong to $P_C(\mathbf{u}^*,\boldsymbol{y}_M^*)$. Hence

(8-37) $\quad \mathbf{p}^*$ belongs to $P_C(\mathbf{u}^*,\boldsymbol{y}_M^*)$.

Now (8-37) and (8-35) together show that the fixed-point allocation and prices indeed define a Pareto-efficient allocation within the competitive sector. From Lemma 3 of the previous section, it follows, as in that section, that conditions (a), (b), (c), and (d′) of D.6 hold, while (8-36) asserts that (e) holds.

From (8-30) and (8-34) it follows, just as in the previous section, that

$$s_h(\mathbf{p}^*,\boldsymbol{w}^*) = 0 \quad \text{for all } h,$$

so that D.6(f) also holds. Thus, $(\mathbf{p}^*,\mathbf{u}^*,\boldsymbol{w}^*)$ form a compensated monopolistic equilibrium.

The difficult points in applying Kakutani's theorem, referred to above, are the following:

(1) The range of the variable $\mathbf{u}$ now depends on $\boldsymbol{y}_M$, since we assume $\mathbf{u}$ belongs to $U(\boldsymbol{y}_M)$; also, as in the previous section, the range need not be a convex set. This can be met by extending the device used there; for each $\boldsymbol{y}_M$, the set $U(\boldsymbol{y}_M)$ can be mapped into a set V for which

$$\mathbf{v} \geqq \mathbf{0}, \qquad \sum_h \mathrm{v}_h = 1.$$

Since $\mathbf{a}$ defines $\boldsymbol{y}_M = \boldsymbol{y}_M(\mathbf{a})$, $\mathbf{a}$ and $\mathbf{v}$ together define $\mathbf{u}$ in $U(\boldsymbol{y}_M)$, the correspondence used above can be considered as defined on $P \times V \times \hat{\boldsymbol{W}}_C \times A$, where P, V, and A are closed bounded convex sets. Similarly, any $\mathbf{u}$ in $U(\mathbf{p},\boldsymbol{w})$ can be mapped into a member of V, with the property that $\mathrm{v}_h = 0$ if and only if $u_h = 0$; it is not difficult to see that $V(\mathbf{p},\boldsymbol{w})$, so defined, is convex.

(2) The set $\hat{\boldsymbol{W}}_C$ is not necessarily convex; we recall that it is the set of allocations in the competitive sector which are feasible for *some* monopolistic production allocation; since the set of monopolistic production allocations is not in general convex, neither is $\hat{\boldsymbol{W}}_C$ in general. However, the image set $\hat{\boldsymbol{W}}_C(\mathbf{u},\boldsymbol{y}_M)$ is always convex. Hence, all that is needed is to pick for the domain of definition a closed bounded convex set of competitive allocations containing $\hat{\boldsymbol{W}}_C$.

From (8-26), (8-28), and Assumption 15 it follows, just as in the previous section, that

$$\sum_h M_h^* > 0.$$

We can define resource-relatedness and indirect resource-relatedness as in the previous section with respect to the competitive sector alone, for any given feasible monopolistic production allocation (which affects the competitive sector as if it were a change in initial endowment).

ASSUMPTION 16. *Every household is indirectly resource-related to every other for any given feasible monopolistic production allocation.*

Then by the argument already given in the previous section, a compensated monopolistic equilibrium is a monopolistic competitive equilibrium.

THEOREM. *Under Assumptions 8–16, a monopolistic competitive equilibrium exists.*

Remark 1. The model presented here is a formalization of Chamberlin's case of monopolistic competition with large numbers (1956, pp. 81–100; originally published in 1933). As Triffin (1940) showed, the essential aspects of monopolistic competition appear as soon as one attempts to introduce some monopolies into a system of general competitive equilibrium. The only previous complete formalization is that of Negishi (1960–61). Negishi assumed that each monopolist produced only one commodity and maximized profits according to a perceived demand curve which was a function of all prices and the allocation but was in particular linear (or piecewise linear) in the price of the commodity. He saw the importance of a formulation of the type of Assumption 14 here, that at equilibrium the monopolist's perceived demand curve should at least pass through the observed price-quantity point. In his formulation, which was originally suggested by Bushaw and Clower (1957, p. 181), the monopolist's price equaled the given one if at the given allocation, supply and demand were equal for that commodity. The assumption made here is considerably weaker, since it need only hold if the competitive sector is in equilibrium. Also Negishi restricted attention to the case where the monopolists have convex production possibility sets, a severe condition since under those circumstances the occurrence of monopoly is unlikely, as Negishi himself noted (p. 199, middle). He raised the possibility of more general assumptions, similar to Assumption 11.

Remark 2. No explicit mention has been made of product differentiation, a central theme of monopolistic competition theory. But note that the model admits the possibility that any monopolistic firm can produce a variety of goods. Suppose that all conceivable goods are included in the list of commodities; even what are usually regarded as varieties of the same good must be distinguished in this list if they are not perfect substitutes in both production and consumption. A monopolist will, in general, find it profitable to produce a number of varieties. The definition of a monopoly implies that, for some reason or another, two different monopolists produce non-overlapping sets of goods, but of course the goods produced by one monopolist may be quite close substitutes for those produced by another. The usual idea in product differentiation that a firm produces just one commodity is not a convenient assumption for general equilibrium analysis, but it is equally certainly not a good description of the real world.

Remark 3. The notion of free entry and with it the famous double-tangency solution of Chamberlin and Robinson (1933, pp. 93–94) have no role here either. The list of monopolists is assumed given, so that in effect there is a scarcity of the appropriate type of entrepreneurship, and there is no reason for profits to be wiped out. No doubt if there are several firms producing products which are close substitutes in consumption and have very similar production possibility sets otherwise, they should behave about the same way, and, if there are enough of them, it may well be that each is making very little in the way of profit. But the question then is the one raised originally by Kaldor (1935): would not the elasticity of demand to the individual firm be essentially zero, so that the situation is essentially one of perfect competition? It cannot be said that this question has been fully answered, since a more specific model defining close substitutes and their production possibilities has not yet been explicitly formulated.[1]

Remark 4. An open and potentially important research area is the specification of conditions under which monopolistic behavior, as expressed in the function, $\mathbf{p}^M(\mathbf{p},w)$, is in fact continuous. The formulation is very general; it is certainly compatible with utility-maximizing behavior (for example, preference for size or particular kinds of expenditures or products) as well as profit-maximizing behavior. However, the assumption of continuity may nevertheless be strong; in effect, it denies the role of increasing returns as a barrier to entry. As the demand shifts upward, the firm might pass from zero output (that is, a purely potential existence) to a minimum positive output.

1. As Robin Marris has pointed out to me, the above discussion presupposes the absence of oligopolistic interdependence, which may well be, in fact, the most likely outcome when there are extremely close substitutes. But the argument was directed against the likely validity of the double tangency solution, which has not hitherto been derived from an assumption of oligopoly.

A zero output must be interpreted as a price decision at a level corresponding to zero demand; but if the demand curve is downward-sloping, then entry at a positive level far removed from zero implies a discontinuous drop in price. The importance of this problem is not easy to assess. The situation can only arise if the (perceived) marginal revenue curve is, broadly speaking, flatter than the marginal cost curve, otherwise entry would be a continuous phenomenon; but then the demand curve must also be relatively flat and therefore the price discontinuity may be mild even if the output discontinuity is large. Also, if there were only a single monopolist who correctly perceived the excess demand correspondence of the competitive sector, he could choose his most preferred point, which would then be an equilibrium; the discontinuity of his behavior would be irrelevant. However, the problem may be important if his perceptions are accurate only at equilibrium or if there are several monopolists; the discontinuity in the behavior of any one affects the perceived demand functions for the others, though again, if the monopolists are relatively separated in markets and each relatively small on the scale of the economy, then the discontinuities involved may be unimportant.

Remark 5. It must always be remembered that monopolistic competition models of the type discussed here ignore the mutual recognition of power among firms, the oligopoly problem.

The Firm as Forecaster: The Existence of Temporary Equilibrium

Hicks (1939, pp. 130–133) introduced the analysis of temporary equilibrium; a more recent methodological discussion is to be found in Hicks (1965, chap. 6). To interpret general equilibrium theory in the context of time, the formally simplest procedure is to regard commodities at different points of time as different commodities. But then we immediately encounter the somewhat unpleasant fact that the markets for most of these commodities do not exist. Since production and consumption both have important dynamic elements, individual agents replace the nonexistent prices for future commodities by expectations (certain or probabilistic). Given these expectations, equilibrium on current markets alone is arrived at (we here neglect the relatively few futures markets). There is, however, at least one current market in addition to those for the usual commodities, namely a market for bonds, to permit individuals to have planned expenditure patterns over time which differ from their income patterns.

We now understand that the components of the possible production and consumption vectors extend over several periods of time. For simplicity, we confine ourselves to two periods, present and future. We assume that the only commodities traded in currently are commodities of the current period plus bonds; a unit bond is a promise to pay one unit of the currency of account in the next period. Let the subscript, b, refer to bonds. We use here the notation $\mathbf{x}^1$ to refer to commodities of the current period, $\mathbf{x}^2$ to those of the future period, and $\mathbf{x}$ to be the vector of commodities currently traded in by households; thus, $\mathbf{x} = (\mathbf{x}^1, x_b)$, *not* $\mathbf{x} = (\mathbf{x}^1, \mathbf{x}^2)$. Similarly, for firms, $\mathbf{y} = (\mathbf{y}^1, y_b)$, where y_b is the supply of bonds issued by firms, and $\mathbf{p} = (\mathbf{p}^1, p_b)$ is the vector of prices on current markets.

Before going into details, the main difficulties in applying the methods of the second section and the strategy for overcoming them will be discussed. The modifications to be made to the definition of and assumptions on the production sets are straightforward except for one particular. Consider some one firm. Its production plan for the future has consequences in current markets because it affects the current value of the firm and the amount it will now borrow. But since there is no current market for the resources of the subsequent period, the availability of resources then cannot be used to argue that production plans are bounded. This creates obvious difficulties, which, however, are partly academic, since one could argue that a firm is "realistic enough" not to plan indefinitely large production. However, it is preferable to incorporate the argument from realism into our construction in a way more in the spirit of the perfectly competitive model. We do this by insisting that the price expectations of firms be "sensible." This is done in Assumption 18(b) below.

As already noted, the plans for future production must have consequences in current markets. We shall in fact assume that each firm offers in the current bond market a quantity of bonds equal to its expected profit in the future. This means that there is a "current" representation of the future plans, which in turn allows us to incorporate these in the framework of the model of the second section. This is made precise in (8-38) and D.8.

When we come to consumers, a number of special problems arise. First, we must decide what we mean by the initial endowment of bonds held by a household. We simply take it to equal its anticipated receipts of the future period; that is, it represents the maximum the household believes it could repay. Note that the household's anticipated receipts may differ from what any other agent would expect them to be, given the household's plans—that is, we allow for differences in price expectations.

The differences in expectations, however, also mean that different households will value any given firm differently. We assume that the actual current market value of any firm is equal to the highest value any agent places on it and suppose that the ownership of the firm will shift to the hands of that household or those households which value it most highly (D.11 and Assumption 20). We therefore now treat d_{hf}, the share of household h in firm f, as a variable of the equilibrium. All this leads to modifications in the manner in which we must write the households' budget constraints (see (8-47) and (8-52)).

We must also ensure that our assumptions about consumption possibility sets, 4 and 5 of the second section, hold when reinterpreted in terms of the current market. This is fairly straightforward; see Assumption 19, (8-53), and D.12.

Lastly there is the following problem. We know that the household utility depends on its future plans, and in the existence proof of the second section the utilities of the households play an important part. Our procedure of incorporating the expected future into arguments about the present is to use a "derived utility function" (D.13). This will be the maximum utility of the household, given its first-period allocation, under an appropriate budget constraint. It will be obvious that this derived function can be treated as a function of current plans only, which is what we want.

We now proceed to detailed argument. Let us consider the behavior of the firm. We take the viewpoint that the firm is an entity which, on its own, has expectations of future prices and maximizes profits in accordance with them. At the end of this section some comments will be made on this assumption.

We retain the assumptions on the production possibility sets of the individual firms with appropriate changes of notation, and add a hypothesis which embodies the possibility of abandoning a productive enterprise without loss.

DEFINITION 7. *The set of possible two-period production vectors for firm f is Y_f^{12}. An element is denoted by $\mathbf{y}_f^{12} = (\mathbf{y}_f^1, \mathbf{y}_f^2)$, where $\mathbf{y}_f^1$ are the components of $\mathbf{y}_f^{12}$ referring to the first period and $\mathbf{y}_f^2$ those referring to the second period. We also refer to $\mathbf{y}_f^1$ and $\mathbf{y}_f^2$ as first-period and second-period production vectors respectively.*

ASSUMPTION 17. *Assumption 1 of the second section holds with $\mathbf{y}_f$ replaced by $\mathbf{y}_f^{12}$ and Y_f by Y_f^{12}. If $(\mathbf{y}_f^1, \mathbf{y}_f^2) \in Y_f^{12}$, then there exists $\mathbf{y}_f^{2\prime} \geqq \mathbf{0}$ such that $(\mathbf{y}_f^1, \mathbf{y}_f^{2\prime}) \in Y_f^{12}$.*

The firm observes current prices, $\mathbf{p} = (\mathbf{p}^1, p_b)$, and is assumed to have subjectively certain expectations for prices in period 2, $\mathbf{p}_f^2$; since there are no futures markets, different firms may have different expectations. A production plan, $(\mathbf{y}_f^1, \mathbf{y}_f^2)$, yields net revenue $\mathbf{p}^1\ \mathbf{y}_f^1$ in period 1 and is expected to yield net revenue $\mathbf{p}_f^2\ \mathbf{y}_f^2$ in period 2. If bonds sell in period 1 at p_b, then a revenue of $\mathbf{p}_f^2\ \mathbf{y}_f^2$ in period 2 is equivalent on perfect markets to a first-period income of $p_b(\mathbf{p}_f^2\ \mathbf{y}_f^2)$. For simplicity, we will assume that the firm actually sells bonds to the extent of its anticipated second-period income, so that its offering of bonds is

(8-38) $\quad y_{fb} = \mathbf{p}_f^2\ \mathbf{y}_f^2,$

and its current receipts from a given production plan are

(8-39) $\quad \mathbf{p}^1\ \mathbf{y}_f^1 + p_b(\mathbf{p}_f^2\ \mathbf{y}_f^2).$

The firm chooses its production plan so as to maximize (8-39) among all production plans $\mathbf{y}_f^{12} \in Y_f^{12}$. Provisionally, we will assume that all price expectations are totally inelastic, that is, that $\mathbf{p}_f^2$ is a datum for the firm independent of current prices. Then (8-38) maps the elements of Y_f^{12} into a set Y_f of $(n + 1)$-dimensional vectors; in effect, with fixed expectations, the firm's future possibilities amount to its ability to produce bonds for today's market.

DEFINITION 8. *The set of possible current vectors,* $\mathbf{y}_f$, *for firm f is the set derived from* Y_f^{12} *by replacing the second-period components,* $\mathbf{y}_f^2$, *by the single element obtained from them by (8-38), that is,*

Y_f is the set of vectors $\mathbf{y}_f = (\mathbf{y}_f^1, y_{fb})$ such that $y_{fb} = \mathbf{p}_f^2\ \mathbf{y}_f^2$ for some $(\mathbf{y}_f^1, \mathbf{y}_f^2)$ in Y_f^{12}.

It is easy to verify from Assumption 17 that

(8-40) Assumption 1 holds for Y_f under D.8.

That is, $\mathbf{0}$ belongs to Y_f (derived from $\mathbf{y}_f^{12} = \mathbf{0}$); Y_f is closed, and Y_f is convex.

From D.8 and (8-39),

(8-41) the firm maximizes $\mathbf{p}\ \mathbf{y}_f$.

Suppose $p_b > 0$, and the firm has chosen a production plan, $\mathbf{y}_f^{12}$, for which there will be negative receipts in the future, $\mathbf{p}_f^2\ \mathbf{y}_f^2 < 0$. Then by the second half of Assumption 17 it is possible to choose another plan with higher profits.

(8-42) If $p_b > 0$, then $\mathbf{p}_f^2\ \mathbf{y}_f^2 = y_{fb} \geqq 0$ at any profit-maximizing plan.

We now make an assumption about the impossibility of production without inputs and about irreversibility which is somewhat stronger than that obtained by simply replacing $\mathbf{y}_f$ by $\mathbf{y}_f^{12}$ and Y_f by Y_f^{12} in Assumption 2. The reason the stronger assumption is needed is that future resource limitations do not directly restrain production, since there are no futures markets on which they appear. We do still have the constraints on first-period resources and in addition we will, in accordance with (8-42), restrict ourselves at certain stages in the argument to plans for which $\mathbf{p}_f^2\, \mathbf{y}_f^2 \geqq 0$, since only those will satisfy our equilibrium conditions.

ASSUMPTION 18. (a) *If* $\Sigma_f\, \mathbf{y}_f^1 \geqq \mathbf{0}$, *then* $\mathbf{y}_f^1 = \mathbf{0}$, *all* f. (b) *The future returns to any production plan requiring no first-period inputs are bounded for any firm, that is,* $\mathbf{p}_f^2\, \mathbf{y}_f^2$ *is bounded as* $\mathbf{y}_f^2$ *varies over all two-period production vectors* $(\mathbf{0}, \mathbf{y}_f^2)$ *in* Y_f^{12} *with no current inputs.*

It will be argued that this assumption is not unreasonable. First, it will have to be understood that any factor availabilities in period 1 as the result of earlier production (for example, durable capital goods or maturing agricultural products) are to be included in the initial endowment of current flows, $\bar{\mathbf{x}}^1$. Hence, the absence of net inputs means the absence of capital, labor, and current raw materials; it is reasonable then to conclude that no production takes place in period 1, that is, $\mathbf{y}_f^1 = \mathbf{0}$, all f. As far as (b) is concerned, if it were not true, then a firm could expect indefinitely large profits in the next period even if it were to shut down today. But then the firm would know that its price expectations are not consistent with any equilibrium, and so it is reasonable to argue that it does not hold any such expectations. Thus (b) is really a weak requirement on the rationality of expectations.

It is convenient to define a two-period production allocation, $(\mathbf{y}_f^{12})$, to be *quasi-feasible* if it is first-period feasible and if the second-period components are not unprofitable to any firm (according to its own expectations), that is, if it satisfies the conditions

$$\sum_f \mathbf{y}_f^1 + \bar{\mathbf{x}}^1 \geqq \mathbf{0}, \qquad \mathbf{p}_f^2\, \mathbf{y}_f^2 \geqq 0, \quad \text{each } f.$$

From Assumption 18, it is possible to prove, analogously to the corresponding discussion in the second section, that

(8-43) the set of quasi-feasible two-period production allocations is closed, bounded, and convex.

In the theory of consumer behavior, we apply again the assumptions made earlier to the intertemporal consumption vectors.

DEFINITION 9. *The set of possible two-period consumption vectors for household h is X_h^{12}, with elements $\mathbf{x}_h^{12} = (\mathbf{x}_h^1, \mathbf{x}_h^2)$, the components being referred to as the first-period and second-period possible consumption vectors, respectively.*

ASSUMPTION 19. *Assumptions 4, 5, and 6 hold under D.9 with $\mathbf{x}_h$, $\bar{\mathbf{x}}_h$, $\bar{\bar{\mathbf{x}}}_h$, and X_h replaced by $\mathbf{x}_h^{12}$, $\bar{\mathbf{x}}_h^{12}$, $\bar{\bar{\mathbf{x}}}_h^{12}$, and X_h^{12} respectively. We also assume that $U_h(\mathbf{x}_h^1, \mathbf{x}_h^2)$ is not satiated in $\mathbf{x}_h^2$ for any $\mathbf{x}_h^1$.*

Like the firm, the household knows current prices, including that of bonds, and anticipates second-period prices, $\mathbf{p}_h^2$. It plans purchases and sales for both periods. In each period there is a budgetary constraint. The two constraints are linked through the purchase of bonds, which constitute an expense in period 1 and a source of purchasing power in period 2 (or vice versa, if the household is a net borrower in period 1). The household can be considered to have an initial endowment of bonds, $\bar{x}_{hb}$, which is precisely its anticipated volume of receipts in period 2. The net purchase of bonds in period 1 is then denoted by $x_{hb} - \bar{x}_{hb}$. Total expenditures for goods and bonds in period 1 are $\mathbf{p}^1 \mathbf{x}_h^1 + p_b(x_{hb} - \bar{x}_{hb})$, while planned expenditures in period 2 are $\mathbf{p}_h^2 \mathbf{x}_h^2$.

The purchasing power available in period 1 is the sum of the sale of endowment, $\mathbf{p}^1 \bar{\mathbf{x}}_h^1$, and receipts from firms in that period. The planned receipts in period 2 equal the planned sale of endowment, $\mathbf{p}_h^2 \bar{\mathbf{x}}_h^2$, plus receipts from firms in period 2, and this sum equals x_{hb}, as remarked. The purchasing power planned to be available in period 2 is the repayment to the household of its net purchase of bonds, x_{hb} minus $\bar{x}_{hb}$, plus planned receipts, and is therefore simply x_{hb}.

There is a feature in this model not present in the static model or its intertemporal analogue with all futures markets. Since different households hold different expectations of future prices, they have different expectations of the profitability of any particular firm. Hence, a market for shares in firms will arise; the initial stockholders may value the firm less highly than some others, and therefore the stock of the firm should change hands.

After the firm has chosen its production plan, $\mathbf{y}_f^{12}$, household h values the plan according to current prices and its expectations of future prices.

DEFINITION 10. *The capital value of firm f according to household h is*

$$K_{hf}(\mathbf{p}, \mathbf{y}_f^{12}) = \mathbf{p}^1 \mathbf{y}_f^1 + p_b(\mathbf{p}_h^2 \mathbf{y}_f^2).$$

The value of the firm in the market is the highest value that any household gives to it.

DEFINITION 11. *The market capital value of firm f is*

$$K_f(\mathbf{p},\mathbf{y}_f^{12}) = \max_h K_{hf}(\mathbf{p},\mathbf{y}_f^{12}).$$

We will assume that, for each production plan for each firm, there is at least one household that values the plan at least as highly as the firm itself does; one might rationalize this by noting that the firm's manager is presumably himself the head of a household.

ASSUMPTION 20. *The market capital value of a firm is at least equal to the maximum profits anticipated by the firm itself; in symbols,*

$$K_f(\mathbf{p},\, \mathbf{y}_f^{12}) \geqq \mathbf{p}\ \mathbf{y}_f, \quad \text{for all } \mathbf{p} \text{ and all } \mathbf{y}_f^{12} \in Y_f^{12}.$$

From D.10 and D.11,

$$K_f = \max_h\, [\mathbf{p}^1\ \mathbf{y}_f^1 + p_b(\mathbf{p}_h^2\ \mathbf{y}_f^2)] = \mathbf{p}^1\ \mathbf{y}_f^1 + p_b \max_h\, (\mathbf{p}_h^2\ \mathbf{y}_f^2),$$

since $\mathbf{p}^1\ \mathbf{y}_f^1$ and p_b are independent of h. Let

(8-44) $$K_f^2(\mathbf{y}_f^2) = \max_h\, (\mathbf{p}_h^2\ \mathbf{y}_f^2).$$

If we recall that $\mathbf{p}\ \mathbf{y}_f = \mathbf{p}^1\ \mathbf{y}_f^1 + p_b(\mathbf{p}_f^2\ \mathbf{y}_f^2)$, then Assumption 20 implies

(8-45) $$K_f - \mathbf{p}\ \mathbf{y}_f = p_b(K_f^2 - \mathbf{p}_f^2\ \mathbf{y}_f^2) \geqq 0.$$

Let $\bar{d}_{hf}$ be the share of firm f held initially by household h; we assume that it sells its shares at the market price and buys others—only, however, in those firms which it values at least as highly as any other household. We assume the absence of short sales. Let d_{hf} be its share of firm f after the stock market has operated. Its net receipts from sale less purchase of stocks (possibly negative, of course) are given by

$$\sum_f (\bar{d}_{hf} - d_{hf})K_f.$$

Also,

(8-46) $$d_{hf} = 0 \quad \text{unless} \quad K_{hf} = K_f.$$

It will be recalled that the current receipts of the firm are given by (8-39) or (8-41); it is assumed that they are all distributed among its new owners, so that household h receives

$$\sum_f d_{hf}(\mathbf{p}\ \mathbf{y}_f).$$

Hence, the budget constraint for period 1 reads:

$$\mathbf{p}^1 \mathbf{x}_h^1 + p_b(x_{hb} - \bar{x}_{hb}) \leqq \mathbf{p}^1 \bar{\mathbf{x}}_h^1 + \sum_f d_{hf}(\mathbf{p}\,\mathbf{y}_f) + \sum_f (\bar{d}_{hf} - d_{hf})K_f. \tag{8-47}$$

In period 2, the household is responsible for its share of the bonds issued by firm f, which total $\mathbf{p}_f^2\,\mathbf{y}_f^2$. But according to its expectations, the firm will receive $\mathbf{p}_h^2\,\mathbf{y}_f^2$. From (8-46), the household only invests in firms whose production plans it values at least as highly as anyone else, so that from (8-44) any firm for which $d_{hf} > 0$ will be expected by household h to have second-period receipts K_f^2. Hence, the anticipated total receipts from firms in period 2 by household h will be

$$\sum_f d_{hf}(K_f^2 - \mathbf{p}_f^2\,\mathbf{y}_f^2).$$

From earlier remarks, then,

$$\bar{x}_{hb} = \mathbf{p}_h^2\,\bar{\mathbf{x}}_h^2 + \sum_f d_{hf}(K_f^2 - \mathbf{p}_f^2\,\mathbf{y}_f^2), \qquad \bar{\mathbf{x}}_h = (\bar{\mathbf{x}}_h^1, \bar{x}_{hb}). \tag{8-48}$$

Then

$$\bar{x}_b = \sum_h \bar{x}_{hb} = \sum_h (\mathbf{p}_h^2\,\bar{\mathbf{x}}_h^2) + \sum_f (K_f^2 - \mathbf{p}_f^2\,\mathbf{y}_f^2). \tag{8-49}$$

Note that $\bar{x}_b$ is a function of the $\mathbf{y}_f^2$s, the second-period production allocation. Note also that, from (8-45), the summation terms in (8-48) and (8-49) are nonnegative.

Define now

$$\bar{\bar{x}}_{hb} = \mathbf{p}_h^2\,\bar{\bar{\mathbf{x}}}_h^2, \; \bar{\bar{\mathbf{x}}}_h = (\bar{\bar{\mathbf{x}}}_h^1, \bar{\bar{x}}_{hb}). \tag{8-50}$$

By a slightly tedious but elementary calculation, it can easily be seen that the vector $\bar{\bar{\mathbf{x}}}_h$, defined for current markets, in fact satisfies the conditions of Assumption 5 if Assumption 19 holds.

$$\bar{\mathbf{x}}_h \geqq \bar{\bar{\mathbf{x}}}_h; \quad \text{if} \quad \bar{\bar{x}}_{hi} > 0, \quad \text{then} \quad \bar{x}_{hi} > \bar{\bar{x}}_{hi}. \tag{8-51}$$

As already remarked, the budget constraint for period 2 is simply

$$\mathbf{p}_h^2\,\mathbf{x}_h^2 \leqq x_{hb}. \tag{8-52}$$

We therefore define:

DEFINITION 12. *The set of current consumption vectors, X_h, consists of all vectors, $\mathbf{x}_h = (\mathbf{x}_h^1, x_{hb})$ such that $x_{hb} \geqq \mathbf{p}_h^2\,\mathbf{x}_h^2$ for some $(\mathbf{x}_h^1, \mathbf{x}_h^2)$ in X_h^{12}.*

In other words, X_h is the set of current market vectors which, at the price expectations of the household, permit a possible two-period consumption vector.

From (8-52) and Assumption 19, $x_{hb} \geqq 0$, also $\bar{\bar{\mathbf{x}}}_h$ belongs to X_h. Assumption 19, (8-51), and D.12 then assure us that

(8-53) Assumptions 4 and 5 hold with the new interpretations of $\mathbf{x}_h$, $\bar{\mathbf{x}}_h$, $\bar{\bar{\mathbf{x}}}_h$, X_h (see (8-48), (8-51), and D.12, respectively).

The maximization of $U_h(\mathbf{x}_h^1, \mathbf{x}_h^2)$ subject to the budget constraints (8-47) and (8-52) can be thought of as occurring in two stages. For any given $\mathbf{x}_h = (\mathbf{x}_h^1, x_{hb})$, we can maximize with respect to $\mathbf{x}_h^2$ subject to (8-52); the maximum is now a function of $\mathbf{x}_h^1$ and of x_{hb}, that is, of $\mathbf{x}_h$, with respect to which it can be maximized subject to (8-47).

DEFINITION 13. *First-period derived utility is*

$$U_h^*(\mathbf{x}_h) = \max U_h(\mathbf{x}_h^1, \mathbf{x}_h^2) \quad \text{subject to } \mathbf{p}_h^2 \, \mathbf{x}_h^2 \leqq x_{hb}.$$

We do have to assume that the maximum in D.13 actually exists. The existence depends primarily on $\mathbf{p}_h^2$, the household's anticipations of future prices. It will be assumed that the household is sufficiently realistic for this purpose; this is not an unreasonable assumption since the household would know, from the fact that a maximum does not exist, that the prices could not be equilibrium prices.

ASSUMPTION 21. *For given $\mathbf{x}_h^1$, the function $U_h(\mathbf{x}_h^1, \mathbf{x}_h^2)$ assumes a maximum subject to the constraint $\mathbf{p}_h^2 \, \mathbf{x}_h^2 \leqq x_{hb}$ for any x_{hb} permitting possible second-period consumption, that is, for any $\mathbf{x}_h \in X_h$.*

From Assumption 19, it is easy to see that U_h^* is continuous. It is also true that it is semistrictly quasi-concave and very easy to establish that U_h^* is locally nonsatiated in $\mathbf{x}_h$. By a suitable choice of origin, we can ensure $U_h^*(\bar{\bar{\mathbf{x}}}_h) = 0$.

(8-54) $U_h^*(\mathbf{x}_h)$ is continuous, semistrictly quasi-concave, and admits no local satiation; $U_h^*(\bar{\bar{\mathbf{x}}}_h) = 0$; U_h^* is strictly increasing in x_{hb} for any $\mathbf{x}_h^1$.

These properties, except for the last, are precisely those of U_h as assumed in Assumption 6.

The aim of the household, then, is to maximize U_h^* subject to (8-47), which can be written

(8-55) $$\mathbf{p}\,\mathbf{x}_h \leqq M_h,$$

where

(8-56) $$M_h = \mathbf{p}\,\bar{\mathbf{x}}_h + \sum_f d_{hf}(\mathbf{p}\,\mathbf{y}_f) + \sum_f (\bar{d}_{hf} - d_{hf})K_f(\mathbf{p},\mathbf{y}_f^1,\mathbf{y}_f^2).$$

Another way of writing (8-56) will be useful. First, rewrite it slightly; then note that by our notation, $\mathbf{p}\,\bar{\mathbf{x}}_h = \mathbf{p}^1\,\bar{\mathbf{x}}_h^1 + p_b\,\bar{x}_{hb}$; then substitute from (8-48):

(8-57) $$M_h = \mathbf{p}\,\bar{\mathbf{x}}_h + \sum_f \bar{d}_{hf}(\mathbf{p}\,\mathbf{y}_f) + \sum_f (\bar{d}_{hf} - d_{hf})(K_f - \mathbf{p}\,\mathbf{y}_f)$$
$$= \mathbf{p}^1\,\bar{\mathbf{x}}_h^1 + \sum_f \bar{d}_{hf}(\mathbf{p}\,\mathbf{y}_f) + p_b[\mathbf{p}_h^2\,\bar{\mathbf{x}}_h^2 + \sum_f \bar{d}_{hf}(K_f^2 - \mathbf{p}_h^2\,\mathbf{y}_f^2)].$$

Recall that $K_f - \mathbf{p}\,\mathbf{y}_f = p_b(K_f^2 - \mathbf{p}_f^2\,\mathbf{y}_f^2)$ by (8-45). One important implication of (8-57) is that the actual final share allocation does not affect the household budget constraints and therefore does not affect the equilibrium. The reason is that, since shares in firms are assumed to be sold to those who value them most highly at a price equal to that value, each potential buyer is in fact indifferent between making the purchase and investing in bonds, and none of his other behavior is affected by the choice.

We now have all the threads of the model in hand. Since equilibrium occurs only on current markets, the only relevant prices are those for current commodities and bonds. Basically, the model is very similar to that of static competitive equilibrium; the aim of the firm is to maximize $\mathbf{p}\,\mathbf{y}_f$ subject to $\mathbf{y}_f \in Y_f$, according to (8-41) and D.8, while the consumer aims to maximize a (first-period-derived) utility function subject to a budget constraint (8-55). The feasibility conditions for the current markets have the same form as before; demand for first-period commodities and for bonds shall not exceed supply, including the initial endowment of bonds as defined. However, there are two complications: (1) the budget constraint, using the definition of M_h in (8-57), is somewhat different from that of the second section and more especially contains variables, the $\mathbf{y}_f^2$s, which are not in the standard system; (2) by (8-49) one component of the social endowment vector, namely $\bar{x}_b$, also depends on the $\mathbf{y}_f^2$s.

Let us formally define competitive and compensated temporary equilibrium.

DEFINITION 14. *Competitive and compensated temporary equilibrium are defined as in the second section (see D.1 and D.2) with the notation introduced in this section, except that (1) the variables* $\mathbf{y}_f^2$ *must be consistent with intertemporal profit maximization, (2) the utility functions,* U_h*, are replaced by* U_h^**, and (3) the budget equations now take the form* $\mathbf{p}^* \mathbf{x}_h^* = M_h^*$*, where* M_h^* *is given by (8-56) or (8-57) in terms of equilibrium magnitudes.*

To prove the existence of compensated equilibrium, the previous mapping has to be only slightly modified; however, the details are omitted here.

We have assumed to this point that all price expectations are totally inelastic; this assumption can easily be relaxed.

ASSUMPTION 22. *For each household and firm, anticipated second-period prices are a continuous function of current prices, that is,* $\mathbf{p}_h^2(\mathbf{p})$ *and* $\mathbf{p}_f^2(\mathbf{p})$ *are continuous functions.*

We now interpret those assumptions which referred to anticipated second-period prices, namely, 18, 20, and 21, to hold for all values of $\mathbf{p}_h^2$ and $\mathbf{p}_f^2$ in the ranges of the anticipation functions, $\mathbf{p}_h^2(\mathbf{p})$ and $\mathbf{p}_f^2(\mathbf{p})$. The various functions and correspondences now depend explicitly on $\mathbf{p}$, through $\mathbf{p}_f^2$ and $\mathbf{p}_h^2$; all the relevant continuity properties are easily seen to hold, and the existence of a compensated temporary equilibrium remains valid for elastic expectations.

Finally, to show that the compensated equilibrium is a competitive equilibrium, we need to redefine the concepts of resource-relatedness. We will say that household h' is *resource-related* to household h'' for given $\bar{x}_b$ and $\mathbf{p}$ if the definition given in the second section holds when Y_f is computed as of a fixed $\mathbf{p}_f^2$ determined by $\mathbf{p}$, U_h^* as of a fixed $\mathbf{p}_h^2$ determined by $\mathbf{p}$, and $\bar{x}_b$ is taken as given. Then household h' is said to be *resource-related* to household h'' without qualification if it is so resource-related for any given $\bar{x}_b$ and $\mathbf{p}$. As before, household h' is *indirectly resource-related* to household h'' if there exists some chain of households, beginning with h' and ending with h'', such that each household in the chain is resource-related to its successor.

ASSUMPTION 23. *Every household is indirectly resource-related to every other.*

With this and the earlier assumptions, a compensated temporary equilibrium is necessarily a competitive temporary equilibrium, so the existence of competitive temporary equilibrium is established.

Remark 1. The theory of the firm used here is somewhere between two currently popular views. It is "managerial" in that only the expectations of managers enter into the firm's decisions; stockholders appear only as passive investors. However, in contradistinction to theories such as those of Marris (1964) and Williamson (1964), I do not ascribe to managers any motives other than profit maximization according to their expectations.

A more general model would introduce a utility function for managers which depends in some more complicated way on the firm's production vector and current and anticipated profits; I have not investigated such a model here.

An alternative theory has the firm maximizing the current market value of its stock. That is, it chooses $\mathbf{y}_f^{12}$ to maximize K_f. This could be included in the present model by identifying $\mathbf{p}_f^2$ with $\mathbf{p}_h^2$ for that household for which K_{hf} is a maximum, where, for each h, K_{hf} has itself been defined by maximizing over Y_f^{12} at given $\mathbf{p}$ and $\mathbf{p}_h^2$. The only difficulty with this theory in the present framework is that as current prices change, different households value the firm most highly, and so $\mathbf{p}_f^2$ might change discontinuously as $\mathbf{p}$ changed. This would be avoided if we assumed that there is in fact a continuum of households, filling up a whole area in $\mathbf{p}_h^2$-space for any given $\mathbf{p}$; then $\mathbf{p}_f^2$ as defined would vary continuously with $\mathbf{p}$. But such a theory requires advanced methods for analysis.

Remark 2. The model here has assumed that there are no debts in the initial period, though there will, in general, be debts at the beginning of the next period. If expectations are falsified, then it can happen that no equilibrium in the next period will exist without bankruptcy, because the distribution of debt which is the result of the present period's choices and therefore the initial distribution for the next period is inappropriate.

Remark 3. Of course, I am here neglecting uncertainty. This is a more serious problem than one might think; for in the presence of uncertainty it is unreasonable to assume that bonds of different firms and households are perfect substitutes. If we are not willing to assume that all individuals have the same probability distributions of prices, then it is reasonable to suppose that any firm or household has more information about matters that concern it most and therefore that a household will have different subjective probability distributions for the bonds of different firms. If a given firm is then the only supplier of a commodity (its bonds) for which there are no perfect substitutes, then the capital markets cannot be assumed perfect.

Remark 4. The restriction to two periods prevents us from examining speculation in the market for shares based on other households' expectations, a matter to which Keynes (1936, pp. 154–159) has called attention in a dramatic passage. In a three-or-more-period model, a household may buy shares in a firm because it has expectations that in the second period others will have expectations which will make it profitable to sell the shares then.

References

Arrow, K. J., and Debreu, G. (1954). "Existence of equilibrium for a competitive economy," *Econometrica,* 22:265–290.

Arrow, K. J., Karlin, S., and Scarf, H. (1958). *Studies in the Mathematical Theory of Inventory and Production* (Stanford, Calif.: Stanford University Press).

Arrow, K. J., and Hahn, F. H. (1971). *General Competitive Analysis* (San Francisco: Holden-Day).

Burger, E. (1963). *Introduction to the Theory of Games* (Englewood Cliffs, N.J.: Prentice-Hall).

Bushaw, D. W., and Clower, R. W. (1957). *Introduction to Mathematical Economics* (Homewood, Ill.: Irwin).

Chamberlin, E. H. (1956). *The Theory of Monopolistic Competition,* 7th ed. (Cambridge, Mass: Harvard University Press).

Cournot, A. A. (1838). *Recherches sur les principes mathêmatiques de la théorie des richesses* (Paris: Rivière).

Debreu, G. (1959). *Theory of Value* (New York: Wiley).

Debreu, G. (1962). "New concepts and techniques for equilibrium analysis," *International Economic Review,* 3: 257–273.

Farrell, M. J. (1959). "The convexity assumption in the theory of competitive markets," *Journal of Political Economy,* 67: 377–391.

Hicks, J. R. (1939). *Value and Capital* (Oxford: Clarendon Press).

Hicks, J. R. (1965). *Capital and Growth* (New York and Oxford: Oxford University Press).

Hoffman, A. J., and Jacobs, W. (1954). "Smooth patterns of production," *Management Science,* 1: 86–91.

Holt, C. C., Modigliani, F., Muth, J. F., and Simon, H. A. (1960). *Planning Production, Inventories, and Work Force* (Englewood Cliffs, N.J.: Prentice-Hall).

Kakutani, S. (1941). "A generalization of Brouwer's fixed-point theorem," *Duke Mathematical Journal,* 8: 451–459.

Kaldor, N. (1935). "Market imperfection and excess capacity," *Economica,* n.s., 2: 33–50.

Kalecki, M. (1939). *Essays in the Theory of Economic Fluctuations* (New York: Farrar & Rinehart).

Keynes, J. M. (1936). *The General Theory of Employment Interest and Money* (New York: Harcourt, Brace).

Marris, R. (1964). *The Economic Theory of 'Managerial' Capitalism* (Glencoe, Ill.: Free Press of Glencoe).

McKenzie, L. (1954). "On equilibrium in Graham's model of world trade and other competitive systems," *Econometrica,* 22: 147–161.
McKenzie, L. (1959). "On the existence of general equilibrium for a competitive market," *Econometrica,* 27: 54–71.
McKenzie, L. (1961). "On the existence of general equilibrium: some corrections," *Econometrica,* 29: 247–248.
Negishi, T. (1960–61). "Monopolistic competition and general equilibrium," *Review of Economic Studies,* 28: 196–201.
Penrose, E. T. (1959). *The Theory of the Growth of the Firm* (New York and Oxford: Oxford University Press).
Robinson, J. (1933). *The Economics of Imperfect Competition* (London: Macmillan).
Rothenberg, J. (1960). "Non-convexity, aggregation, and Pareto optimality," *Journal of Political Economy,* 68: 435–468.
Schlesinger, K. (1933–34). "Über die Produktionsgleichungen der ökonomischen Wertlehre," *Ergebnisse eines mathematischen Kolloquiums,* 6: 10–11.
Starr, R. (1969). "Quasi-equilibria in markets with nonconvex preferences," *Econometrica,* 37: 25–38.
Tompkins, C. B. (1964). "Sperner's lemma and some extensions," chap. 15 in E. F. Beckenbach (ed.), *Applied Combinatorial Mathematics* (New York, London, and Sydney: Wiley).
Triffin, R. (1940). *Monopolistic Competition and General Equilibrium Theory* (Cambridge, Mass.: Harvard University Press).
Wald, A. (1936). "Über einige Gleichungssysteme der mathematischen Ökonomie," *Zeitschrift für Nationalökonomie,* 8: 637–670. English translation (1951), "On some systems of equations of mathematical economics," *Econometrica,* 19: 368–403.
Williamson, O. E. (1964). *The Economics of Discretionary Behavior* (Englewood Cliffs, N.J.: Prentice-Hall).

9 General Economic Equilibrium: Purpose, Analytic Techniques, Collective Choice

Coordination and Efficiency of the Economic System

From the time of Adam Smith's *Wealth of Nations* in 1776, one recurrent theme of economic analysis has been the remarkable degree of coherence among the vast numbers of individual and seemingly separate decisions about the buying and selling of commodities. In everyday, normal experience, there is something of a balance between the amounts of goods and services that some individuals want to supply and the amounts that other, different individuals want to sell. Would-be buyers ordinarily count correctly on being able to carry out their intentions, and would-be sellers do not ordinarily find themselves producing great amounts of goods that they cannot sell. This experience of balance is indeed so widespread that it raises no intellectual disquiet among laymen; they take it so much for granted that they are not disposed to understand the mechanism by which it occurs. The paradoxical result is that they have no idea of the system's strength and are unwilling to trust it in any considerable departure from normal conditions. This reaction is most conspicuous in wartime situations with radical shifts in demand. It is taken for granted that these can be met only by price control, rationing, and direct allocation of resources. Yet there is no reason to believe that the same forces that work in peacetime would not produce a working system in time of war or other considerable shifts in demand. (There are

---

Reprinted by permission from *Les Prix Nobel en 1972* (Stockholm: Nobel Foundation, 1973), pp. 206–231.

undesirable consequences of a free market system, but sheer unworkability is not one of them.)

I do not want to overstate the case. The balancing of supply and demand is far from perfect. Most conspicuously, the history of the capitalist system has been marked by recurring periods in which the supply of available labor and of productive equipment available for the production of goods has been in excess of their utilization, sometimes, as in the 1930s, by very considerable magnitudes. Further, the relative balance of overall supply and demand in the postwar period in the United States and Europe is in good measure the result of deliberate governmental policies, not an automatic tendency of the market to balance.

Nevertheless, when all due allowances are made, the coherence of individual economic decisions is remarkable. As incomes rise and demands shift, for example, from food to clothing and housing, the labor force and productive facilities follow suit. Similarly, and even more surprising to the layman, there is a mutual interaction between shifts in technology and the allocation of the labor force. As technology improves exogenously, through innovations, the labor made redundant does not become permanently unemployed but finds its place in the economy. It is truly amazing that the lessons of both theory and more than a century of history are still so misunderstood. On the other hand, a growing accumulation of instruments of production raises real wages and in turn induces a rise in the prices of labor-intensive commodities relative to those which use little labor. All these phenomena show that by and large and in the long view of history, the economic system adjusts with a considerable degree of smoothness and indeed of rationality to changes in the fundamental facts within which it operates.

The problematic nature of economic coordination is most obvious in a free enterprise economy but might seem of lesser moment in a socialist or planned society. But a little reflection on the production and consumption decisions of such a society, at least in the modern world of complex production, shows that in the most basic aspects the problem of coordination is not removed by the transition to socialism or to any other form of planning. In the pure model of a free enterprise world, an individual, whether consumer or producer, is the locus both of interests or tastes and of information. Each individual has his own desires, which he is expected to pursue within the constraints imposed by the economic mechanism; but in addition he is supposed to have more information about himself or at least about a particular sphere of productive and consumptive activity than other individuals. It might be that in an ideal socialist economy, all individuals will act in accord with some agreed ideas of the common good, though I personally find this concept neither realistic nor desirable, in that it denies the fact and value of individual diversity. But not even the most ideal socialist society will obviate the diversity of information about productive methods that must obtain simply because the acquisition of information is costly. Hence, the need for coordination, for some means of seeing that plans of diverse agents have balanced totals, remains.

How this coordination takes place has been a central preoccupation of economic theory since Adam Smith. A reasonably clear answer was provided in the 1870s by the work of Jevons, Menger, and above all, Léon Walras: it was the fact that all agents in the economy faced the same set of prices that provided the common flow of information needed to coordinate the system. There was, so it was argued, a set of prices, one for each commodity, which would equate supply and demand for all commodities; and if supply and demand were unequal anywhere, at least some prices would change, while none would change in the opposite case. Because of the last characteristics, the balancing of supply and demand under these conditions may be referred to as *equilibrium* in accordance with the usual use of that term in science and mathematics. The adjective *general* refers to the argument that we cannot legitimately speak of equilibrium with respect to any one commodity; since supply and demand on any one market depend on the prices of other commodities, the overall equilibrium of the economy cannot be decomposed into separate equilibria for individual commodities.

Now even in the most strictly neoclassical version of price theory, it is not precisely true that prices alone are adequate information to the individual agents for the achievement of equilibrium, a point that will be developed later. One brand of criticism has put more stress on quantities themselves as signals, including no less an authority than the great Keynes (1936); see especially the interpretation of Keynes by Leijonhufvud (1968, especially chap. 2). More recently the same argument has been advanced by Kornai (1971) from socialist experience. Nevertheless, although the criticisms are, in my judgment, not without some validity, they have not given rise to a genuine alternative model of detailed resource allocation. The fundamental question remains: how does an overall total quantity, say demand, as in the Keynesian model, get transformed into a set of signals and incentives for individual sellers?

If one shifts perspective from description to design of economies it is not so hard to think of nonprice coordinating mechanisms; we are in fact all familiar with rationing in one form or another. Here, the discussion of coordination shades off in that of efficiency. There has long been a view that the competitive price equilibrium is efficient or optimal in some sense that rationing is not. This sense and the exact statement of the optimality theorem were clarified by Pareto (1909, chap. 6, secs. 32–38) and in the 1930s by my teacher, Harold Hotelling (1938), and by Abram Bergson (1938). An allocation of resources is *Pareto-efficient* (or *Pareto-optimal*) if there is no other feasible allocation which will make everyone better off (or, as more usually stated, will make everyone at least as well off and at least one member better off). Then, by an argument that I shall sketch shortly, it was held that a competitive equilibrium necessarily yielded a Pareto-efficient allocation of resources.

It was, of course, recognized, most explicitly perhaps by Bergson, that Pareto efficiency in no way implied distributive justice. An allocation of resources could be efficient in a Pareto sense and yet yield enormous riches to some and dire poverty to others.

The Hicks-Samuelson Model of General Equilibrium

I will state more formally the model of general competitive equilibrium as it had been developed by about 1945, primarily through the detailed developments and syntheses of John Hicks (1939) and Paul Samuelson (1947). Competitive analysis is founded on two basic principles: optimizing behavior on the part of individual agents in the presence of prices taken as given by them and the setting of prices so that, given this individual behavior, supply equals demand on each market. The outcome of the competitive process is then to be evaluated in terms of Pareto efficiency and additional conditions on the resulting distribution of goods.

The maximizing behavior of individuals has been well surveyed by Samuelson in his Nobel lecture (1971), and I will not go over that ground here. I just want to remind the reader of a few elementary points. The first is that the consumer's choices are subject to a budget constraint. The consumer starts with the possession of some quantities of economically valuable goods, such as labor of particular types, land, or other possessions. Let us imagine there are n commodities altogether, and let $\bar{x}_{hi}$ be the amount of commodity i owned initially by individual h (this may well be zero for most commodities). If p_i is the price of the ith commodity, then his total income available for expenditure is

$$\sum_{i=1}^{n} p_i \bar{x}_{hi}.$$

Hence, he can choose for consumption any bundle of goods, $x_{h1}, \ldots, x_{hn}$, which cost no more than his income,

$$\sum_{i=1}^{n} p_i x_{hi} \leqq \sum_{i=1}^{n} p_i \bar{x}_{hi}.$$

Within this budget set of possible consumption bundles, the individual is presumed to choose his most preferred bundle. The most usual interpretation of "most preferred" in this context is that there is a preference ordering over all possible bundles, according to which, for every pair of bundles, one is preferred to the other or else the two are indifferent; and these pairwise judgments have the consistency property known to logicians as "transitivity"; thus, for example, if bundle *A* is preferred to bundle *B* and *B* to *C*, then *A* will be preferred to *C*. This "ordinalist" view of preferences was originally due to Pareto and to Irving Fisher, about 1900, and represented an evolution from the earlier "cardinalist" position, according to which a measurable satisfaction or "utility" was associated with each bundle, and the consumer chose that bundle which maximized utility within the budget set. Obviously, a cardinal utility implies an ordinal preference but not vice versa; and if the only operational meaning of utility is in the explanation of consumer choice, then clearly two utility functions which defined the same preference ordering would be operationally indistinguishable.[1]

The most preferred bundle then is a function, $x_{hi}(p_1, \ldots, p_n)$ of all prices. Notice that, from this viewpoint, all prices clearly enter into the determination of the demand for any one commodity. For one thing, the rise in any one price clearly diminishes the residual income available for all other commodities. More specifically, however, the demands for some commodities are closely interrelated with others; thus, the demand for gasoline is perhaps more influenced by the use of automobiles and therefore by their price than it is by its own price. The interrelation of all demands is clearly displayed here.

The characterization of consumer choice by optimization can, as we all know, be made more explicit. Let us recall Hicks's definition of the *marginal rate of substitution* between two commodities for any individual. For any given bundle, $(x_1^0, \ldots, x_n^0)$, consider all bundles indifferent to it, that is, neither preferred to it nor inferior to it. If we hold all but two commodity

1. The ordinalist view in fact only began to have wide currency in the 1930s, and indeed the treatments of Hicks and Samuelson, along with a paper of Hotelling's (1935), did much to make the ordinalist view standard. Interestingly enough, both Hicks and Samuelson have studied consumer choice by alternative axiom systems even weaker than ordinalism; see Hicks and Allen (1935) and Samuelson (1938).

quantities constant, say $x_k = x_k^0 (k \neq i,j)$, we can consider x_i as a function of x_j on this indifference surface. Then $-dx_i/dx_j$, evaluated at the point $x_i = x_i^0$, all i, is the marginal rate of substitution of commodity j for commodity i; it is, to a first approximation, the amount of commodity i that would be required to compensate for a loss of one unit of commodity j. The optimizing consumer will equate this marginal rate of substitution to the price ratio, p_j/p_i; for if the two were unequal, it would be possible to move along the indifference surface in some direction and reduce spending.

But since the marginal rate of substitution for any pair of commodities is equal to the price ratio for all individuals, it is also true that the marginal rate of substitution for any two commodities is the same for all individuals. This suggests in turn that there is no possibility that two or any number of individuals can gain by trading with each other after achieving a competitive equilibrium. The equality of the marginal rates of substitution means that a trade which would leave one individual on an indifference surface would do the same to the other. Hence, a competitive equilibrium satisfies the same kinds of conditions that are satisfied by a Pareto optimum.

(It will be observed that the stated conditions for a consumer optimum and for a Pareto optimum are first-order conditions in the differential calculus. Hotelling, Hicks, and Samuelson also developed the second-order conditions which distinguish maxima from minima and showed that these had important implications.)

Evaluation of the performance of an economy with regard to distributive justice was far less studied, not surprisingly, since the deepest philosophical issues are at stake. Incorporated in the Anglo-American tradition was one viewpoint, tacitly accepted though rarely given much prominence—the utilitarian views of Bentham and Sidgwick, given formal expression by Edgeworth. The criterion was the maximization of the sum of all individuals' utilities. This criterion only made sense if utility was regarded as cardinally measurable. With the rise of ordinalist doctrines, the epistemological basis for the sum-of-utilities criterion was eroded. It was to this issue that Bergson's famous paper (1938) was addressed. As already noted, a given preference ordering corresponds to many different utility functions. For any given set of preference orderings for the members of the economy, choose for each ordering one of the utility functions which imply that preference ordering, and then the social welfare is expressed as some function, $W(U_1, \ldots, U_n)$ of the individual utilities. The function W will change appropriately if the utility indicator for the given preference orderings is changed, so that the entire representation is consistent with the ordinalist interpretation. However, the function W is not uniquely prescribed, as in the Edgeworth-Bentham sum of utilities, but is itself an expression of social welfare attitudes which may differ from individual to individual.

So far I have, for simplicity, spoken as if there were no production, an omission which must be repaired. A productive unit or firm is characterized by a relation between possible outputs and inputs. A firm may have, of course, more than one output. Then firm f may be characterized by its transformation surface, defined by an equation, $T(y_{f1}, \ldots, y_{fn}) = 0$, where y_{fi} is taken to be an output if positive and input if negative; the surface is taken to define the efficient possible input-output vectors for the firm, that is, those which yield maximum output of one commodity for given inputs and given outputs of other commodities. The optimizing behavior of the firm is taken to be the maximization of profit among the points on its transformation surface. Because of the sign conventions for inputs and outputs, the firm is seeking to maximize

$$\sum_{i=1}^{n} p_i y_{fi}.$$

It is assumed in the treatment by Hicks and by Samuelson in the books referred to that the transformation surface is differentiable, so that the maximum-profit position is defined by suitable marginal equalities, and that the result is a function, $y_{fi}(p_1, \ldots, p_n)(i = 1, \ldots, n)$.

Two remarks should be made at this point. (1) Clearly, if all prices are multiplied by the same positive constant, the budget constraint for households is really unchanged, and hence so are the consumer demands. Similarly, the profits are multiplied by a positive constant, so that the profit-maximizing choice of a firm is unchanged. Hence, the functions $x_{hi}(p_1, \ldots, p_n)$ and $y_{fi}(p_1, \ldots, p_n)$ are homogeneous of degree zero in their arguments. (2) The firms' profits have to be treated as part of the income of the households that own them. This causes a modification of the previous budget constraint for the individual, which I will not spell out in symbols here but will refer to below.

For any commodity i, there will be some demands and some supplies at any given set of prices. Following Hicks, we will speak of the *excess demand* for commodity i as the sum over all individuals and firms of demands and supplies, the latter being taken as negative. The demand by individual h is $x_{hi}(p_1, \ldots, p_n)$, so that the total demand by all households is

$$\sum_{h} x_{hi}(p_1, \ldots, p_n).$$

The supply by households is the aggregate amount they have to begin with, that is,

$$\sum_h \bar{x}_{hi}.$$

Finally, the aggregate supply by firms is

$$\sum_f y_{fi}(p_1, \ldots, p_n);$$

some firms may be demanders rather than suppliers, but the sign convention assures that the above sum gives the aggregate *net* supply by firms, that is, after canceling out demands by one firm which are supplied by another. Hence, the market excess demand for commodity i is

$$z_i(p_1, \ldots, p_n) = \sum_h x_{hi}(p_1, \ldots, p_n) - \sum_h \bar{x}_{hi} - \sum_h y_{fi}(p_1, \ldots, p_n).$$

Since each term is homogeneous of degree zero, so is the total, z_i. Further, the satisfaction of the budget constraint for each individual also restricts the excess demand functions. Since for each individual the monetary value of expenditures planned at any set of prices equals the monetary value of his initial endowments plus his share of the profits, we have in the aggregate that the money value of planned expenditures by all households equals the money value of total endowments plus total profits, or

$$\sum_h \sum_{i=1}^{n} p_i x_{hi}(p_1, \ldots, p_n) = \sum_h \sum_{i=1}^{n} p_i \bar{x}_{hi} + \sum_f \sum_{i=1} p_i y_{fi}(p_1, \ldots, p_n),$$

or, from the definition of excess demand,

$$\sum_i p_i z_i(p_1, \ldots, p_n) \equiv 0,$$

where the identity symbol reminds us that this relation, which Lange (1942) called Walras' law, holds for all values of the prices.

The general equilibrium of the economy is then the set of prices which equate all excess demands to zero,

$$z_i(p_1, \ldots, p_n) = 0 (i = 1, \ldots, n).$$

These appear to be n equations in n unknowns; but there are two off-setting complications in the counting. On the one hand, since the equations are homogeneous, no solution can be unique, since any positive multiple of all prices is also a solution. In effect, the equations really only determine the $n-1$ price ratios. On the other hand, the equations are not independent; if $n-1$ are satisfied, then the nth must be by Walras' law.

The Need for Further Development

There were, however, several directions in which the structure of general equilibrium theory was either incomplete or inconsistent with doctrines which had strong currency in economic theory.

(1) There was no proof offered that the system of equations defining general equilibrium had a solution at all; that is, it was not known that there existed a set of prices which would make excess demand zero on every market. This was the most serious unresolved problem.

(2) The assumptions on production were not the same as those used in the analysis of production itself. In the latter, a common, though not universal, assumption was that of constant returns to scale; if any production process can be carried out, with given inputs and outputs, then the process can be carried out at any scale. That is, if the inputs are all multiplied by the same positive number, then it is possible to produce the same multiple of all the outputs. But in this case, there cannot be a unique profit-maximizing position for any set of prices. For suppose there were a position which yielded positive profits. Then doubling all inputs and outputs is feasible and yields twice as great profits. Hence, there would be no profit-maximizing position, since any one could be improved upon. On the other hand, zero profits can always be obtained by having no inputs and no outputs. It can be concluded that, if prices are such that there is some profit-maximizing set of inputs and outputs not all zero, the corresponding profits must be zero, and the same profits can be achieved by multiplying all inputs and outputs by any positive number.

Therefore, under constant returns to scale, there is never a single-valued function, $y_{fi}(p_1, \ldots, p_n)$ defining inputs and outputs as a function of prices; rather, for any given set of prices, either there is no profit-maximizing input-output vector or else there is a whole ray of them. But then the notion of equating supply and demand must be redefined.

Of somewhat lesser importance in this regard is the fact that the transformation surface need not be differentiable in very plausible circumstances. A frequently held view was that production of a given output required prescribed amounts of each input; in some circumstances, at least, it is impossible to reduce the need for one input by increasing the amount of another. This is the fixed-coefficient technology. In this case, it can easily be seen that though the transformation surface is well defined, it is not differentiable but has kinks in it.

(3) The relation between Pareto-efficient allocations and competitive equilibria was less clearly formulated than might be desired. What had really been shown was that the necessary first-order conditions for Pareto efficiency were the same as the first-order conditions for maximization by firms and individuals when the entire economy is in a competitive equilibrium.

(4) Actually, the condition for individual optimization (equating of marginal rates of substitution to price ratios) required some modification to take care of corner maxima. It is obvious to everyday observation that for each individual there are some (indeed, many) commodities of which he consumes nothing. Similarly, for every firm, there are some commodities which are neither inputs to nor outputs of it. But then the argument that the marginal rate of substitution must equal the price ratio for each individual breaks down. For consider an individual for whom the marginal rate of substitution of commodity j for commodity i is *less* than the price ratio, p_j/p_i, but the individual consumes nothing of commodity j. A small increase in the consumption of j with a compensating decrease in i to stay on the same indifference surface would involve an increase in costs. The only way to achieve a decrease in cost without moving to a less preferred position would be to decrease the consumption of j; but this is impossible, since consumption cannot fall below zero. It is true, however, that the marginal rate of substitution of j for i cannot *exceed* the price ratio.

Similarly, if one individual consumes nothing of commodity j, it is possible to have Pareto efficiency with his marginal rate of substitution of j for i less than that for some other individual. Since marginal rates of substitution do not have to be equated across individuals either for competitive equilibria or for Pareto-efficient allocations, the relation between the two concepts was seen to need further study.

(5) Still another question is whether supply and demand are necessarily equal. Clearly, demand cannot exceed supply, for there would have to be unfulfilled demands. But as we look around us, we see that there are goods, that is, flows which we prefer to have, which nevertheless are so abundant that we have no desire for more. Air and sunlight come immediately to mind. Characteristically, such highly abundant goods are free; no price is charged for their use.

This elementary observation has been made a number of times by economists. A distinction was drawn between *scarce goods* and *free goods,* the former alone being the proper subject matter of economics. But it is easy to see from a mathematical viewpoint that the classification of goods in this way is not a given but depends on those parameters of the system which govern tastes, technology, and initial supplies. Suppose, for example, that we have two commodities, *A* and *B*, which serve as factors of production only. Suppose further it so happens that the two factors are always used together and always in the same proportion, say, one unit of *A* with two units of *B*. Finally, suppose that *A* and *B* are not themselves produced goods but are natural resources available in equal quantities. Then clearly commodity *B* is the bottleneck; commodity *A* is a free good in the usual economic sense, since a small change in the quantity available would have no effect on production. But this classification of the two goods into free and scarce is relative to the technology and to the initial supplies of the two goods. If a technological innovation reduced the need for *B* so that one unit of *A* required the cooperation of less than one unit of *B*, *B* would become the free good, and *A*, the scarce one; and the same would happen if the initial supply of *A* were reduced, perhaps by some catastrophe, to less than half of that of *B*.

The conditions for equilibrium then have to be modified. We require now that excess demand be nonpositive and that, for any commodity for which it is negative, the price be zero. In symbols,

$$z_i(p_1, \ldots, p_n) \leqq 0 \; (i = 1, \ldots, n),$$

if

$$z_i(p_1, \ldots, p_n) < 0, \quad \text{then} \quad p_i = 0.$$

The commodities for which the inequality holds are the free goods. Equilibria in which there are free goods are referred to as *corner equilibria.*

The problem just raised illustrates a general tendency in the evolution of general equilibrium theory for a shift from a local to a global analysis. If we consider small shifts in the parameters which determine tastes, technology, and initial supplies, the classification of goods into free and scarce remains unchanged. Hence, from a local viewpoint, the list of scarce goods could legitimately be taken as given. We need not debate here the relative virtues of local and global analysis: clearly a global analysis is always preferable if it is possible, but a local analysis will normally produce more specific implications. But it turns out that the first of the problems raised, that of the existence of equilibrium prices, cannot be handled at all except from a global viewpoint; and the realization of the possibility of corner equilibria turned out to be an indispensable step in the development of an existence proof.

To avoid a misinterpretation of this list of the needs for further development, two points should be stressed: (1) the general aims and structure of general equilibrium theory have remained those already set forth by Hicks, and the subsequent development would have been impossible and indeed meaningless except on his foundations; (2) I have summarized here only the most general and foundational aspects of the work of Hicks and Samuelson, since those are most relevant for my present purpose, but the primary interest of both was rather in the laws of working of the general equilibrium system, results not summarized above, than in the questions of existence and the like.

The German-Language Literature

We now turn from the Anglo-American work to a variant strand of neoclassical thought, published primarily in German, and written to a considerable extent by mathematicians rather than economists. The whole literature might be described as an extended commentary on a formulation of general equilibrium theory by Cassel (1918), a statement rather different in nature from that of Hicks. In particular, maximizing behavior hardly appeared in Cassel's model. With regard to individual consumers, Cassel also assumed that the demand of individual households was a function of prices; he did not, however, seek to derive this demand from a preference or utility maximization. With regard to production, he assumed a fixed-coefficient technology, so that there was in effect no scope for profit maximization by firms; the demands for inputs were completely defined by the outputs, independent of prices. More explicitly, Cassel differentiated commodities into produced goods and primary factors, the two classes being assumed distinct. Individuals owned initially only primary factors, and they demand only produced goods. Produced goods were made by inputs of primary factors; let a_{ij} be the amount of factor j used in the production of one unit of good i. Let $\boldsymbol{P}$ be the set of produced goods, $\boldsymbol{F}$, that of factors.

At any set of prices, the total demand for produced good i is

$$\sum_h x_{hi}(p_1, \ldots, p_n) = x_i;$$

the demand for factor j by the industry producing good i is then $a_{ij}x_i$, and the total demand for factor j is obtained by summing this demand over all producing industries. On the other hand, the initial supply of factor j is $\Sigma_h \bar{x}_{hj}$, so that the condition for equality of supply and demand for factor j is

$$\sum_h \bar{x}_{hj} = \sum_{i \in P} a_{ij} x_i.$$

As j varies over $\boldsymbol{F}$, we have a system of linear equations in the x_i's. Now von Stackelberg (1933) observed that this system might easily have no solution, for example, if there are more factors than produced goods.

Cassel completed the system by using the condition that, under constant returns to scale, there must be zero profits. Then, for each produced good, the price must equal the cost of the factors used in making one unit, or

$$p_i = \sum_{j \in F} a_{ij} p_j (i \in \boldsymbol{P}).$$

About contemporaneously with von Stackelberg, Neisser (1932) showed that it could easily be true that the complete Cassel system could be satisfied only if some factor prices were negative.

It was at this point that the Viennese banker and amateur economist, K. Schlesinger (1933–34), decisively affected the subsequent discussion. He observed that the criticisms raised by von Stackelberg and by Neisser could be met by recognizing the possibility of corner equilibria, particularly with regard to primary factors. Some may simply be superfluous and have to be regarded as free goods. Thus, the equality of supply and demand for factors has to be replaced by the following conditions:

$$\sum_h \bar{x}_{hj} \geqq \sum_{i \in P} a_{ij} x_i, \qquad p_j = 0$$

if the strict inequality holds ($j \in \boldsymbol{F}$).

With this amendment, Schlesinger conjectured, it could be shown that there existed an equilibrium in which all prices were nonnegative. He interested the mathematician Abraham Wald in this problem, and the latter showed in a brilliant series of papers (1933–34, 1934–35), summarized in 1936, that equilibrium indeed existed, though rather strong assumptions had to be made and the analysis was confined to variations of the Cassel model. Wald's reasoning was formidably complex, and his work was published in a German language mathematics journal; it was only some ten years later that American mathematical economists began to be aware of it.

Within the same period, the mathematician John von Neumann published a paper (1937) which had in the longer run a deeper impact, though its subject matter was less relevant. This was a development of Cassel's model of steady growth of the economy. The aim was to show the existence of a growth path with maximum proportional expansion in all commodities. From an economic point of view the model was somewhat strange in that there was no consumption at all; the outputs of one period were inputs into activities which generated the outputs of the next period. There were three noteworthy points which had great influence on the development of general equilibrium theory. First, the structure of production was characterized in a novel way. It was assumed that there was a fixed set of activities, each being characterized by a vector of possible inputs and outputs and each being technologically capable of operation at any scale. This generalized the fixed-coefficient model, in which there was one activity for each output. The feasible combinations of activities were those for which the total usage of each input did not exceed the amount available from previous production. Second, the maximum growth path could be characterized as a sort of competitive equilibrium, in the sense that it was mathematically possible and meaningful to introduce a new set of variables, which could be regarded as prices. Any activity that was run at all yielded zero profits; other activities yielded zero or negative profits. Hence, the choice of activity levels could be described as profit-maximizing, where the maxima may involve some corners. Further, the price of any commodity for which the demand as input fell short of the amount available had to be zero; hence, the competitive equilibrium could require corners. Third, the method of proof of the existence of prices and relative quantities which yielded a maximum growth rate required the use of a tool from combinatorial topology, a generalization of Brouwer's fixed point theorem. From a mathematical viewpoint, the existence of equilibrium in the von Neumann growth model was a generalization of the minimax theorem for zero-sum two-person games, which von Neumann had studied a few years earlier. The interest in game theory following the publication of the great book of von Neumann and Morgenstern (1944) was a strong collateral force in introducing new mathematical techniques, particularly in the theory of convex sets, into general equilibrium theory.

A simplification of von Neumann's fixed point theorem was developed a few years later by S. Kakutani (1941) and has become the standard tool for proving existence theorems. Let us review briefly the fixed point theorems of Brouwer and Kakutani. Recall that a set of points is said to be compact if it is closed and bounded and to be convex if every line segment joining two points of the set lies entirely within the set. Let $\boldsymbol{C}$ be a compact convex set. Let $f(x)$ be a vector function which assigns to every point of $\boldsymbol{C}$ a point of $\boldsymbol{C}$. Then Brouwer's theorem asserts that if the mapping $f(x)$ is continuous, then there is at least one point, x^*, which is mapped into itself, that is, for which $f(x^*) = x^*$.

In the indicial notation which we have used hitherto, we have n real-valued functions $f_i(x_1, \ldots, x_n)$ of n variables. If these functions are continuous and if the point $(f_1, \ldots, f_n)$ lies in some compact convex set $\boldsymbol{C}$ whenever $(x_1, \ldots, x_n)$ lies in that set, then the system of equations, $f_i(x_1, \ldots, x_n) = x_i$, has at least one solution in $\boldsymbol{C}$.

The relevance of such a mathematical tool to the problem of existence is obvious. However, we have already noted above that once we permit constant returns to scale, we have to allow for the possibility that the profit-maximizing choice of production process may be a whole set, all equally profitable, for some given set of prices. Hence, instead of dealing with functions, we need to concern ourselves with the more general notion of a point-to-set mapping, or *correspondence,* as it is sometimes termed. Kakutani's theorem deals with this more general situation. To every point $x = (x_1, \ldots, x_n)$ in a compact convex set $\boldsymbol{C}$, we associate a subset of $\boldsymbol{C}$, say $\Phi(x)$. We say that x^* is a *fixed point* of this correspondence if the point x^* belongs to the set associated with x^*, that is, to $\Phi(x^*)$.

Kakutani's theorem tells us that such a fixed point will exist if two conditions are fulfilled: for each x, $\Phi(x)$ is a convex set; and as x varies, $\Phi(x)$ is continuous in a certain sense, more technically, that it has the property known as *upper semicontinuity.*

Pareto Efficiency, Competitive Equilibrium, and Convexity

My own interest first centered on the relations between Pareto efficiency and competitive equilibrium. In particular, there was considerable discussion among economists in the late 1940s about the inefficiencies resulting from rent control and different proposals for arriving at the efficiency benefits of a free market by one or another transition route. Part of the informal efficiency arguments hinged on the idea that under rent control people were buying the wrong kind of housing, say, excessively large apartments. It struck me that an individual bought only one kind of housing, not several. The individual optima were at corners, and therefore one could not equate marginal rates of substitution by going over to a free market. Yet diagrammatic analysis of simple cases suggested to me that the traditional identification of competitive equilibrium and Pareto efficiency was correct but could not be proved by the local techniques of the differential calculus.

I soon realized that the theory of convex sets, and, in particular, the separation theorem, was the appropriate tool. Start with a Pareto-efficient allocation, and consider all logically possible allocations which would be preferred to it by everyone. Of course, no such allocation can be feasible; otherwise the allocation we started with would not be Pareto-efficient. Each such allocation is a statement of demand or supply of each commodity by each individual or firm. Hence, by summing over individuals and firms, with appropriate attention to signs, we can define the excess demand for each commodity. Let $\boldsymbol{Z}$ be the set of all excess demand vectors $(z_1, \ldots, z_n)$ generated this way. Since they are all infeasible, it must be true for each one that there is positive excess demand for at least one commodity. In the language of set theory, the set $\boldsymbol{Z}$ is disjoint from the nonpositive orthant, that is, the set of vectors $(z_1, \ldots, z_n)$ such that $z_i \leq 0$ for all i.

The separation theorem for convex sets asserts that if two convex sets are disjoint, there is a hyperplane which separates them, so that one set is on one side and the other set on the other. In symbols, if $\boldsymbol{C}_1$ and $\boldsymbol{C}_2$ are disjoint convex sets in n-dimensional space, there exist numbers $p_i (i = 1, \ldots, n)$, not all zero, c, such that $\Sigma_{i=1}^n p_i x_i \geqq c$ for all $x = (x_1, \ldots, x_n)$ in $\boldsymbol{C}_1$, $\Sigma_{i=1}^n p_i x_i \leqq c$ for all x in $\boldsymbol{C}_2$. Let us apply this theorem to the present case. The nonpositive orthant is obviously a convex set; let us assume for the moment that $\boldsymbol{Z}$ is convex. Then we can find numbers $p_i (i = 1, \ldots, n)$, not all zero, c, such that

$$\sum_{i=1}^{n} p_i z_i \geqq c \quad \text{for } z = (z_1, \ldots, z_n) \text{ in } \boldsymbol{Z},$$

$$\sum_{i=1}^{n} p_i z_i \leqq c \quad \text{if} \quad z_i \leqq 0 \quad \text{for all } i.$$

From the second condition, it can easily be seen that we cannot have $p_i < 0$ for any i. Hence, p_i is nonnegative for all i and (since there is at least one nonzero p_i) positive for at least one i. This is customarily expressed by saying that the vector $p = (p_1, \ldots, p_n)$ is *semipositive.*

It follows that

$$\sum_{i=1}^{n} p_i z_i \leqq 0 \quad \text{if } z_i \leqq 0 \quad \text{for all } i,$$

and therefore we can assume without loss that $c \leqq 0$. On the other hand, if we set $z_i = 0$ for all i, we see that $c \geqq 0$. Hence, we can set $c = 0$.

The conditions for a Pareto-efficient allocation then become

$$\sum_{i=1}^{n} p_i z_i \geqq 0 \quad \text{for } z \text{ in } \boldsymbol{Z}, p \text{ semipositive.}$$

Let $z^0 = (z_1^0, \ldots, z_n^0)$ be the vector of excess demands defined by the Pareto-efficient allocation under consideration. It is feasible, so that $z_i^0 \leqq 0$, all i, and therefore,

$$\sum_{i=1}^{n} p_i z_i^0 \leqq 0.$$

Now assume, as is usually reasonable, that there are points in $\boldsymbol{Z}$ as close as one wishes to z^0. Then clearly we must have

$$\sum_{i=1}^{n} p_i z_i^0 = 0,$$

and hence, since $z_i^0 \leqq 0$, all i, $p_i \geqq 0$, all i, that

$$\text{if} \quad z_i^0 < 0, \qquad p_i = 0.$$

We begin to see that a Pareto-efficient allocation is an equilibrium of supply and demand in the generalized sense which includes corners.

We also see that

$$\sum_{i=1}^{n} p_i (z_i - z_i^0) \geqq 0 \quad \text{for } z \text{ in } \boldsymbol{Z}.$$

Let us go back to the definition of excess demand, as a sum of individual and firm demands and supplies:

$$z_i = \sum_h x_{hi} - \sum_h \bar{x}_{hi} - \sum_f y_{fi},$$

where $y_f(y_{f1}, \ldots, y_{fn})$ is a technologically possible vector of inputs and outputs for firm f and $x_h = (x_{h1}, \ldots, x_{hn})$ is a possible vector of consumptions for individual h. In particular, the excess demands defined by the Pareto-efficient allocation can be written in this form:

$$z_i^0 = \sum_h x_{hi}^0 - \sum_h \bar{x}_{hi} - \sum_f y_{fi}^0;$$

and then, if z belongs to $\boldsymbol{Z}$, we must have, for each h, that the consumption vector of individual h, $(x_{h1}, \ldots, x_{hn})$ is preferred to that under the Pareto-efficient allocation $(x^0_{h1}, \ldots, x^0_{hn})$. Then

$$\sum_h \left(\sum_{i=1}^n p_i x_{hi} - \sum_{i=1}^n p_i x^0_{hi} \right) - \sum_f \left(\sum_{i=1}^n p_i y_{fi} - \sum_{i=1}^n p_i y^0_{fi} \right) \geqq 0$$

if, for each h, x_h is preferred by individual h to x^0_h.

Now the elementary point about this inequality is that the variable vectors x_h, y_f are independent of each other. It is not hard to see that this inequality can hold only if it holds for each individual and each firm separately. For a firm f, this means that

$$\sum_{i=1}^n p_i y^0_{fi} \geqq \sum_{i=1}^n p_i y_{fi} \quad \text{for all possible } y_f,$$

that is, if we interpret the p_i's as prices, each firm is maximizing its profits. The corresponding interpretation for individuals is somewhat less simple; it is that the consumption vector prescribed by the given Pareto-efficient allocation is the cheapest way of deriving that much satisfaction.

Taken altogether, it has been shown that if $\boldsymbol{Z}$ is a convex set, the Pareto-efficient allocation can be achieved as a competitive equilibrium of the market, in the sense that prices and a suitable initial allocation of resources can be found such that each individual is achieving his satisfaction level at minimum cost, each firm is maximizing profits, and the markets are all in equilibrium in the generalized sense which permits corner equilibria.

The need to assume that $\boldsymbol{Z}$ is convex puts in sharper focus the convexity assumptions which had always implicitly underlain neoclassical theory. The convexity of $\boldsymbol{Z}$ could be derived from the following two assumptions: (1) for each individual, the set of consumption vectors preferred to a given vector is convex; (2) for each firm, the set of technologically possible vectors is convex.

The result states that, under suitable convexity conditions, a necessary condition for an allocation to be Pareto-efficient is that it be realizable in the market as a competitive equilibrium. A by-product of the investigation was the proof of the converse theorem: a competitive equilibrium is always Pareto-efficient, and this theorem is true without any convexity assumption.

These results were embodied in an earlier paper (Arrow, 1951a). But the idea that the theory of convex sets was the appropriate tool was clearly in the air. While I was working at Stanford, Gerard Debreu (1951) obtained very much the same results at the Cowles Commission for Research in Economics at Chicago.

The Existence of Competitive Equilibrium

Again working independently and in ignorance of each other's activities, Debreu and I both started applying Kakutani's fixed point theorem to the problem of existence. In this case, we exchanged manuscripts in sufficient time to realize our common efforts and also to realize the need for relaxing an excessively severe assumption we had both made (Arrow and Debreu, 1954).

An essential precondition for our studies was the basic work of Tjalling Koopmans (1951) on the analysis of production in terms of activity analysis. In this he extended von Neumann's work into a systematic account of the production structure of the economy. He saw it as a set of activities, each of which could be operated at any level but with the overall levels constrained by initial resource limitations. The crucial novelty was the explicit statement of the assumptions which ensured that the feasible set of outputs would be bounded for any finite set of initial resources. It turned out that this limitation is a "global" property. That is, conditions on the nature of individual activities (for example, that every activity had to have at least one input) were not sufficient to ensure the boundedness of the economy as a whole. It was necessary to require that no combination of activities as a whole permitted production without inputs.

The first question is the definition of equilibrium when the behavior of firms is described by a correspondence rather than a function. For simplicity, I will continue to assume that the decisions of individual consumer h can be represented by single-valued functions of prices, $x_h(p)$. A set of prices defines a competitive equilibrium if supply and demand balance on each market, including the possibility of corners, with *some* choice of the profit-maximizing input-output vector for each firm. Formally, we will say that a price vector p^*, an input-output vector y_f^* for each firm, and a consumption vector, $x_h^* = x_h(p^*)$, for each individual together constitute a competitive equilibrium if the following conditions hold:

(a) p^* is semipositive;

(b) for each commodity i,

$$\Sigma_h \bar{x}_{hi} + \Sigma_f y_{fi}^* \geqq \Sigma_h x_{hi}^*;$$

(c) for any commodity for which the strict inequality holds in (b), we must have $p_i^* = 0$;

(d) y_f^* is one of the input-output vectors which maximizes profits, $\Sigma_{i=1}^n p_i^* y_{fi}$, among all the input-output vectors technologically possible for firm f.

It is, of course, understood that the demand function for individuals, $x_h(p)$, is defined, as before, as the most preferred consumption pattern consistent with the budget constraint,

$$\sum_{i=1}^{n} p_i x_{hi} \leqq \sum_{i=1}^{n} p_i \bar{x}_{hi}.$$

For the present purposes, I will ignore the possibility that individuals' incomes also include profits; this modification can be handled at the cost of some analytic complexity but no true difficulty.

It will be assumed that (1) the set of possible input-output vectors for any firm is convex, and (2) the individual demand functions are continuous; this assumption will be discussed again below.

Since the total production possibilities of the economy are bounded, it can be shown there is no loss of generality in assuming that the set of possible input-output vectors for each firm is bounded (actually, we assume the set to be compact). Then for any set of prices there is at least one profit-maximizing input-output vector, but in general there may be a whole set of them, say $\boldsymbol{Y}_f(p)$. However, this set is certainly convex and further, as p varies, the correspondence so defined is upper semicontinuous.

Define an excess demand correspondence as follows: For each f, consider any possible selection of a vector y_f from the profit-maximizing correspondence $\boldsymbol{Y}_f(p)$. For each such selection for each firm, form the excess demand for each commodity for the entire economy,

$$z_i = \sum_h x_{hi}(p) - \sum_f y_{fi} - \sum_h \bar{x}_{hi}.$$

Let $\boldsymbol{Z}(p)$ be the set of all vectors $(z_1, \ldots, z_n)$ which can be formed by all possible selections of the vectors y_f from the profit-maximizing correspondence $\boldsymbol{Y}_f(p)$, the selections for different firms being made independently of each other. It is not hard to show that $\boldsymbol{Z}(p)$ is convex for each p and is an upper semicontinuous correspondence for p as a variable. It is also true and important that Walras' law holds; that is, if z belongs to $\boldsymbol{Z}(p)$, then

$$\sum_{i=1}^{n} p_i z_i = 0.$$

The correspondence $\boldsymbol{Z}(p)$ assigns to each price vector a set of excess demands; an equilibrium price vector p^* would be one such that $\boldsymbol{Z}(p^*)$ has at least one element for which $z_i \leq 0$, all i. We now introduce a mapping from excess demands; very roughly, we want low excess demands to have low or more precisely zero prices. Since the whole system is homogeneous of degree zero in the prices, the general level of the prices can be set arbitrarily with no loss of generality. It will be assumed then that

$$\sum_{i=1}^{n} p_i = 1.$$

Since prices are semipositive, it is also assumed that $p_i \geq 0$, all i; the set of price vectors satisfying these conditions will be denoted by $\boldsymbol{P}$, the price simplex. Then we define the following correspondence, assigning to each vector of excess demands, a subset of the price simplex: for any $z = (z_1, \ldots, z_n)$, let $\bar{z}$ be the largest of the components z_i; then define $\boldsymbol{P}(z)$ to be the set of price vectors in the unit simplex for which $p_i = 0$ for all commodities i for which $z_i < \bar{z}$. In words, total prices must add up to one, but this total is to be distributed only over those commodities with maximum excess demand. This rule is somewhat artificial, but it suffices for the proof.

Consider the set of all pairs (z, p) of vectors, one an excess demand vector and one a price vector. To any such pair we assign a set of pairs, $\boldsymbol{Z}(p) \times \boldsymbol{P}(z)$ (for any pair of sets, $\boldsymbol{S}$, $\boldsymbol{T}$, the notation $\boldsymbol{S} \times \boldsymbol{T}$ means the set of ordered pairs of vectors obtained by taking any vector from $\boldsymbol{S}$ followed by any vector from $\boldsymbol{T}$). With some further argument, it can be shown that Kakutani's theorem applies. The mapping of pairs has a fixed point, (z^*, p^*) belonging to $\boldsymbol{Z}(p^*) \times \boldsymbol{P}(z^*)$. By definition,

$$z^* \in \boldsymbol{Z}(p^*), \qquad p^* \in \boldsymbol{P}(z^*).$$

Let $\bar{z}^*$ be the largest component of $z^* = (z_1^*, \ldots, z_n^*)$. Then $p_i^* = 0$ for $z_i^* < \bar{z}^*$. Therefore,

$$p_i^* z_i^* = p_i^* \bar{z}^*.$$

By Walras' law,

$$0 = \sum_{i=1}^{n} p_i^* z_i^* = \sum_{i=1}^{n} p_i^* \bar{z}^* = \bar{z}^* \sum_{i=1}^{n} p_i^* = \bar{z}^*;$$

since the largest excess demand is zero, all excess demands are nonpositive, and therefore p^* is indeed an equilibrium price vector.

Many variations of this argument are possible and are illuminating in different ways. Independently of my work with Debreu, Lionel McKenzie (1954) proved the existence of equilibrium; he simply assumed the existence of supply and demand functions rather than analyzing them in terms of the underlying production and consumption structures. For systematic presentations of the existence theorems for competitive equilibrium, see Debreu (1959) and Arrow and Hahn (1971, chaps. 2–5).

There is one loose end that should now be picked up. It has been assumed that the demand functions of the individual are continuous. But one of the surprising discoveries that Debreu and I made in the course of our study was that even under all the usual strong assumptions about the behavior of individuals, this cannot be true everywhere in the price simplex except under very artificial conditions. The trouble is that the individual's income also depends on prices, and if the prices of those commodities which the individual owns originally fall to zero, his income falls to zero. When some prices and income are zero, however, the demand for the now-free goods may jump discontinuously. To illustrate, suppose an individual owned initially only one good, say, labor. So long as the price of that good was positive, he might retain some for his own use, but in any case could never consume more than he had initially. But when the price fell to zero, he could demand the same labor from others and in any amount he chose.

The existence of competitive equilibrium, then, does depend on assumptions which ensure that for each individual there is at least one commodity he owns initially which is bound to have positive value. I will not state these assumptions here; the original set in Arrow-Debreu has been refined through the work of Gale (1957), McKenzie (1959, 1961), and Arrow and Hahn (1971, chap. 5, section 4).

General Equilibrium and Uncertainty

Once the broad approach to the analysis of existence was set, it could be applied in many different directions. One was the analysis of models which represented in one way or another imperfections in the competitive system. The requirement of proving an existence theorem in each case leads to the need for a rigorous spelling out of assumptions, a requirement which seems to be proving very fruitful. Much of this work is now going on, in such areas as the analysis of futures markets, expectations, and monetary theory, but this is not the place to comment on what is in any case a rapidly changing field.

Another approach is to retain the competitive assumptions but interpret them in new contexts. One example of this is the extension of general equilibrium theory to uncertain outcomes (Arrow, 1953; Debreu, 1959, chap. 7). Suppose there is some uncertainty in production due, for example, to the weather. One type of weather will benefit one kind of producer and injure another, while another type will do the opposite. If we assume that individuals are averse to risk, there is room for a mutually profitable trade in insurance. Even apart from risk aversion, individuals and firms in planning for an uncertain future may want to make sure that their demands and outputs are mutually compatible. Thus, if there is uncertainty about the supply of grain, a miller may prefer to make future contracts for labor contingent on that uncertainty.

We take from the theory of probability the concept of a *state of the world,* which is a description of the world so precise that it completely defines all initial holdings of goods and all technological possibilities. Uncertainty is not knowing which state will in fact hold. The initial holdings of commodity i by individual h if state s should hold can be designated by $\bar{x}_{his}$. Similarly, the set of possible input-output vectors for a firm may depend on the state s; let $y_{fs} = (y_{f1s}, \ldots, y_{fns})$ be a possible input-output vector for firm f if s is the state.

The feasibility of any allocation will then depend on the state s, and therefore commitments to consumption and production must vary similarly. Hence the decision by any individual must be a separate vector $x_{hs} = (x_{h1s}, \ldots, x_{hns})$ for each state s. But clearly it is optimal for all concerned to make all these decisions simultaneously, in advance of knowing which state of the world will in fact prevail; it is this advance decision which permits the possible gains from insurance, from the reduction in risk bearing. Hence, we should really think of the vector x_h, which, for fixed h, contains components x_{his} where i and s range over commodities and states of the world, respectively.

What we are led to is considering the same physical commodity in different states of the world as economically different commodities. The procedure is exactly analogous to Hicks's analysis of present and future goods (1939); the same physical commodity at different points of time defines different commodities.

The whole previous analysis can then be applied, with a suitable reinterpretation. Commodities in the ordinary sense are replaced by *contingent commodities,* promises to buy or sell a given commodity if, and only if, a certain state of the world occurs. The market will then determine contingent prices. Clearing of the markets means clearing of the contingent markets; the commitments made are sufficiently flexible so that they can always be satisfied.

It should be noted that preference orderings over vectors of contingent commodities contain elements of judgment about the likelihoods of different states of the world as well as elements of taste in the ordinary sense. Other things being equal, one will invest less heavily in a demand contingent upon a state deemed unlikely.

One can work out the implications of this model. Clearly, the contingent commodities called for do not exist to the extent required, but the variety of securities available on modern markets serves as a partial substitute. In my own thinking, the model of general equilibrium under uncertainty is as much a normative ideal as an empirical description. It is the way the actual world differs from the criteria of the model which suggests social policy to improve the efficiency with which risk bearing is allocated.

In fact, it is not a mere empirical accident that not all the contingent markets needed for efficiency exist, but a necessary fact with deep implications for the workings and structure of economic institutions. Roughly speaking, information about particular events, even after they have occurred, is not spread evenly throughout the population. Two people cannot enter into a contract contingent on the occurrence of a certain event or state if only one of them in fact will know that the event has occurred. A particular example of this is sometimes known as "moral hazard" in the insurance and economic literature. The very existence of insurance will change individual behavior in the direction of less care in avoiding risks. The insurance policy that would be called for by an optimal allocation of risk bearing would only cover unavoidable risks and would distinguish their effects from those due to behavior of the individual. But in fact all the insurer can observe is a result, for example, a fire or the success or failure of a business, and he cannot decompose it into exogenous and endogenous components. Contingent contracts, to speak generally, can be written only on mutually observed events, not on aspects of the state of the world which may be known to one but not both of the parties.

Although I cannot argue the point here, I would hold that the allocational difficulties arising from the inequality in information are of importance in such diverse fields as medical care and racial discrimination (see Arrow, 1963a, 1972). The difficulty of achieving optimal allocation of risk bearing because of differences in information was first stated in a general form by Roy Radner (1968).

The Theory of Social Choice

General competitive equilibrium above all teaches the extent to which a social allocation of resources can be achieved by independent private decisions coordinated through the market. We are assured indeed that not only can an allocation be achieved, but the result will be Pareto-efficient. But, as has been stressed, there is nothing in the process which guarantees that the distribution be just. Indeed, the theory teaches us that the final allocation will depend on the distribution of initial supplies and of ownership of firms. If we want to rely on the virtues of the market but also to achieve a more just distribution, the theory suggests the strategy of changing the initial distribution rather than interfering with the allocation process at some later stage.

Thus even under the assumptions most favorable to decentralization of decision making, there is an irreducible need for a social or collective choice on distribution. In point of fact, there are a great many other situations in which the replacement of market by collective decision making is necessary or at least desirable. In their different ways, both political scientists and economists have discussed the necessary role of the state. Among economists, these discussions have revolved around the concepts of externalities, increasing returns, and market failure; the clarification and application of these ideas have been among the major achievements of modern economic thought, but here I will merely recall them as helping to create the need for normative and descriptive analysis of collective decision making.

In the context of social choice, each individual may be assumed to have a preference ordering over all possible social states. This ordering expresses not only his desire for his own consumption but also social attitudes, his views on justice in distribution or on benefits to others from collective decisions. The ordinalist viewpoint forbids us from ascribing a definite quantitative expression to this preference, at least a quantitative expression which would have any interpersonal validity.

Classical utilitarianism specifies that choices among alternative social states be judged in terms of their consequences for the members of the society; in the present terminology, this means in terms of the individual preference scales for social choices. This is obviously not a sufficient basis for choice in view of the diversity of individual preferences. It is implicit in classical utilitarianism and explicit in Bergson's work that there is a second level where the individual judgments are aggregated into what might be termed a welfare judgment.

Thus the formation of welfare judgments is logically equivalent to what I will call a *constitution.* Specifically, a constitution is a rule which associates to each possible set of individual preference orderings a social choice rule. A social choice rule, in turn, is a rule for selecting a socially preferred action out of any set of alternatives which may be feasible.

So far, I would hold that the description of a constitution is a tautology, at least if we start from the view that social choice has to be based on the individual preference orderings. The real question is what conditions are to be imposed on the constitution.

One condition, which is already contained in Bergson's work, is that for any given set of individual preferences, the social choice rule defined by them shall satisfy the technical conditions of an ordering; that is, that all possible alternative social states should be capable of being ranked and then the social choice from any particular set of alternatives should be the most preferred alternative, according to the ordering, in the available set. This is sometimes called the condition of collective rationality.

A second condition, again in agreement with Bergson, is the Pareto principle; the social choice process shall never yield an outcome if there is another feasible alternative which everyone prefers according to his preference ordering.

A third, hardly controversial, condition is that of non-dictatorship; the constitution shall not be such that there is an individual whose preferences automatically become those of society regardless of anyone else's preferences.

The fourth condition which I have suggested, that of the independence of irrelevant alternatives, is more disputable, though I would argue that it has strong pragmatic justification: the social choice made from any set of alternatives will depend on only the orderings of individuals among alternatives in that set. To see what is at stake, suppose that a society has to make a choice among some alternatives and does so. After the decision is made, an alternative which has not previously been thought of is mentioned as a logical possibility, although it is still not feasible. The individuals can expand their preference orderings to place this new alternative in its place on their ranking; but should this preference information about an alternative which could not be chosen in any case affect the previous decision?

Any form of voting certainly satisfies the condition of independence of irrelevant alternatives; the preferences of voters as between candidates and noncandidates or as between noncandidates are, of course, never asked for or taken into account.

It turns out that these four reasonable sounding requirements are contradictory (Arrow, 1951b, 1963b). That is, if we devise any constitution, then it is always possible to find a set of individual orderings which will cause the constitution to violate one of these conditions. In one special form, this paradox is old. The method of majority voting is an appealing method of social choice. Like any other voting method, it satisfies independence of irrelevant alternatives and certainly the Pareto principle and the condition of non-dictatorship. But as Condorcet pointed out as far back as 1785, majority voting may not lead to an ordering. More specifically, intransitivity is possible. Consider the following example. There are three alternatives *x*, *y*, and *z*, among which choice is to be made. One-third of the voters have the ranking *x*, *y*, *z*; one-third, the ranking *y*, *z*, *x*; and one-third, the ranking *z*, *x*, *y*. Then a majority of the voters prefer *x* to *y*, a majority prefer *y* to *z*, and a majority prefer *z* to *x*. Unfortunately, this result is not due to a removable imperfection in the method of majority voting. The four conditions on social choice are mutually contradictory.

The philosophical and distributive implications of the paradox of social choice are still not clear. Certainly, there is no simple way out. I hope that others will take this paradox as a challenge rather than as a discouraging barrier.

References

K. J. Arrow (1951a). "An Extension of the Basic Theorems of Classical Welfare Economics," in J. Neyman, ed., *Proceedings of the Second Berkeley Symposium on Mathematical Statistics and Probability,* Berkeley and Los Angeles 1951, 507–532.

K. J. Arrow (1951b). *Social Choice and Individual Values,* New York 1951.

K. J. Arrow, "Le Rôle des Valeurs Boursières pour la Repartition la Meilleure des Risques," *Econometrie,* Colloques Internationaux du Centre National de la Recherche Scientifique, vol. 11, 1953, 41–47.

K. J. Arrow (1963a). "Uncertainty and the Welfare Economics of Medical Care," *Amer. Econ. Rev.,* Dec. 1963, 53, 941–973.

K. J. Arrow (1963b). *Social Choice and Individual Values,* New York 1963.

K. J. Arrow, "Models of Racial Discrimination," in A. H. Pascal, ed., *Racial Discrimination in Economic Life,* Lexington 1972.

K. J. Arrow and G. Debreu, "Existence of an Equilibrium for a Competitive Economy," *Econometrica,* July 1954, 22, 265–290.

K. J. Arrow and F. H. Hahn, *General Competitive Analysis,* San Francisco 1971.

A. Bergson, "A Reformulation of Certain Aspects of Welfare Economics," *Quart. J. Econ.,* Feb. 1938, 52, 310–334.

K. G. Cassel, *Theoretische Sozialökonomie,* Erlangen 1918.

Marquis de Condorcet, *Essai sur l'application de l'analyse à la probabilité des décisions rendues à la pluralité des voix,* Paris 1785.

G. Debreu, "The Coefficient of Resource Utilization," *Econometrica,* July 1951, 19, 273–292.

G. Debreu, *Theory of Value,* New York 1959.

D. Gale, "General Equilibrium of Linear Models," unpublished, 1957.

J. R. Hicks, *Value and Capital,* Oxford 1939.

J. R. Hicks and R. G. D. Allen, "A Reconsideration of the Theory of Value," *Economica,* Feb. 1934, 1, 52–76, 196–219.

H. Hotelling, "Demand Functions with Limited Budgets," *Econometrica,* Jan. 1935, 3, 66–78.
H. Hotelling, "The General Welfare in Relation to Problems of Taxation and Railway and Utility Rates," *Econometrica,* July 1938, 6, 242–269.
S. Kakutani, "A Generalization of Brouwer's Fixed-Point Theorem," *Duke Mathematical J.,* 1941, 8, 451–459.
J. M. Keynes, *The General Theory of Employment Interest and Money,* New York 1936.
T. C. Koopmans, "Analysis of Production as an Efficient Combination of Activities," in T. C. Koopmans, ed., *Activity Analysis of Allocation and Production,* New York 1951, chap. 3.
O. Lange, "Say's Law: A Restatement and Criticism," in O. Lange et al., eds., *Studies in Mathematical Economics and Econometrics,* Chicago 1942, 49–68.
A. Leijonhufvud, *On Keynesian Economics and the Economics of Keynes: A Study of Monetary Theory,* New York 1968.
L. McKenzie, "On Equilibrium in Graham's Model of World Trade and Other Competitive Systems," *Econometrica,* Apr. 1954, 22, 147–161.
L. McKenzie, "On the Existence of General Equilibrium for a Competitive Market," *Econometrica,* Jan. 1959, 27, 54–71.
L. McKenzie, "On the Existence of General Equilibrium: Some Corrections," *Econometrica,* Apr. 1961, 29, 247–248.
H. Neisser, "Lohnhöhe und Beschäftigungsgrad im Marktgleichgewicht," *Weltwirtschaftliches Archiv,* 1932, 36, 415–455.
J. von Neumann, "Über ein ökonomisches Gleichungssystem und eine Verallgemeinerung des Brouwerschen Fixpunktsatzes," *Ergebnisse eines Mathematischen Kolloquiums,* 1937, 8, 73–83.
J. von Neumann and O. Morgenstern, *Theory of Games and Economic Behavior,* Princeton 1944.
V. Pareto, *Manuel d'Économie Politique,* Paris 1909.
R. Radner, "Competitive Equilibrium under Uncertainty," *Econometrica,* Jan. 1968, 36, 31–58.
P. A. Samuelson, "A Note on the Pure Theory of Consumer Behavior," *Economica,* Feb. 1938, 4, 61–71.
P. A. Samuelson, *Foundations of Economic Analysis,* Cambridge, Mass. 1947.
P. A. Samuelson, "Maximum Principles in Analytical Economics," in *Les Prix Nobel en 1970,* Stockholm 1971, 273–288.
K. Schlesinger, "Über die Produktionsgleichungen der ökonomische Wertlehre," *Ergebnisse eines Mathematischen Kolloquiums,* 1933–34, 6, 10–11.
H. von Stackelberg, "Zwei Kritische bemerkungen zur preistheorie Gustav Cassels," *Zeitschrift für Nationalökonomie,* 1933, 4, 456–472.
A. Wald, "Über die eindeutige positive Lösbarkeit der neuen Produktionsgleichungen," *Ergebnisse eines Mathematischen Kolloquiums,* 1933–34, 6, 12–20.
A. Wald, "Über die Produktionsgleichungen der ökonomische Wertlehre," *Ergebnisse eines Mathematischen Kolloquiums,* 1934–35, 7, 1–6.
A. Wald, "Über einige Gleichungssysteme der mathematischen Ökonomie," *Zeitschrift für Nationalökonomie,* 1936, 7, 637–670.

10 Cost-theoretical and Demand-theoretical Approaches to the Theory of Price Determination

In the state of flux of economic theory preceding the publication of Adam Smith's *Wealth of Nations,* there were several writers (such as Condillac and Turgot) who maintained that the value of goods was partly determined by their usefulness or the demand for them. Indeed, in an isolated development, Isnard proposed a genuine general-equilibrium model in which each individual spends a fixed proportion of his income on each final good, the income being derived from sale of assets (Isnard assumes each individual holds at most one asset), and production of goods from factors takes place under fixed coefficients.[1] It is clear that the equilibrium prices of this system are determined by both demand and supply conditions — more specifically, by the proportions in which the individuals divide their incomes among final goods and the input–output coefficients.

But the role of demand in the determination of prices was essentially disregarded by the classical school stemming from Adam Smith and continuing with Ricardo, John Stuart Mill, and Marx. If one takes a consistent labor theory of value, as is suggested by Smith's famous example of the deer

1. A. N. Isnard, *Traité des richesses* (1781); see the account of his work in R. Theocharis, *Early Developments in Mathematical Economics* (London, 1961), pp. 66–70.

This chapter was written with David Starrett. Reprinted from *Carl Menger and the Austrian School of Economics,* ed. J. R. Hicks and W. Weber (Oxford: Clarendon Press, 1973), pp. 129–148.

and the beavers, the classical position can be explained, if not defended. That is, there is a simple model of the economic system in terms of which prices are determined solely by the technological conditions of production. The model is simply this: There is one primary factor of production. All other goods are produced under conditions of fixed coefficients with one output, the inputs being the primary factor and possibly other produced goods. Finally, competition enforces zero profits. Hence, to each produced good, there corresponds one equation defining its price to be equal to its cost, which is determined by the prices of the one primary factor and of other produced goods. In symbols, let p_i be the price of produced commodity i, v the price of the primary factor, a_{ij} the amount of commodity j used in the production of one unit of commodity i, and b_i the amount of the primary factor in the production of one unit of commodity i. Then the condition of zero profits is

$$p_i = \sum_j a_{ij} p_j + b_i v, \tag{10-1}$$

since the right-hand side is the cost of producing one unit of commodity i. As we let i vary over the produced commodities, we have a system of equations in the unknown prices, p_i, v. The equations are homogeneous, so that if there is one solution, we can obtain others by multiplying all prices (including that of the primary factor) by the same positive constant. If we fix v, the price of the primary factor, we can consider Eqs. (10-1) to be a system of equations in the prices of the produced commodities, p_i. There are as many equations as unknowns. The classical economists implicitly and Leontief explicitly solved for these prices in terms of v; thus the price of each commodity is a constant multiple of v, and the multiple is completely determined by the input–output coefficients a_{ij} and b_i. We find then that under the assumptions made, the relative prices of all commodities are completely determined by the technology of the system.

(Modern theoretical economists have learned to ask more penetrating questions and to demand more rigor in the reasoning. They wish to be assured that solutions to the equations (10-1) actually exist; this is not guaranteed merely by equal numbers of equations and unknowns. They are also concerned to show that the solutions are economically meaningful; in this case, that the prices found are positive. It has been shown that both of these questions have affirmative answers but only provided that a natural condition is placed on the matrix of input–output coefficients. Designate an output level, x_i, for each produced commodity i; call this the *gross output* of that commodity. The production of other commodities requires inputs of commodity i; the difference between the gross output and the interindustry demand is called the *net output* of commodity i for the system. In symbols, the net output, y_i, is defined by

$$y_i = x_i - \sum_j a_{ji} x_j.$$

For an arbitrary choice of gross-output levels, it can easily happen that the net output of one or more commodities is negative. We shall say that the input–output matrix is *productive* if there is at least one system of gross outputs, x_i, for which all net outputs are positive. In this definition, we are ignoring any limitations on the primary factor. Then if there are fixed coefficients and if each industry produces only one output, so that a_{ij} is never negative, it can be shown that if the input–output matrix is productive, Eqs. (10-1) have a unique solution which is nonnegative.)

To repeat, the assumptions here made are fixed coefficients, one primary factor, and no joint production. The assumptions made by the classical economists are a little hard to pin down at times, but certainly a world in which labor is the sole primary factor is one interpretation which bears some relation to classical thought. Then the relative prices of commodities are exactly proportional to the amounts of labor directly or indirectly embodied in them.

The system of equations (10-1) is not, from the modern point of view, a complete system, for it says nothing about quantities. It can, of course, be completed by adding functions expressing consumer demand as a function of prices and income, where the income of a consumer is the amount of the primary factor he holds multiplied by v. But the point is that Eqs. (10-1), though a subsystem of the complete set of equations of general equilibrium, form a complete system in the prices alone.

The Ricardian system in a simple form (without capital) appears to have two factors of production, labor and land. But in fact the Malthus–Ricardo theory of labor supply makes labor a produced commodity. Labor, far from being a primary factor, is in perfectly elastic supply at a fixed real wage in terms of grain, at least in the long run. Hence, labor is properly to be thought of as a produced commodity; so is grain, which is produced from land and labor. Land is the only primary factor, and the static Ricardian theory implies that the relative prices of all commodities are determined by the amounts of land directly or indirectly embodied in them.[2]

2. For this interpretation of Ricardo, see P. A. Samuelson, "A Modern Treatment of the Ricardian Economy," *Quarterly Journal of Economics*, 73 (1959), 217–231.

The introduction of capital into these static classical models was never really accomplished consistently. Sraffa has interpreted Ricardo's determination of the rate of interest as being purely technological.[3] According to Sraffa, Ricardo assumed that there was at least one process by which grain could be used, for planting and for feeding workers, to produce a crop of marginal and therefore rent-free land. This rate of return then ruled the entire economy. However, if there is to be also a theory of land value, there must be at least two processes for producing grain, one using marginal land and the other using land with a higher contribution to productivity. Such a theory can certainly be constructed, but we are no longer in a world of fixed coefficients. Marx's attempt to introduce capital into an otherwise standard classical model led only to the famous contradiction between the models of volume 1 and of volume 3 of *Capital.*

Apart from the problem of capital, the classical structure gradually faced new challenges, partly due to more detailed study of the real world, partly due to changes in that world. By the middle of the nineteenth century the course of real wages was certainly inconsistent with any subsistence theory. The value placed by the market on labor could not be explained by its cost of production; the most natural alternative was to explain wages by the productivity of labor, an explanation only useful if labor was intrinsically scarce. In short, labor had to be treated like land. Also, the only explanation of relative wages in a classical model was Smith's doctrine of equalizing differences, due to unpleasantness, riskiness, and the like. Individuals were supposed to have equal abilities but were not indifferent among alternative jobs. But this is already a multifactor model; not only raw labor but also willingness to do unpleasant work or to engage in risk bearing are scarce primary factors. Further, the most casual observation of the world suggested that equalizing differences were an inadequate explanation of relative wages; it was frequently remarked that the most highly paid positions were the most, not the least, preferred. When Cairnes started talking about "non-competing groups," the classical model was completely vitiated. The multiplicity of primary factors required a new theory.

The great founders of the neoclassical school, Carl Menger, W. S. Jevons, and Léon Walras, and their precursors, A. A. Cournot and H. H. Gossen, understood the glaring omission of demand from the classical model. They

---

3. P. Sraffa, Introduction to *Works and Correspondence of David Ricardo,* ed. P. Sraffa and M. H. Dobb (Cambridge, 1951–55), vol. 1, pp. xxxi–xxxii.

took as an expository point of departure a model which was the polar opposite of the classical, the model of pure exchange. They recognized the importance of production, but Menger and Jevons especially put stress on the notion of exchange as expressing the essence of the economic system; production to some extent appeared merely as an indirect way of exchanging initial holdings.

If a classical model of production is completed by adding a system of demand relations, the prices are determined purely by technological or cost considerations. Then the quantities are completely determined by the demands at those prices. In a model of pure exchange, the direction of causation is almost completely reversed. The total quantities of the goods are given; the demand conditions determine the prices as that set that will cause demand to equal the given supply for all goods.

General Equilibrium and Nonsubstitution Theorems

From a formal point of view, all possibilities are encompassed in a general equilibrium model. The technology, the demand conditions, and the initial resource availabilities jointly determine all prices and quantities. But like all generalities, statements of this kind are not very informative. It would be more useful to be able to say that there are some relations in the system that depend on only some but not all of the parameters of the system. As far as this chapter is concerned, the question is whether there exist any propositions about prices in which only the technology parameters of the economy enter.

Intuitively, it is clear that such propositions are possible only if some specific assumptions about the technology are made. Clearly, in a world of diminishing returns in each industry, the relative prices are going to be governed by the outputs, which in turn depend on demand. Even under constant returns, it will be necessary to have some sense of a clear distinction between primary factors and produced goods. On the other hand, we must maintain the multiplicity of factors; we cannot retreat from that essential feature of the neoclassical revolution.

We may expect, and this turns out to be the case, that we can establish a link between the prices of factors and those of produced goods, where the parameters in this relation are purely technological. This generalizes the one-factor classical determination of prices. It can first be seen most clearly by changing the input–output model given above only to the extent of having several primary factors. Let k be the index for a primary factor, v_k its price, and b_{ik} the amount of factor k used in the production of one unit of commodity i. Then Eqs. (10-1) are replaced by

$$p_i = \sum_j a_{ij} p_j + \sum_k b_{ik} v_k. \tag{10-2}$$

Now fix all the factor prices, v_k. Then Eqs. (10-2) are exactly the same as Eqs. (10-1) except for the constant terms. Hence, we can solve for the goods prices, p_i, for any given set of values of factor prices. (The same argument as before shows that if the input–output matrix is productive, the price solution exists and is always nonnegative if the factor prices are.) As the factor prices change, the commodity prices will, of course, change; but for any given set of factor prices, the goods prices are determined by a relation that involves only technological parameters.

Under these conditions the economic system can be reduced to a model that is formally identical with a model of pure exchange, where, however, only the primary factors are considered. For any given set of prices for the factors, the incomes of the consumers are determined. At the same time, by the method of the preceding paragraph, the prices of final goods are determined. The demand conditions then determine the demands for final goods. In an input–output system, these demands in turn determine demands for primary factors uniquely. Hence, we have expressed demands for primary factors as functions of their prices alone (all other prices having been expressed in terms of factor prices). The supplies of factors are given, so that the model of derived demand for factors leads to a formulation abstractly isomorphic to that of pure exchange.

The assumptions about production made so far, to repeat, have been fixed coefficients of production and no joint production. It is a somewhat surprising fact that the first assumption is unnecessary. This was shown independently by Paul Samuelson and Nicholas Georgescu-Roegen.[4] They stated their results for the case of one primary factor, but they can be reinterpreted to express the technological determination of the prices of produced goods by those of factors.

More precisely, it is supposed that each produced good can be produced in

4. N. Georgescu-Roegen, "Some Properties of a Generalized Leontief Model," in T. C. Koopmans (ed.), *Activity Analysis of Allocation and Production* (New York, 1951), chap. 10; P. A. Samuelson, "Abstract of a Theorem Concerning Substitutability in Leontief Models," in T. C. Koopmans (ed.), ibid., chap. 7. See also chaps. 8 and 9 by T. C. Koopmans and K. J. Arrow in the same volume.

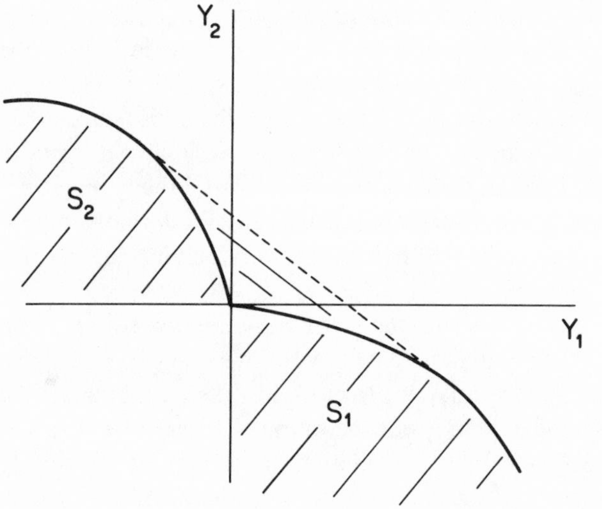

Figure 10.1

a number of alternative ways, but that constant returns and convexity hold and that no production process has more than one output. The model can be represented diagrammatically as in Figure 10.1. Assume there is only one primary factor; call it "labor" for definiteness. Commodity 1 can be produced by any one of a set of alternative activities from labor and commodity 2, and similarly commodity 2 from labor and commodity 1. Now consider all possible production vectors having commodity 1 as output and using *all* of the labor. This set is represented by S_1 on the diagram; in general, commodity 2 is an input, so vectors in this set have positive y_1-coordinates and negative y_2-coordinates. (Here, we let y_1 and y_2 be outputs of commodities 1 and 2, respectively, inputs being regarded as negative outputs.) Similarly, S_2 is the set of possible vectors representing the production of commodity 2 by the use of commodity 1 and all of the available labor. In fact, the labor will be divided between two production vectors, one for each output. Under constant returns to scale a production vector with a fraction a of the total labor is obtained by multiplying both the y_1- and the y_2-coordinates by a. If the fraction $1-a$ is then assigned to another production vector, a similar multiplication takes place. The net result, from the viewpoint of the entire economy, is obtained by adding the two resulting vectors. If one vector is chosen from S_1 and one from S_2, this amounts to taking a line segment joining any vector in S_1 with any vector in S_2; any point on that line segment is a technologically possible production vector for the entire economy. However, this social production vector is feasible only if the values of y_1 and y_2 are nonnegative, for there are no outside sources for these commodities. The socially feasible production-possibility set is then defined as consisting of all vectors which (1) lie on a line segment joining a vector in S_1 with one in S_2, and (2) fall in the nonnegative orthant. Finally, the social production frontier consists of all such points that are not dominated (that is, for which there does not exist another feasible production vector which produces more of both outputs).

A glance at Figure 10.1 shows that the feasible production frontier is in fact a straight line. This is a remarkable fact, with interesting implications. For one thing, it shows that the relative prices of the different outputs must be constant for all possible demands, for the marginal rates of transformation are constant. It follows then that relative prices are determined by technological conditions only; they are cost-determined or at least supply-determined. Further, the activity used in producing any particular commodity is independent of the demands; it is that production vector in S_1 or S_2, as the case may be, that lies on the frontier, after adjustment for scale. Indeed, one might as well assume fixed coefficients; the only practical difference from the fixed-coefficient case is that the input-output coefficients for every industry will change if there is technical change in any one industry in the present case of alternative activities, while, by definition, they will change only in the one industry in the fixed-coefficients case.

The absolute prices of the final goods vary in proportion to the price of the one factor. Since the relative output prices are cost-determined, each final goods price is a constant multiple of the factor price.

The Samuelson–Georgescu-Roegen theorem, as stated, assumes constant returns to scale, no joint production, and one primary factor, but, unlike the fixed-coefficients case, permits alternative activities for the production of a commodity. However, it can easily be reinterpreted to provide a statement of the extent to which prices are determined by technology, analogous to the relation that holds in the case of fixed coefficients. Choose any set of prices for the primary factors, and hold them constant for the moment. Then we can treat all the primary factors as a single composite commodity, in the manner that we have learned from Hicks. The Samuelson–Georgescu-Roegen theorem then assures us that the relative prices of the produced goods are completely determined by technology, and the methods of production used are also so determined. If the factor prices are changed, then there is a new determination of relative prices and of production vectors in each industry. It can easily be seen that the relative prices of the produced goods vary continuously with factor prices and also that the absolute prices of the produced goods are homogeneous of degree one in the factor prices.

Let us restate this important conclusion: *If there are constant returns to scale and no joint production, then for each produced good, its price and its production vector are continuous functions of factor prices, determined by technology alone, price being homogeneous of degree one and the production vector homogeneous of degree zero in factor prices.*

This result gives a precise statement of the ways in which technology and demand affect the determination of prices. Start with a set of factor prices. With these and the given factor supplies, individual incomes are now determined. At the same time, the prices of produced goods are determined; in conjunction with the incomes, household demands for produced goods are determined. Since methods of production are also determined by factor prices, the derived demands for factors are determined. Thus factor demands are well-defined functions of factor prices, while factor supplies are given. The price system of the entire economy then can be determined from equilibrium in the factor markets, and the latter is formally isomorphic to equilibrium in a pure exchange model.

In a many-factor world, then, demand considerations affect the determination of prices through their effects on demand for factors. If there are two commodities, however different they may be from each other, which make the same direct and indirect demands on factors, then their prices are going to be equal no matter what the demands for them are. But if commodities use primary factors in differing proportions, then shifts in demand among them change the demands for primary factors and these changes, in turn, change the relative prices of the commodities.

Since such strong use has been made of the assumption that there is no joint production, it may be well to illustrate what the consequences of permitting it are. In Figure 10.2 we consider the general case of joint production with one primary factor; the set S_{12} consists of all pairs of outputs which can be produced with a given volume of the one primary factor. In equilibrium, the ratio of the prices of the produced goods is equal to their marginal rate of transformation, and this varies from point to point along the production frontier. Hence, the price ratio will depend on both cost and demand conditions. The extreme case where the two products are produced jointly in fixed proportions is illustrated in Figure 10.3. Here, the quantities of the two produced goods are fixed, and their relative prices are completely demand-determined.

A special case of some interest is that where joint production is possible,

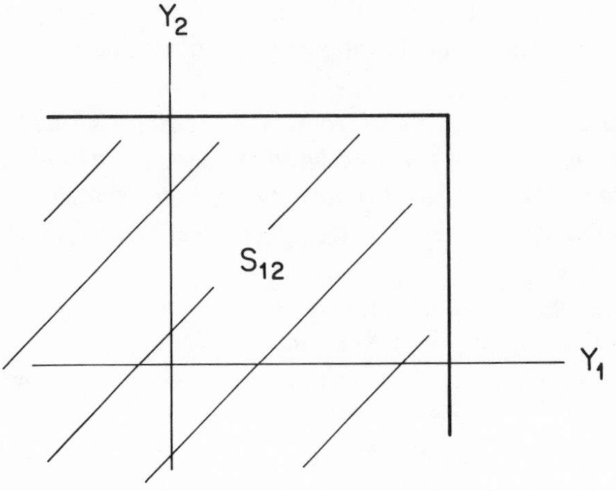

Figure 10.2

but there is also a set of alternative processes for producing one of the two products. This is illustrated in Figure 10.4. The social production set then is obtained, as in Figure 10.1, by drawing all possible line segments joining points in S_1 (the production vectors having commodity 1 as sole output and using all of the primary factor) with points in S_{12}. The feasible production frontier then consists partly of a straight line and partly of the curved boundary of S_{12}. Thus, if demand conditions are such as to require the use of some production of commodity 1 alone, the prices of the produced goods

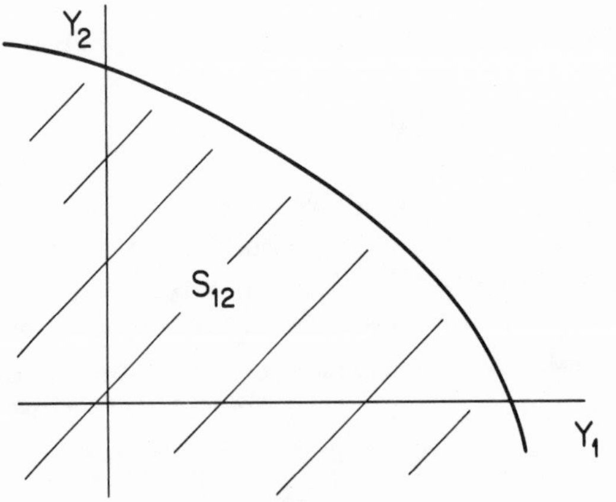

Figure 10.3

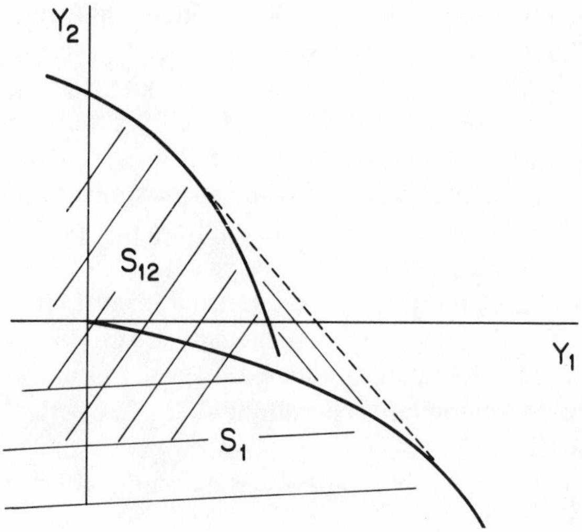

Figure 10.4

are technologically determined. But if demand so shifts that only joint production processes are employed, then prices are jointly determined by supply and demand; in the extreme case where joint production occurs only in fixed proportions, the prices become purely demand-determined.

So far, the model presented has been static in nature. Time has not entered in any way; indeed, it has been tacitly assumed that production takes no time. However, we can incorporate the basic considerations of capital theory into our framework with little difficulty. But before doing so, it is convenient to introduce the special case of a pure capital model.

The Pure Capital Model

The last few decades have seen the development of a new one-factor model, this time with capital as the sole primary factor, and therewith a new version of determination of prices by cost considerations alone. As the multiplicity of current and ancient debates has revealed, capital in the abstract sense is not an identifiable commodity like labor, land, or specific capital goods; it is rather the willingness to wait.[5]

5. Carl Menger sharply distinguished between specific capital goods and capital in the abstract; see F. A. Hayek, Introduction to *Collected Works of Carl Menger,* vol. 1, no. 17, in Reprints of Scarce Tracts in Economic and Political Science (London School of Economics and Political Science, 1934), p. xxvi.

The essential assumption is stated in the title of Piero Sraffa's influential exposition;[6] all commodities are produced. Some commodities, capital goods in particular, have a special role in production. But since they are themselves produced, they cannot play an ultimate role in the determination of values.

First, let us consider some elementary definitions and assumptions. When we speak of capital as a factor of production, we are implying that production takes time, that inputs precede outputs. By a device due to John von Neumann,[7] we can assume that all production takes the same length of time, which we take as one time unit. There is no loss of generality; if a production process takes two units of time, we regard the state of the good in process after one time unit as a distinct commodity, the output of the first period's work and an input into the second.

A production process, then, consists of inputs of certain goods, which we shall call capital goods, and outputs of both capital goods and consumption goods. The supply of a capital good at any moment is the output of a production process which started one period earlier; the demand for that good is the total input of that good in all processes starting at that moment. Feasibility requires that demand not exceed supply. As before, we assume that the production of each kind of good occurs under conditions of constant returns to scale and no joint production, but alternative methods of production may exist.

What the modern theorists assert is that under these conditions, costs determine prices in the long run. Clearly, if initially the supplies of different kinds of capital goods are arbitrarily given, production possibilities over the next few periods are constrained by them, and relative prices will actually be affected by demand. But the emphasis of Sraffa and of Joan Robinson,[8] and earlier of von Neumann,[9] is on states of *balanced growth* of the system, in

6. P. Sraffa, *Production of Commodities by Means of Commodities* (Cambridge, 1963).

7. J. von Neumann, "Über ein ökonomisches Gleichungssystem und eine Verallgemeinerung des Brouwerschen Fixpunktsatzes," *Ergebnisse eines Mathematischen Kolloquiums,* 8 (1937), 73–83.

8. Sraffa, *Production of Commodities;* J. Robinson, *The Accumulation of Capital* (London, 1958).

9. von Neumann, "Über ein ökonomisches Gleichungssystem." It should be remarked that the von Neumann model is more general and permits joint production. By this fact, it does not bear directly on the issue of this chapter. It is true that in the original von Neumann model, prices are technologically determined; but this is so because there is nothing but technology in the model, consumption being absent. The model has been modified to permit consumption

which the initial supplies of capital goods are such that relative prices are constant over time and quantities of capital and consumption goods are growing at the same constant rate. It seems to be implicitly assumed that a system starting from an arbitrary configuration of capital goods will tend to a state of balanced growth, an assumption which surely does not hold in general and should be validated in any given case. We shall show here how in a pure capital model with no joint production, the balanced growth prices are indeed determined purely by technology. However, we must enter one reservation immediately. The very existence of a state of balanced growth is possible only if some restrictions are placed on demand. Demand here refers both to choice over time and choice of consumption goods at a given instant of time. In a pure capital model, it may well be that per capita incomes are rising; it is implied that at constant prices both the savings ratio and the relative demands for consumption goods are constant. At a logical level, therefore, demand affects prices if only to the extent that demand must satisfy certain conditions if the balanced growth path is to exist.[10]

The types of conclusion possible are well illustrated by a simple model in which there are two goods, a consumption good and a capital good, each produced one time unit after an input of the capital good. Since the capital-good-producing process has the same physical good as input and output, the rate of interest is equal to the excess of output over input for a unit input in that process. The price of the consumption good relative to that of the capital good is simply the ratio of their capital inputs per unit output. Prices are indeed technologically determined. Demand conditions determine the real magnitudes of the system; in balanced growth, they are the rate of growth of the capital stock and the ratio of consumption to capital in each time period (these are not independent). The rate of interest equals the maximum possible rate of growth of the system that would occur if there were no consumption.

The properties of this example generalize to a situation with arbitrarily

---

by J. G. Kemeny, O. Morgenstern, and G. L. Thompson, "A Generalization of the von Neumann Model of an Expanding Economy," *Econometrica,* 24 (1956), 115–135, especially 132–133. But then in general relative prices and indeed the rate of interest will be affected by the consumption levels.

10. Empirically, the savings ratio may indeed be sensibly constant over time, but Engel's laws show that relative demands for produced goods certainly change with income. As the analysis of this chapter suggests, the crucial point is whether or not the shift in commodity demands causes a shift in demands for different capital goods. It surely does have this effect, and therefore balanced growth seems to have limited use as a tool of long-run analysis.

many consumption and capital goods (and choice of technique) if we assume no joint production and in addition that the available technologies for producing capital goods are *indecomposable.* The assumption of indecomposability requires roughly that it should not be possible to split the capital goods up into two groups such that elements of one group can be produced without using any capital goods from the other group.

Under this interdependence assumption, it can be shown that the interest rate and the relative prices of capital goods are indeed completely determined by the technology. The interest rate is equal to the fastest rate of pure capital accumulation possible given the technology, and the only competitive activities will be those that would generate this maximal capital growth.

Once the capital goods prices are known, it is clear that the consumption goods prices are uniquely determined; for each consumption good, the activity chosen will be the one which is cheapest in its use of capital goods, valued at the known capital goods prices. *Thus, all balanced growth prices in an indecomposable pure capital model with no joint production are determined by the technology.* This conclusion is justified in greater detail in the Appendix.

We also show in the Appendix that demand conditions will determine the relative demands for different consumption goods and the demand for capital goods as a whole relative to consumption goods; the latter ratio in turn determines the rate of growth of the system. Indeed, with relative prices fixed, we can treat consumption and capital as composite commodities, and the simple two-commodity model discussed before applies.

Critique of the Pure Capital Model

The basic difficulties with the pure capital model are those that led to the downfall of the classical theory—the failure to explain either absolute or relative wages. In many varieties of growth models labor is exogenously given, but then, of course, it is a nonproduced primary factor even in the long run, and the preceding analysis fails. Relative prices then are partially demand-determined.

A pure capital model has two alternatives: to treat labor as a produced good, or to ignore its role as a limiting factor. The former approach has, to our knowledge, been tried seriously only by von Neumann, who in effect revived the Ricardo-Malthus subsistence theory. But even then labor appears as jointly produced with other goods. Certainly, under modern conditions, there is no clear relation between the economic resources available to parents and the number of their children. When one considers in addition that children are consumption goods for their parents as well as capital goods in later years, it would appear that there is no way of treating labor as a produced commodity without also permitting joint production in an essential way. But then the argument that leads to cost determination of prices is completely vitiated.

In Joan Robinson's version, the condition of equality of supply and demand on the labor market is dropped from the system. Keynesian assumptions are projected into the long run. Permanent and indeed relatively growing unemployment is possible. Then (if land is disregarded), a pure capital model is possible.

In a purely neoclassical version, permanent unemployment would require a zero wage. In Robinson's model, market-clearing forces do not operate on the labor market, though they do on all other markets. Real wages are then determined by social and institutional considerations, or by a structural need of the system for demand by workers.

We merely wish to present this view, not to comment on it. It does involve a complete divorce between wages and the scarcity of labor.

Finally, we note that in terms of the pure capital model, relative wages can be determined only by investments of human capital. Actually, this hypothesis does not go far to explain actual relative wage levels. It is true, for example, that on the average individuals with college degrees earn more than those without them, and the rate of return is even comparable to the market rate. But the use of averages conceals a very large variance within each one of the two categories. This variance may be due to chance, but it is certainly also due in part to varying performance abilities which are acquired genetically or in the family and general culture and which cannot be described as produced or acquired under market conditions.

In short, the supplies of labor in general and with particular skills cannot be regarded as completely purchased within the economic system, and therefore the pure capital model seems inadequate. The demand element in the formation of prices seems to us ineradicable.

We now consider briefly a more general capital model, in which original factors of production appear. In order to make use of the framework and analysis of the second section, we drop the distinction between consumption and capital goods. With interest (r) now being paid on circulating capital and exogenous resource inputs, Eqs. (10-2) become (note that we are again restricting ourselves to balanced growth):

$$p_i = \left(\sum_j a_{ij} p_j + \sum_k b_{ik} v_k\right)(1 + r).$$

Now if we hold the prices of exogenous resources *and the interest rate* fixed, we can perform the analysis of the second section just as before.[11] We conclude that the prices of goods are uniquely determined once the prices of factors *and the interest rate* are determined. Thus, if we think of the interest rate as the "price" of an original factor "time," we are asserting that all relative variation in final demand will be reflected in the relative prices of "original" factors. This is precisely the operational meaning of Samuelson's factor-price frontier.[12]

Remark. The assumption of no joint production excludes the possibility of fixed capital. By a well-known argument, used by von Neumann and attributed by Sraffa to Torrens (1818),[13] the capital goods remaining at the end of a production period are to be considered as jointly produced with the output of the process in the usual sense. But as shown in the second section (see Figure 10.4 and the discussion based on it), as long as capital goods are also being produced independently in some positive quantities, the Samuelson – Georgescu-Roegen theorem is still applicable; hence the present generalization as well as the results of the third section are still valid in this case.

In the system as now constituted, the rate of time preference may have considerable influence on relative prices and the particular choice of technique, since the rate of time preference enters into the determination of the rate of interest; for different rates of interest relative to other factor prices, we naturally get different commodity prices and different production programs. This is simply one more manifestation of our general conclusion that the theory of value cannot be divorced entirely from demand considerations.

Appendix

We sketch here briefly the determination of the balanced-growth prices and magnitudes in the pure capital model. A collection of activities, one for producing each commodity, will be referred to as a *realization* of the technology. We can represent a realization by a pair of matrices, columns of which are production activities. Let C be the matrix of these production

11. This analysis is rigorously carried out by M. Morishima, *Equilibrium, Stability and Growth* (Oxford, 1964), chap. 4. Also, see P. A. Samuelson, "A New Theorem on Nonsubstitution," in *Money, Growth and Methodology* (Lund, 1961), pp. 407–423.

12. See P. Samuelson, "Parable and Realism in Capital Theory," *Review of Economic Studies*, 29 (1962), 193–206.

13. Sraffa, *Production of Commodities*, pp. 94–95.

vectors for consumption goods and K the matrix of production vectors for capital goods. When necessary, we shall use a superscript to index realizations. Both C and K are nonnegative in every realization; we assume that K is also *indecomposable* (every capital good is used directly or indirectly in the production of every other capital good) in every realization.

We show first that regardless of the pattern of demand (subject to the caveats mentioned above), the balanced-growth price system and realization are uniquely determined by the technology. Concentrate first on the prices for capital goods. For any realization K, the zero profit condition for capital goods production processes can be written

(A-1) $$q = (1 + r)qK,$$

where r is the rate of interest. It is well known that the system (A-1) has a unique nonnegative solution for r and q whenever K is indecomposable.[14]

In this solution r is the maximal rate of capital expansion which can be achieved using these activities. It remains to show that among all the possible realizations, only one can be competitive over all the others. We will argue that this is indeed true and that the surviving realization is the one with the largest internal expansion factor. Let δ be this largest expansion factor (with associated realization K^δ) and suppose that σ is some smaller competitive interest factor (with associated realization K^σ and price vector q^σ). Now if K^σ is to be profit-maximizing over all realizations at prices σ, q^σ, we must have

(A-2) $$\sigma q^\sigma K^\delta \geqq q^\sigma.$$

But since K^δ is indecomposable, it is well known that its unique interest factor δ satisfies the condition

$$\delta = \min \{\lambda | \lambda q K^\delta \geqq q, \quad \text{some} \quad q \geqq 0\}.$$[15]

Therefore, since we assumed $\sigma < \delta$, (A-2) cannot be satisfied for any $q^\sigma \geqq 0$.

Hence, the only competitive realization in the capital goods industries involves using the von Neumann activities for the technology as a whole.[16]

---

14. This is a simple consequence of Frobenius' theorem for nonnegative matrices.

15. See, for example, R. Bellman, *Introduction to Matrix Analysis* (New York, 1960), p. 278, theorem 2.

16. Of course, it is possible that the von Neumann activities are not unique. However, even if this is so, it can be shown that the competitive price system is still unique.

Once q^δ is thus determined, the only competitive activities for producing consumption goods are those which minimize the capital costs per unit, computed at the prices q^δ. With the consumption realization thus determined, consumption goods prices can be computed uniquely by the equations

$$p = \delta q^\delta C^\delta. \tag{A-3}$$

Thus, the price system is indeed determined by the technology alone, regardless of the pattern of consumption demand (as long as it is balanced).

Making use of the condition of equality of supply and demand for each capital good at each time point, we can determine the rate of growth and the production rates for capital goods as functions of the rate of saving and the relative demands for consumption goods.

Let g be the growth factor for the system, x^0 the vector of capital goods needed at time 0, and y^0 the vector of consumption goods desired at time 0. Then, the vector of capital goods supplied at time t is x^0g^t, and the vectors of capital goods and consumption goods, respectively, desired at time $t + 1$ are x^0g^{t+1} and y^0g^{t+1}. The equality of supply and demand for capital goods can be written

$$g^{t+1}Cy^0 + g^{t+1}Kx^0 = g^tx^0.$$

Dividing through by g^t and rearranging terms,

$$(I - gK)x^0 = gCy^0. \tag{A-4}$$

By well-known theorems about Leontief-Metzler matrices, the above equations always have a nonnegative solution in x^0 for any nonnegative y^0 provided that g is less than δ.

To determine the rate of growth, multiply through in (A-4) by q to get

$$(q - gqK)x^0 = gqCy^0.$$

Then multiply through by δ and substitute for δqK and δqC from (A-1) and (A-3), respectively. This yields

$$(\delta - g)qx^0 = gpy^0 \quad \text{or} \quad \frac{g}{\delta} = \frac{qx^0}{py^0 + qx^0};$$

the rate of growth of the system is determined by the ratio of gross savings to gross national income.

11 The Genesis of Dynamic Systems Governed by Metzler Matrices

The literature on dynamic systems in economics is vast, and an important part of it deals with systems of differential or of difference equations where the Jacobian of the right-hand side is a Metzler matrix, that is, a matrix whose off-diagonal elements are nonnegative. Such matrices have a wide range of applicability in dynamic economic models, in input-output analysis, in stability analysis of systems of excess demands governing price changes, and in multisector and multinational Keynesian income determination models. Oskar Morgenstern early perceived the importance of such models and encouraged research in them, as seen in papers by Y. K. Wong and M. A. Woodbury (Morgenstern, 1954). For a later survey, see McKenzie (1960).

The bulk of this work, as indeed the bulk of the work on dynamic systems in general, concerns what might, in theological terms, be called the *eschatology* of the system, the questions of the end or final state of the system. In this chapter I want to concentrate on the behavior of the system in its initial phases, its *genesis*. The problems revolve mainly around the presence of off-diagonal zeros in the matrix governing the system and of zeros in some components of the initial conditions and of the forcing terms. If the matrix were strictly positive, for example, then any initial impulse anywhere immediately (or with a lag of one time period in a difference equation system) produces a positive response everywhere. But if there are some zeros

Reprinted from *Mathematical Economics and Game Theory,* ed. R. Henn and O. Moeschlin (Berlin: Springer-Verlag, 1976), pp. 629–644.

in the matrix, then the transmission of the impulses is delayed. In the case of differential equation systems, the effect appears as a lower rate of growth of the component; instead of increasing linearly, it may increase quadratically or even with a higher power from its initial value of zero.

The discussion of this subject involves what appears to be a new concept, that of *first-positivity*. A sequence is first-positive if the first nonzero element is positive. Similar definitions can be given for sequences of vectors and matrices. The methods bring together a number of elementary concepts from diverse fields, including matrix algebra, the theory of relations, and the theory of differential equations.

In the first section of this chapter the concept of first-positivity is introduced, and some elementary properties developed. In the second section there is a digression on some properties of relations which will be useful in the sequel. The third section studies first-nonzero and connectivity properties of the sequence formed by the powers of a matrix; at this stage, there is no restriction to Metzler matrices. The fourth section discusses a property of matrix exponentials, which are used in expressing the solution to a system of differential equations. In the fifth section the previous results are drawn together in application to the first-positivity and connectivity properties of the sequence of powers of a Metzler matrix.

The results to which the earlier sections were leading are contained in the sixth and seventh sections. These sections characterize the geneses of systems of difference equations and of differential equations, respectively. In the first, the time of first-positivity of a specific component is expressed in terms of the connectivity properties of the matrix, the specification of the positive components of the starting values, and the first-positivity properties of the forcing function. In the second, the order of increase of a specific component is expressed in terms of the same factors.

First-Positivity

In the following, "D" is used as an abbreviation for "Definition." In general, lowercase letters, such as x, stand for sequences (functions on the nonnegative integers) of scalars or vectors; a capital letter, such as A, stands for a sequence of matrices; $x(n)$ or $A(n)$ will be the value of x or A, respectively, at integer n; x_α or $A_{\alpha\beta}$ will be the scalar sequence formed by considering only the component α of the vector or the element (α,β) of the matrix sequence.

DEFINITION 1. *For a scalar sequence x, define $v(x) = \min \{n|x(n) \neq 0\}$. We refer to $v(x)$ as the nonzero index of x.*

Note that the nonzero index is not necessarily defined, since x might be identically zero. This problem of lack of definition occurs persistently but can be dealt with, as will be noted later.

DEFINITION 2. $x^{\nu} \triangleq x[\nu(x)]$.

Thus x^{ν} is the value of the first element in the sequence x which is not zero. The symbol $\triangleq$ is read "equals by definition."

DEFINITION 3. *(x is first-positive)* $\triangleq (x^{\nu} > 0)$.

Now let x be a sequence of vectors. Each of the above definitions is still allowed to hold, but must be applied to each component. That is, for each component α of the vector, x_{α} is a scalar sequence. Then $\nu(x_{\alpha})$ is defined by D.1, and similarly, $(x_{\alpha})^{\nu}$ by D.2. It will be useful to interpret x to be a function from a finite domain (the domain of its components) to the space of scalar sequences. Let F be this domain. Then $\nu(x)$ will be interpreted as a *function,* the value for α being $\nu(x_{\alpha})$. It must be emphasized, however, that $\nu(x)$ might not be defined for all elements of F, for it can happen that the sequence x_{α} is identically zero for some α, and therefore $\nu(x)(\alpha) = \nu(x_{\alpha})$ is not defined for that value of α.

DEFINITION 4. *If x is a sequence of vectors, the function* $\nu(x)$ *is defined by the relation* $\nu(x)(\alpha) = \nu(x_{\alpha})$.

DEFINITION 5. $x^{\nu}(\alpha) = x_{\alpha}[\nu(x_{\alpha})] = x_{\alpha}^{\nu}$, *so that the function* x^{ν} *has the same domain of definition as* $\nu(x)$.

The analogue of D.3 for vectors is a vector inequality, that is, we regard a sequence of vectors as first-positive if each component is. However, we have to account for the possibility that the domain of definition of x might not be the entire possible domain F. We need a convention for the meaning of an expression like $f(\alpha) > 0$, or, more generally, for an expression, $f(\alpha) > g(\alpha)$, where one or both of the functions f and g may be undefined at a particular point α. We shall regard the inequality as holding if f is undefined at α and g is defined there or if both are defined and $f(\alpha)$ is indeed bigger than $g(\alpha)$, and not otherwise.

CONVENTION 1. *If the functions f and g are both defined at* α, *then the expression* $f(\alpha) > g(\alpha)$ *has its usual meaning; otherwise, it holds if and only if f is not defined at* α *and g is.*

A similar convention will hold for equality.

CONVENTION 2. *If the functions f and g are both defined at* α, *then the* *expression $f(\alpha) = g(\alpha)$ has its usual meaning; otherwise, it holds if and only if neither f nor g is defined at α.*

If we use the usual symbol,

DEFINITION 6. *dom $f = \{\alpha | f(\alpha)$ is defined$\}$,*

then Convention 1 says that $f(\alpha) > g(\alpha)$ if $\alpha \in$ dom g and $\alpha \notin$ dom f, while Convention 2 implies that $f(\alpha) = g(\alpha)$ if $\alpha \notin$ dom f, $\alpha \notin$ dom g.

Inequality among *functions* has the usual meaning that the inequality holds for all values of the argument, except that the conventions above are observed. From the foregoing remarks it is easy to note that $f \leq g$ implies dom $f \subset$ dom g.

With these conventions, the definition of first-positivity, D.3, remains valid for sequences of vectors. It means that each component is first-positive if not identically zero.

The following simple lemma holds for adding first-positive sequences, whether of vectors or of scalars.

LEMMA 1. *If x^i is first-positive for each i, then $\Sigma_i x^i$ is first-positive, and $\nu(\Sigma_i x^i) = \min_i \nu(x^i)$.*

Proof. Let $\bar{\nu} = \min_i \nu(x^i)$, $P = \{i | \nu(x^i) = \bar{\nu}\}$. If $n < \bar{\nu}$, then $n < \nu(x^i)$ for all i, so that $x^i(n) = 0$ for all i, by D.1, and therefore $\Sigma_i x^i(n) = 0$. On the other hand, $x^i(\bar{\nu}) = x^{i\nu} > 0$ for $i \in P$, by D.2 and then D.3, $\nu(x^i) > \bar{\nu}$ for $i \notin P$, and therefore $x^i(\bar{\nu}) = 0$ for $i \notin P$. Hence, $\Sigma_i x^i(\bar{\nu}) > 0$, so that the lemma holds.

Although the proof has been stated for scalars, it holds, with suitable interpretation, for vectors; the operator, $\min_i$, in the statement of the lemma must be taken to hold component-wise.

In addition, it is useful to note how the conventions are used. The proof as given seems to require that $\nu(x^i)$ be defined for all i. If, however, it is defined only for some i, then $\bar{\nu}$ is taken as the minimum over all i for which it is defined. That indeed is the interpretation implied by Conventions 1 and 2. Then the argument is valid in every detail; in particular, if $\nu(x^i)$ is not defined for some i, then certainly, by Convention 1, $\nu(x^i) > \bar{\nu}$. On the other hand, in just that case, $x^i(n) = 0$ for all n, and therefore certainly, $x^i(\bar{\nu}) = 0$. In the future, all proofs will be carried on as though all functions were defined; the correction for the cases of lack of definition can easily be supplied by the reader.

The same definitions will be needed for sequences of matrices; however, since a matrix can be thought of as a vector, there is no need for additional definitions. (Square) matrices can be thought of as functions on a domain of the form $F \times F$, where F is finite and $\times$ denotes Cartesian product. In this case, if A is a sequence of matrices, $\nu(A)$ is a function of two variables, representing the rows and the columns.

A useful concept in expressing the solution of systems of difference equations is the *convolution* of two sequences, a term borrowed from probability theory. It is the same as the expression for the distribution of the sum of two independent nonnegative random variables.

DEFINITION 7. *If x and y are two sequences, then the sequence x^*y is defined by*

$$(x^*y)(n) = \sum_{j=0}^{n} x(j)\, y(n-j).$$

First, suppose x and y are scalar sequences. From D.1, $x(j) = 0$ if $j < \nu(x)$, and $y(n-j) = 0$ if $n - j < \nu(y)$, or, equivalently, $j > n - \nu(y)$. Hence,

$$x(j)\, y(n-j) = 0 \quad \text{unless} \quad \nu(x) \leqq j \leqq n - \nu(y).$$

If $n < \nu(x) + \nu(y)$, then $\nu(x) > n - \nu(y)$, so that $x(j)\, y(n-j) = 0$ for all j, and therefore $(x^*y)\,(n) = 0$. If $n = \nu(x) + \nu(y)$, then $x(j)\; y(n-j) = 0$ except for $j = \nu(x) = n - \nu(y)$, so that $(x^*y)\,(n) = x[\nu(x)]\, y[\nu(y)] = x^\nu y^\nu \neq 0$, by D.2 and D.1. Hence, for scalar sequences, $(x^*y)\,(n) = 0$ for $n < \nu(x) + \nu(y)$, $\neq 0$ for $n = \nu(x) + \nu(y)$, so that, by D.1, $\nu(x^*y) = \nu(x) + \nu(y)$, and, by D.2, $(x^*y)^\nu = x^\nu y^\nu$. If it is also assumed that x and y are first-positive, then, by D.3, $x^\nu > 0$, $y^\nu > 0$, and therefore $(x^*y)^\nu > 0$, so that x^*y is first-positive.

LEMMA 2. *If x and y are scalar sequences, then $\nu(x^*y) = \nu(x) + \nu(y)$, and $(x^*y)^\nu = x^\nu y^\nu$. If in addition x and y are first-positive, then so is x^*y.*

The definition of a convolution can be applied not only to scalars but also to vectors and pairs consisting of matrices and vectors, with the proper interpretation of multiplication in the definition. Let x and y be vector sequences, each vector being of the same number of components, and let multiplication be interpreted as the taking of an inner product,

$$x(j)\, y(n-j) = \sum_{\beta} x_\beta(j)\, y_\beta(n-j),$$

so that

$$(x^*y)\,(n) = \sum_{j=0}^{n} \sum_{\beta} x_\beta(j)\, y_\beta(n-j) \tag{11-1}$$

$$= \sum_{\beta} \sum_{j=0}^{n} x_\beta(j)\, y_\beta(n-j) = \sum_{\beta} (x_\beta{}^* y_\beta)\,(n).$$

Suppose in addition that x and y are first-positive. Then, for each β, x_β and y_β are first-positive, and therefore $x_\beta{}^*y_\beta$ is first-positive, by Lemma 2, and x^*y is first-positive by Lemma 1. From Lemmas 1 and 2,

$$\text{(11-2)} \qquad \begin{aligned} v(x^*y) &= \min_\beta v(x_\beta{}^*y_\beta) \\ &= \min_\beta [v(x)(\beta) + v(y)(\beta)]. \end{aligned}$$

We will apply this result to multiplication of a matrix sequence A by a sequence of conforming column vectors, x, where both A and x are first-positive. Equation (11-2) can be applied, with each row of A, in turn, replacing x, and x replacing y. The sequence A^*x is a sequence of column vectors.

LEMMA 3. *Let A be a first-positive sequence of matrices, and x a first-positive sequence of column vectors conforming with A. Then $v(A^*x)(\alpha) = \min_\beta [v(A)(\alpha,\beta) + v(x)(\beta)]$, and A^*x is first-positive.*

Relations, Their Powers, and Chains

A relation is simply a set of ordered pairs. In the main application in this chapter, the relation $C(A)$ is defined by the condition that $\alpha\ C(A)\ \beta$ if and only if $A_{\alpha\beta} \neq 0$, for a given matrix A; thus $C(A)$ is the set of all ordered pairs for which this condition holds. Typically, then, a relation R is some subset of $F \times F$. In this section, however, the relation R is arbitrary.

A particularly interesting relation is the identity relation, E.

DEFINITION 8. $(\alpha\ E\ \beta) \triangleq (\alpha = \beta)$.

Following Quine (1965, p. 213), the *relative product* of two relations, R and S, is defined by

DEFINITION 9. $(\alpha\ R|S\ \beta) \triangleq$ *(for some* γ, $\alpha\ R\ \gamma$ *and* $\gamma\ S\ \beta)$.

Like any other form of multiplication, the relative product can be used to define the powers of a relation inductively.

DEFINITION 10. $R^0 = E,\ R^{n+1} = R^n|R$.

This definition can be given a useful alternative form by introducing the concept of an R-chain.

DEFINITION 11. *(σ is an R-chain of length n from α to β) $\triangleq$ (σ is a function defined on the intergers $0, \ldots, n$, $\sigma(0) = \alpha$, $\sigma(n) = \beta$, and $\sigma(i-1)\ R\ \sigma(i)$ for $i = 1, \ldots, n$).*

In short, an R-chain is an ordered sequence of $n + 1$ elements, such that the relation R holds between every successive pair.

It is intuitively obvious and can easily be proved by induction that the relation R^n holds if and only if there is an R-chain of length n connecting the two elements.

LEMMA 4. *$\alpha R^n \beta$ if and only if there exists an R-chain of length n from α to β.*

For a given α and β, there may be R-chains of different lengths from one to the other. (Of course, it is also possible that there are no R-chains of any length from α to β.)

DEFINITION 12. *(σ is a shortest R-chain from α to β) $\triangleq$ (for some n and all $m < n$, σ is an R-chain of length n from α to β and there is no R-chain of length m from α to β).*

Shortest chains have a property which will be useful later.

LEMMA 5. *A shortest R-chain is a one-one function.*

Proof. We seek to prove that if σ is a shortest R-chain from α to β and if $\sigma(i_1) = \sigma(i_2)$, then $i_1 = i_2$. Let $\underline{i} = \min(i_1, i_2)$, $h = \max(i_1, i_2) - \underline{i}$. Clearly, $h \geqq 0$ by definition; we seek to prove that $h = 0$, or, equivalently, that $h \leqq 0$. To this end, we construct an R-chain of length $n - h$ from α to β, where σ is an R-chain of length n; since σ is a shortest R-chain, it follows by definition that $n - h \geqq n$, or $h \leqq 0$. By assumption,

(11-3) $\quad \sigma(\underline{i}) = \sigma(\underline{i} + h).$

Define a function, σ', on the integers $0, \ldots, n - h$, as follows:

(11-4a) $\quad \sigma'(i) = \sigma(i), 0 \leqq i < \underline{i},$

(11-4b) $\quad = \sigma(i + h), \underline{i} \leqq i \leqq n - h.$

If $\underline{i} = 0$, then from (11-4b) and (11-3), $\sigma'(0) = \sigma(h) = \sigma(0)$. If $\underline{i} > 0$, then $\sigma'(0) = \sigma(0)$ from (11-4a), so that $\sigma'(0) = \sigma(0)$ in either case. Also, from (11-4b), $\sigma'(n - h) = \sigma(n)$. Since σ is an R-chain of length n from α to β, $\sigma(0) = \alpha$ and $\sigma(n) = \beta$; hence, we have shown that $\sigma'(0) = \alpha$ and $\sigma'(n - h) = \beta$.

To show that σ' is an R-chain of length $n - h$ from α to β, it remains, by D.11, to show that $\sigma'(i - 1) \; R \; \sigma'(i)$, $1 \leqq i \leqq n - h$. If $i < \underline{i}$, this follows immediately from (11-4a). If $i > \underline{i}$, then $i - 1 \geqq \underline{i}$; by (11-4b), $\sigma'(i - 1) = \sigma(i + h - 1)$, $\sigma'(i) = \sigma(i + h)$, and, since σ is an R-chain, $\sigma(i + h - 1) \; R \; \sigma(i + h)$, and therefore $\sigma'(i - 1) \; R \; \sigma'(i)$.

Finally, let $i = \underline{i}$; then $\underline{i} > 0$. In this case, $\sigma'(i-1) = \sigma(i-1)$, while $\sigma'(i) = \sigma(i+h) = \sigma(\underline{i}+h) = \sigma(\underline{i}) = \sigma(i)$, by (11-4a), (11-4b), and (11-3). Since σ is an R-chain, $\sigma(i-1)\,R\,\sigma(i)$; hence, $\sigma'(i-1)\,R\,\sigma'(i)$. Therefore all the conditions of D.11 are satisfied for σ', so there is an R-chain of length $n-h$ from α to β, and therefore $h \leqq 0$, verifying the lemma.

To any fixed β, there is associated the set $\{\alpha | \alpha R\ \beta\}$; we introduce the notation $R\beta$ to stand for this set. More generally, if there is a set of values of β, say S, then RS will stand for the union of the sets $R\beta$, for $\beta \in S$.

DEFINITION 13. $RS \triangleq \{\alpha | \text{for some } \beta,\ \alpha\ R\ \beta \text{ and } \beta \in S\}$.

It is easy to see that

$$(11\text{-}5) \qquad R(S \cup T) = (RS) \cup (RT),$$

where $A \cup B$ is the union of the sets A and B.

More generally, if S_i is an indexed set of sets, with i varying over a set,

$$(11\text{-}6) \qquad R \bigcup_i S_i = \bigcup_i RS_i,$$

where $\bigcup_i S_i$ is the union of the sets S_i.

Connectivity of a Matrix and Nonzero Index for the Sequence of Powers of a Matrix

The following *connectivity relation* can be associated in a natural way with any given matrix A.

DEFINITION 14. *$[\alpha\ C(A)\ \beta] \triangleq (A_{\alpha\beta} \neq 0)$.*

The connectivity relation for a power of A will also be of interest.

The sequence of powers of a matrix, A^n, $n \geq 0$, where $A^0 = I$, is a particular sequence, and a nonzero index function can be associated with that sequence. As a matter of notation, we must distinguish between a particular element of the sequence and the name of the sequence. For this purpose, we borrow the *functional abstractor* notation from mathematical logic (see for example Quine, 1965, p. 226). In general, for any function which takes on the value $f(x)$ at the point x, we will mean by $\lambda_x f(x)$ the name of the function which takes on these values. In this chapter the notation will be applied only to sequences, where the variable is n.

DEFINITION 15. *$\lambda_n f(n)$ is the function which takes on the value $f(n)$ when the argument takes on the value n.*

Thus, $\lambda_n A^n$ is the sequence of powers of A. Associated with this sequence is a nonzero index function, $\nu(\lambda_n A^n)$, defined over ordered pairs. By D.1, D.4, and D.14,

(11-7) $\quad \nu(\lambda_n A^n)(\alpha,\beta) = \min\{n \mid \alpha\ C(A^n)\beta\}.$

Note that

(11-8) $\quad C(A^0) = C(I) = E,$

so that $\alpha\ C(A^0)\beta$ holds if and only if $\alpha = \beta$; therefore,

(11-9) $\quad \nu(\lambda_n A^n)(\alpha,\beta) = 0 \quad \text{if and only if} \quad \alpha = \beta.$

In view of (11-7), $\nu(\lambda_n A^n)$ is defined for a particular pair (α,β) if and only if $\alpha C(A^n)\beta$ for some n. In set-theoretic language, define the relation $K^\nu(A)$ by the following definition:

DEFINITION 16. $K^\nu(A) = \bigcup_{n=0}^{\infty} C(A^n),$

where $\bigcup_{n=0}^{\infty}$ is the union of the relations $C(A^n)$; remember that a relation is a particular kind of set. Then,

(11-10) $\quad K^\nu(A) = \text{dom}\ \nu(\lambda_n A^n) = \text{dom}\ (\lambda_n A^n)^\nu.$

We will explore the effect, on the nonzero index and related concepts for a sequence of powers of a matrix, of altering the matrix by adding a constant to the diagonal elements. As a preliminary, we note that the binomial theorem is valid for pairs of matrices which commute with each other.

$$(A + B)^n = \sum_{r=0}^{n} \binom{n}{r} A^r B^{n-r} \quad \text{if} \quad AB = BA.$$

Let B be a scalar multiple of the identity matrix, $B = sI$ for some scalar s. Then sI commutes with every matrix A. Note that $(sI)^{n-r} = s^{n-r}I^{n-r} = s^{n-r}I.$

(11-11) $\quad (A + sI)^n = \sum_{r=0}^{n} \binom{n}{r} s^{n-r} A^r.$

DEFINITION 17. $(A \equiv B \bmod I) \triangleq (A - B = sI$ *for some scalar* $s)$.

Note that the relation is symmetric. Suppose it holds for two matrices, A and B. From (11-11),

(11-12) $\quad (B^n)_{\alpha\beta} = \sum_{r=0}^{n} \binom{n}{r} s^{n-r} (A^r)_{\alpha\beta} \quad$ for some scalar s.

Clearly, if $(B^n)_{\alpha\beta} \neq 0$, then it must be that $(A^r)_{\alpha\beta} \neq 0$ for some $r \leq n$. In particular, let $n = \nu(\lambda_n B^n)(\alpha,\beta)$. Then it follows that

$$\nu(\lambda_n A^n)(\alpha,\beta) \leqq \nu(\lambda_n B^n)(\alpha,\beta).$$

But since the relation $A \equiv B \bmod I$ is symmetric, this must hold with A and B interchanged; also, it holds for any α and β:

$$\nu(\lambda_n A^n) = \nu(\lambda_n B^n).$$

If two functions are equal, they have the same domain of definition, by Convention 2; hence, from (11-10), $K^\nu(A) = K^\nu(B)$. Further, if we set $n = \nu(\lambda_n A^n)(\alpha,\beta) = \nu(\lambda_n B^n)(\alpha,\beta)$, then, by (D.1), $(A^r)_{\alpha\beta} = 0$ for $r < n$; from (11-12), $(B^n)_{\alpha\beta} = (A^n)_{\alpha\beta}$. By D.5,

$$(\lambda_n A^n)^\nu = (\lambda_n B^n)^\nu.$$

THEOREM 1. *If* $A \equiv B \bmod I$, *then* (a) $\nu(\lambda_n A^n) = \nu(\lambda_n B^n)$; (b) $(\lambda_n A^n)^\nu = (\lambda_n B^n)^\nu$; *and* (c) $K^\nu(A) = K^\nu(B)$.

The relation $C(A)$ measured what might be termed the direct connectivity of the matrix. Two elements may be indirectly connected through a chain of direct connections. In view of Lemma 4, it is natural to define the *connectivity index* of a matrix (a function, not a number) as the smallest power of $C(A)$ which holds between two elements.

DEFINITION 18. $\delta(A)(\alpha,\beta) = \min \{n | \alpha[C(A)]^n\beta\}$.

Note that, since $[C(A)]^0 = E$, $\delta(A)(\alpha,\beta) = 0$ if and only if $\alpha = \beta$. Also, if $A_{\alpha\beta} \neq 0$ and $\alpha \neq \beta$, then $\alpha[C(A)]^1\beta$ while not $\alpha\ C(A)^0\beta$, so that $\delta(A)(\alpha,\beta) = 1$. From D.18, the domain of definition of the connectivity index is precisely the set of ordered pairs for which the relation $[C(A)]^n$ holds for some n. Define

DEFINITION 19. $K^\delta(A) = \bigcup_{n=0}^{\infty} [C(A)]^n$.

Then,

(11-13) $\quad K^\delta(A) = \text{dom}\ \delta(A)$.

It is convenient to introduce the following notation:

(11-14) $\quad \Sigma(A)(\alpha,\beta,n)$ is the set of $C(A)$-chains of length n from α to β.

Then, from Lemma 4,

(11-15) $\quad \alpha[C(A)]^n\beta$ if and only if $\Sigma(A)(\alpha,\beta,n)$ is nonempty.

We now investigate the effect on the connectivity index of a change in the diagonal elements of the matrix. (Although for our later purposes only a constant change is relevant, the results hold for any change in the diagonal elements.) Suppose therefore $A - B$ is a diagonal matrix; note again that this relation is symmetric. Let σ be a $C(A)$-chain of length $\delta(A)(\alpha,\beta)$. By D.18, it is a shortest $C(A)$-chain from α to β, and therefore σ is a one-one function by Lemma 5. In particular, $\sigma(i-1) \neq \sigma(i)$, $1 \leqq i \leqq \delta(A)(\alpha,\beta)$. Since $A - B$ is diagonal,

$$A_{\sigma(i-1),\sigma(i)} = B_{\sigma(i-1),\sigma(i)}. \tag{11-16}$$

Since σ is a $C(A)$-chain, $\sigma(i-1)\ C(A)\ \sigma(i)$ for all i, or, by D.14, $A_{\sigma(i-1),\sigma(i)} \neq 0$, for all i. By (11-16), $B_{\sigma(i-1),\sigma(i)} \neq 0$ for all i, so that σ is a $C(B)$-chain. In the notation of (11-14),

$$\Sigma(A)(\alpha,\beta,\delta(A)(\alpha,\beta)) \subset \Sigma(B)(\alpha,\beta,\delta(A)(\alpha,\beta)).$$

If $\delta(A)$ is indeed defined at (α,β), then the left-hand set is nonempty and therefore so is the right-hand set. By D.18 and (11-15), $\delta(B)(\alpha,\beta) \leqq \delta(A)(\alpha,\beta)$. This statement also holds if $\delta(A)$ is undefined at (α,β) by Conventions 1 and 2. By the symmetry, the inequality holds with A and B interchanged, so that $\delta(A) = \delta(B)$. Since the two functions are equal, they have the same domain of definition. From (11-13), then, we have

THEOREM 2. *If $A - B$ is a diagonal matrix, then $\delta(A) = \delta(B)$ and $K^{\delta}(A) = K^{\delta}(B)$.*

Matrix Exponentials

As is well known, solutions to systems of linear differential equations with constant coefficients can be expressed simply in terms of the exponential of the matrix of coefficients.

DEFINITION 20. $e^A \triangleq \sum_{n=0}^{\infty} A^n/n!$

The infinite series converges absolutely for all A, so that e^A is defined and the series can be rearranged at will. If we add the scalar multiple of the identity matrix to A, the value of the exponential can be expressed with the aid of (11-11).

$$e^{A+sI} = \sum_{n=0}^{\infty} (A + sI)^n/n! = \sum_{n=0}^{\infty} (1/n!) \sum_{i+j=n} (n!/i!j!) s^i A^j$$

$$= \sum_{n=0}^{\infty} \sum_{i+j=n} (s^i/i!)\,(A^j/j!)$$

$$= \left(\sum_{i=0}^{\infty} s^i/i!\right)\left(\sum_{j=0}^{\infty} A^j/j!\right)$$
$$= e^s e^A.$$

LEMMA 6. *If $A \equiv B$ mod I, then $e^B = pe^A$ for some positive scalar p.*

COROLLARY 1. *If $A \equiv B$ mod I, then $e^A \geqq 0$ if and only if $e^B \geqq 0$.*

COROLLARY 2. *If $A \equiv B$ mod I, then $C(e^A) = C(e^B)$.*

First-Positivity and Connectivity of Nonnegative and Metzler Matrices

First, make the obvious observation that if $A \geqq 0$, then $\alpha C(A)\beta$ if and only if $A_{\alpha\beta} > 0$. Recall that $(A^{n+1})_{\alpha\beta} = \Sigma_\gamma (A^n)_{\alpha\gamma} A_{\gamma\beta}$. If $A \geq 0$, then $A^n \geq 0$ for all n. Hence, the right-hand side is a sum of nonnegative terms and is positive if and only if at least one is positive. Therefore, $\alpha C(A^{n+1})\,\beta$ if and only if, for some γ, $(A^n)_{\alpha\gamma} A_{\alpha\gamma} > 0$, or, equivalently, if and only if, for some γ, $\alpha C(A^n)_\gamma$ and $\gamma C(A)\beta$. In the notation of D.9,

(11-17) $\quad C(A^{n+1}) = C(A^n)|C(A).$

LEMMA 7. *If $A \geqq 0$, $C(A^n) = [C(A)]^n$.*

Proof. For $n = 0$, we know that $C(A^0) = E = [C(A)]^0$. Suppose the lemma is true for n. Then, from (11-17),

$$C(A^{n+1}) = [C(A)]^n|C(A) = [C(A)]^{n+1},$$

by D.10.

From (11-7) and the definition of $\delta(A)$, D.18, Lemma 7 immediately implies that $\nu(\lambda_n A^n) = \delta(A)$ when $A \geqq 0$; the two functions have the same domain of definition, so that $K^\nu(A) = K^\delta(A)$ by (11-10) and (11-13).

Since $A^n \geqq 0$, it follows immediately from D.5 that $(\lambda_n A^n)^\nu \geqq 0$; but by D.4, it must be that $(\lambda_n A^n)^\nu$ $(\alpha,\beta) \neq 0$ for all (α,β) in the domain of definition, so that $(\lambda_n A^n)^\nu > 0$, that is, the matrix sequence, $\lambda_n A^n$, is first-positive.

Finally, from the definition of an exponential, D.20, $e^A \geqq 0$ when A $\geqq 0$. Since the defining series is a sum of nonnegative terms, $(e^A)_{\alpha\beta} > 0$ if and only if $(A^n)_{\alpha\beta} > 0$ for some n, so that

$$C(e^A) = \bigcup_{n=0}^{\infty} C(A^n) = K^\nu(A),$$

by D.16.

LEMMA 8. *If $A \geqq 0$, then $\lambda_n A^n$ is first-positive, $\nu(\lambda_n A^n) = \delta(A)$, $e^A \geqq 0$, and $K^\nu(A) = K^\delta(A) = C(e^A)$.*

The main mathematical result of the chapter is that this lemma holds not merely for nonnegative but for all Metzler matrices. We recall the following definition:

DEFINITION 21. *A is Metzler if $A_{\alpha\beta} \geqq 0$ for $\alpha \neq \beta$.*

A simple and useful relation between Metzler and nonnegative matrices is the following:

(11-18) A is Metzler if and only if there exists $B \geqq 0$ such that $A \equiv B \bmod I$.

THEOREM 3. *If A is Metzler, then $\lambda_n A^n$ is first-positive, $\nu(\lambda_n A^n) = \delta(A)$, $e^A \geqq 0$, and $K^\nu(A) = K^\delta(A) = C(e^A)$.*

Proof. Choose B as in (11-18). Then, from Theorem 1, Lemma 8, and Theorem 2, $\nu(\lambda_n A^n)^\nu = \nu(\lambda_n B^n)^\nu = \delta(B) = \delta(A)$. From Theorem 1 and Lemma 8, $(\lambda_n A^n)^\nu = (\lambda_n B^n)^\nu > 0$. From Lemma 8, $e^B \geqq 0$, and therefore from Corollary 1, $e^A \geqq 0$. Finally, from Corollary 2, Lemma 8, and Theorem 1, $C(e^A) = C(e^B) = K^\nu(B) = K^\nu(A)$, while from Lemma 8 and Theorem 2, $K^\nu(B) = K^\delta(B) = K^\nu(A)$.

The importance of this theorem is that the qualitative behavior of the powers and the exponential of a Metzler matrix can be inferred solely from its connectivity properties. These depend only on the location of the off-diagonal zeros and are independent both of the diagonal elements and of the magnitudes of the nonzero off-diagonal elements. Thus, if we raise a Metzler matrix to successively higher powers we know that in each place in the matrix, the first nonzero element (if any) will be positive and the power for which the nonzero entry occurs is equal to the length of the shortest chain from the row element to the column element through nonzero entries.

A side consequence of the analysis is a pair of what are apparently new necessary and sufficient conditions for a matrix to have the Metzler property.

THEOREM 4. *Each of the following conditions is necessary and sufficient that A be a Metzler matrix:* (a) *$\lambda_n A^n$ is first-positive;* (b) *$e^{At} \geqq 0$ for all $t > 0$.*

Proof. (a) Necessity has already been shown in Theorem 3. Suppose, then, that the sequence $\lambda_n A^n$ is first-positive. The pairs (α,β) can be classified according as $\nu(\lambda_n A^n)$ (α,β) is 0, 1, or greater than 1. In the first case, as remarked in (11-9), $\alpha = \beta$. In the second, we must have $(A^1)_{\alpha\beta} \neq 0$, by definition, and therefore $A_{\alpha\beta} > 0$, since $\lambda_n A^n$ is first-positive. In the third case, $(A^1)_{\alpha\beta} = 0$ by definition of the nonzero index. Hence, if $\alpha \neq \beta$, $A_{\alpha\beta} \geqq 0$, so that A is a Metzler matrix.

(b) If A is Metzler and $t > 0$, a scalar, then At is also Metzler, and $e^{At} \geqq 0$ by Theorem 3. Conversely, suppose that $e^{At} \geqq 0$ for all $t > 0$. Note that $e^{At} = I$ when $t = 0$, that

$$\frac{d(e^{At})}{dt} = Ae^{At},$$

so that

$$\left.\frac{d(e^{At})}{dt}\right|_{t=0} = \mathrm{A},$$

and that, by definition,

$$\left.\frac{d(e^{At})}{dt}\right|_{t=0} = \lim_{t\to 0} \frac{(e^{At} - I)}{t}.$$

From the hypothesis and (11-18), $e^{At} - I$ is Metzler for $t > 0$, and therefore $(e^{At} - I)/t$ is a Metzler matrix for $t > 0$. Hence, A is a limit of Metzler matrices; since the set of Metzler matrices is clearly closed, from the definition, A must be a Metzler matrix.

Genesis of a System of Difference Equations with Metzler Matrix as Jacobian

We consider the system of difference equations

(11-19) $$x(n + 1) = Ax(n) + b(n),$$

where we assume that A is a Metzler matrix, b a first-positive sequence, and $x(0) \geqq 0$. To express the solution compactly, define a vector sequence c by,

(11-20) $$c(n) = x(0) \text{ for } n = 0 \quad \text{and} \quad c(n) = b(n - 1) \text{ for } n > 0.$$

Then (11-19) can be written,

$$x(n + 1) = Ax(n) + c(n + 1), \qquad x(0) = c(0).$$

By induction, it is easy to verify that

$$x(n) = \sum_{j=0}^{n} A^j c(n-j),$$

or, in the notation introduced in D.7,

(11-21) $\quad x = (\lambda_n A^n)^* c.$

Since b is first-positive, it is easy to see from (11-20) that c is first-positive. (If $x_\beta(0) > 0$, then $c_\beta(0) > 0$, so that c_β is certainly first-positive; if $x_\beta(0) = 0$, then the first nonzero element in the sequence c_β is the first nonzero element of b_β with nonzero index increased by 1, and must be positive since b is first-positive.) If A is Metzler, $\lambda_n A^n$ is first-positive by Theorem 3. Hence, by Lemma 3, x is first-positive, and

(11-22) $\quad \nu(x)(\alpha) = \min_{\beta} [\nu(\lambda_n A^n)(\alpha,\beta) + \nu(c)(\beta)].$

Define, for any vector x,

DEFINITION 22. *$P(x) \triangleq \{\alpha | x_\alpha > 0\}$.*

In (11-22), for each β, either $\beta \in P[x(0)]$ or $\beta \notin P[x(0)]$. The minimum can be taken separately over the two subsets and then the minimum of the two taken. Note that if $\beta \in P[x(0)]$, then, from (11-20), $\nu(c)(\beta) = 0$, while if $\beta \notin P[x(0)]$, then $\nu(c)(\beta) = \nu(b)(\beta) + 1$. Further, from Theorem 3, $\nu(\lambda_n A^n)(\alpha,\beta) = \delta(A)(\alpha,\beta)$. Substitution into (11-22) yields the following theorem:

THEOREM 5. *If A is a Metzler matrix, b a first-positive sequence of vectors, $x(n+1) = Ax(n) + b(n)$, and $x(0) \geqq 0$, then x is a first-positive sequence, and*

$$\nu(x)(\alpha) = \min\left\{ \min_{\beta \in P[x(0)]} \delta(A)(\alpha,\beta), 1 + \min_{\beta \notin P[x(0)]} [\delta(A)(\alpha,\beta) + \nu(b)(\beta)] \right\}.$$

Note that Theorem 5 implies that each component is positive before it can become negative. Further, a given component can be positive in two different ways. One is ultimately due to a positive initial component β which is linked to the given component α directly or indirectly. The other is through the emergence of a positive element in one component of the forcing term $b(n)$, which is then linked to the given component, α. The shortest of all these routes determines the length of time before the positive effect appears.

Genesis of a System of Differential Equations with Metzler Matrix as Jacobian

As a preliminary, we note, in the notation introduced in D.13 and D.22,

LEMMA 9. *If $A \geqq 0$ and $x \geqq 0$, then $P(Ax) = C(A)\,P(x)$.*

Proof. $(A_\alpha) = \Sigma_\beta A_{\alpha\beta} x_\beta$. Since all terms are nonnegative by assumption, $(Ax)_\alpha > 0$ if and only if, for some β, $A_{\alpha\beta} > 0$ and $x_\beta > 0$; but this holds if and only if, for some β, $\alpha C(A)\beta$ and $\beta \in P(x)$.

Now consider the system of differential equations

(11-23) $\dot{x} = Ax + b(t)$,

where A is a Metzler matrix, $b(t) \geqq 0$ for all t, and $x(0) \geqq 0$. This clearly has the solution,

(11-24) $$x(t) = e^{At}x(0) + \int_0^t e^{A(t-u)}b(u)du,$$
$$= y(t) + z(t),$$

where

(11-25) $y(t) = e^{At}x(0)$,

(11-26) $$z(t) = \int_0^t e^{A(t-u)}b(u)du.$$

By Theorem 4, $e^{At} \geqq 0$ for all $t > 0$, so that, from (11-25), $y(t) \geqq 0$ for all $t \geqq 0$. Also, $e^{A(t-u)} \geqq 0$ for $t > u$; since $b(u) \geqq 0$ for all u, by assumption,

(11-27) $e^{A(t-u)}b(u) \geqq 0, \quad 0 \leqq u < t$,

and therefore $z(t) \geqq 0$ from (11-26). Combining these statements we see that

(11-28) $x(t) \geqq 0$, and $P[x(t)] = P[y(t)] \cup P[z(t)]$, all $t > 0$.

From Lemma 9, $P[y(t)] = C(e^{At})P[x(0)]$, all $t > 0$. From Theorem 3, $C(e^{At}) = K^\delta(At)$ for $t > 0$; but since obviously $C(At) = C(A)$ for any matrix A and any scalar $t \neq 0$, it follows from the definition of $K^\delta(A)$, D.19, that $K^\delta(At) = K^\delta(A)$ for all $t > 0$.

(11-29) $P[y(t)] = K^\delta(A)P[x(0)]$ for $t > 0$.

In particular, $P[y(t)]$ is independent of t for $t > 0$. Hence, as far as the effects of initial conditions go, any component that is going to be positive eventually is positive immediately. However, as will be seen below, the delay effects of the connectivity of the matrix affect the solution but in a different way.

If, for some component $\alpha, (e^{A(t-u)}b(u))_\alpha = 0$ for all u, $0 \leqq u < t$, then obviously, from (11-26), $(z(t))_\alpha = 0$. On the other hand, if b is assumed continuous, then if

$$(e^{A(t-u)}b(u))_\alpha > 0 \quad \text{for some } u, \qquad 0 \leqq u < t,$$

it is positive in some interval and hence from (11-27) and (11-26), $(z(t))_\alpha > 0$. In symbols,

$$\text{(11-30)} \quad P[z(t)] = \bigcup_{0 \leqq u < t} P[e^{A(t-u)}b(u)] = \bigcup_{0 \leqq u < t} C(e^{A(t-u)})P[b(u)]$$

$$= \bigcup_{0 \leqq u < t} K^\delta(A)P[b(u)]$$

$$= K^\delta(A) \bigcup_{0 \leqq u < t} P[b(u)], \quad \text{for} \quad t > 0.$$

The steps are the same as those leading to (11-29), together with a final step which uses (11-6).

The result can be made still more transparent with the aid of a nonzero index for functions of a continuous variable.

DEFINITION 23. *$\zeta(b)(\beta) = inf\{t | t \geqq 0,\ b_\beta(t) \neq 0\}$.*

If $u < \zeta(b)(\beta)$, then $b_\beta(u) = 0$, and therefore $\beta \notin P[b(u)]$. Therefore, if $t \leqq \zeta(b)(\beta)$, $\beta \notin P[b(u)]$ for all u, $0 \leqq u < t$, and therefore

$$\text{if } t \leqq \zeta(b)(\beta), \qquad \beta \notin \bigcup_{0 \leqq u < t} P[b(u)].$$

Suppose now $t > \zeta(b)(\beta)$. Then, by D.23, there exists u,

$$\zeta(b)(\beta) \leqq u < t, \qquad \beta \in P[b(u)],$$

and therefore

$$\beta \in \bigcup_{0 \leqq u < t} P[b(u)].$$

Hence,

$$\text{(11-31)} \quad \beta \in \bigcup_{0 \leqq u < t} P[b(u)] \quad \text{if and only if } 0 \leqq \zeta(b)(\beta) < t.$$

For fixed b, $\zeta(b)$ is a function over a finite set. For any function f, $f^{-1}(y)$

means the set $\{x|f(x) = y\}$; for any set S in the range of f, $f^{-1}(S)$ means the set $\{x|f(x) \in S\}$. In this notation,

$$0 \leqq \zeta(b)(\beta) < t \quad \text{if and only if} \quad \beta \in [\zeta(b)]^{-1}\,(<0, t)),$$

where $<0, t)$ is the interval closed on the left and open on the right. Then,

$$\bigcup_{0 \leqq u < t} P[b(u)] = [\zeta(b)]^{-1}(<0,t)).$$

In combination with (11-30), (11-29), and (11-28), we can state the following:

THEOREM 6.[1] *Suppose A is a Metzler matrix, b continuous and nonnegative, $\dot{x}(t) = Ax(t) + b(t)$ for all $t \geqq 0$, and $x(0) \geqq 0$. Then $x(t) \geqq 0$, all $t \geqq 0$, and $P[x(t)] = K^{\delta}(A)\{P[x(0)] \cup [\zeta(b)]^{-1}(<0,t))\}$ for $t > 0$.*

Notice again that the signs of all the components are completely determined by the sign patterns of the matrix of the initial conditions, A, and of the forcing function, b. At any time t, we find all components which are either positive at time 0 or have been nonzero at some time point before t; then take all components linked to them directly or indirectly by chains of nonzero entries in the matrix A. This set is precisely the set of positive components at time t.

This theorem actually relates to more than the genesis of the dynamic system. The next result will study behavior at the starting point, specifically, the qualitative behavior of the successive time derivatives of the different components of $x(t)$ at the point $t = 0$.

First, the nonnegativity of a function and the first-positivity of the sequence of its derivatives are related.

LEMMA 10. *An infinitely differentiable vector function f is nonnegative for $t \geqq 0$ if and only if, for each $t \geqq 0$, the sequence $\lambda_n f^{(n)}(t)$ is first-positive.*

Proof. Suppose $f(t) \geqq 0$, all $t \geqq 0$, but for some $t_0 \geqq 0$, the sequence $\lambda_n f^{(n)}(t_0)$ is not first-positive. Then there exist β and n so that $f_\beta^{(r)}(t_0) = 0$ for $r < n$, $f_\beta^{(n)}(t_0) < 0$. But if $n = 0$, then $f_\beta(t_0) < 0$, contrary to hypothesis; if $n > 0$, then $f_\beta(t) < 0$ in some right-hand neighborhood of t_0, again contrary to hypothesis.

Conversely, suppose $\lambda_n f^{(n)}(t)$ is first-positive for all t. Then in particular, it

1. The conclusion that $x(t) \geqq 0$ already appeared in Arrow (1960), Theorem *, p. 14.

is impossible that $f_\beta(t) < 0$ for any t and β, for then $f_\beta^{(0)}(t) < 0$, in which case the sequence $\lambda_n f^{(n)}(t)$ would not be first-positive.

Differentiate the system of differential equations (11-23) n times, and then set $t = 0$.

$$x^{(n+1)}(0) = Ax^{(n)}(0) + b^{(n)}(0). \tag{11-32}$$

By Lemma 10, the sequence $\lambda_n b^{(n)}(0)$ is first-positive; the matrix A is Metzler by assumption; and $x^{(0)}(0) = x(0) \geqq 0$, by assumption. Hence, (11-32) constitutes a system of difference equations which satisfies all the hypotheses of Theorem 5.

THEOREM 7. *Under the hypotheses of Theorem 6, the sequence $\lambda_n x^{(n)}(0)$ is first-positive, and*

$$\begin{aligned} &v(\lambda_n x^{(n)}(0)) \\ &= \min\left\{\min_{\beta \in P[x(0)]} \delta(A)(\alpha,\beta), 1 + \min_{\beta \notin P[x(0)]} [\delta(A)(\alpha,\beta) + v(\lambda_n b^{(n)}(0))]\right\} \end{aligned}$$

Thus, a positive initial component causes every component indirectly connected to it to become positive in the right-hand neighborhood of the origin, but the order of growth (linear, quadratic, or whatever) depends on the length of the connecting chain through the matrix. Similarly, a forcing term will cause an order of growth in a component of x which is greater by one than the sum of the order of growth of the forcing term at zero and the length of the shortest chain to the x-component. These remarks are only valid for the first effect on the given component.

To illustrate, for an x-component which is initially zero, the growth is linear if either there is a chain of length 1 to a positive x-component or the forcing term for the given component is positive. The growth is quadratic if neither of these conditions hold and if one of the following three conditions is valid: (1) there is a chain of length 2 to a positive initial component; (2) there is a chain of length 1 to a component whose forcing term is increasing linearly from zero; (3) the forcing term for the given component is increasing quadratically.

References

Arrow, K. J. 1960. "Price-Quantity Adjustments in Multiple Markets with Rising Demands." In K. J. Arrow, S. Karlin, and P. Suppes (eds.), *Mathematical*

Methods in the Social Sciences, 1959. Stanford, Calif.: Stanford University Press. Pp. 3–15.
McKenzie, L. 1960. "Matrices with Dominant Diagonals and Economic Theory." In K. J. Arrow, S. Karlin, and P. Suppes (eds.), *Mathematical Methods in the Social Sciences, 1959.* Stanford, Calif.: Stanford University Press. Pp. 47–62.
Morgenstern, O. (ed.). 1954. *Economic Activity Analysis.* New York: Wiley.
Quine, W. van O. 1965. *Mathematical Logic* (rev. ed.). Cambridge, Mass.: Harvard University Press.

12 Quantity Adjustments in Resource Allocation: A Statistical Interpretation

Resource allocation is part of the general theory of constrained optima. Any method of successive approximation seeks to approximate a solution of the Lagrangian conditions (if we ignore nonnegativities and the possibility of slack in the constraints).

The following notation is used:

x is a column vector of n *decision variables;*

$f(x)$ is the *objective function,* to be maximized;

$g(x)$ is a column vector function defining constraints, specifically, $g(x) = 0$;

f_x is the gradient of x, the row vector with components $\partial f/\partial x_j$;

g_x is the matrix of gradients of the constraint functions, with components $(\partial g_i/\partial x_j)$;

primes denote transpose.

Then the optimization problem is

$$\text{maximize } f(x) \text{ subject to } g(x) = 0. \tag{12-1}$$

If the matrix g_x has full row rank, then the solution to (12-1) satisfies the Lagrangian conditions, namely, there exists a row vector p such that

---

(12-2) $$f_x + pg_x = 0,$$

(12-3) $$g(x) = 0.$$

In the standard discussion of decentralized resource allocation, attention is concentrated on adjustments in the Lagrange parameters, p. At each stage, an approximation to p is given. Then x is chosen to satisfy (12-2); this can be interpreted as choosing x to maximize

(12-4) $$L = f(x) + pg(x),$$

if $f(x)$ and $g(x)$ are assumed concave. However, unless p is already that associated with the constrained optimum, (12-3) will not be satisfied. The deviation of $g(x)$ from 0 is used to guide changes in p. A specific adjustment process in differential equation form is suggested by interpreting $g_i(x)$ as the excess supply of primary factor i when the productive activities are determined by the decision variables x. Then we wish to lower p_i if $g_i(x) > 0$ and raise it otherwise; specifically, the adjustment process might take the form

(12-5) $$\dot{p} = -g(x),$$

where the dot denotes differentiation with respect to time.

This process will in fact converge to the constrained optimum under suitable hypotheses, which we will not investigate here (Arrow and Hurwicz, 1960, pp. 70–71, 84–85). The idea is standard in the theory of market socialism. It is usually defended on the grounds that not only does it converge, but it is also informationally economical. At each stage, the decision on x requires knowledge only of the gradients of $f(x)$ and $g(x)$ (which can be interpreted as marginal productivities and marginal input requirements). The decision to adjust p, in turn, requires only the simple reflection of the x-decision on resource limitations through $g(x)$.

Marglin (1969) challenged the view that price adjustments have any unique virtues. He considered a very simple case, with one resource: decision variables were taken to be the allocations of the resource to different uses, so that

(12-6) $$g(x) = r - \sum_j x_j,$$

where r is the total resource availability, and $\partial f/\partial x_j$ can be interpreted as the marginal productivity of the resource in its jth use. In the price adjustment process, satisfaction of (12-2) implies that all the marginal productivities are equal throughout the adjustment process. Marglin suggested instead that at each stage the allocation x be chosen so as to be feasible (to satisfy (12-3)). Then, if the allocation is not optimal, (12-2) will not be satisfied. He suggested that each x_j be adjusted so as to increase L, that is,

(12-7) $$\dot{x} = L'_x,$$

where L is defined by (12-4); in computing L as a function of x, p is to be so chosen that feasibility is maintained when x is adjusted in accordance with (12-7).

In his special case, Marglin argued that the proposed quantity adjustment system is guaranteed to converge and that the amount of information transmitted at each stage is comparable to that in the price adjustment system.

One interesting implication of the Marglin process is that the adjustment equations can be stated in statistical terminology. Specifically, (12-7) turns out to say that x_j should be adjusted in proportion to the difference between the marginal productivity of the resource in its jth use and the average marginal productivity of the resource in all uses. Further, the rate of increase of the objective function is proportional to the variance of the marginal productivities, which, naturally, falls to zero when (12-2) is satisfied.

Do these conclusions generalize to the case of many resources? In particular, what is the generalization of the "statistical" interpretation of the Marglin process?

Actually, the notion of quantity adjustments had appeared earlier in studies of methods of approximating constrained optima; see Forsythe (1955) and Arrow and Solow (1958, sec. 3). The interest of these studies lay rather in the fact that convergence was valid under less stringent conditions than in questions of informational economy. However, the results developed earlier can be reinterpreted to give rise to a generalized statistical interpretation.

Specifically, the tentative prices and the quantity adjustments in a quantity-adjustment process can be thought of as determined by a regression. Each "observation" is taken to correspond to one component of the decision vector. For the jth observation, the value of the dependent variable is taken to be $\partial f/\partial x_j$, while the value of the ith independent variable is $\partial g_i/\partial x_j$. That is, given any tentative values for the decision variables, the marginal gains to the different decision variables are regressed against the marginal inputs. The regression coefficients can then be interpreted as the (tentative) prices, while the residuals in the regression are the rate of adjustment of the decision variables. Finally, the rate of growth of the objective function is precisely the square of the standard error of estimate multiplied by the number of decision variables.

In the following section, the Marglin model is reviewed in the present language. In the third section, the generalization to any number of resources is given, and the results in the preceding paragraph proved. In the last section, some comments are made relating the quantity adjustment process to decentralization and informational economy.

The Marglin Quantity Adjustment Process

We will now reexamine Marglin's model in somewhat more general form. He assumed that $f(x)$ was additively separable, an issue important for decentralization (see the fourth section below) but not necessary to his main results.

If $g(x)$ has the special form (12-6) and if we insist that the resource allocation be feasible at every moment of the adjustment process, that is, that (12-3) hold throughout, then we are requiring that

$$\sum_j x_j(t) \equiv r. \tag{12-8}$$

This condition will hold if and only if the following two statements are valid:

$$\sum_j x_j(0) = r; \tag{12-9}$$

$$\sum_j \dot{x}_j(t) \equiv 0. \tag{12-10}$$

From (12-6), the Lagrangian can be written

$$L(x,p) = f(x) + p(r - \sum_j x_j), \tag{12-11}$$

where p is now a scalar, so that

$$\partial L/\partial x_j = (\partial f/\partial x_j) - p,$$

and the adjustment process for any component x_j is defined by

$$\dot{x}_j = (\partial f/\partial x_j) - p. \tag{12-12}$$

To make sure that (12-10) holds, p has to be selected appropriately at any time t. Substitute (12-12) into (12-10), and solve for p:

$$p = \sum_j (\partial f/\partial x_j)/n, \tag{12-13}$$

that is, p is the *average* marginal productivity of the resource in all uses. Then (12-12) asserts that the rate of change of the resource allocation to any use is the difference between its marginal productivity in that use and the average over all uses.

We will also compute the rate of growth of the objective function itself:

$$\dot{f} = \sum_j (\partial f/\partial x_j)[(\partial f/\partial x_j) - p] = ns^2,$$

where s^2 is the sample *variance* of the marginal productivities about their mean.

So long as the Lagrange condition (12-2) is not satisfied, the marginal productivities will not all be equal. Hence s^2 will be positive, and therefore so will $\dot{f}$. It is clear, then, that the process can only come into equilibrium at a point where (12-2) is satisfied as well as (12-3). Since the path is a path of resource allocations, it must be bounded and therefore must have a limit point. It is easy to see that $\dot{f} = 0$ at any limit point, and from this it can be shown that an adjustment path starting from any initial point which is feasible, that is, which satisfies (12-9), will converge to a point satisfying (12-2) and (12-3).

Remark. The adjustment process (12-7) is arbitrary with regard to the choice of adjustment speeds. The rate of change of any particular x_j could be thought of as proportional to $\partial L/\partial x_j$, rather than equal to it. However, in that case, a suitable change of units in measuring x_j will restore the form given.

The General Case without Nonnegativity or Slack

Let us revert to the general constrained maximization problem. We will follow the discussion in Arrow and Solow (1958, sec. 3) but reinterpret the results.

We now wish to require that (12-3), the feasibility condition, hold throughout the adjustment process and therefore as an identity in time:

(12-14) $g[x(t)] \equiv 0.$

Expression (12-14) will hold for all t if and only if (1) it holds for $t = 0$ and (2) its derivative with respect to time is identically zero.

(12-15) $g[x(0)] = 0;$

(12-16) $dg[x(t)]/dt \equiv 0.$

By the chain rule, (12-16) becomes

(12-17) $\quad g_x \dot{x} \equiv 0.$

From (12-4), the definition of L,

$$L_x = f_x + p g_x.$$

Hence, the adjustment process for the resource allocation (12-7) is

(12-18) $\quad \dot{x} = f_x' + g_x' p'.$

The vector p is to be chosen, at any time t, so that (12-17) holds. Write (12-18) as

(12-19) $\quad f_x' = -g_x' p' + \dot{x}.$

We are, then, seeking a linear combination of the columns of a matrix, $-g_x'$, such that the difference between a given vector, f_x', and the linear combination is orthogonal to every column of the given matrix (note that the rows of g_x are the columns of g_x'). This is precisely the defining characteristic of the vector of regression coefficients estimated from a sample, where the columns of the matrix represent different independent variables and the given vector represents the dependent variable.

In more detail, let a regression of y be fitted to variables $z_1, \ldots, z_m$. Let u_j be the residual in the jth observation. Then the linear regression model asserts that, for each j $(=1, \ldots, n)$,

$$y_j = \sum_i \beta_i z_{ji} + u_j,$$

where β_i is the regression coefficient of z_i, z_{ji} is the jth observation on the independent variable z_i, and u_j is an error term. Let b_i be the least squares estimate of β_i and v_j the jth estimated residual. Then, by definition of estimated residual,

$$y_j = \sum_i b_i z_{ji} + v_j,$$

or, in matrix-vector notation,

(12-20) $\quad y = Zb + v.$

The estimates b satisfy the normal equations

$$Z'Zb = Z'y,$$

which can be written

$$Z'(y - Zb) = 0,$$

or, from (12-20),

$$Z'v = 0. \tag{12-21}$$

The analogy is now obvious. In (12-20) and (12-21) replace y by f'_x, Z by $-g'_x$, b by p', and v by $\dot{x}$; then (12-20) translates into (12-19) and (12-21) into (12-17) (after multiplying by -1).

Hence, at any stage t, there is an approximation, $x(t)$, to the optimal allocation. At this value of the decision vector, compute the marginal benefit vector, f'_x, and the marginal input vectors for all inputs, forming the matrix $-g'_x$. Take the regression, across decision variables, of marginal benefits on marginal inputs. The estimated regression coefficients are the approximation at stage t to the resource prices; the calculated residuals are the rates of adjustment of the individual decision variables.

Further, we can easily relate the rate of increase of the objective function to the standard error of the residuals. With the aid of (12-17) and (12-19), we have

$$\begin{aligned}\dot{f} &= f_x\dot{x} = (\dot{x}' - pg_x)\dot{x} \\ &= |\dot{x}|^2 - pg_x\dot{x} = |\dot{x}|^2 = ns_E^2,\end{aligned}$$

where

$$s_E = \left[\left(\sum_j \dot{x}_j^2\right)/n\right]^{1/2}$$

is the standard error of estimate (since the regression has no constant term, the deviations are taken from zero rather than from the sample mean).

As in the simple Marglin case, the objective function continues to increase so long as the regression does not fit perfectly. The path cannot come to an equilibrium unless the Lagrange conditions (12-2) are satisfied. Suppose the adjustment path is bounded. Then by standard use of Lyapunov's second method (see Letov, 1961, pp. 7–9 or Arrow and Hahn, 1971, chap. 11, sec. 4), with $f(x)$ as the Lyapunov function, $x(t)$ must converge to a limit at which condition (12-2) holds; (12-3) has been required to hold for all points on the path. Under suitable concavity conditions (or even quasi-concavity conditions), conditions (12-2)–(12-3) are sufficient as well as necessary for a constrained optimization.

When will the adjustment path be bounded? Let

$$F = \{x | f(x) \geqq f[x(0)]\}.$$

Since $f[x(t)]$ is increasing, $x(t)$ must belong to F for all t. Hence, the boundedness of F is sufficient for that of the path $x(t)$.

Alternatively, it has been ensured by construction that $x(t)$ is feasible for all t. If the set of feasible resource allocations is bounded, then again the path must be bounded.

THEOREM. *Let g_x have full row rank. Then the quantity adjustment process defined as a path $x(t)$, $p(t)$ satisfying the conditions*

(a) $g[x(t)] \equiv 0$,

(b) $\dot{x} = L'_x$,

where $L = f(x) + pg(x)$ is well defined if the initial point satisfies the condition $g[x(0)] = 0$. If, for each $x = x(t)$, the regression across decision variables of the components of the gradient of f on the corresponding components of the gradients of the constraint functions $g_i(x)$ $(i = 1, \ldots, m)$ is taken, then the estimated regression coefficients are the components of $p(t)$, and the estimated residuals are the components of $\dot{x}$. If s_E is the standard error of estimate (about zero), then $\dot{f} = ns_E^2$.

If either the set $\{x | f(x) \geq f[x(0)]\}$ or the feasible set $\{x | g(x) = 0\}$ is bounded, then the path converges to a point that satisfies the Lagrangian condition, $L_x = 0$, as well as the feasibility condition, $g(x) = 0$.

Observations on Decentralization, Information, and Computation

Let us take the case most favorable to the possibility of decentralization, that in which both the objective function and the constraint functions are additively separable, that is,

$$f(x) = \sum_j f^j(x_j), \qquad g(x) = \sum_j g^j(x_j). \tag{12-22}$$

Here, x_j might be interpreted as an activity level, and, for given j, the functions $f^j(x_j)$ and $g_i^j(x_j)$ $(i = 1, \ldots, m)$ define the final output and intermediate outputs (or inputs, with sign reversed) of a nonlinear activity. In that case, the information in the jth "observation," that is, $\partial f / \partial x_j$ and $\partial g_i / \partial x_j$ $(i = 1, \ldots, m)$, is solely a function of x_j and hence can be determined by the jth activity manager without other information. Therefore, the information can be transmitted to the central authority. Indeed, in some sense, the information transmitted is less expensive than the demands and supplies needed under a price adjustment mechanism, for the latter requires optimization and hence global knowledge by the activity manager, while the former requires only information on the production structure of the jth activity in the neighborhood of the present point.

Hence, from the information point of view, Marglin's thesis is valid in the more general case. The information to be transmitted by the activity managers is not greater and may even be less in the quantity adjustment process than in the price adjustment process.

But a different valuation must be made when we consider computing costs at the center. In the price adjustment model, all that is needed is aggregate excess demand; this is computed by simply adding up the excess demands of the individual activities. In the quantity adjustment model, *per contra,* the central authority has to fit a regression, a much more complicated operation. Indeed, it involves, among other steps, the inversion of a matrix whose order equals the number of resources. The Marglin model, which involves only one resource, thus gives an unrepresentatively favorable impression of the computational problem, since the regression estimation reduces to computing the mean.

It should also be noted that any commodity which enters into the production of another commodity is a "resource" from this point of view; that is, the resources which are constrained include both primary resources and intermediate goods. Thus, the number of resources is apt to be almost the same as the number of commodities.

These cursory remarks do leave some issues unresolved. For example, if the production structure is marked by constant coefficients (as in a Leontief structure), then the inversion need only be done once, not repeated at each iteration. It is clear that we need a more sophisticated theory of computational and informational efficiency, in which a priori knowledge of production and utility structures is used to reduce the need for calculation. But if we stick to the conventional rules for evaluating alternative optimal resource allocation mechanisms, in which the central authorities know no more of the activity structures than what is transmitted to them, the quantity adjustment process appears to be inferior in terms of the computational load on the center, though not in terms of the costs of information transmission.

References

K. J. Arrow and F. H. Hahn. 1971. *General Competitive Analysis.* San Francisco: Holden-Day.

K. J. Arrow and L. Hurwicz. 1960. "Decentralization and computation in resource allocation." In R. W. Pfouts (ed.), *Essays in Economics and Econometrics.* Chapel Hill, N.C.: University of North Carolina Press. Pp. 34–104.

K. J. Arrow and R. M. Solow. 1958. "Gradient methods for constrained maxima, with weakened assumptions." In K. J. Arrow, L. Hurwicz, and H. Uzawa, *Studies in Linear and Non-Linear Programming.* Stanford, Calif.: Stanford University Press. Pp. 166–176.

G. E. Forsythe. 1955. "Computing constrained maxima with Lagrangean multipliers." *Journal of the Society for Industrial and Applied Mathematics* 3:173–178.

A. M. Letov. 1961. *Stability in Nonlinear Control Systems,* trans. J. G. Adashko. Princeton, N.J.: Princeton University Press.

S. Marglin. 1969. "Information in price and command systems of planning." In J. Margolis and H. Guitton (eds.), *Public Economics.* New York: St. Martin's Press. Pp. 54–77.

13 The Future and the Present in Economic Life

Armen Alchian's refusal to be coerced by prevailing orthodoxies has again and again been of the greatest use in clarifying economic analysis. This happy end has frequently come to pass by the acceptance of his ideas on a wide scale; equally often it has been achieved by reaction against them. What matters in the history of thought is that the concepts advanced be important, that both their affirmation and their negation matter and that either be fruitful.

In this chapter I want to examine one line of thought that Alchian has stressed and that has become increasingly dominant in recent thought, especially but not exclusively with regard to macroeconomic policy. I refer to the emphasis on the economic future as against the present. The present is viewed as a small and relatively unimportant portion of the economic life of any agent. Economic decisions are seen as mostly concerned with decisions on holdings of assets rather than on choices of flows. Perishable goods are limiting forms of durable goods with high depreciation rates. Supplies of assets are largely constrained by the past and only changeable incrementally. Decisions to hold assets and to acquire increments are determined by the future or, more precisely, by anticipations of the future. In particular, some have emphasized the role of anticipations of price changes. Precisely because supplies are changing slowly, price movements have to be such as to induce the economy to hold present stocks, and therefore there can be no

Reprinted from *Economic Inquiry,* 16 (1978):157–170.

anticipated profits to change on the average; hence, price movements take the form of random walks or something similar.

This emphasis on the fleeting nature of the present and the dominance of the anticipated future has led to an argument strongly held in some quarters, that policy to offset economic fluctuations is essentially impossible. If the policy has been anticipated, then individual agents in the economy have already offset its effects. Thus, if an increase in the money supply is anticipated, individuals will promptly raise prices in the same proportion so that there is no change in the real money stock and hence no effect on real magnitudes. Or, to take an even more striking argument, a reduction in taxes with expenditures constant will induce each individual to anticipate higher future taxes to service and repay the debt. Hence, his net change in wealth, the difference between his current increase in disposable income and the discounted value of his future increases in taxes, is zero. Since for a rational individual current consumption is determined by total wealth rather than by current income, a cut in taxes should lead to no change in consumption.

The emphasis on stocks and on anticipations as governing present behavior is a most salutary corrective to an exclusive preoccupation with flows such as marked much post-Keynesian thinking. But I want to suggest in this chapter that much too drastic consequences are being drawn. Perhaps this is a necessary tendency in any shift in theoretical understanding; it may be necessary in convincing both oneself and others of the importance of a new viewpoint that its differences with previous viewpoints be exaggerated. Certainly the successes of Keynesian economics and, in the last century, of marginalism in economics were both marked by extreme assertions of novelty in theory and policy which were only gradually discarded; compare, for example, Jevons' denunciations of Ricardo with Marshall's appreciation nineteen years later.

The role of time in economic affairs has of course been stressed many times. The developers of capital theory, Böhm-Bawerk, Walras, Fisher, and Marshall, each in his own way, emphasized the place of stocks in economic analysis. Above all, Frank Knight stressed the omnipresence of capital. The importance of anticipations in determining present economic decisions was implicit and even explicit, particularly in Fisher. Business-cycle analysts also brought similar emphasis; to some, indeed, cyclical fluctuations were little else than the natural outcome of alternating moods of optimism and pessimism. In itself, this is hardly much of a theory. Keynes, too, though stressing flow equilibrium at underemployment levels, had as a basic component of his theory a demand for investment based on anticipations. Like many earlier business-cycle theorists, Keynes gave greatest weight to the instability of expectations.

Hicks's *Value and Capital* gave the most systematic treatment to that date combining the general equilibrium theory of the economy, the importance of capital and other forward-looking economic decisions, and the formation of expectations. He introduced the device of regarding commodities at different dates as different commodities, which permitted the already-developed tools of static analysis to be applied to intertemporal decisions. To make price expectations part of the analysis instead of exogenous to it, he took them to be a function of current prices. Hence, the stability of the economy was dependent in part on the responsiveness of expected to current prices.

If expectations are thus important, the mode of their formation becomes critical. The simple Hicksian relation was not satisfactory empirically; clearly, price forecasts depended on extrapolation of rates of change and not merely on previous levels. A number of hypotheses appeared in the literature from 1947 on, but the one which showed the greatest usefulness on empirical grounds was that introduced independently by Koyck and Chenery and which came to be known as "adaptive expectations": at each time point, the previous forecast was compared with the actual, and the new forecast was the old forecast plus an adjustment in the direction of the actual. Equivalently, the price forecast was a weighted average of past actual values with geometrically declining weights.

The formal development of general equilibrium theory pointed in a different direction. Using Hicks's device of dating commodities, Debreu and I, in our proof of existence of competitive equilibrium, proved the existence of present and future prices which jointly equilibrated supply and demand on all markets, present and future. This was presented in greater richness by Debreu in his *Theory of Value.* Taken literally, this procedure implied the existence at the initial moment of markets for all future as well as present transactions, that is, a set of futures markets for all commodities for all future dates.

An alternative interpretation of the model is to assume that the consumers and producers forecast future prices perfectly. If they use as forecasts the equilibrium values, then as the economy passes through successive dates, it will find at each one of them that supplies and demands are in fact equilibrated at the anticipated prices. The existence theorem for general intertemporal equilibrium can be taken as a proof that perfect foresight is at least a consistent theory.

It is a weaker form of this hypothesis that has become widely current. If we recognize that forecasting must be uncertain, that we can never know the future in detail, then the requirement of perfect foresight cannot hold literally. However, we can ask that foresight be accurate on the average. The future price (or other economic magnitude) has to be thought of as a random variable with a probability distribution. In particular, the future price has an expected value (in the sense of probability theory, that is, an average). A moderate version of the rational expectations hypothesis is that the anticipated price equal the expected price. A stronger version is that the economic agent know that the price is a random variable and use in his decisions the true distribution. (The stronger hypothesis is significant if the agent is a risk averter, so that his decisions are not determined merely by knowledge of the expected value.) This rational expectations hypothesis was introduced by John Muth in 1961 and has become the basis of much current thinking.

I have dwelt thus long on the doctrinal development because I believe it brings out some latent assumptions. The most important, and perhaps the most surprising in view of the policy implications that have been drawn, is that the emphasis on anticipations and stocks minimizes the role of markets as equilibrating mechanisms. The crucial empirical point is that markets for most future commodities do not exist. It is an interesting and illuminating question why they do not exist, but this is not the place to examine that. But in their absence behavior on current markets largely reflects anticipations of the future if the present is unimportant. It is true that the rational expectations hypothesis implies that the outcomes on future markets are well anticipated, but it is hard to see why this should be true. The very concept of the market and certainly many of the arguments in favor of the market system are based on the idea that it greatly simplifies the informational problems of economic agents, that they have limited powers of information acquisition, and that prices are economic summaries of the information from the rest of the world. But in the rational expectations hypothesis, economic agents are required to be superior statisticians, capable of analyzing the future general equilibria of the economy.

I will develop this theme in four specific sets of methodological remarks in the following sections. (1) Certainly one requirement of theory-making is that it account for the existence of economic fluctuations; theories which imply the impotence of government policy seem also to imply the absence of fluctuations. (2) The economic world is complex and varied, and each agent in it has access only to limited information, differing across agents. It does not pay the agents to use general information in the formation of their anticipations. (3) In any case, the predictions of effects of government policy have to be done consistently with general theory. This has not been done, though it is probably a less significant difficulty than the others. (4) Since disequilibria do occur, they must be anticipated. Hence, future quantities as well as future prices must be anticipated. Once this amendment is introduced, government policy becomes reinstated.

To make my position clear, I am not necessarily arguing that government contracyclical policy is necessarily optimal or efficient or necessarily even in the right direction. But I would argue that the question is not whether or not the government could, in principle, have an effective policy. It is rather whether or not the government's bureaucratic organization and political structure permit effective policies to be carried out.

The Existence of Economic Fluctuations

The interest in macroeconomic policy stems from the long-standing observation that there are cyclical fluctuations in economic activity in every well-developed capitalist economy. Certainly since the extensive observations of Clement Juglar (1859), it has been accepted that there are fluctuations in economic activity, with positive but imperfect correlation of the different sectors of the economy, which show distinct persistence in time. The fluctuations are certainly not periodic in any strict sense of that term but rather are like irregular waves of varying amplitude and varying time interval from peak to peak (or trough to trough). Further, these cycles are characterized at least at their lower levels by what certainly appear to be disequilibria, failures to equate supply and demand. Some labor and some capital goods stand idle while other, apparently identical, workers and tools are used.

The combination of emphasis on stocks and the rational expectations hypothesis can seem to imply that there is no possibility of change which lasts more than a short period of time. There can be no anticipated unemployment, for presumably wages would have adjusted to prevent it. Suppose then there is some unanticipated shift in the system, most likely some effect on aggregate spending. (In a Keynesian model, this might be a collapse of the demand for investment; in a monetarist model, this might be an unexpected reduction in the supply of money which affects spending.) Consumption, determined according to the permanent or life-cycle income hypotheses, will change but little. Anticipations are revised, and on the average, they will now be correct; there is no reason, under the assumption of rational expectations, to suppose they will be persistently wrong. With correct anticipations, investment will be "correct"; there is no reason to expect serial correlation in unemployment or other indices of general economic activity.

This is the line of argument used to show that government policy is impotent if anticipated and only temporarily effective otherwise. But there is no reason to confine the argument to government action; from the viewpoint of an individual economic agent, any behavior on the part of another agent, whether the government or another private agent, impinges equally. Hence, the same arguments that suggest weakness of government policy will suggest lack of sustained response to any unanticipated perturbation in the market.

Indeed, an interesting question is raised as to the informational basis of individual decision making. In a perfectly competitive system, with all markets operating, there is no information needed beyond the prices on all markets (this is not strictly true in the case of constant returns; see the fourth section below). However, when there are no futures markets, anticipations of prices on those markets may be based on all sorts of additional information. In particular, it appears to be assumed that the individual agent reads the published figures on the government money stock, tax rates, spending, and so forth. He does not, as is suggested in Keynesian analysis, merely notice that his disposable income has been increased, but observes that the increase is due to a reduction in taxes. His inferences as to future disposable income, then, may be different from what they would be if the increase came from a wage or profit increase. The inferences may also differ depending on the announcements (verbal behavior) that accompany the tax changes, which proclaim them to be temporary or permanent.

But once we go down the path of permitting inferences to be drawn, there are more and more subtle possibilities. One may regard a strong government monetary policy to be significant, not merely for itself but because it is an indication of the government's determination to do something about the current depressed situation. On this basis, the reaction might be much stronger than would be justified by the objective facts. Arguments of this kind were popular at one time with regard to rediscount rate policy on the part of central banks; it was the signaling effect rather than the objective impact on the economy that was dominant.

But why should we confine ourselves to information about government behavior? Suppose there is a spate of investment activity. Why should not the individual economic agent infer that it is likely to come to an end as the natural limits come into play and therefore restrict his response?

Let me also approach the matter in a different way. Economic theory and policy making may have unduly minimized stocks and anticipations; but one can err in the opposite direction. Economic theory implies that price anticipations are relevant in decisions about capital formation but not in flow decisions. In allocating consumption today, the future price of a completely perishable good is irrelevant (strictly speaking, this is true only if consumption bundles of different periods are separable in utility). An extreme example of a perishable commodity is labor-time. The laborer is durable, but the hours he can work are not. Hence, there is essentially no reason for anticipations of future wage increases, correct or incorrect, to affect the present supply of labor. Yet one finds models which argue that statistical unemployment is wholly or partly a voluntary withholding of labor because of unduly optimistic expectations!

I just hedged a bit by saying that there was "essentially" no effect of wage anticipations on the current supply of labor. It is true that there is virtually no economic decision, including that to supply labor, which has no capital component. Apart from the training aspects which have been so much discussed in the human capital literature, sheer location has a capital component. Taking one job may possibly increase the cost of taking or looking for another one tomorrow; hence, it is conceivable that an expectation of rising wages may induce an individual to wait rather than incur the additional transfer costs. But this effect seems to me very minor indeed and applicable only to a relatively small number of workers. It is hardly comparable to the genuinely dominant speculative motives in highly durable goods, commodity futures, or securities.

To digress a moment, the modeling of unemployment presents, as always, a problem. Whatever influences behavior on current markets, it is assumed in many models that they must clear. To explain the statistical phenomenon of unemployment, these models must assume that it is voluntary, in spite of the definitions used in collecting the data. The explanations offered are the speculative motive just discussed, which has virtually no basis in economic theory, the search motive (to which Alchian has contributed so much), or the alternative opportunities of unemployment compensation or welfare. In the absence of a detailed and workable model of these phenomena, it is not unreasonable to approximate their effects by Friedman's assumption of a "natural rate of unemployment," though the fact that this is only an approximation should never be forgotten. But what is one to make of a model, such as has been proposed, in which the natural rate of unemployment is a random variable following a stochastic process in no way influenced by other economic variables, whether governmental or private? This is Molière's dormitive principle indeed.

To return to the main thread of the argument, it has been noted that price anticipations affect only some of the current markets. This observation weakens the case for the rational expectations hypothesis. Essentially, there are two arguments for that hypothesis. One is a severe market argument: if a good is durable, then speculation will take place until there is no expected profit (beyond normal interest rates) in holding the good. The second is simply that it pays any individual to be well-informed about the future and therefore to invest in the information and analysis to enable him to predict better. Thus, the future price of a perishable good is relevant as part of his general ability to purchase goods in the future and hence affects saving. Perhaps more important, the future wage level is important in estimating future income and hence present wealth. But unlike the case of durable goods, there is no market pressure driving expectations of price changes in a particular direction.

If the markets for durable goods are peculiarly sensitive to price anticipations, while those for perishable goods are more sensitive to current prices, then there is a little more scope for explaining economic fluctuations. Suppose some shift occurs in some underlying parameters, possibly even a relatively temporary shift. The demand for perishables, being controlled primarily by wealth, may remain relatively unchanged. The demand for durables may be affected considerably by anticipated price changes; but if, in view of rational expectations, the expected price change must wind up being zero, then it is the quantities demanded and supplied that have to adjust. Hence, as we have always observed in the business cycle, it is the quantities supplied and demanded of durable goods that show the greatest volatility. That being so, the initial supply of durable goods in the next period, say the supply of capital goods, will be different. Hence, the parameters underlying the future have also shifted, and therefore the effect of the initial fluctuation will continue in time. No doubt in some very long run, the effects of the initial disturbance may gradually disappear, but that is hardly of concern when one is trying to explain the business cycle.

The Economic Agent as an Economizer of Information

As already indicated in the introductory paragraphs, the usual view of the competitive economy is that the average economic agent wants pretty much to economize on information. In defenses of the free enterprise system such as Hayek's, great emphasis is placed on the particularity of knowledge in different agents. It is objected to planning that broad general information about the future of the economy does very little good in defining the allocation of resources.

I suggest that the lessons of this observation are sometimes forgotten in current model building, particularly in the emphasis on rational expectations formed in a rather sophisticated way.

I disagree with the widely accepted proposition that econometric models should have expectations consistent with them. To the extent, it is argued, that the economic theory underlying the model involves anticipations, the anticipations that appear in the model as determining individual behavior should be equal to the forecasts made from the model. More generally, in fact, I would disagree with the weaker proposition that anticipations made by individuals should be necessarily dependent on broadly available general data about the economy and in particular about government actions.

Let me take up the first proposition. It is the essence of the decentralized economy that individuals have different information. Each individual is specialized in certain activities and has in general specialized knowledge about those activities. There is no reason, therefore, why his forecasts should be based only on the rather general kind of information which the econometrician can use. Let me cite a study of inventory cycles made a number of years ago by Lovell. It was based on a simple accelerator model; the desire to stock an inventory for the next period was a fixed fraction of anticipated sales. The demand for flows of inventories, then, was the difference between a desired stock and the current actual stock. The model had to be completed by some equation expressing anticipated sales in terms of other variables. Lovell tried several simple formulations and then suggested a very simple hypothesis, that anticipated sales were in fact actual sales. This turned out to give the best fit of all. My first reaction, and I suppose that of whatever readers the article had, was bewilderment. After all, the firm could not know its future sales, so how could they determine the present actions? It then occurred to me, however, that the firm probably had access to a great deal more information than the econometrician. Although the firm was undoubtedly making a forecast, the information at its disposal included a good deal of direct observation of its customers.

In short, one objection to what may be called the consistent expectations hypothesis (the hypothesis that the anticipations embedded in any model should be the best forecast from that model) is that this is very far from a set of rational expectations for any given agent. Each agent ought rationally to base his anticipations on all the information at his disposal, and this may include a great many facts and observations not available to others. Indeed it is of the essence of the decentralized economic system, as I have already said, that this should be so. Thus the anticipations of the different economic agents are not only not based on the same general economic model, but they should in general differ considerably from each other.

I am sure that an objection will be raised to this argument that if two economic agents have different abilities at forecasting a given price, the one with the higher ability will sooner or later take over the entire market. But I do not think this argument is at all conclusive. In the first place, the survival process has random elements in it, so that there is no reason in a finite length of time for this superiority to predominate for sure. With a steady turnover of population, each member of which has a finite life, the steady-state equilibrium will still require individuals of varying ability to forecast. In the second place, the fact that individuals have different information does not imply that one is necessarily superior to the other on the average; it may just be that sometimes one is superior and sometimes the other. But third and most important, the survival argument requires a freedom to arbitrage which is in many respects inconsistent with a specialized economy. Supposing it is true, as most economists have always held, that prices are more nearly determined by supply considerations than by those of demand. Then in general, sellers will probably be better able to forecast prices than buyers, since the former are more aware of cost changes. However, the only way that sellers can manifest this superior knowledge is by taking over the buying role as well; thus leather sellers would buy out shoe-manufacturing firms. But clearly there are many factors in the success of shoe manufacturing quite apart from predicting the price of leather, and so the ability to take advantage of this particular skill at forecasting is nonexistent.

So far, I have argued that forecasts will be based on more information than is contained in econometric models and in general on information differing from agent to agent. I also want to argue that they will not necessarily use all the information contained in an econometric model. In fact, the two propositions are intimately linked though they seem to move in opposite directions. We have to assume that information-processing ability is scarce. As I have already said, this is one of the main justifications for and explanations of a decentralized economy. But then it follows that an individual concentrates on acquiring the information most useful to him and will have to crowd out the information which is less useful. In particular, information that is broadly pertinent to the economy as a whole may have very little predictive power for the future of an individual.

Consider, for example, Barro's argument that a tax cut will not affect a consumer's perceived wealth, for the consumer will regard the increased debt as an obligation that he will have to pay out of future taxes. But for any given individual, the extent of his tax obligation for future debt is very hard to predict. It depends on his future income; it depends on how the tax burden will be distributed in the future; and, to the extent that it falls upon his heirs, it depends on their income status and tax burden. Hence a knowledge that the national debt has increased is only a modest predictor of an individual's future burden. What he is really interested in is his whole future income of which the tax due to service of the public debt is going to be a relatively small fraction. Even within the realm of tax burdens, variations in other government expenditures are likely to be more important. In addition, of course, variations in his own earning status, returns on his private security holdings, and so forth, will be much more significant in affecting his future wealth. Therefore, to the extent that he has limited resources for prediction, he will pay little attention to the public debt and far more to these other factors. The arguments about cancellation assume their force in a relatively simple world of one or two commodities with no distributional questions and with an absence of other uncertainties about the future.

Present Policies Affect the Future

The argument that anticipated future reactions will nullify any effects of the present ignores the possibility that the present policies may irreversibly alter the future. Let me give two illustrations of this portentous-sounding statement.

The first was suggested to me by my student Laurence Weiss. Suppose we have an increase in money stock. Then, it is usually argued, the next period the stock of money will be higher and therefore prices will be higher in the same proportion, so that there is no net effect on real economic activity. But the initial introduction of the new money stock requires a lowering of the rate of interest. In fact the anticipated price rise will mean that the real rate of interest declines even more. Therefore in the first period, there will be additional investment, so that the stock of capital in the future will be larger. It is conceivable that prices will fall rather than rise; it is the money gross national product that will increase in the same proportion as the stock of money.

The point of this little story is that the process by which the change takes place, in this case the increase in the stock of money, will imply other changes as well. In particular, we would expect, as suggested in the first section, that the accompanying effects will be mostly in the realm of durable goods so that initial conditions for the future are in fact different than they otherwise would be.

For a second illustration, let me take again the Barro argument about the government debt. Supposing I ignore the considerations of the second section. Each individual in fact fully takes account of the government debt in calculating his future tax liabilities. Even then I would argue that there are offsetting possibilities. Let us consider the situation from the point of view of the future. Imagine two alternate futures, one with a higher and one with a lower government debt. Will the economies proceed otherwise unchanged? In particular, would one expect the future course of government expenditures to be unchanged by the existence of a public debt? I think the answer is clearly no. Intuitively, one would expect a resistance to other government expenditures if service on the public debt is larger. While the aggregate of government expenditures may not remain absolutely fixed, one would expect to have some degree of pressure on other expenditures; nor is this in any way irrational. The representative taxpayer-voter is buying two kinds of services, those supplied by the usual government expenditures and those supplied by the holders of the public debt. Obviously I am assuming here that the debt is not uniformly distributed across the population but that there are individuals with varying incomes and varying time streams of needs. In that case, once the debt exists, the individual may prefer to spend some of his resources in maintaining it. But then his income available for other expenditures, government and private, is reduced, and he will therefore rationally reduce the portion he spends on government expenditures as well as the portion he consumes. This effect is reinforced if one recognizes that the taxes to repay the government debt have welfare losses associated with them. In that case, the wiping out of the debt, even of the uniformly distributed debt, will involve a net welfare loss which the individual will not want to undertake.

I do not wish to overstress the points in this section. I think it fair to say to a first approximation, the debt considered as an asset to its holders is approximately offset by the indebtedness of others. I have introduced here what I think are more like second-order qualifications. The arguments in the other sections are more important.

Quantity Constraints in the Present and in the Future

I have spoken of anticipations in general but concentrated on price anticipations. In this I reflect the literature which is being analyzed. It has put, for the most part at any rate, most exclusive stress on prices. Individuals are regarded as responding solely and exclusively to present and anticipated prices, very much in the spirit of textbook neoclassical theory.

With due regard to the defects of Keynesian theory, I think one lesson is valid, in the interpretation due to Clower and Leijonhufvud. At any moment of time there are really disequilibria; individuals are not able to carry out all the transactions they want to at the current set of prices. Most strikingly, workers are not able to sell in the market all the labor they would like to at the going wage. Hence the income on which they base their purchasing decisions is not the income they will receive by selling all the labor they want, as it would be in Walrasian or Marshallian equilibrium theory, but rather by selling the labor for which there is an effective demand.

This point will, of course, be sharply contested. It will be argued that the unemployed are different from those who are employed, that they are asking wages above those which they could receive on the basis of market considerations and are therefore voluntarily unemployed. Even if this assumption were valid, I think there would be a confusion of categories. An individual failing to sell his labor because he misapprehends the price he could receive for it is not really in the same position as someone who voluntarily chooses leisure over labor at the going wage. Many rational expectations models would probably not deny this point but would regard the associated unemployment as being transitory. An individual, not being employed, will recognize his error and form new and more realistic expectations. My own judgment, however, is that the matter cannot be so easily explained. Those unemployed are essentially identical with others who are currently employed; indeed, most periods of unemployment are relatively brief; those unemployed at any moment have been and will be employed at the same wages as others who do not share the period of unemployment.

To be sure, the element of time and the future modify the simpler statements of the quantity-restricted theory. Consumption of an individual at any moment is not actually restricted by his current income. It is a function, in large measure at any rate, of long-run income, according to the theories of Friedman or of Modigliani and his collaborators. But the empirical application of these theories shows that the expectations of future income, which govern current consumption, are affected by unemployment. They are in fact responsive to cyclical fluctuations, though in a more muted form than the simpler Keynesian models would have postulated. But individuals certainly regard themselves as constrained in the future as well as in the present by their income opportunities. Indeed it would appear that they extrapolate their futures from current considerations, for permanent income seems well approximated by an average of income for the last three years.

It is perhaps helpful to remark that even the strictest of neoclassical models cannot completely exclude quantity signals. Under constant returns to scale the output of any one firm is not determined by prices, even though the aggregate output for the industry is. In the context of investment, this means that each firm must forecast its future outputs. Hence quantity anticipations must play a role in any case. It is of course clear that in fact all empirically fitted theories of investment have required output anticipations. This is true not merely of the simplest accelerator model but of the more sophisticated versions, like Jorgenson's, which allow for variable capital-labor ratios and for lags between decisions and realizations in capital formation. Relative factor prices enter, but only to determine the capital-labor and capital-output ratios; the actual amount of capital formation still depends on quantity anticipations.

We must further recognize that firms do not perceive themselves as able to sell unlimited quantities at going prices. Not only do they anticipate limits on output in the future but they perceive current sales as also limited. Indeed it would be hard otherwise to explain why firms lay off workers. Since their capital costs are sunk in the short run, they should prepare to sell so long as their prices cover variable costs. But in fact it does not appear to be the case. Most evidence suggests that prices cover normal costs of operation plus a markup. Why do firms not reduce their prices? One explanation clearly is that they feel their sales are rationed and that price cutting would have relatively little influence. This is not the place to review the burgeoning literature which elaborates this position and which is, in many respects, a revival of the monopolistic competition literature of forty years ago. Suffice it to say that the hypothesis of rationally perceived quantitative constraints on sales of goods and of labor appears to be fruitful enough for further study.

As a final aspect of quantity constraints I would surmise that the time is ripe for the revival of the old hypothesis of credit rationing. The extension of credit is hardly an arm's-length transaction in which each party looks only at the price. The bank clearly looks at the viability of the loan and enters into a direct relation with a debtor. The conditions of this relation vary with business circumstances and, in particular, with the ability of the banking system to extend credit. It could be argued that one social function of banking is precisely to specialize in information about the quality of credit risks. The only way, indeed, that I have been able to understand the monetarist position that the stock of money is very important but that the interest rate is not, is to assume it based on widespread credit rationing.

As may be suggested by these remarks, the monetarist and Keynesian positions come relatively close together in contrast with the new views based on rational anticipations and the unimportance of the present. Like Modigliani in his presidential address before the American Economic Association, I would regard them rather as belonging to the same model with different estimates of the parameters. Neither, as I interpret them, denies the possibility of disequilibria in the labor or other markets. Both stand in contrast to a world in which prices and their anticipations are everything.

In conclusion, I do not wish to minimize the intellectual contribution of the newer thought. I have omitted a number of qualifications that have been made in various places. The doctrine of rational anticipations seems to at least be one of those bold hypotheses which can lead to simplification. Clearly, we do not expect people to be consistently wrong in their judgments, at least as based on data available to them. I recognize also that the influence of the future on the present is powerful and that many actions of a short-run nature can be expected to have little effect when they can be so easily offset when anticipated. But an appropriate development of macroeconomic theory and its reconciliation with microeconomic foundations demands more complete attention to the information bases of anticipations and how they differ from individual to individual in a dispersed economy.

14 Pareto Efficiency with Costly Transfers

The theoretical notion of Pareto efficiency has been an important clarifying concept in comparing alternative resource allocations, both in theory and in the formation of economic policy. In particular, the close link between Pareto efficiency and competitive equilibrium is the central result for both analysis and policy. The equivalence of the two concepts is stated in the form of two theorems.

FIRST THEOREM OF WELFARE ECONOMICS. *Every competitive equilibrium is Pareto-efficient.*

SECOND THEOREM OF WELFARE ECONOMICS. *For every Pareto-efficient allocation of resources, there is a redistribution of the endowments such that the given Pareto-efficient allocation is a competitive equilibrium for the new endowment distribution.*

The second theorem in particular implies that problems of equity can be separated from those of efficiency; if the existing distribution of welfare is judged inequitable, rectification should proceed by redistributing endowments ("lump-sum transfers") and then allowing the market to work unimpeded rather than by direct interference with the market in the form, say, of price controls or rationing.

I have not stated the well-known hypotheses for the validity of the two

Reprinted from *Studies in Economic Theory and Practice*, ed. J. Łos (Amsterdam: North-Holland, 1981), pp. 73–86.

theorems; these hypotheses, roughly the existence of all relevant markets (including those for externalities) and convexity, at least on the production side, are of course frequently violated, and the theory of government policy is an attempt to suggest one class of remedies. This literature is vast, and I will not tread that ground here.

Another objection to the application of the two theorems is also widely known, but its analysis has not yet been well explored. I refer to the impossibility of distributing the endowments without some cost. Apart from poll taxes, which certainly have no appeal as instruments for achieving equity, we have no effective means of transferring endowments from one individual to another without some loss due to incentives. Any tax that is proposed will usually fall on some margin of the individual's choice and cause a price distortion. The redistribution itself, then, will cause an inefficiency; even if the market is allowed to operate without impedance after the transfers, the final state of the system will be inefficient.

Once it is recognized that redistributive transfers are costly, the concept of Pareto efficiency needs modification to take account of losses during the redistribution process. Hence, whether a given allocation is Pareto-efficient or not will in general depend on the amount of transferring needed to achieve it and therefore on the initial distribution of endowments.

In this chapter I seek to initiate a general discussion of Pareto efficiency and its relation to competitive equilibrium when transfers are costly. For simplicity, I confine the discussion to a pure exchange economy (no production).

It is necessary to specify a *transfer technology,* a concept that has already appeared in the literature in connection with competitive equilibrium in the work of Foley (1970), Hahn (1971), and others. Here, it is applied to transfers through extra-market means (primarily government compulsion) as well as through the market. For this initial study, we will make the simplest possible assumption, that the losses in transferring a given commodity are in terms of that commodity and proportional to the transfer.

In this model, it is then straightforward to characterize allocations which are Pareto-efficient relative to a given endowment allocation. We can define an allocation as being Pareto-efficient without qualification if it is Pareto-efficient for *some* endowment allocation. The class of Pareto-efficient allocations can be characterized in an interesting way in terms of a cycle condition, that a sequence of pairwise trades between successive elements of a closed cycle of economic agents not be advantageous.

It is easy to demonstrate that if the market transfer technology is the same as the redistributive transfer technology, then the first theorem of welfare economics remains valid. However, the second is clearly false, so that the trade-off between efficiency and equity becomes unavoidable.

Allocations That Are Pareto-efficient with Respect to Initial Endowments

The following notation will be used in this chapter:

x^i_k = amount of commodity k used by individual i
x = allocation of commodities to individuals, with components x^i_k
x^i = commodity vector of individual i, that is, with components x^i_k for fixed i
ω^i_k = amount of commodity k in individual i's endowment
ω = endowment allocation of commodities to individuals, with components ω^i_k
ω^i = endowment commodity vector of individual i
$U^i(x^i)$ = utility of individual i from commodity vector x^i. I assume U^i to be differentiable.
U^i_k = $\partial U^i / \partial x^i_k$
u^i = commodity vector of withdrawals from individual i
u = allocation of withdrawals, with components u^i_k
v^i = commodity vector of transfers to individual i
v = allocation of transfers to individuals, with components v^i_k

The two transfer vectors u^i and v^i are taken to be nonnegative. From the notation, final and endowment allocations are related by

(14-1) $$x^i = \omega^i - u^i + v^i, \quad \text{all } i.$$

We will have to require that $x^i \geqq 0$.

DEFINITION 1. *The set of admissible pairs (u, v) of allocations of withdrawals and transfers is termed the transfer technology, T.*

Under the usual assumptions of costless transfer, the transfer technology is defined by the conditions

$$u^i \geqq 0, \qquad v^i \geqq 0, \quad \text{all } i; \qquad \sum_i u^i \geqq \sum_i v^i.$$

DEFINITION 2. *The transfer technology is said to be simple if, for each k, there exists a parameter, β_k, such that the transfer technology T is defined by the relations*

(14-2) $u^i \geqq 0, \quad v^i \geqq 0, \quad \text{all } i;$

(14-3) $\sum_i v_k^i \leqq \beta_k \sum_i u_k^i, \quad \text{all } k.$

The parameter, β_k, is the proportion of goods taken from some individuals which is still available to be given to others. We assume, of course, that

(14-4) $0 < \beta_k < 1,$

so that transfer is possible but with some possible loss. The loss may differ among commodities.

(In a more general transfer technology, the transfer of one set of goods will be at the expense of other goods rather than itself. The present case is treated only because of its simplicity.)

DEFINITION 3. *The allocation x is said to be attainable from ω if there exists a pair of withdrawal and transfer allocations (u, v) belonging to the transfer technology for which Eq. (14-1) holds with*

(14-5) $x^i \geqq 0.$

DEFINITION 4. *The allocation x is said to be Pareto-efficient with respect to the endowment allocation ω if x is attainable from ω and if there does not exist x′ attainable from ω such that*

$$U_i(x'^i) \geqq U_i(x^i), \quad \text{all } i, \qquad U_j(x'^j) > U_j(x^j), \quad \text{some } j.$$

Let

$$A(\omega) = \{x | x \text{ attainable from } \omega\}.$$

Since T is defined in a way independent of ω, we have

(14-6) $A(\omega) = (\{\omega\} + T) \cap X^+,$

where $\{\omega\}$ is the set consisting of ω alone, and $X^+ = \{x | x \geqq 0\}$.

Pareto efficiency with respect to ω means simply Pareto efficiency over $A(\omega)$. Then, if the utility functions are quasi-concave and satisfy some additional regularity properties, x is Pareto-efficient over a convex set if and only if there exist nonnegative multipliers, λ_i, not all zero, such that x maximizes

(14-7) $\sum_i \lambda_i U^i(x^i)$

over that set. In view of the structure of $A(\omega)$, x is Pareto-efficient over $A(\omega)$

if there exist $\lambda_i \geqq 0$, not all zero, u^i, v^i, which maximize Exp. (14-7) subject to Eqs. (14-2), (14-3), and (14-5), with x^i defined by Eq. (14-1).

Let p_k be the Lagrange multiplier associated with the constraint Eq. (14-3), and q_{ik} that associated with the constraint, $x^i_k \geqq 0$, Eq. (14-5). The Lagrangian can then be written

$$L = \sum_i \lambda_i U^i(\omega^i - u^i + v^i) + \sum_k p_k(\beta_k \sum_i u^i_k - \sum_i v^i_k) + \sum_i \sum_k q_{ik}(\omega^i_k - u^i_k + v^i_k). \tag{14-8}$$

Since the variables u^i_k, v^i_k are constrained to be nonnegative, necessary conditions for an optimal allocation are that, for all i and k,

(14-9a) $\quad \partial L/\partial u^i_k \leqq 0, \quad$ with equality if $u^i_k > 0$,

(14-9b) $\quad \partial L/\partial v^i_k \leqq 0, \quad$ with equality if $v^i_k > 0$.

In addition, the inequalities (14-3) and (14-5) must hold; the corresponding Lagrange parameters must be nonnegative, and, if any are positive, the corresponding inequality must become an equality. These conditions, together with Eq. (14-9), constitute a system of linear equations and inequalities in the Lagrange parameters for a given transfer; the solvability of this system is equivalent to the Pareto optimality (with respect to the initial endowment ω) for the allocation x defined by the given transfers u, v according to Eq. (14-1).

We now write out the system of inequalities explicitly. From Eqs. (14-9a) and (14-8),

$$-\lambda_i U^i_k + \beta_k p_k - q_{ik} \leqq 0, \quad \text{all } i \text{ and } k,$$

or

(14-10a) $\quad \lambda_i U^i_k + q_{ik} \geqq \beta_k p_k, \quad$ for all i and k;

and

(14-10b) $\quad \lambda_i U^i_k + q_{ik} = \beta_k p_k, \quad$ if $\quad u^i_k > 0$.

Similarly, if we replace i by j in Eq. (14-9b), we find,

(14-11a) $\quad \lambda_j U^j_k + q_{jk} \leqq p_k, \quad$ all j and k;

(14-11b) $\quad \lambda_j U^j_k + q_{jk} = p_k, \quad$ if $\quad v^j_k > 0$.

The inequalities on the Lagrange parameters are

(14-12a) $\lambda_i \geqq 0$, all i;

(14-12b) $\lambda_j > 0$, some j;

(14-13a) $p_k \geqq 0$, all k;

(14-14a) $q_{ik} \geqq 0$, all i and k.

If $p_k > 0$, then constraint (14-3) must hold with equality for the corresponding k.

(14-13b) $\sum_i v^i_k = \beta_k \sum_i u^i_k$, if $p_k > 0$.

Similarly, $q_{ik} > 0$ implies that constraint (14-5) must hold with equality for the corresponding i and k. In the contrapositive form, this statement reads

(14-14b) $q_{ik} = 0$, if $x^i_k > 0$.

Note that the marginal utilities U^i_k and U^i_k in Eqs. (14-10) and (14-11) are evaluated at x^i, as defined by Eq. (14-1).

Let us postulate that there is no satiation for any set of goods. That is,

(14-15) $U^i_k > 0$, all i and k, for all x^i.

From Eqs. (14-12b) and (14-15), $\lambda_j U^i_k > 0$, for all k, for some j. Since $q_{jk} \geqq 0$, by Eq. (14-14a), it follows from Eq. (14-11a) that $p_k > 0$, for all k. Hence, Eqs. (14-13a, b) can be rewritten,

(14-16a) $p_k > 0$, all k,

(14-16b) $\sum_i v^i_k = \beta_k \sum_i u^i_k$, for all k.

Suppose for some i and k, we had both $u^i_k > 0$ and $v^i_k > 0$ (that is, an individual both gave and received commodity k). Then from Eqs. (14-10b) and (14-11b) (replacing j by i in the latter), we must have $p_k = \beta_k p_k$. But this is impossible, since $p_k > 0$ by Eq. (14-16a) and $\beta_k < 1$, by Eq. (14-4).

(14-17) For all i and k, it cannot be that both $u^i_k > 0$ and $v^i_k > 0$.

If we review the system of inequalities (14-2), (14-10), (14-11), (14-12), (14-14), and (14-16), we observe first that the endowments ω do not appear explicitly. The primal variables appearing explicitly are x, u, and v. These determine ω, for, from (14-1),

(14-18) $\omega^i = x^i + u^i - v^i$.

This suggests that a natural rephrasing of the original question is to start with a given x, u, v and ask whether x is Pareto-efficient for the corresponding ω. In a still further rephrasing, we can start with a (final) allocation x and ask for the set of endowments ω such that x is Pareto-efficient with respect to ω. (This set may, of course, be empty.) This is equivalent to seeking the solution of the system in the Lagrange parameters and the variables u and v.

Since the endowment allocation must be nonnegative, it follows from (14-18) that the transfers u and v must satisfy

(14-19) $\quad x^i + u^i - v^i \geqq 0, \quad \text{all } i.$

It is also to be observed that, except for Eq. (14-16b) and the inequalities (14-2), the variables u and v enter only through their signs (in Eqs. (14-10b) and (14-11b)). Consider first, then, the remainder of the system, that is, Eqs. (14-10a), (14-11a), (14-12), (14-14), and (14-16a). For fixed x, the coefficients U^i_k and U^j_k are given. Call this the *inner system.* The variables are just the Lagrange parameters. The inner system may or may not be solvable. If it is not, then clearly x is not Pareto-efficient for any endowment ω. If it is, take any solution. Rewrite Eqs. (14-10b) and (14-11b) in contrapositive form:

(14-20) $\quad u^i_k = 0, \quad \text{if} \quad \lambda_i U^i_k + q_{ik} > \beta_k p_k,$

(14-21) $\quad v^i_k = 0, \quad \text{if} \quad \lambda_j U^i_k + q_{jk} < p_k.$

Then, given the Lagrange parameters which solve the inner system, we have a system of equations and inequalities in u and v, namely, Eqs. (14-2), (14-16b), (14-19), (14-20), and (14-21), which may be termed the *outer system.* Note that this system always has at least one solution, namely, $u^i = v^i = 0$, for all i. In this case, we have $\omega = x$. Thus, if the inner system is solvable, then x is Pareto-efficient with respect to itself.

However, for any given solution of the inner system, there are in general many solutions of the outer system. For each solution, there is a corresponding ω, defined by Eq. (14-18). More detailed properties of these solutions, and a useful necessary and sufficient condition for solvability of the inner system, will be found in the following sections. In the meantime, the results found thus far can be summarized in the following definition and theorems.

DEFINITION 5. *The allocation x is said to be Pareto-efficient (without qualification) if it is Pareto-efficient with respect to some ω.*

THEOREM 1. *The allocation x is Pareto-efficient if and only if it is Pareto-*

efficient with respect to itself. A necessary and sufficient condition that x be Pareto-efficient is that the following system of equations and inequalities have a solution in the variables λ_i, p_k, q_{ik}:

(a) $\lambda_i U^i_k + q_{ik} \geqq \beta_k p_k$,
(b) $\lambda_j U^j_k + q_{jk} \leqq p_k$,
(c) $\lambda_i \geqq 0$, all i,
(d) $\lambda_j > 0$, some j,
(e) $q_{ik} \geqq 0$,
(f) $q_{ik} = 0$, if $x^i_k > 0$,
(g) $p_k > 0$.

Here, U^i_k is evaluated at x^i. The system (a)–(g) will be referred to as the *inner system* (for x).

THEOREM 2. *Let x be Pareto-efficient. For any solution, λ_i, p_k, q_{ik} to the corresponding inner system, let u and v satisfy the following system of equations and inequalities:*

(a) $u^i \geqq 0$,
(b) $v^i \geqq 0$,
(c) $\Sigma_i v^i_k = \beta_k \Sigma_i u^i_k$,
(d) $x^i + u^i - v^i \geqq 0$,
(e) $u^i_k = 0$, if $a_{ik} > \beta_k$,
(f) $v^i_k = 0$, if $a_{ik} < 1$,

where

(g) $a_{ik} = (\lambda_i U^i_k + q_{ik})/p_k$.

Then if $\omega^i = x^i + u^i - v^i$, x is Pareto-efficient for ω.

The system (a)–(f) will be referred to as the *outer system.*

It is interesting to note that the outer system depends on the solution of the inner system only through (e) and (f), which designate zero values for certain transfers.

Simplification of the Outer System

For a given solution of the inner system, the outer system can be given a somewhat simplified form. Let

(14-22) $\bar{a}_k = \max_i a_{ik}, \qquad \underline{a}_k = \min_i a_{ik}.$

From Theorem 1(a) and (b), $\bar{a}_k \leqq 1$, $\underline{a}_k \geqq \beta_k$, so that $\underline{a}_k/\bar{a}_k \geqq \beta_k$. Suppose the strict inequality holds. Then either $\underline{a}_k > \beta_k$ or $\bar{a}_k < 1$. In the first case $a_{ik} > \beta_k$, all i, so that $u^i_k = 0$ for all i, by Theorem 2(e). Therefore, $\Sigma_i v^i_k = 0$, from Theorem 2(c); since $v^i \geqq 0$ by Theorem 2(b), we must have $v^i_k = 0$ for all i. In the second case, $v^i_k = 0$ for all i, by Theorem 2(f), so that by corresponding reasoning $u^i_k = 0$ for all i. In either case,

(14-23) $\quad$ if $\underline{a}_k/\bar{a}_k > \beta_k$, then $u^i_k = v^i_k = 0$ for all i.

Now suppose $\underline{a}_k/\bar{a}_k = \beta_k$. Then $\underline{a}_k = \beta_k$, $\bar{a}_k = 1$. From the definitions (14-22), this means there is at least one individual i for which a_{ik} takes on its least possible value, β_k, and at least one for which it takes on its greatest possible value, 1. Let

(14-24) $\quad \underline{S}_k = \{i | a_{ik} = \beta_k\}, \qquad \bar{S}_k = \{i | a_{ik} = 1\}.$

From Theorem 2(e)–(f),

(14-25) $\quad u^i_k = 0, \ \text{if} \ i \notin \underline{S}_k, \qquad v^i_k = 0, \ \text{if} \ i \notin \bar{S}_k.$

Theorem 2(c) now becomes,

(14-26) $\quad \sum_{i \in \bar{S}_k} v^i_k = \beta_k \sum_{i \in \underline{S}_k} u^i_k.$

If $i \notin \bar{S}_k$, then Theorem 2(d) reduces to the statement, $x^i_k + u^i_k \geqq 0$, which is automatically satisfied. For $i \in \bar{S}_k$, Theorem 2(d, b) becomes the statement,

(14-27) $\quad 0 \leqq v^i_k \leqq x^i_k \quad \text{for} \quad i \in \bar{S}_k.$

If we refer back to the definition of ω^i in (14-18) and make use of Eq. (14-25), we see that

(14-28) $\quad u^i_k = \omega^i_k - x^i_k, \ \text{for} \ i \in \underline{S}_k, \qquad v^i_k = x^i_k - \omega^i_k, \ \text{for} \ i \in \bar{S}_k.$

Formulas (14-23)–(14-28) together can be restated as the following theorem.

THEOREM 3. *Let x be Pareto-efficient, and let $T(x)$ be the set of solutions (λ_i, p_k, q_{ik}) to the inner system for x. For any element of $T(x)$, let*

(a) $\quad a_{ik} = (\lambda_i U^i_k + q_{ik})/p_k,$
(b) $\quad \underline{S}_k = \{i | a_{ik} = \beta_k\}, \qquad \bar{S}_k = \{i | a_{ik} = 1\}.$

Define $\Omega(x, \lambda_i, p_k, q_{ik})$ to be the set of endowment allocations ω satisfying the following conditions (c)–(e):

(c) *for any commodity k for which* $\min_i a_{ik} > \beta_k \max_i a_{ik}$,

$\omega^i_k = x^i_k$ *for all individuals;*

(d) *for all other commodities i,* $\omega^i_k \geqq x^i_k$ *for* $i \in \underline{S}_k$,
$0 \leqq \omega^i_k \leqq x^i_k$ *for* $i \in \overline{S}_k$,
$\omega^i_k = x^i_k$ *if i belongs to neither* $\underline{S}_k$ *nor* $\overline{S}_k$*;*

(e) $\sum_{i \in \overline{S}_k} \omega^i_k + \beta_k \sum_{i \in \underline{S}_k} \omega^i_k = \sum_{i \in \overline{S}_k} x^i_k + \beta_k \sum_{i \in \underline{S}_k} x^i_k.$

Then x is Pareto-efficient for ω *if and only if* $\omega \in \Omega(x, \lambda_i, p_k, q_{ik})$ *for some solution* $(\lambda_i, p_k, q_{ik}) \in T(x)$.

Simplification of the Inner System and a Criterion for Pareto Efficiency

We now analyze the inequality system of Theorem 1. In particular, it can be reduced to a system of inequalities in the utility weights, λ_i, alone. Since $q_{jk} \geqq 0$ by Theorem 1(e),

(14-29) $\lambda_j U^j_k \leqq p_k$, all j and k.

From Theorem 1(a) and (f),

(14-30) $\lambda_i U^i_k \geqq \beta_k p_k$ if $x^i_k > 0$.

It will be useful to distinguish those individuals, if any, for which $x^i = 0$. These individuals are excluded in effect from all goods. In particular, therefore, Eq. (14-30) does not apply to them for any commodity k.

(14-31) $E = \{i | x^i = 0\}$.

If $i \notin E$, then $x^i_k > 0$, some k, and therefore, from Eq. (14-30),

(14-32) $\lambda_i > 0$, if $i \notin E$.

If we assume that $j \notin E$, then we can divide (14-30) by (14-29) to find

(14-33) $(\lambda_i U^i_k / \lambda_j U^j_k) \geqq \beta_k$, if $x^i_k > 0$, $j \notin E$.

Let $\Lambda(x)$ be the projection of $T(x)$ on the subspace of variables $\lambda_i (i \notin E)$, that is,

(14-34) $\Lambda(x) = \{\lambda_i, i \notin E | (\lambda_i, p_k, q_{ik}) \in T(x)$
for some $\lambda_i (i \in E)$, some p_k and some $q_{ik}\}$.

Then we have shown that any element of $\Lambda(x)$ satisfies Eq. (14-33). Conversely, however, we shall show that for any solution of Eq. (14-33), with $\lambda_i > 0$, all $i \notin E$, we can find $\lambda_i (i \in E)$, p_k, q_{ik} such that the inner system is satisfied. For given $\lambda_i (i \notin E)$, satisfying Eq. (14-33), we have to show that Theorem 1(a), (b), (e), (f), and (g) can be satisfied. We exhibit such a solution, namely,

(14-35) $\lambda_i = 0, \quad \text{for} \quad i \in E,$

(14-36) $p_k = \max_{j \notin E} \lambda_j U^j_k,$

(14-37) $q_{ik} = \max\,(\beta_k p_k - \lambda_i U^i_k, 0).$

From Eq. (14-37), it is immediately obvious that Theorem 1(e) holds; from Eq. (14-36), Theorem 1(g) is true. Suppose $x^i_k > 0$. From Eq. (14-33),

$$\lambda_i U^i_k \geqq \beta_k \lambda_j U^j_k, \quad \text{for all } j \notin E.$$

In particular, choose j to maximize $\lambda_j U^j_k$; from Eq. (14-36),

$$\lambda_i U^i_k \geqq \beta_k p_k,$$

so that, from Eq. (14-37), $q_{ik} = 0$ when $x^i_k > 0$, verifying Theorem 1(f).

Add $\lambda_i U^i_k$ to both sides of Eq. (14-37):

(14-38) $\lambda_i U^i_k + q_{ik} = \max(\beta_k p_k, \lambda_i U^i_k).$

It follows immediately that Theorem 1(a) is verified.

If $\lambda_i U^i_k > \beta_k p_k$, then $i \notin E$, from Eq. (14-35), and

$$\lambda_i U^i_k + q_{ik} = \lambda_i U^i_k \leqq p_k,$$

by Eqs. (14-38) and (14-36). If $\lambda_i U^i_k \leqq \beta_k p_k$, then

$$\lambda_i U^i_k + q_{ik} = \beta_k p_k < p_k,$$

from Eq. (14-38) and the fact that $\beta_k < 1$. Thus Theorem 1(b) also holds, and we have verified that

(14-39) $\Lambda(x)$ is characterized by Eq. (14-33).

We now restate Eq. (14-33):

(14-40) $\lambda_i / \lambda_j \geqq \beta_k (U^j_k / U^i_k), \quad \text{if} \quad x^i_k > 0, \qquad j \notin E.$

Let

(14-41) $K_i = \{k | x^i_k > 0\}.$

If $i \notin E$, the set K_i is nonempty. Since k appears only on the right-hand side of Eq. (14-40), the inequalities in Eq. (14-40) can be expressed by replacing the right-hand side by its maximum over k.

(14-42) $$\lambda_i/\lambda_j \geqq \max_{k \in K_i} \beta_k(U^j_k/U^i_k), \quad \text{if} \quad i, j \notin E.$$

Now take logarithms of both sides of Eq. (14-42). Let

(14-43) $$\mu_i = \log \lambda_i,$$

(14-44) $$b_{ij} = \log \max_{k \in K_i} \beta_k(U^j_k/U^i_k).$$

Equation (14-42) becomes

(14-45) $$\mu_i - \mu_j \geqq b_{ij}.$$

The conditions for solvability of the system of linear inequalities, Eq. (14-45), have already been obtained by Afriat (1963); they are conditions on the numbers b_{ij}. To state them we need some new terminology.

By a chain σ of individuals of length n will be meant an assignment of an individual to each of the numbers 0, . . . , n; thus, $\sigma(r)$ is the individual numbered r in the chain. If the chain has length 1, its coefficient will be b_{ij} with $i = \sigma(0)$, $j = \sigma(1)$. For longer chains, the *chain coefficient* will be the sum of the coefficients of the successive links. Thus,

$$v(\sigma) = \sum_{r=1}^{n} b_{\sigma(r-1),\sigma(r)}$$

is the chain coefficient for a chain σ of length n.

A particular kind of chain is a *cycle,* where the beginning and end of the chain are the same, that is, where $\sigma(0) = \sigma(n)$, where n is the length of σ. Then Afriat has shown (1963, theorem 7.2, p. 131, slightly restated) that a necessary and sufficient condition for the solvability of inequalities (14-45) is that $v(\sigma) \leqq 0$ for all cycles σ.

It is useful to interpret this condition. First of all, the term

$$\max_{k \in K_i} \beta_k(U^j_k/U^i_k)$$

indicates the most efficient way of improving individual j's welfare by transferring from individual i. Let $k(i, j)$ denote the commodity permitting the most efficient transfer. Then, by using the definition of $v(\sigma)$ and taking antilogarithms, the condition that $v(\sigma) \leqq 0$ becomes

(14-46) $$\prod_{r=1}^{n} \beta_{k[\sigma(r-1),\sigma(r)]} \{U^{\sigma(r)}_{k[\sigma(r-1),\sigma(r)]}/U^{\sigma(r-1)}_{k[\sigma(r-1),\sigma(r)]}\} \leqq 1.$$

If Eq. (14-46) were violated for a cycle σ, then there would be successive sets of transfers around a cycle which would improve the lot of the initial individual and not hurt anyone else, a clear violation of Pareto efficiency.

THEOREM 4. *A necessary and sufficient condition that x be Pareto-efficient is that condition (14-46) hold for any cycle of individuals. If it holds, then all solutions of the inner system of Theorem 1 can be obtained as follows: Let* $E = \{i | x^i = 0\}$. *Then find* $\lambda_i (i \notin E)$ *as the solutions of the system of inequalities,*

$$\text{(a)} \qquad \lambda_i / \lambda_j \geqq \max_{k \in K_i} \beta_k (U^j_k / U^i_k), \qquad \lambda_i > 0, \quad \text{for } i, j \notin E.$$

Then for any given solution of (a), choose $\lambda_i (i \in E)$, p_k, q_{ik}, *to satisfy Theorem 1 (a), (b), (e), (f), and (g).*

Pareto Efficiency and Competitive Equilibrium under Costly Transfer

Suppose there is a market, rather than direct redistribution. Suppose, however, that the costs of transfer are the same, that is, a sale of commodity k to the market permits purchases of a proportion of only β_k. Then buying and selling prices must be related correspondingly. The conditions for competitive equilibrium are obvious and coincide with those for Pareto efficiency.

THEOREM 5. *Suppose that in a competitive market only a fraction* β_k *of the sales of commodity k are available for purchase. Then a competitive equilibrium for a given endowment allocation* ω *is Pareto-efficient for that endowment.*

References

Afriat, S. N. (1963). The system of inequalities $a_{rs} > X_r - X_s$. *Proc. of the Cambridge Philosophical Society,* 59, pp. 125–133.

Foley, D. K. (1970). Economic equilibrium with costly marketing. *J. Economic Theory,* 2, pp. 276–291.

Hahn, F. H. (1971). Equilibrium with transaction costs. *Econometrica,* 39, pp. 417–439.

Index

Abstract economy, 69, 71
Accelerator model, 283
Activity analysis, 1–4
Adaptive expectations, 277
Additivity axiom for production, 62
Adjustment of prices, 124, 266, 269, 271
Adverse selection, 142
Afriat, S. N., 301
Alchian, A., 275
Allais, M., 47
Allen, R. G. D., 114
Allocation: efficient, 34; of risk, 46–57; feasible, 161; resource, 265; attainable, 293
Anticonsumer, 59
Arbitrage, 52
Attainable allocation, 293
Aumann, R., 120, 137

Balanced growth, 58, 113, 129, 238–239
Banfield, E. C., 151
Bargaining costs, 138, 142
Barro, R., 285–286
Bentham, J., 204
Bergson, A., 202, 204, 223–224
Binary shift in demand, 127
Black, D., 150
Bliss point, 22
Block, H. D., 125
Blocked allocation, 121
Bonds, 185–186
Boundedness of consumption, 73–74
Brouwer's fixed point theorem, 114, 116, 169, 212–213
Buchanan, J., 145, 150
Budget constraint, 136, 164, 202–203
Business cycles, 279–282

Cairnes, J. E., 230
Capacity, 94
Capital model, 237–238
Cassel, G., 87–88, 111–112, 210–212
Chains, 250–251, 301
Chamberlin, E. H., 46, 139, 159, 183
Chenery, H., 92
Clark, J. B., 110
Classical economics, 108–109, 156, 227, 229
Classical welfare economics, 15
Coalition, 121, 141
Coase, R. H., 145
Collective action, 150–152
Comparative dynamics, 129
Comparative statics, 111, 126–127, 129
Compensated equilibrium, 164
Competitive system, 15, 25, 37; equilibrium, 59, 109–111, 135–136, 164, 290
Complementary factors of production, 79
Complementary slackness, 112
Composit commodity, 128
Concave function, 52

Condorcet paradox, 225
Cone, convex, 62
Connectivity of a matrix, 252–255
Conspicuous consumption, 40
Constant returns to scale, 2, 41, 62, 118, 157, 207, 211, 233, 235
Constitution, 223
Constrained optimization, 265
Contingent commodities, prices and markets, 221
Continuity of a multivalued function, 70
Contract curve, 111
Convex cone, 62
Convexity assumption, 41–42, 49, 64, 119, 135, 158
Convex sets, 42–43
Convolution of sequences, 249
Core, 111, 120–122, 129
Core equivalence theorem, 122
Corner solution, 4n, 39, 208–211
Correspondence principle, 115
Costs of bargaining, 138
Costs of computation in resource allocation, 273
Costs of information transmission, 273
Costs of redistribution, 291
Cournot, A. A., 108, 109, 156, 230
Credit rationing, 289
Cycles, 301. *See also* Business cycles

Debreu, G., 58–59, 70, 114, 121, 137, 158, 217, 220, 277
Decentralization, 272–273
Demand, excess, 67, 174–175, 205–206, 209
Demsetz, H., 139, 142, 145
Difference equations, 258–259
Differential equations, 260–263
Diminishing returns to scale, 62n, 122
Discontinuity of the supply curve for labor, 79
Disposal, free, 31, 37
Distribution: of goods, 15, 20; of income, 158
Distributive justice, 202, 204
Dominant diagonal of a matrix, 126
Dominated allocation, 120–121
Downs, A., 150
Duality, 85–86
Duesenberry, J. S., 40
Dynamic systems, 245

Edgeworth, F. Y., 111, 126, 137, 140, 204
Efficiency, 290. *See also* Pareto efficiency
Efficient allocation, 34
Endowment, 65, 161, 162, 202, 290
Entrepreneurship, 122, 157
Entry, 158, 184
Equilibrium: existence of, 58–90, 160–172; competitive, 59, 109–111, 135–136, 164, 290; stability, 110–115, 124–129; uniqueness, 123–124, 129; partial, 127–128; over time, 128–130; compensated, 164; monopolistic competitive, 180; temporary, 185
Equity, 290
Exceptional case, 25, 30, 39
Excess demand, 67, 174–175, 205–206, 209
Exchange economy, 145, 231
Exclusion principle, 146
Existence of equilibrium, 58–90, 160–172; historical review, 87–90
Expectations, 185–187; adaptive, 277; rational, 278
Exports, 93
Externality, 145

Farrell, M. J., 120, 137, 159
Feasible allocation, 161
Firms, 156–197
First-positivity, 246–250
Fisher, I., 111, 203
Fixed coefficients in production, 79, 87–88, 156, 208, 210, 228
Fixed point theorem, 114, 116, 169, 212–213, 219
Foley, D. K., 291
Forsythe, G. E., 267
Free disposal, 31, 37
Free goods, 30–31, 67, 88, 116, 208–211
Free rationed goods, 62n
Friedman, M., 47, 281
Frisch, R., 129

Gale, D., 119, 123, 125
Game Theory, 113–114, 139
Georgescu-Roegen, N., 232

Giffin's paradox, 125
Goods: free, 30–31, 67, 88, 116, 208–211; public, 145
Gossen, H. H., 230
Graph of a multivalued function, 70
Growth, balanced, 58, 113, 129, 238–239

Hagstrom, K. G., 151
Hahn, F. H., 126, 160, 291
Harsanyi, J. C., 140
Hicks, J. R., 18, 41, 114–115, 128–129, 185, 202–207, 277
Hicksian matrix, 115, 123
Hicks-Leontief aggregation theorem, 128
Hicks-Samuelson model, 202–207
Hirshleifer, J., 144
Homogeneity of supply and demand, 116, 205, 206
Hotelling, H., 47, 58, 114, 150, 202, 204
Hurwicz, L., 125, 266

Imports, 92–93; optimal program, 96
Impossibility theorem, 224
Income distribution, 158
Increasing returns to scale, 57, 119, 134, 137
Indecomposability of technologies, 240
Independence of irrelevant alternatives, 224
Indifference surface, 204
Indivisibilities, 119; and uncertainty, 56
Industrial organization, 4, 8, 10
Information, 143; in prices, 201, 280; costs of transmission, 273
Inner system, 296–297
Insurance, 221
Interior solution, 17
Invisible hand, 107
Irreducible economy, 119
Irreversibility of production, 62–63

Jacobian matrix, 123, 126
Jenkin, F., 109
Jevons, W. S., 109, 201, 230–231
Joint production, 2, 229, 235
Juglar, C., 279

Kakutani fixed-point theorem, 114, 169, 212–213, 219
Kaldor, N., 139, 184
Kalecki, M., 159
Kaysen, C., 144
Keynes, J. M., 46, 201
Knight, F. H., 145
Koopmans, T. C., 1, 4, 34, 41, 217
Kuhn, H. W., 17n
Kuznets, S., 18

Labor theory of value, 108, 227–228
Lagrangian conditions, 265, 294
Lange, 0., 16, 206
Law of supply and demand, 67, 71
Leibenstein, H., 40
Leijonhufvud, A., 201
Leontief model, 1, 92
Leontief, W. W., 1, 93, 128
Lerner, A. P., 16
Life-cycle permanent income hypothesis, 279
Linear programming, 1, 17n, 96
Lovell, M., 283

Malthus, T. R., 108, 229
Marginal productivity, 266, 267
Marginal rate of substitution, 15, 203–204, 208
Marglin, S., 266–269
Markets: optimal allocation of risk, 52; failure, 134, 148; universality, 135; contingent, 221
Market socialism, 266
Marris, R., 159, 196
Marschak, J., 47, 144
Marschak, T., 149
Marshall, A., 123
Marx, K., 108, 227, 230
McKenzie, L., 58–59, 114, 119, 121, 158, 219
Meade, J. E., 145
Menger, C., 109, 112, 201, 230–231
Metzler, L. A., 115
Metzler matrix, 245–263
Mill, J. S., 108–109
Minimax theorem, 212
Monopolistic competition, 139, 172–185; equilibrium, 180
Monopoly, 122, 138, 172–185
Moral hazard, 143, 222

Morgenstern, O., 113, 129, 140, 150, 212, 245
Morishima, M., 125, 127, 242
Musgrave, R. A., 146
Muth, J., 278

Nash equilibrium, 69–70
Nash, J. F., 58, 69–70, 140
Natural rate of unemployment, 281
Negishi, T., 126, 139, 172, 183
Neisser, H., 88–89, 112, 211
Neoclassical economics, 230–231
New welfare economics, 40–41
Nikaidô, H., 114, 123
Non-dictatorship, 224
Nonprice coordinating mechanisms, 25, 150–152, 201–202, 290
Non-tâtonnement stability, 126
Norms of social behavior, 151–152
Numéraire, 110

Optimal allocation of risk, 46–57
Optimal distribution, 15, 21
Optimal imports, 96
Outer system, 296–297

Pareto efficiency, 121, 136, 202, 204, 208, 213–217, 290
Pareto, W., 111, 203
Partial equilibrium, 127–128
Penrose, E. T., 159
Perfect foresight, 129, 277–278
Permanent income hypothesis, 279
Potential income, 68
Preference ordering, 203; over social states, 223
Prices, 23–24; nonnegativity, 67; information in, 201, 280; contingent, 221; adjustment, 266
Primary factors, 210–211
Product differentiation, 183
Production: joint, 2, 229, 235; fixed coefficient, 79, 87–88, 156, 208, 210, 228
Production possibility set, 62
Productive economy, 229
Profit maximization, 63, 164–165, 210
Public goods, 145
Pure exchange economy, 145, 231

Quantity adjustment, 267
Quasi-concave function, 49, 65

Radner, R., 142, 222
Rate of adjustment, 124, 269, 271
Rate of time preference, 242
Rational expectations, 278
Rationing, 25, 126, 202, 290; credit, 289
R-chain, 250–251
Recontracting, 126
Redistribution, 290–291
Relatedness, 163
Relations, 250–252
Relative product of relations, 250
Resource allocation, 265
Resource relatedness, 163
Returns to scale: constant, 2, 41, 62, 118, 157, 207, 211, 233, 235; increasing, 57, 119, 134, 137; diminishing, 62n, 122
Revealed preference, 113, 124, 125, 148
Ricardian system, 229–230
Ricardo, D., 108, 227, 229
Risk, allocation of, 46–57
Risk aversion, 221
Robbins, L., 79
Robertson, D. H., 145
Robinson, J., 46, 159, 238, 241
Rothenberg, J., 120, 137, 150, 159

Samuelson, P. A., 1–4, 67, 114–115, 124, 145, 202–207, 232, 242
Satiation, 22, 64, 162, 295
Savage, L. J., 47
Scarce goods, 209
Scarf, H., 121, 125, 137
Schelling, T., 144
Schlesinger, K., 89, 113, 157, 211
Schumpeter, J., 150
Scitovsky, T., 145
Selten, R., 140
Separation theorem, 214
Shapley, L. S., 122, 140
Shubik, M., 121, 137
Sidgwick, H., 204
Slutzky relations, 85
Small numbers problem, 146
Smith, A., 107–108, 201, 227, 230
Social choice theory, 222–225

Socialism, 200–201
Social norms, 151–152
Social welfare function, 204–205
Solow, R. M., 97, 269
Speed of adjustment, 124, 269, 271
Sraffa, P., 230, 238
Stability of equilibrium, 110–115, 124–129; global vs. local, 125
Stackelberg, H., 88, 89, 112, 211
Starr, R., 137, 162
Starrette, D., 227
State contingent claims, 50, 221
State of nature, 48, 221
Stationary equilibrium, 113, 129
Steady growth economy, 211
Structural unemployment, 80n
Stubblebine, W. C., 145
Subjective probability, 47–48
Substitutes, 123, 125
Substitution theorems, 4, 8

Tatonnement, 110–111
Temporary equilibrium, 185
Time preference, 242
Tintner, G., 40
Transaction costs, 134, 149
Transfer technology, 291–292
Transformation surface, 20, 205; differentiability, 207–208
Triffin, R., 139, 183
Tucker, A. W., 17n
Tullock, G., 150

Uncertainty, 142–143, 196, 220–222
Unemployment, 281, 287
Uniqueness of equilibrium, 123–124, 129
Universality of markets, 135
Upper semi-continuity, 167, 213
Utilitarianism, 204, 223
Utility, 64, 203; individual, 20, 40
Utility maximization, 20, 21, 66, 164
Uzawa, H., 114, 125–126

Veblen, T., 40
von Neumann, J., 58, 113, 140, 150, 210–212, 217, 238
von Neumann-Morgenstern theorem, 51
Voting, 224–225

Wald, A., 47, 58, 60, 89–90, 113, 123–124, 157, 211
Walrasian equilibrium, 59, 109–111. *See also* Competitive equilibrium
Walras, L., 59, 109–111, 126, 156, 201, 230
Walras' law, 110, 206–207
Welfare economics: classical, 15–17, 85, 120–122, 290; new, 40–41
Wicksteed, P., 110
Williamson, O. E., 196

Young, A. A., 145

Zero profit condition, 108, 110
Zeuthen, F., 88–89, 112, 140